EROGENEITY AND LIBIDO

Other Books by Robert Fliess

THE PSYCHOANALYTIC READER (ed.)

THE REVIVAL OF INTEREST IN THE DREAM

SYMBOL DREAM AND PSYCHOSIS

EGO AND BODY EGO

EROGENEITY and LIBIDO

Addenda to the Theory
of the Psychosexual Development of the Human

VOLUME ONE
PSYCHOANALYTIC SERIES

ROBERT FLIESS, M.D.

INTERNATIONAL UNIVERSITIES PRESS, INC.
New York

Manufactured in the United States of America

TO BUNNY:

Celtic heart, Latin mind.

CONTENTS

FOREWORD xiii

PART ONE

Chapter I

A BRIEF EXAMINATION OF THREE FUNDAMENTAL, IF CONTROVERSIAL, HYPOTHESES

I. FREUD'S DUALISTIC THEORY OF THE INSTINCTS: A FEW DATA IN ITS SUPPORT   3

II. FREUD'S ASSUMPTION OF PHYLOGENETIC INHERITANCE   8

    A. A CONDENSATION OF SUPPORTING ARGUMENT   9

    B. THE TRANSCRIPT OF AN "ARCHAIC" EXPERIENCE: ON A FRAGMENT OF DIALOGUE BETWEEN "LITTLE HANS" AND HIS FATHER   12

        1. Preliminary Remarks   14

        2. The Analysis of the Background . . .   16

        3. The Analysis of the Passage Proper . .   18

          a. The Body as Phallus   18

          b. The Enigma of the "Stone" . .   19

            (i) Bismarck's Dream   19

            (ii) Leonardo's Drawing . . .   22

            (iii) Freud's Dream   26

            (iv) The Experience of a Patient   26

            (v) Concluding Argument in re "Stone"   28

          c. The Bleeding to be Limited . .   30

          d. A Symbolic Modulation . . .   31

          e. The Inconsistency is Explained .   32

            (i) A Superego in Statu Nascendi   34

            (ii) The Voice of the Superego   35

        4. Conclusion   40

    C. PHYLOGENETIC INHERITANCE: CONCLUDING ARGUMENT   40

        1. Freud's Three Concepts of Repression   41

        2. An Addendum to the Theory of "Primal Repression"   41

        3. On the Nature and Inhibition of Archaic Affect   43

III. FREUD'S HYPOTHESIS OF THE LIBIDO: THREE DIF-
      FERENT DEFINITIONS OF THE CONCEPT   44
      A. THE FIRST DEFINITION   45
      B. THE SECOND DEFINITION   46
      C. THE DISTINCTION BETWEEN EROGENEITY AND
         LIBIDO   48
      D. THE THIRD DEFINITION   49

PART TWO

Chapter 2

THE FIRST ORAL PHASE

I.   THE UNIT OF MOUTH AND EYE   55
II. THE PROBLEM OF ACTIVITY   60
III. ON THE ROLE OF THE FIRST ORAL PHASE IN RE-
     GRESSIVE CONDITIONS   65
     The Handkerchief of Desdemona   66
IV. ON THE INCEPTION OF EGO   69

Chapter 3

THE SECOND ORAL PHASE

I.   NASCENT EGO AND OBJECT: THEIR IDENTITY AND
     THEIR DELIMITATION   71
II. NARCISSISTIC IDENTITY AND REGRESSIVE IDENTI-
     FICATION   75
III. THE SUBJECTIVE REALITY OF THE CANNIBALISTIC
     ACT AND THE PERSISTENCE OF THE CANNIBALISTIC
     DESIRE IN THE INDIVIDUAL   78
     A. ON THE RELATIVE ABSENCE OF CANNIBALISTIC
        MANIFESTATIONS IN THE CHILD   78
     B. PORTIA'S (FIRST) INJUNCTION AGAINST THE
        CANNIBALISM OF SHYLOCK   80
        1. Shylock's Suggestive Influence on An-
           tonio   82
        2. The True Shylock   85
        3. The Meaning of Portia's Injunction .   86

C. THE DEATH INSTINCT AND THE REGRESSIVE RE-VIVAL OF THE ORAL-SADISTIC MOUTH 86

D. CANNIBALISTIC AIM INHIBITION AND AIM DIS-PLACEMENT 88

E. CANNIBALISTIC RE-INCORPORATION 90

IV. A TYPICAL RE-ENACTMENT OF THE "WEANING TRAUMA" IN THE TRANSFERENCE 92

V. ON THE COLLECTIVE PERSISTENCE OF THE CANNI-BALISTIC DESIRE 97

VI. THE EYE-MOUTH UNIT OF PRIMARY IDENTIFICA-TION. "EMPATHY" AND SCOPTOPHILIA 101

VII. THE BEGINNING OF SPEECH: BISYLLABIC REDUPLI-CATION 104

VIII. THE CANNIBALISTIC AFFECT: IMPATIENCE . . . 107

Chapter 4

THE ANAL-SADISTIC PHASES

I. ON THE PERSISTENCE OF ORALITY IN THE ANAL PHASES 111

A. ANAL-EROTIC ELABORATION UPON CANNIBAL-ISTIC AND ORAL-EROTIC LIBIDO 111

B. ORAL QUALITIES OF THE ANAL-EROTIC OBJECT 116

II. SPHINCTER CONTROL AND THE CONTROL OF AR-CHAIC AFFECT 121

A. THE FIRST "MORALITY": THAT OF THE SPHINC-TER 121

Portia's (Second) Injunction 125

B. THE ANAL REVERSAL 125

III. ON THE MOTOR CHARACTERISTICS OF THOUGHT . . 128

IV. ANAL-SADISTIC DEVELOPMENT AND THE EAR . . . 131

A. THE PERSISTENCE OF ORALITY (MOUTH, EYE, HAND) IN LANGUAGE 132

B. THE SPOKEN WORD AS A PART OF THE BODY, WHOSE LOSS AND WHOSE (AUDITORY) RE-ENTRY IS FEARED 134

C. THE WORD AN OBJECT TO THE UNCONSCIOUS IN THE CASE OF THE NAME 137

D. THE CONTROL OF SPEECH AND POSTURE (UP-
    RIGHT GAIT) BY THE EAR   137

E. THOUGHT AND MUSICAL THOUGHT   139

Chapter 5

THE PHALLIC PHASE

I.   INTRODUCTION   144

II. ON THE PERSISTENCE OF EARLIER PHASES IN THE
     PHALLIC PHASE   145

     A. ANAL-SADISTIC PHASES   145

         1. The Second Anal Phase   145

             a. A Phallic Pleasure-Physiological
                Copy of the Rectum   145

             b. On Some Typical Ideas of In-
                feriority   147

         2. Both Anal Phases   150

         3. First Anal Phase   150

     B. ORAL PHASES   151

         1. Second Oral Phase   151

             a. On the Urethral-Erotic Discharge
                of Cannibalistic Libido   152

                 (i) Ambition   152
                 (ii) The Urge to Talk   153
                 (iii) The "Preservation of Fire"   154
                 (iv) Further Clinical Material .   155

             b. Consequences of the Discharge for
                the Ego Organization   158

             c. Résumé: The Analysis of Shylock's
                Forensic Speech   163
                 (i) The Speech   164
                 (ii) The Analysis of the Speech   165

         2. The First Oral Phase   168

III. SOME PRIMAL FANTASIES CONCERNING THE PHAL-
     LIC PHASE   169

     A. THE FANTASY OF PREGNANCY THROUGH A FILL-
        ING OF THE "MOTHER'S BELLY" WITH URINE,
        AND OF ERECTION THROUGH A FILLING OF THE
        PENIS WITH URINE   169

B. THE FANTASY OF CLITORIS URINATION . . . 170

C. THE FANTASY OF AN "UNCASTRATED" CONSTITUTION 171

D. THE FANTASY OF A PHALLUS EQUIPPED WITH A MOUTH 176

    1. *The Devouring Paternal Phallus* . . . 177

    2. *The Devouring Maternal Phallus* . . 180

IV. A TRANSFERENCE DELUSION CONCERNING THE CASTRATION COMPLEX: THE DÉJÀ RACONTÉ 182

V. CONCLUSION 194

Chapter 6

THE GENITAL PHASE

I. THE PERSISTENCE OF EARLIER PHASES IN THE GENITAL PHASE 196

II. A NEW EROGENIC ZONE, DISCHARGING AN OLD PARTIAL LIBIDO 199

III. A PRIMITIVE EROGENIC MODEL 201

IV. ELABORATION UPON THE MODEL 203

A. THE CONCEPT OF PARTIAL SUBJECT AND PARTIAL OBJECT 204

B. THE FEMALE GENITAL PARTIAL SUBJECT: PART I 208

C. REPRESENTATIONS OF THE PARTIAL SUBJECT . 212

    1. *A Direct Representation: "The Spot"* . 212

    2. *Indirect Representations* 216
       a. "Mother Comes In" 216
       b. The "Wave Dream" 221

D. THE ORALITY OF THE LIBIDO EMPLOYED . . . 230

    1. *Menstrual Dreams* 230

    2. *A Typical Complaint Concerning the First Menstruation* 235

    3. *Pregnancy and Giving Birth* 238

E. THE FEMALE GENITAL (PROCREATIVE) PARTIAL SUBJECT: PART II 242

    1. *A Review of the Preceding Examples in Regard to the Discharge of Affect* . . 243

2. *A Second Review of the Same Examples with Regard to the Subject or Object Respectively of the Oral-Sadistic or Defused Aggression* 246

3. *Regressive Anal-Sadistic Interference with Menstruation* 247

4. *Oral-Sadistic Interference with Menstruation: The "Kreuz"* 252

F. ON THE MALE GENITAL PARTIAL SUBJECT . . 266

V. TOWARD A THEORY OF COITION 272

VI. POSTSCRIPTUM: NOTES ON AN ARIA AND DIALOGUE FROM "THE MAGIC FLUTE" 276

PART THREE

Chapter 7

ON EROGENIC (REGRESSIVELY PARTIAL-EROTIC) LANGUAGE

ON EROGENIC (REGRESSIVELY PARTIAL-EROTIC) LANGUAGE 285

I. INTRODUCTION 286

II. URETHRAL-EROTIC LANGUAGE 288

    A. INCONTINENCE TYPE 288

    B. PHALLIC TYPE 289

    C. MIXED TYPE 289

III. ANAL-EROTIC LANGUAGE 290

IV. ORAL-EROTIC SILENCE 293

Bibliography 297

Index 305

FOREWORD

The small series of monographs, of which this is the first, is not intended to be either critical or didactic; it is devoted to certain results of psychoanalytic research.

The *method* of my research need not be explained since its description is contained in the seventeen volumes of Freud's works. I may merely mention that with rare exceptions, it is directly applicable to neurotic disturbances only, and may quote Freud who once wrote: "Strictly speaking—and why should one not speak about this as strictly as possible?—only that analytic endeavor deserves the recognition as correct psychoanalysis that has succeeded in removing the amnesia obscuring to the adult the knowledge of his childhood, i.e. from about the second to the fifth year of life."[1]

This method is not easy to learn, and it is still more difficult to employ it toward original contributions. Apropos of this last, I remember how, as a young man, I mentioned to Freud one of his older followers whom I had found inspiring in spite of his indulging in flights of fancy. Freud, impatient, waved me aside: "Ach, das können wir nicht brauchen. Wir setzen doch Stein auf Stein . . ." ("Oh, we have no use for that. After all, we put stone upon stone . . ."). A few years ago, I looked through a newly published anthology in English of this man's writings, and saw how little of any value had remained.

Psychoanalysis, although in its infancy, is still a natural science; it already has entered, as do other natural sciences from time to time, a period of *Einzelforschung*, that is, of research on

[1] *'A Child Is Being Beaten'* (1919). Col. P., II.

special problems. The methodological difficulties of such research, if it concerns the analytic observation of adults, need hardly be enumerated: one cannot select a particular subject, nor can one "pursue" one in the sense of systematic follow-up. One cannot bend material to one's interest, let alone experiment with it: one has to take what each patient presents and subordinate one's own scientific interests to his therapeutic needs. In other words, chance alone dictates what grist comes to the mill; and one must therefore resign onself to that "fragmentary treatment of a subject" that Freud has once called his "personal predilection." One's attention, as I have expressed it previously, arrested here or there in the course of one's clinical work, becomes focused, and allows one to abstract from observation only so far as to place the abstraction in a context that is, in itself, fragmentary and inhomogeneous.

I am making so much of this in order to explain the necessitous disparity of the findings laid down in these volumes.

I have said that my purpose is not didactic. Were it so, it would have to feature the observations of others, and to strive for coherence; as it is my report cannot be but incoherent, since it limits itself, in the main, to what I believe I have observed. In so doing my observations are apt upon occasion to stray into fields where I am not an expert, and I have, therefore, to restrict myself to the briefest remarks, hoping that they may at some time stimulate future specialists. In addition, while some observations and the abstractions derived from them are definite, others are tentative; others again merely point to questions that, although they lie in my own field, I cannot answer.

Where I am definite, nothing is rash or unsubstantiated; my interest in all of the topics treated is of a fifteen to twenty years' duration, so that there has been much time to discard and revise. Nothing, of course, can be verified by the reader except through his own observation; but I have made it my business never to state anything without furnishing *clinical illustration*. In an attempt to offset the interruptions of theoretical discussions by the interpolation of clinical material, the former will be found, wherever possible, to continue directly after the (frequent) insertion of the latter.

There is one particular type of illustration that I have found to be, often I must confess with a sense of wonder approaching the eery, equivalent to the clinical one: *the Shakespearean portrait of man*. I must briefly justify its unusually frequent use.

The reader knows that this poet's knowledge and profundity in so many different fields has baffled many; which explains the layman's recurring desire to prove that Shakespeare was not himself but must have been someone else. Volumes have been written to try to show that he was a sailor, a soldier, a statesman, etc., because only then could he have known that much about sailoring, soldiering, or statescraft. Well, one could write another book proving that he was an analyst! For there is hardly anything that Freud has taught us, or that we have found for ourselves, that we do not encounter in the work of Shakespeare. To explain how this is possible would be to explain genius; I for one cannot even explain how a Freud was able to make the discoveries that he did in "Dora's" two months of analysis, or in the one-and-a-half-year one of the "Wolf Man." At any rate, here is a literally inexhaustible fund of "clinical" illustration, every bit as cogent as the correct interpretation of the patient's associations; and I have felt at liberty to employ it.[2]

2 The edition of Shakespeare's works generally in use, the so-called "Globe" edition, is a nineteenth-century "corruption." I use, therefore, the First Folio, reprinted by the Nonesuch Press in 1953, and collated by Herbert Fargeon and Ivor Brown, with the Quartos as well as with the "Globe." (These editors have replaced the antique letters, the S's, F's, V's, etc., for us an unnecessary obstacle, with modern typography.) The study of the work of Dr. G. B. Harrison of the University of Wisconsin has taught me how to correct obvious printer's errors in the Folios, and to choose what would appear to be the authentic reading of a given disputed version. (As the reader probably knows, no manuscript of any play in its author's hand exists; plays were made into working "scripts," in the modern sense of the word, and the originals were not preserved.)

I need hardly add that practically all italics in passages quoted are mine; the Folio uses them for names alone.

There is one more thing: Elizabethan and Jacobean spelling, punctuation, and typesetting are predominantly not *grammatical* but *dramatic*. This means that they assist language (in its literal meaning: "audible, articulate human speech as produced by the action of the tongue and adjacent vocal organs": Webster), not syntax; imitate affect rather than ideation. This opinion is held by some editors (Harrison), and rejected by others (Kittredge). Nevertheless, it is the

The analytic observation of the adult is, of course, complementary to the direct observation of the child; but it is not replaceable by the latter. The early development is, as Freud wrote with regard to the second year of life, and the last part of the first, "traversed so rapidly that direct observation could probably never have succeeded in grasping its fleeting forms."[3] I believe that this remark is valid for much of the first five years of life.

The introduction, occupying the first part of this volume, is —as is the foreword—one to the series. Freud's hypotheses, discussed introductorily, are prerequisite to whatever fragments of theory I shall advance. In attempting to add to Freud's work, I differ sometimes from him in minor, but hardly ever in fundamental matters. Of those there are only two for which the study of his writings has not prepared me.

With regard to the first of them I am apparently not quite alone; Anna Freud reports from direct child observation that she and those working with her found themselves "at variance with established analytic findings concerning *chronology*. Penis envy," she goes on to say, "which we expected to see in girls in the phallic phase, appeared with extreme violence according to some of our recordings in girls between eighteen and twenty-four months. In these cases, the responsible factor may have been the bodily intimacy between boys and girls as it exists in a residential nursery . . . It is less easily explained why in some cases infants showed definite reactions of disgust *before* toilet training had started, as well as reactions of shame long after exhibitionism had been interfered with."[4] The analysis of adults, brought up in homes, not institutions, confirms observations such as these, and extends them to almost every manifestation characteristic for the development of the child. Everything

conviction of the present writer that without its adoption—unequivocal and complete in spite of the coexistence of the many obvious typographical errors— the thorough analysis of many a Shakespearean line remains futile.

[3] *Introductory Lectures on Psycho-Analysis* (1916/17). Lecture XXI, p. 287.

[4] Anna Freud: *Observations on Child Development*. Psa. Study of the Child, VI, 1951.

happens, in general, earlier than analytic tradition would have it.[5]

With regard to the second matter, it will be remembered that Freud first took all the fantasies of his patients for memories, until he learned to distinguish between the two. My impression is that in so doing he went too far in *favoring fantasy at the cost of memory,* if my material is at all comparable to his, which in all other respects it has certainly proven to be. I do not mean to invalidate his classical finding that the neurotic suffers from his (unconscious) fantasies; but I do mean to say that the amnesia removal uncovers much more frequently than Freud's writings lead one to expect, *memories* of which there can be doubt as to their authenticity, yet which are of so bizarre a nature that, if one followed the general trend of these writings, one would declare them—erroneously—as *fantasies* of the polymorphously perverse child. Finding this, I found also the cause. It lies in *the unbelievable frequency of the (undiagnosed) ambulatory psychosis.* When one is able to diagnose it, one sees relatively few families of one's patients that are entirely free of it; and one recognizes that the patient in need of a long and thorough analysis would appear to be, by and large, someone who had been damaged by and has identified with a psychotic parent.

There is no place here to deal with the inexhaustible subject of the psychosis; I can therefore say only in passing that the child of such a parent becomes the object of defused aggression (maltreated and beaten almost within an inch of his life), and of a perverse sexuality that hardly knows an incest barrier (is seduced in the most bizarre ways by the parent, and, at his or her instigation, by others). Among the damages one may single out one as perhaps the severest: it appears as though the child takes over all of the feelings of guilt over incest that the parent

[5] Freud himself hints at an, undoubtedly phallic, "arousal of libido" in response to seeing his mother in the nude "between the ages of two and two and a half." Freud: *The Origins of Psychoanalysis* (1887-1902), ed. M. Bonaparte, A. Freud, E. Kris. New York: Basic Books, 1954.

should have had, but being psychotic, *did not.* This promotes an excessive unconscious need for punishment, of which Freud has said that it "sets the most stringent limitations to our therapeutic endeavor." We work, consequently at times, in a paradoxical situation: those who need us most often appear actually to want us least. I have made these remarks here because without them some readers might take exception, on the grounds of credibility, to some of my clinical illustrations.[6]

There are, finally, a few more remarks to be made.

With regard to the *title* of the present volume, it is, of course, but an approximation. The erogenic zone—charged with, discharging or inhibiting the discharge of libido—is obviously a part of the body. Its psychic representation is consequently a part of the body-ego and as such not without influence on the ego. I had therefore at many points to deal with the latter and, in so doing, to anticipate the second volume whose title is *Ego and Body-Ego*.

The distinction between erogeneity and libido is Freud's: "erogeneity" is the functioning of an erogenic zone, mentioned above; and "libido" is, for one thing, the energy of the sexual instincts. However, it is more than that; a discussion of the ambiguity of this indispensable concept will be found on pp. 44-49.

With regard to the *style* of these monographs, I have been told, on occasion, that my writing is sometimes so condensed that it is hard to follow my thought. I admit to an occasional excess of condensation. However, I feel that a science which

---

6 The appearance of Freud's biography compels me further to append a remark that I would not otherwise make. However, the initiative is no longer mine. In the first volume of his biography Jones gives a description of my father that enables the psychiatric reader to make his own diagnosis. Some of these readers, perhaps defending themselves against acknowledging the above-mentioned incidence in their own families, may therefore be tempted to dismiss what I have observed as a form of projection. For their benefit: following Freud's advice to the analyst to re-enter analysis, I have clarified the picture of my father in two expert and thorough analyses, the last in middle age with Ruth Mack Brunswick; and I have had an extended conversation with Freud himself about his onetime friend.

strives to reduce observable phenomena ultimately to hypothetical displacements of hypothetical quanta of cathectic energy inside the mental apparatus, and in so doing must do (at the present time) without the benefit of measuring these quanta and of expressing the economic results in mathematical language, is hard pressed for an adequate means of expression. If it commands none other than language, it will be forced to tool it toward one end: precision. It is astonishing, but illustrable by the prose of the greatest writers in any field (e.g., Pascal, Shakespeare, Benjamin Franklin in his letters), that the extreme refinement of language manifests without fail one particular characteristic of the primary process: condensation (cf., e.g., Freud's own style in the *Two Principles,* his *Negation,* or the *Outline*). I beg the reader's indulgence where I have tried to learn, in however modest a measure, from these great men and failed.

As for the subjects of my clinical illustrations, I have sacrificed specificity to anonymity: and, instead of allowing patients to come alive on the printed page, have in most cases reverted to the very "autopsic" designation of "a male," or "a female" that I have elsewhere decried.[7]

As to the *translations of Freud,* in quoting from them I have often found it necessary to approximate the original somewhat more closely; and when faced with the choice between a more idiomatic English and a more accurate rendering of the original I have preferred the latter. (In the case of untranslatable terms or idioms I have put the German in bracket or parenthesis behind the English approximation.) The result is, of course, that the reader looking up a passage will not always find it identical with my quotation.

With regard to the few sayings of Freud that have come down to me *by word of mouth*: my informants are no longer alive. I had therefore, after judging upon the accuracy of a given quo-

[7] See R. Fliess: *The Autopsic Encumbrance. Some Remarks on an Unconscious Interference with the Management of the Analytic Situation.* Int. J. Psa., XXXV, 1954.

tation, to decide when a particular one of my colleagues would have liked credit for it by name, and when he would have preferred anonymity; and so to be governed.

As to my *dispensing with a number of theoretical concepts* that have lately become *en vogue,* such as for example the "neutralization of instinctual energy," I am hesitant to sound critical because of my utter devotion to freedom of thought. Their proponents have as much right to promulgate these hypotheses as I have to reject them. I do so because they are, as far as I can see, unsupported—and I fear, at present at least, unsupportable—by any persuasive clinical observation.

With regard, finally, to the dilution that analysis has gradually undergone and the ensuing confusion in the minds of most—including, I am afraid, the better part of my readers—as to what is, and what is not analysis, I need not say much, but can instead recommend Maxwell Gitelson's essay *Psychoanalyst, USA, 1955* to their attention. I would like, however, to quote from the author's "credo," which he laid down in his short paper: "Psychoanalysis . . . with its technique"—consisting, I may add, in the interest of defining my own position, aside from adroit "management," of *free association* by the patient, *free-floating attention* on the part of the analyst, and *correct interpretation* by him—"has made and can continue to make its unique contribution to the sum total of our knowledge about the nature of man. . . . [*It*] . . . *cannot sustain extensive modifications without impairing the particular perspective which the scientific ordering of (the analytic) material requires . . . Psychoanalytic technique as a clinical method is at one and the same time our most fundamental psychological research method . . .* [and] . . . there are those whose special capacities and interests lead them to devote themselves to the basic psychoanalytic method and to some of these it is given to advance the discoveries begun by Freud."[8]

Reading this warms the heart at a time when originality in

8 Am. J. Psychiat., CXII, 1956. Italics mine.

clinical observation, however small, is by many as much frowned upon as is practicing strictly the "classical" Freudian method by others.

R.F.

New York,
Summer, 1956

EROGENEITY AND LIBIDO

PART ONE

1.

A BRIEF EXAMINATION OF THREE FUNDAMENTAL, IF CONTROVERSIAL, HYPOTHESES

Prerequisite to the theory of the psychosexual development of the human—as well as to all psychoanalytic theory—are certain hypotheses which, although convincing to Freud and to many of his students, have remained unconvincing to others. They are therefore, in general, looked upon as controversial. They must consequently be reviewed here, and their adoption by the present writer explained.

I. FREUD'S DUALISTIC THEORY OF THE INSTINCTS: A FEW DATA IN ITS SUPPORT

With regard to the first of these, *the dualistic hypothesis of the instincts,* the writer remembers a conversation with Freud. He said: "When, originally, I had this idea I thought to myself: this is either something altogether erroneous [*etwas ganz Abwegiges*], or something very important. . . . Well," he went on with a smile, "lately I have found myself more inclined toward the second alternative." This quotation implies proper argument: a hypothesis is justified solely by necessity. If one can no longer think without it, that is, if relinquishing it leads either to contradictory thought or to thought less economical, one adopts it.

Much that the analyst observes are phenomena consequent to regression; and it is some of these in the first place that remain unaccountable for without resorting to the dualistic hypothesis of the instincts. In a natural science the method of testing

3

thought is abstracting from observation. Rightfully I should therefore postpone testing this hypothesis to the clinical parts of this book and restrict myself introductorily to reflection. But I am forced to break the restriction as soon as I set it down. It is impossible for a scientist to "reflect" without observation; and the analytic theoretician is in no different a position. If, for example, he merely confesses that the monistic assumption of the production, by one basic instinct, of derivatives as antithetic as libido and aggression, and of transformation of those derivatives into each other, coerces his thought, whereas the dualistic assumption of *two* basic instincts, and their fusion and defusion, does not—he may be answered that others experience no such imposition. He has therefore no choice but to support his argument by clinical observation.

A brief review of the development of the analytic thought on the *suicide of the melancholic* may serve as an illustration. The first step naturally, was Freud's (53), who asked himself which one of the three factors, that he had found operative in melancholia, is specific for it. Two excluded themselves: the introjection as existing in many other conditions, and the ambivalence as appearing in the compulsive self-reproaches upon the death of beloved persons. One remained: (a) the regression to orality of the libido. The next steps were Abraham's (7): (b) the melancholic regresses to a fixation point at the second oral stage, with a tendency to regress further, and to escape from the tortures inflicted upon the object of the libido of this stage, to the peace of that of the first. Furthermore, (c) the self-reproaches are not only, as Freud discovered, reproaches originally directed by the person against the lost object but also by the lost object against the person. I believe that this clinically verifiable observation should lead one to assume a twofold and intertwined topography for the lost object: (d) its seat is not only the ego but the superego as well. Finally, (e) the libido regression is, as Freud has shown, accompanied by a defusion of instincts liberating enormous quantities of death instinct, and allowing (f) for their deposition in the superego, which becomes thereby a "pure culture of the death-instinct" in the melancholic (61A).

This leaves the question: what becomes of the libido? The above appears therefore, at first sight, to support a monistic hypothesis, for the answer seems practically implied: there is no libido left; the transformation of it into aggression is virtually complete. But a hypothesis cannot be tested *ad hoc*; and this one is not in accord with others of proven value with regard to pathological superego-ego relations (unconscious need for punishment, punishment dreams, etc.).

The dualistic hypothesis can do better. If the suicidal melancholic seeks the timeless peace of the passive first oral stage, obtainable later only temporarily by the use of drugs, his libido has regressed to this stage. The hypothesis of defusion allows for a distribution of aggression, manifest originally in the second oral stage, and libido, manifest originally in the first, with the superego the seat of the former, and the ego the seat of the latter.[1]

Thus, while defusion and libido regression are extreme, the superego that destroys is historically less regressive than the ego that is destroyed. This constellation renders the instinctual aim of the two opposed institutions in effect identical and permits a joint action, executive of a superego that annihilates an ego, desiring dissolution after the fashion of the first oral phase in which it did not exist. It is enough for the moment to stress the economy and the harmony of thought afforded by this hypothesis, and to cite, for the first that the much discussed problem of self-preservation is not even encountered; and for the second, that the replacement of the "constancy principle" by the "Nirvana principle" (which had recommended itself to Freud for reasons other than the existence of suicide), finds here its supreme application. It might naturally be possible to cover the same ground with a monistic theory of the instincts, but it would certainly not be either as economic or as harmonious.

Spitz, in a most instructive article (135), full of original observations, has described the original model of melancholia and suicide in the infant in response to the mother's removal. In

[1] For this and the following I must assume the responsibility; for I have read it nowhere and I cannot be certain how many analysts, if any, would be prepared to see it my way. Spitz (135), for instance, without relinquishing the dualistic hypothesis, elaborates theoretically in a different way.

the present context it is noteworthy that the disturbance does not arise before the child has entered the oral-sadistic phase, while "finger-sucking increased conspicuously" before, and still more so during, the depression.

Why then, one is forced to ask, is the dualistic theory controversial? I believe in the last analysis, because the theoretician is human. Prone, as is everyone, to fear death, and incapable, as are we all, of imagining his own, he avoids the fear, again as do we all, through a denial, whose perhaps subtlest form is while knowing that one *will* die, to ignore that one *must*. Death as accident does not imply death as necessity; it is not, at least in principle, inescapable, even if it be so in fact.

If, however, the fear of death is, as Freud believed it to be, a matter between ego and superego, the theoretician, compelled by his scientific conscience to accept the hypothesis of the death instinct, is, at the same time, compelled to accept, instead of denying death. He is thereby exposed to fear. It would seem that the imminence of this fear has made an indeterminate number of analysts phobic toward what Freud has called "the ubiquitousness of non-erotic aggression and destruction," and has prevented them from "granting [those instinctual manifestations] their due position in life" (70A).

Two phenomena, one from *public,* one from *private* life might be selected to illustrate the undeniability of such aggression.

(a) It would seem that in all of recorded history war has outweighed peace, because the death instinct prevails, as it does in the individual, eventually over Eros. Peoples are seized periodically by the urge to destroy: they break forth, with or without ideology, kill and torture; and the history of their seizures is the better half of the history of mankind:

"¶ 1:   Let me have war say I, it exceeds peace as far as day does night: it's spritely walking, audible, and full of vent. Peace is a very apoplexy, lethargy, mull'd, deaf, sleepy, insensible, a getter of more bastard children, than war's a destroyer of me.

"¶ 2:   'Tis so, and as war's in some sort may be said to be a ravisher, so it cannot be denied, but peace is a great maker of cuckolds.

"¶ 1:   Ay, and it makes men hate one another.

"¶ 3:   Reason, because they then less need one another: the wars for my money" (117A).

As for that half of our history, where "men hate one another" because libido and aggression are no longer distributed between groups opposing friend to foe, one need merely point to the frequent precipitation of aggression in members of a professional group, engaged in sublimated pursuits yet treating each other in the end, as infant brothers.

(b) One historic example may take the place of many recountable from direct observation.

According to the story, Leonardo da Vinci "was passing the Spini bank, hard by the church of Santa Trinita, [where] several notables were there assembled, who were discussing a passage in Dante, and seeing Leonardo, they bade him come and explain it to them. At the same time Michelangelo passed, and on one of the crowd calling to him, Leonardo said, 'Michelangelo will be able to tell you what it means.' To which the latter, thinking this had been said to entrap him, replied, *'Nay, do thou explain it thyself, horse-modeller that thou art—who, unable to cast a statue in bronze, was forced with shame to give up the attempt.'* So saying, he turned his back on them and departed" (80).

The example contains all the distinctive elements of the aggressive outbreak under consideration: the subject (Michelangelo) is singularly qualified to appreciate the superiority of the object (Leonardo) whom he must not only attack, but "destroy." Leonardo's existence as an artist is negated; what is left of him is an artisan, and an unsuccessful one at that.

It is true that the incident is misleading in two points—Leonardo's being the older, and the actuality of a contest between the two for a commission. Both these circumstances are, however, extrinsic: the incident could have occurred had their ages been the reverse, and had there been no competition. I have, in fact, often wondered at the "Platonic" character of the destructive intent, and failed to perceive of the gain through its gratification, until Freud gave eventually the better part of the answer. "The older brother," he wrote but a few years before his death, in the draft of a letter that has remained little known (75), "is the natural rival; it is to him that the smaller one proffers an elemental, unfathomably deep hostility, for which later years may find adequate the designation death-wish, intent to murder. To remove Joseph [his older brother], to take his place, to become Joseph himself must have been the strongest striving [*Gefühlsregung*] of the small child, Napoleon. It is strange, but it is secured through observation: infantile strivings as excessive as these are particularly apt to transform themselves into opposites. The hated rival becomes beloved; . . . the primal hatred [*Urhass*] has then been overcompensated . . . ! One must add that the process is a reversible one: primal hatred is likely to erupt again when the individual is confronted with the existence of an 'older brother'; his annihilation is the instinctual aim and the gain from it is the restoration of the original narcissism of the child."[2]

II. FREUD'S ASSUMPTION OF PHYLOGENETIC INHERITANCE

With regard to the second "controversial" hypothesis—the assumption of *phylogenetic inheritance* of "dispositions" (i.e., modes of reaction) and "content" (i.e., memory traces of expe-

[2] Speaking of the death instinct and citing in exemplification Leonardo da Vinci I cannot refrain from quoting him directly, because his notebooks contain a description of the death instinct, as concise and complete as Freud's, and identical in detail. Both the existence and the "mute" nature of man's "longing for his own destruction" are formulated; the antithesis between Eros and Thanatos is implied, and the "elasticity" of the instinct is recognized in the constant "desire to return to its source":

"Behold now the hope and desire to go back to our own country, and to return to our former state, how like it is to the moth with the light! And the man who with perpetual longing ever looks forward with joy to each new spring and each new summer, and to the new months and the new years, deeming that the things he longs for are too slow in coming, does not perceive that he is *longing for his own destruction. But this longing is the quintessence and spirit of the elements, that finding itself imprisoned within the life of the human body, desires continually to return to its source.* And I would have you know that *this very same longing is that quintessence inherent in nature,* and that man is a type of the world" (100). (Italics this writer's.)

riences of past generations)—it is impossible to be more eloquent in its defense than was Freud.

A. A CONDENSATION OF SUPPORTING ARGUMENT

If the priority for this hypothesis belongs to Jung, if Freud was slow in adopting it, it was because he regarded it "as a methodological error to seize upon a phylogenetic explanation before the ontogenetic possibilities have been exhausted," and because "obstinately disputing the importance of infantile prehistory while at the same time freely acknowledging the importance of ancestral prehistory" (55A), as did Jung, seemed to him arguing against reason.

Phylogenesis with Freud, is, methodologically speaking, a remainder. "It is only," he sums up, "in the prehistory of the neuroses that we see the child lay hold of this phylogenetic experience where his experience fails him. He fills in the lacunae in individual truth with prehistoric truth; he puts this experience of his ancestors in the place of his own" (55A). In other words, the hypothesis is again, as was the previous one, necessitated by clinical observation. "In studying reactions to early traumata we often find to our surprise that they do not keep strictly to what the individual himself has experienced, but deviate from this in a way that would accord much better with their being reactions to genetic events and in general can be explained only through such an influence" (78A). This phylogenetic event, however, the "motives" issuing from it and the "productions" elaborating upon it, "show themselves in need of elucidation which in quite a number of instances they can obtain from the individual's childhood!" (55A). The "primal fantasies," upon which we find the child act and which the neurotic perpetuates in his symptoms, are those that his ancestors have perpetuated in their mythologies and have acted upon—so we are forced to assume—in their collective childhood. Thus "the phylogenetically inherited schemata, which, like the categories of philosophy, are concerned with the business of 'placing' the impressions derived from actual experience [become] precipitates from this history of human civilization. . . . Wherever [such] experiences fail to fit in with the hereditary schema, they [i.e., the experiences] become remodelled in the imagination" (55B).

"If we accept the continued existence of . . . memory traces in our archaic inheritance, then we have bridged the gap between individual and mass psychology and can treat peoples as we do the individual neurotic" (78A). But "we also do something else. We diminish the overwide gap human arrogance in former times created between man and beast. If the so-called instincts of animals—which from the very beginning allow them to behave in their new conditions of living as if they were old and long-established ones—if this instinctual life of animals permits of any explanation, it can only be this: that they carry over into their new existence the experience of their kind; that is to say, that they have preserved in their minds memories of what their ancestors experienced. In the human animal things should not be fundamentally different. His own archaic heritage, though different in extent and character, corresponds to the instincts of animals" (78A).

Hence, for instance, the "sort of hardly definable knowledge" quasi "preparatory to an understanding" which Freud first observed in the "Wolf Man" (55B) reacting at the age of one and a half to the probable experience of and again, at four, to the reactivation of the primal scene.

Anna Freud (25), without mentioning her father's hypothesis, gives some clinical illustrations of what she calls "innate attitudes." She reports coitus play of young children in a nursery who could not have seen their parents alone together, or any other adults in sexual intimacy, or have even known a private bedroom. She describes the complete change in the behavior of boys toward their mother substitutes during the transition from the anal to the phallic phase. They "developed masculine qualities and a protective, often overbearing, sometimes indulgently affectionate attitude toward the woman which—under normal conditions—would have been classified invariably as a close imitation of the father and an identification with him." Yet these children lived without fathers. And, finally, she observed the development of "family attitudes" in the course of a few days in nursery children placed for adoption. "Our most instructive case in this respect," she writes, "was a boy who had entered the Nursery as a small baby, had never known his (or any other) family and was visiting for adoption at the age of four-and-a-half. His prospective parents were an affectionate couple, very eager to adopt a child. On the second or third morning, at breakfast, when the man kissed his wife before going to work, the boy had a fit of 'oedipal' jealousy and tried to 'separate the parents.' "

Finally, "this instinctive factor would then [generally] be the nucleus of the unconscious, a primitive kind of mental activity, which would later be dethroned and overlaid by human reason, when that faculty came to be acquired, but which in some people, perhaps in every one, would retain the power of drawing down to it the higher mental processes. Repression would be the return to this instinctive stage, and man would thus be paying for his great new acquisition with his liability to neurosis, and would be bearing witness by the possibility of the neuroses to the existence of those earlier, instinct-like, preliminary stages. But the significance of the traumas of early childhood would lie in the fact that to this unconscious they would contribute material which would save it from being worn away by the subsequent course of development" (55B).

It is a curious experience[3] to present these profound ideas to students of psychoanalysis, and to find them rather unreceptive. It does not seem to occur to them that the hypothesis of *phylogenetic* inheritance deserves consideration if for no other reason but that it was conceived by the man who had exploited *ontogenetic* acquisition to the limit. They appear little impressed by the fact that it is the originator of a method for the removal of

[3] The following section, under the titles: *Phylogenetic Vs. Ontogenetic Experience: Notes on a Passage of Dialogue between 'Little Hans' and His Father*, was published in the International Journal of Psycho-Analysis, Volume XXXVII, 1956, pp. 46-60, and is reprinted here with the kind permission of Dr. W. Hoffer, Editor.

the amnesias of childhood, and the discoverer of the repetition compulsion, who declares himself, even when satisfied with the removal of those amnesias, nevertheless as dissatisfied with the explanation that childhood experiences are repeated, unless childhood itself is looked upon as, in the last analysis, a repetition. One is likely to fail in persuading them that it is necessary to learn the method, to become able to trace repetition, and to have reduced much of the patients' present to their past, before one's experience has enabled one to achieve this dissatisfaction.

Although it is true that the hypothesis is supported by typical and easily available data, such as, e.g., intense sibling rivalry in an only child, or symbols lacking all admixture of picturization, as, e.g., wood for the mother, these data become evidence in its favor only after one has done much analytic work, and has learned that *more* does not furnish the missing explanations.

B. THE TRANSCRIPT OF AN "ARCHAIC" EXPERIENCE

In at least one place in Freud's clinical papers an archaic experience has, to my ear, been transcribed. It is a portion of dialogue between Little Hans and his father. The passage[4] loses much of its pregnant and affective quality in translation. The reader, acquainted with Freud's *Analysis of a Phobia in a Five-Year-Old Boy* (38) is familiar with the protagonists and the action. The sensitive and affectionate father, with a remarkable understanding of analytic thought, is the first "child analyst," and in "supervision" with Freud. The son, frank, vivacious, and original, as are most unintimidated children, is questioned, and answers or recounts spontaneously in many small "sessions" at home or on the occasion of walks. The dialogue under consideration consists altogether of questions and answers. It follows

---

[4] To read it for its word-by-word meaning one needs not only German, of course, but also the Austrian vernacular of the time. My retranslation, besides occasionally exchanging American for British English, is an attempt to approximate the original somewhat more closely at certain points, than does the text in the *Collected Papers*. I have italicized the decisive words or phrases, and when resorting to substitution of circumlocution, I have given the German in brackets. The parentheses are the father's as they occur in the original text.

an attack of fear suffered by the child while he observed a carriage passing in front of the house; he was afraid "because the horses are so proud, that they will fall down." The background: Little Hans, in his oedipal excitation, wants, apparently, to castrate both parents: the father in order to hold him at bay while he takes his place with the mother; and the mother in order to exchange her phallus for the castrated genital by whose virtue she can, in his imagination, be sexually possessed. The passage I have in mind is flanked by the admissions of these two castrative desires: the former concealed in the fear of the falling of the "proud" horses,[5] and the latter in the playful application of the knife "that Mamma has had" to the doll.[6]

This is the passage proper (38A):

" 'I asked him who it actually was that was so *proud*.

" '*He:* "*You are, when I come into bed with Mummy.*"

" '*I:* So you want me to fall down?"

" '*He:* "You should as a naked one (he means: barefoot, as Fritzl had been at the time) *knock up against a stone, and there blood must flow,* and at least I can be alone with Mummy a little. When you come up into the apartment I can quickly run away from Mummy, so that you don't see it."

" '*I:* "Can you remember who it was that knocked up against the stone?"

" '*He:* "Yes, Fritzl."

" '*I:* "When Fritzl fell down, what did you think?"

" '*He:* "That you should (stumble and) *hurl yourself against the stone.*" [*Dass du am Steine hinfliegen sollst.*]

" '*I:* "In other words, you would like to go to Mummy."

" '*He:* "Yes!"

---

5 Cf. the notes of "April 21."

6 Cf. the notes of "April 22." It was a rubber doll whom he called "Grete"; I suspect in memory of the previous "Grete, my Grete" from G......, whom he had shown in fantasy what his Mommy did when she was "completely naked in her shirt." (Notes of March 15) Hans pushed a small penknife into the doll, through the opening to which the little tin whistle, or squeaker, had once been attached, and then tore its feet and legs apart, so as to let the knife drop out, between the legs, and saying to the nurse: "Look there is the weeweemaker."

" *'I:* "Actually, why do I scold you?"

" *'He:* "I don't know that." (!!)

" *'I:* "Why?"

" *'He:* "Because you scold me so hard." [*Weil du eifern tust.*]

" *'I:* "But that is not true!"

" *'He:* "Yes, that is true, you do so get excited, and scold [*du tust eifern*]. I know it. *That must be true.*"

" 'My explanation that only little boys come into bed with their Mommies and that big ones sleep in their own beds had, evidently, not impressed him very much.' " (Italics this writer's.)

1. *Preliminary Remarks*

With regard to its form the texture of Hans's language changes at the point of his second answer abruptly. While preserving the homely idiom of a child as warp, it acquires a woof, a cross-threading that is almost biblical it is so forceful, original and adult. The father is pronounced "proud" (*stolz*), and is compared to a strutting horse where he ordinarily would be named as angry, grouchy, or cross. Instead of "barefoot" (a simple word which the child either knows or could easily circumlocute) he is imagined as "A naked one" (*als Nackter*), and *subjected to a punitive, gravely declaimed command.*[7] The latter gains by its repetition; it becomes more violent, and more injurious. The father is finally accused of *eifern*—an untranslatable verb which in adjectival form is also Luther's for the "jealousy" of the Lord. ("*Ich Dein Gott bin ein eifriger Gott.*")

With regard to its content, the text is both illogical and inconsistent. It does not quite follow that Hans can be with his mother if the father, like Fritzl, stubs his bare foot on a stone; and the child who had, a moment before, all but admitted that the father's displeasure with him is *a posteriori*, i.e., a consequence of his getting into the mother's bed, maintains suddenly that it is *a priori* and that he is ignorant of the reason. When

[7] The *style soutenu* of the passage tempts one to translate it: "*Thou shalt* as a naked one, etc."

the father reminds him that the jealous scolding is not true, the boy opposes him with "Yes, that is true, you do *eifern,* I know it." And, most enigmatically, "That *must* be true."

I believe that one hears him speak under the impact of phylogenetic experience.

To support this belief I can only attempt the analysis of the passage, and through reducing manifest content to latent thought perhaps raise a "reasonable doubt" in the reader's mind with regard to a purely ontogenetic origin of the ideas which forced the child to such unusual forms of expression. Not that the ontogenetic material is lacking; it covers practically every single point. "Proud" horses had actually been on the street. "The coachman," Hans's father explains "was reining (them) in tight, so that they were trotting with short steps and holding their heads high—they had really a proud gait"; and their "falling," displaced upon them from the father's desired death and the mother's observed pregnancy and anal "delivery" on the toilet, has been elucidated by Freud. Hans's playmate Fritzl had actually run barefoot and bled when he hit a stone, giving Hans the idea that the same fate might be his father's. When the mother took Hans into bed the father had actually objected and the parents had argued. As for the rest of it and the subsequent play with the doll, Freud has made it clear that Hans's observation of his parents' intercourse, while unconfirmed, is not necessarily excluded; and, one may add, neither is that of his mother's menstruation.

It is simply that this material does not either explain the unusual choice of expression, restore logic, or resolve the apparent contradiction.

In order to do that, one is forced to supplement individual with collective experience, historic with prehistoric material. This requires that one has absorbed what of it Freud has discovered, that one has gained in addition one's own impressions, some distinct and some indistinct, and that one is unafraid of sounding fantastic. It is characteristic of phylogenetic vestiges that they tax the imagination, and while they certainly should not be believed *quia absurdum,* they should be acknowledged *in spite* of appearing absurd. The relation of ontogenetic material to phylogenetic experience is comparable to that of the material of the dream to the wish in it. In either instance the latter expresses itself in the medium of the former. In the dialogue quoted above the ontogenetic material seems, however, at certain points insufficient for such an expression, and it is here that the speech of the child becomes particularly enigmatic.

I append the analysis of the passage.

2. *The Analysis of the Background*

The horse is not only, as Freud has found, a totemistic representation (58) for the parent but, as one finds in analysis, a symbol for him or her: either parent can be symbolized by the horse; and Hans's transference of them upon it is supported by a symbolization. The proud, erect horses drawing the carriage are the phallic parents in the primal scene. (The symbolization of the phallus through the body is so familiar to the analyst that it need not be pointed out.) Yet the scene is tinged by the preceding anal-sadistic wish of little Hans to beat his mother with the carpetbeater (cf. notes of April 17), i.e., to beat the dirt ("*Lumpf*") out of the mother. There is, consequently, the coachman who rules the horses, holds them back, cracks the whip, and so it seems, makes them defecate while making them trot.[8] Pregnancy finds in the scene a double allusion expressible by the double meaning of "carriage": the horses' gait alludes to the lordotic carriage (i.e., the posture) of pregnant women, which is why they "are so proud that they (will) fall down" (= so pregnant they will give birth); and the carriage (i.e., the vehicle), by being a wagon, alludes to the "boxcarts, furniture,

---

[8] Is it a coincidence that the doctor, still ready to "purge" his patient at the slightest provocation, considers himself a disciple of Hippocrates, the "ruler of horses"? (The name is derived from ἱπποκρατέω, to be superior in horse [ἵππος, horse, κραταίος, strong, mighty].) I am indebted to Professor Ostwald of the Classical Department, Columbia University, for the confirmation of this derivation.

vans and coal wagons" of which Hans had declared, immediately after wanting to beat the mother, that they were "storkbox wagons." Yet both coachman and horses are further overdetermined: the former, onlooker at the primal scene, represents Hans himself in the father's role; and the latter are a symbolization of the mother.

These overdeterminations and the excessive condensation to which they contribute require a few remarks.

Freud has made us aware that little Hans's fantasy, during the period in question, creates in the sign of *Verkehr*, i.e., that its products are concerned with transportation, traffic and intercourse, all of which are denoted by the one German word. The *Verkehr* in the passage is at first vehicular (carriage), then pedestrian (Fritzl and father), and in the end sexual (coming to Mommy); but in each instance Freud's remark, made on the occasion of another fantasy, that the father partakes in the boy's imaginary gratification, applies in some measure. I believe that the condensation in the figure of the coachman, of the passive onlooker to the primal scene and the active partner to it, is indicative of a typical identification of the oedipal child with the father for the purpose of an incestuous gratification. Freud formulates: "I would like to do something with Mama, something forbidden, I do not know what, but I do know you do it too." It appears that one may continue: "And I could do it if you would teach me, lend me your faculties, have me be you." This is equivalent to an introjection of the father into the ego, a collateral to that into the superego. It is not, however, the same as the "putting oneself in a masculine fashion in the place of the father" of Freud's description (63); for in the latter instance the father is, as Freud words it, "soon felt as an obstacle"; in the former he is imagined as of assistance. One may regard this identification with what I may be permitted to call the "assistive father" as a prerequisite to normal puberty where masturbation, so apt to retain the mother object unconsciously at the price of objection by the superego (guilt feelings), and the conviction of castration by the parent (physical damage),[9] is eventually exchanged for sexual intercourse, with the result that the boy is, as it were, the father in spite of his renunciation of the mother.

The symbolization of the mother through two categorically identical individuals (two men, two women, two strangers, etc.) is rather common, and the knowledge of it affords not infrequently the immediate grasp of an unconscious idea (19). It is here two horses that represent the mother engaged by the coachman, the father. That they move a carriage (i.e., that the mother is pregnant) is expressive of the idea, so consistently found in the child, of the production of a full-blown pregnancy during and simultaneous with the act.

So much for the background.

3. *The Analysis of the Passage Proper*

a. The Body as Phallus

Proud, etc.—The father is "proud" because he has an erection, both competitively and assistively (see above) when Hans comes into his mother's bed.

As a naked one, etc.—A symbolic representation of the phallus through the body. All symbolization proper is, as Freud has pointed out, phylogenetic; to explain it as ontogenetic is, one might add, reducing it to allusion or picturization. While the symbolized element and the symbol may separately be explainable on the basis of individual experience, the sameness of their unconscious equation in everybody is not. In the present instance the symbolic interpretation restores logic and justifies the choice of expression. The paternal phallus ready to act is a *"naked one,"*[10] and "there" blood would flow, i.e., if the father were injured there the mother, ready for him, would instead receive Hans "a little," i.e., for a sexual span of time.

9 A coarse but colorful description of this twofold consequence was a famous American evangelist's threat to young men who drank, smoked, or masturbated, that they would both get syphilis and go to Hell.

10 Anyone who prefers to follow the father instead of Hans and to interpret "barefoot" exchanges of course only one symbolization of the phallus for another.

Knock up against . . .—The act of knocking bears much over-determination. I have once tried to demonstrate, in an only partially successful study (17) of the ritual of "knocking on wood," that "knocking" may discharge in attenuation, libidinal ("knocking up") and aggressive ("knocking down") strivings directed against the mother. An extensive comment here is out of place, for the present material does not either permit a convincing verification nor compel one to resort to phylogenetic assumptions.

b. The Enigma of the "Stone"

A stone and there . . . must flow.—This is different both with regard to the "stone" and the "flowing." The connection between these two elements and the element "horse" is so typical yet so puzzling that it would be difficult to be intelligible about them were we not at least in the possession of the analysis of "Bismarck's Dream" (31A).

(i) *Bismarck's Dream:* This analysis is Hanns Sachs's; its significance lies in Freud's approval, for he quoted it in its entirety and verbatim. Besides remarking upon a symbol, Freud points to the dream as "an excellent example of the representation of thoughts, serious and far removed from anything sexual, through infantile sexual material." The present task is to support the impression that this material is, in part, phylogenetic. The reader, interested in the subject, will familiarize himself with the dream and its analysis in order to understand the following comment, which is confined to the few pertinent parts.[11]

---

11 In spite of the fact that the dream text alone cannot render my comment intelligible, I will quote it: "I dreamt (as I related the first thing next morning to my wife and other witnesses) that I was riding on a narrow Alpine path, precipice on the right, rocks on the left. The path grew narrower, so that the horse refused to proceed and it was impossible to turn round or dismount, owing to lack of space. Then, with my whip in my left hand, I struck the smooth rock and called on God. The whip grew to an endless length, the rocky wall dropped like a piece of stage scenery and opened out a broad path with a view over hills and forests, like a landscape in Bohemia [*"auf Hügel und Waldlandschaft,"* a grammatical ambiguity with the plural not necessarily implied. It could mean: "upon hill and woodland as in Bohemia"]. There were Prussian troops with

Ad: Bismarck's dream. There is the rock (*the "stone"*) and the *"horse"*; the latter "refusing" (to proceed) while "turning round and dismounting . . . are impossible" i.o.w. bridling and assuming a posture closely resembling that of the *"proud"* horses of Little Hans. The smooth rock is *struck* (knocked against) with the riding whip and *God is called (for assistance)* whereupon the whip grows to endless length, the rock *tumbles* and the Bohemian landscape behind it ("hills and woodlands") is seen and entered.

Ad: Sachs's analysis of the dream. It is the missing element "flowing" that the interpreter has—in Freud's opinion: correctly—supplied. Sachs divides his interpretation, schematically, into that of three layers. In the most superficial one the fulfillment of a "logistic" wish from the present: the invasion of Austria by the Prussians. In the deepest layer: a pleasurable infantile masturbation (the use of the riding whip in the hand and its elongation), practiced against its prohibition as sin (the "left" hand) and in secret ("In the manifest content God is called on as though to deny, as ostentatiously as possible, any thought of a prohibition or secret"). In the middle layer: an identification of the dreamer "who came from a Bible-loving Protestant family" with the leader Moses. "The whole process of the miraculous liberation from a need through the striking of a rock with its simultaneous drafting of God as a helper bears a conspicuous resemblance to the Biblical scene in which Moses struck water from a rock for the thirsting Children of Israel." The connection between middle and deepest layer: on the one hand, the similarity between Bismarck's situation at the time of the dream, and that of Moses in the Biblical story; on the other, the fact that "the Bible passage contains several details very well employable for the masturbation phantasy: seizing of the—in the dream unambiguously phallic—rod against God's prohibition, the production of fluid from it . . . [and] the threat of death (an-

---

banners, and even in my dream the thought came to me at once that I must report it to your Majesty. This dream was fulfilled, and I woke up rejoiced and strengthened . . ." (31A, p. 378).

nounced to Moses by God)." Furthermore: "Of the two proph-
ecies made by God to Moses—that he should see the Promised
Land but that he should not enter it—the first is clearly represented as fulfilled ("the view over hills and forests"), while the
second, highly distressing one was not mentioned at all. The
water was probably sacrificed to the requirements of secondary
revision [cf. p. 388 ff.], which successfully endeavored to make
this scene and the former one into a single unity; instead of
water, the rock itself fell." Finally: "A dream such as this of
victory and conquest is often a cover for a wish to succeed in an
erotic conquest; certain features of the dream, such as, for instance, that an obstacle was set in the way of the dreamer's advance but that after he had made use of the extensible whip a
broad path opened out, might point in that direction, but they
afford an insufficient basis for inferring that a definite trend of
thoughts and wishes . . . ran through the dream."

Revisory Comment. Sachs's paper was published in 1913; the
last statement is, in the light of present-day knowledge, invalid.
The "trend of thought and wish [running] through the dream"
is the sexual conquest of the mother, the instinctual object of
masturbatory gratification. But the mother, reduced to her
sexual parts[12] finds a double representation in the dream, as
does consequently the masturbation. Once she is represented as
path (vagina), hill (mons veneris) and woodland (region distinguished by pubic hair) which are seen (cf. Abraham's remark on
the incest prohibition in the Bible as an exhibitionist-scopto-
philic injunction), and entered (by proxy). The masturbation
concerned with this partial object is undoubtedly *puberty* masturbation. Yet there is, simultaneously, another representation
of partial object and masturbatory gratification which belongs
to the *phallic* phase. The path narrows, it is no longer negoti-
able; riding the horse (incest object, see above) becomes impossible, as does dismounting or turning back. Here the dreamer

12 I believe that the term "partial object" is a suitable one for denoting this
reduction.

meets with an impasse, flanked by rock and abyss. The meaning of the second of these two elements is familiar; it represents the maternal vulva, qualified by the phallic ignorance of the vagina and the phallic knowledge of childbirth: it threatens the dreamer with falling down (*niederkommen*—see above) in identification with the mother object. The significance of the first element poses the problem.[13] Since the aggregate to which it belongs is phallic, the original vaginal path impenetrable and narrow, the symbolic allusion to childbirth excretory (see above) and since water issues from it, one is prepared to find its nature urethral-erotic.

Familiar with the circuitous course of analytic investigation, the reader will bear with me if I interpolate at this point two descriptions: (1) one of a piece of evidence published by Freud, and (2) the other of the experience of a patient of my own.

(ii) *Leonardo's Drawing:* Freud, in discussing the sexual abstinence dominating Leonardo da Vinci's life and work (40), reproduces by way of a footnote a sexual drawing of the artist, and its discussion by Reitler. He calls the drawing, unique in the artist's work, a "representation of the sexual act in sagittal cross section" and the discussion as containing some strange (remarkable) errors," bearing out his characterization of Leonardo. I abstract Reitler's comment, which of course must be examined while viewing the drawing itself:

(a) The male body is drawn in its totality, the female only in part.

(b) The man's head with its long wavy locks appears female.

(c) The female breast has two defects: it is "ugly" and "pendulous"; and the mamilla has only one milk duct, extending far into the abdominal cavity (cysterna Chyli?) and "perhaps having some kind of connection with the sexual

---

[13] The typical occurrence of this element has caught Freud's attention; its mysterious nature escaped him. He writes: "The complicated topography of the female genitalia renders it understandable that they are very frequently represented as landscape with rock, woods, and water. . . ." Through woods and water, yes; but why such unambiguously soft parts through rock?

organs." The latter error, Reitler points out, might be explained by the prohibition against dissection in Leonardo's time and possibly by an intent of the draughtsman to represent anatomically, the coincidence of the beginning of lactation with the ending of gestation.

(d) This, however, explains hardly the selectively neglectful treatment of the female genital: "while the vagina and an

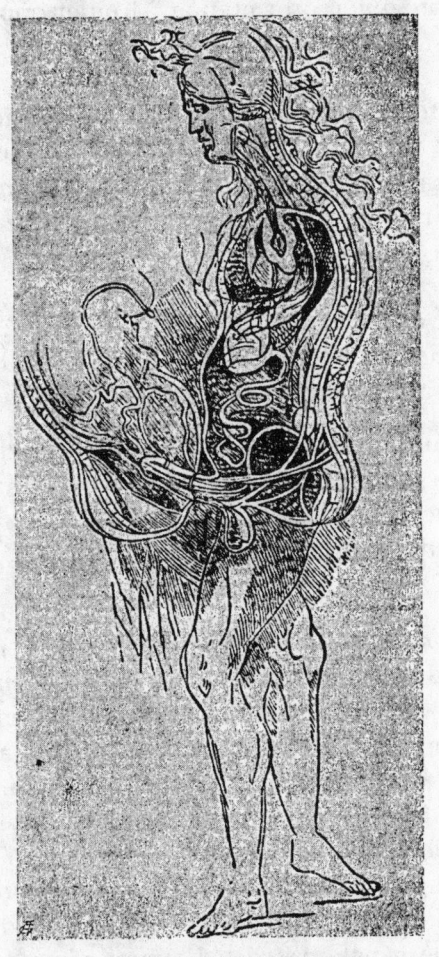

LEONARDO'S DRAWING

From Freud: *Gesammelte Werke*, Vol. VIII, p. 137

intimation of the portio uteri are discernible the womb itself is drawn in utterly confused lines." (The male genital is, in contrast, represented much more correctly and in detail.)

(e) It is "extremely strange" that the "coitus is performed" standing up. "A particularly strong sexual repression must be believed to have caused this singular (*solitären*), almost grotesque representation." Reitler opposes the lying to the standing position as expressive of a wanting to enjoy.

(f) The features of the man's feminine head show unwillingness and rejection. He "frowns, glances sideways with an expression of (shameful) timidity, the lips are compressed and their corners drawn downwards." The countenance, far from conveying pleasure or transport, expresses but reluctance and disgust.

(g) The feet of the two partners are exchanged: the male has a left, the female a right foot—which is the opposite of what their position in the drawing requires.

Freud confines himself to remarking that Reitler's presentation was criticized because it has been held inadmissible to draw such serious conclusions from a cursory drawing and because it was not even certain that its fragments really belong together.

Revisory Comment. The "remarkable errors," i.e., those not due to the lack of dissective practice, become understandable when one frees oneself from the prepossession engendered by Freud's caption. The drawing does not represent a cross-section of the "sexual act," but of *masturbation*. The man is standing, seen in profile from the left, the cross-section, confined to neck and trunk, relieves the (left-handed) draughtsman of the necessity of revealing arm and hand. The man's countenance is a guilty one and his posture befits the shy, sideward glance. The fragment of the female, restricted almost completely to pelvis and breast, is a representation of the "partial object" mentioned above, i.e., of the (mother) object, reduced to her sexual parts. The representation, however, is here again in part genital and in part phallic. The vagina, mature and easily passable, is combined with a youthful, attractive breast. (Reitler's description of it as "ugly and pendulous" must be due to an affective interference with his judgment indicative of an empathic unconscious recognition of the female as the mother.) The complete lack of anal as well as urethral apertures has apparently struck no one; noticing it, one is inclined to regard it as allusive of a continence problem and the "error" in the drawing of the mamilla as the result of a displacement upon the latter of the clitoris in the state of erection. Tracing the course of the vagina, one finds the "path" actually becoming narrow and impassable at precisely the point where the phallus impinges upon ("knocks" against) the phallic cervix. (This is achieved by a shading of the shorter fornix anterior so that only the longer fornix posteriori continues the vaginal tract.) Of the uterus proper, in contrast to portio and vagina, it appears that the "utterly confused lines" render it as a twin of the bladder, with the result that the woman, instead of having two breasts and one bladder, has two bladders and one breast. This formulation is justifiable on the grounds that the presence of the breast is a gratuitous one in the first plase; the "mamma" should not, of course, be visible in a median section. Standing up, facing each other, I have always found to be representative in dreams of an oral-erotic activity between the two partners. Whether or not the legs of the latter belong to the drawing is immaterial. If they do, Leonardo in drawing has exchanged right and left; if they do not, someone else has empathically done so in joining. The exchange is in either instance, symptomatic of an "anal reversal";[14] which in its turn is symbolic of a cathectic displacement from

[14] This phenomenon—the exchange of front and back or its equivalent such as that of right and left—has first been described by Jones. Abraham (4) has supplied its meaning, the cathectic displacement from the genital to the anal zone. Mine is the term, and the clinical observation that the displacement symbolized by the anal reversal, and effecting overcathexis of the powerful anal sphincter, occurs in the interest of the preservation of continence.

the genital to the anal zone (Abraham) for the purpose of preserving continence in the face of an imminent urethral-erotic
discharge of phallic libido.

I need not append a comparison of the dream with the drawing. The equivalence of all essential details cannot have escaped
the student. It is merely the "stone" that appears in the dream
and does not appear in the drawing.

(iii) *Freud's Dream:* Is it an accident that this stone is sup-
pliable if one looks for a dream treating the subject of the
drawing? Freud, in one of his own (31B), after dissecting his
own pelvis, rides through a passage that with a sharp turn at its
end (association: lobby of his house with baby carriages) and
walks subsequently "with an Alpine guide . . . through a changing landscape" on "swampy" and "slippery" ground, arriving
eventually at a "small wooden house ending in an open window." The dream concludes with an elaborate "bridge symbolism": two boards put on the window sill in order to bridge a
chasm, provide a narrowing of the path pursued by the dreamer,
but change subsequently into two benches with two men and
two children lying on them. In the dream hut, boards and
benches are of wood (the mother in the mentality of the genital
phase); in the association hut and benches become stone, a
narrow vacated Etruscan burial chamber with two *stone
benches.* ("The inside of the wooden house in the dream looks
exactly like it, except that stone is replaced through wood.") I
refrain from pointing to the many details in which this dream
resembles Bismarck's (both dreamers are, e.g., carried through
Alpine territory; one by a horse, the other by a *Führer*=guide
and leader, etc.) and the drawing by Leonardo (e.g., two stone
benches instead of two bladders where the path narrows, etc.).
But I venture upon the opinion that the stone belongs to the
phallic phase and to the representation, in the urethral-erotic
mentality of this phase, of the mother.

(iv) *The Experience of a Patient:* A woman patient found
herself on a walk in a beautiful, semicircular little bay filled

with water and rocks. Wanting to urinate, she went about looking for a "secret place," felt a mounting excitement and became
aware that both urge and search were of a sexual nature. For a
fleeting moment she imagined an older woman friend as an onlooker to the impending urination but was soon seized by the
fantasy of her mother to whom she was showing herself squatting and urinating most forcefully as though the stream had the
power of penetration. She had the choice, her report continues,
between two kinds of rocks filling the inlet, split rocks with
crevices underneath which "one could hear the water rumble"
and whole rocks with a smooth surface; she selected eventually
one of the latter and describes it as of granite, "so that it could
not be hurt." She squatted and indulged in a forceful and sexually pleasurable urination on the rock with the afterthought of
exhibiting toward the sun which might burn the area, not ordinarily so exposed. The episode was concluded by an only partly
enjoyable masturbation, accompanied by one fleeting and one
extensive fantasy. She imagined at first, while sitting on the
stones, a little boy urinating proudly into the wide open ocean,
giving him, as it were, her maternal blessing, and subsequently,
a certain man doing so most forcefully and with a tremendous
stream, while she intensely watched him and the spray whipped
up by the surf, "looking for the best vantage point to observe
him in profile." The report on this incident was followed abruptly by another about some intensely emotional experiences
with horses, which had at no other time been of concern to the
patient. In these experiences both the masturbation and the
fantasy with it were repeated symbolically. The dissection (cf.
Bismarck's opening up of the landscape, Leonardo's median
section, Freud's dissecting his pelvis) was supplied in her association to the fantasy about her mother. When the mother prepared, as she frequently did, a chicken by cutting it up via the
anus in order to take out its intestines, the child by way of a
standing joke, used to commiserate with "the poor chicken" as
though "it were still alive."

One cannot, in view of the greater import and the longer

persistence of the preoedipal sexuality in the female, expect to be able to show the phallic behind the genital representation of the mother-object as clearly as in the previous examples concerning males. Yet I believe it is present. The sea, in particular with a concave coastline and often a promontory (which was in this case not missing), is a *genital* representation; the small bay with the rumbling water and the secret place, allusive of the typical phallic ignorance of from where urine issues in the girl,[15] appears *phallic*. It is the latter representation that here, again, employs the "stone."

(v) *Concluding Argument in re: "Stone":* I have never been able to obtain associations to this element, typical in a phallic urethral-erotic representation of the mother object. I assume that the element is a "mute" one, i.e., a symbol. I believe that symbols, in the psychoanalytic sense of the term, represent in the last analysis "sexual" parts or functions.[16] If the "stone" is a symbol, what does it symbolize? Is the symbolized element nameable; and if not, where is one led in the search? The material presented above suggests a bladder stone, i.e., a stone in the bladder as the phallic urethral-erotic precursor of the child in the womb.[17] While rejecting this as absurd one remembers that the oath bearing the name of Hippocrates juxtaposes the prohibition of lithotomy and that of abortion.[18] Cutting a stone

15 Overdetermined by the secret place which, in contrast to the boy, she has to find for the purpose of urination.

16 A statement, correct only in close approximation; an elaboration upon it could not, however, contribute to the present subject.

17 There was, and in some places still is, a recurring use of stones, among a variety of peoples (Syria, Sicily, Brittany, Swabia, parts of Africa, Japan, and the Southern Archipelago, particularly New Caledonia), for a variety of purposes (including fertility and childbirth), and especially to influence tree *fertility* by hanging stones on them, to influence *crops* by placing stones in the fields, to improve the yield of *fishing*, and last but not least—to make *rain* (22).

18 Castiglioni's translator and editor (13) quotes the oath in his own as well as in someone else's translation: "I will not give to a woman a pessary to produce abortion. With purity and holiness I will pass my life and practice my art. I will not cut persons laboring under the stone, but will leave this to be done by men who are practitioners of this work. . . ." "The injunction," the author states in an attempt to provide explanation, ". . . was probably due to an agreement that such an operation should be practiced only by specialists, or perhaps

from the bladder is equivalent to aborting a child from the womb. The oath, as is so much Greek writing of the period, is "modern"; it still graces the physician's office; its commands and injunctions are still valid, except for the prohibition to cut those "laboring under the stone." It is here that one is reminded of the Orphic origin of the oath.[19] Orphic rites, Webster says, "include ceremonies of great antiquity and probably savage origin"; for the mysterious injunction against lithotomy one is thus referred to the early or earliest history of mankind. Since this history and the individuals figuring in it are unknown, we can hardly expect to be in the position of interpreting an occasional vestige.

The analytic argument leads to the same point as the historical one.[20] An element, symbolized by a symbol, is an element of the (pleasure-physiological) body-ego. Yet even if a bladder stone were to represent itself in the latter[21] in such a fashion that it could be endowed with the phallic meaning rendered above it would not in so doing assist the solution of the mystery of the "stone." For both symbols and symbolized elements are ubiquitous; and the latter are normal parts of the body-ego; even those belonging to infantile sexual organizations (phallus,

---

arose from the known danger of producing sterility (functional castration) by this operation." In a footnote a further authority (Dr. Savas Nittis, Bulletin of the History of Medicine, VII, 1939, p. 719) is cited as translating the verb *temeo* as "castrate" rather than "cut," with the last sentence quoted above then reading: "I will not castrate, indeed not even sufferers from the stone, and I will keep apart from men engaging in this deed," which in Castiglioni's words "was regarded as an abomination."

19 Castiglioni: "The hieratic character of this oath, and the clear allusion to medical art as a doctrine of the initiated, all show how it is derived directly from the rites of the Pythagoreans, the Orphics, and other sects of initiates" (13, p. 155).

20 It may here be recalled that two phenomena, belonging to phallic sexuality and urethral-erotic discharge respectively, have caused Freud to draw inferences concerning the prehistory of mankind. He believed that the termination of infantile sexuality in this phase, followed by latency, made it probable that we are descended from an animal that matured at the age of five. With regard to urethral eroticism he suggested that the shame reaction to urethral incontinence pointed toward a period of human development preceding those whose vestiges are preserved in myths and folklore.

21 Freud himself has pointed to the creation of "organ representations" by morbid formations.

cloaca) are, e.g., under the impact of an unconscious infantile dream wish, revivable in the normal adult. The bladder stone is of limited incidence, and pathological. It would therefore demand that one postulate the case of a symbol ("stone") that, by being ubiquitous, does, and of a symbolized element (bladder stone) that by being infrequent and abnormal, does not, fulfill the conditions present in symbolization. Since this is arbitrary and insupportable by observation, I refuse so to postulate. Instead I am led to assume that the missing element, symbolized by the stone, is unknown and unimaginable because it belongs to a prehistoric ancestor of unknown and undivinable constitution.

c. The Bleeding to be Limited

And there blood must flow, etc.—It is evidently not much blood that flows, for it gives Hans only a little time with his mother; and it does not prevent his father from coming up into the apartment (= entering her. Cf., e.g., Freud's analysis of his "Dream of the Staircase"). Some will be satisfied that this limitation of bleeding is a compromise between a wish and its rejection; others, without doubting this, will want more of an explanation. I believe that the limitation is a typical element in the primal fantasy of castration.

Unable to prove this, I can only illustrate it, abortively by way of a few hints; two (i, ii) from a patient's associations and two others (iii and iv) from the literature of the world.

(i) The archaic reaction to defloration, described by Freud (54), found a symbolic expression in the parapraxia of a patient who, in depicting it, employed several elements of the fantasy of Little Hans. After her first intercourse, during which she has been anesthetic, both she and her partner were standing in the nude ("as a naked one") when she inadvertently smashed a glass. Splinters hit the man's foot (cf. Fritzl, "barefoot"), making it bleed. The scene struck her as ludicrous, and she insisted that the man leave the house (cf. Hans's father) after the wound had been bandaged. Her report ends with the gratuitous information, rendered in a peculiarly factual, and yet wistful tone: *"It was only a little blood. . . ."*

(ii) A male patient, when the analysis had, for the first time, restored his full potency, told of a parapraxia of his wife which was understandable only if one considered it as a reactive symbolic action. Before going to bed the next time with the intent of having intercourse, she stubbed her toe (Fritzl) on the bathroom door so that it bled somewhat. He reported this with the same words: *"Oh, it was just a little blood. . . ."*

(iii) Rashi has Abraham, who is forbidden to kill his son Isaac, suggest instead, no less gratuitously, a symbolic castration (89A):

(Abraham to the Angel:) "I shall make him a wound and draw forth from him a *small amount of blood.*"

(The Angel to Abraham:) "Do not do anything to him, [that is] do not make in him a defect . . ." (89).

(iv) Conversely, the sleepwalking Lady Macbeth's initial attempt to "undo" Duncan's murder by hallucinating the conversation with her husband previous to it:

Fye My Lord, fie, a Souldier and affear'd? What need we feare? Who knoes it, when none can call our powre to accompt. . . .

breaks down with her sudden awareness of the bleeding *without limitation*

Yet who would have thought the olde man to have *so much blood* in him [123A].

One wonders, is the limitation of bleeding a mark, distinguishing castration from murder?

d. A Symbolic Modulation

". . . you should (stumble and) hurl yourself against the stone."—Here castration has become murder. The transformation is brought about by an employment of symbolism, reminiscent of what the musician calls "enharmonic" modulation. In

the ambiguous "as a naked one" as well as in the unambiguous "coming up into the apartment" ("*Wenn du in die Wohnung heraufkommst*"= if you enter the mother) the paternal phallus is symbolized by the father's body. By retaining this symbolization while changing the "knocking" *(anstossen* into the allusively fatal "hurling" [*hinfliegen*]) the parricide is achieved.

e. The Inconsistency is Explained

"*'I don't know that.' (!!)*"—The father's double exclamation mark expresses evidently his astonishment at the apparent inconsistency, mentioned above (p. 14). How is it possible in the present context that the child, without lying, declares himself ignorant as to why he is scolded? Had he not been explicit a moment before as to why the father is "proud"? The inconsistency disappears when one appreciates that the "pride" of the father is mute, and his "scolding" is vocal; and acknowledges that the disapproval expressed in the former is not the same as the disapproval expressed in the latter. One is externally, and the other internally, real; one belongs to the father, and the other is projected upon him: the reproachful gesture is that of the actual father, the reproachful voice is the *"voice of the superego."*

Before entering the discussion of this concept it is convenient to consider the rest of the conversation and to explain, introductorily, three German expressions translatable only in approximation; (1) *eigentlich,* (2) *schimpfen,* (3) *eifern.* (1) *Eigentlich* is closely approximated by "actually," except that it seems somewhat stronger; for it denotes a reference to the very core of the matter. (2) *Schimpfen* is to scold, except that its relation to an object is looser. One usually, in present usage, scolds *someone* (German—*jemanden ausschimpfen)* while one may, in contrast (e.g., when one is drunk) just stand there, or walk around and *schimpfen.* (3) *Eifern* is untranslatable. *Eifrig* is eager; *Eifer* is zeal; *eifersüchtig* is jealous. (Cf. p. 14.) In circumlocuting the verb one would have to use a definition listed by Webster under "zeal," and designated as both Biblical and obsolete.

Eifern is the vocal and verbal expression of "ardor of feeling taking the form of jealousy, indignation, or the like"; whereby jealousy besides its current meaning has the obsolete one of a "wrathful" or "ireful" state. In the Viennese vernacular of the time the word was apparently not exclusively Biblical but enjoyed an infrequent colloquial use. The boy could, for instance, have picked it up from a maid.[22] However, in view of the content of the passage and the fact that the father does not employ the word anywhere while the boy uses it only in this one place and, finally, in view of the boy's emphatic conviction that it explains the imaginary, synonymous *"schimpfen,"* I do not believe that this invalidates any of my comment. On the contrary, it confirms, in the case of a particular word, what was said in general of the stylistic texture of the passage (cf. p. 14) as a whole, with its warp of idiom, and its woof of *style soutenu*.

The father used *"eigentlich"* twice in the fragment of dialogue under consideration and each time in the course of a question. The first question is rational and a product of forethought; the father had learned from Freud that his person had been displaced by the son onto the horse, and he tries to undo the displacement. In so doing he is successful, and by the standards of an analysis we would call his procedure correct. The second question is irrational and asked on the spur of the moment. There has been no previous talk of *schimpfen;* the subject is injected into the conversation precipitately and from nowhere, by the father who a moment later denies categorically that it even exists. ("But that is not true!") He is unsuccessful, gains from his patient but an irrational answer which he does not understand ("Because you do *'eifern'* ") and by the standards of an analysis I would call his procedure symptomatic of a sudden, although transient, "counteridentification." I have suggested (19) this term for the—unconscious and technically undesirable—identification of the analyst with a constituent part of the patient's ego; I shall now explain what I believe to be expressed on the basis of other clinical observations, in this

22 I am indebted to Dr. Marianne Kris for this information.

last, irrational part of the conversation between Little Hans and his father.

(i) *A Superego in Statu Nascendi.*—Hans is in the process of developing a superego. He is about to introject the father and to equip the new structural part of his ego thus gained with the aggression directed against the father, in response to the latter's demand to inhibit the libidinal strivings toward the mother. However, the process is not completed. The situation is therefore most instructively complicated by the fact that the father's person in the outside world is simultaneously still the object of that aggression. It is thus necessary, although confusing, that the subsequent discussion reflect this simultaneity by treating the establishment of a superego as both accomplished and impending.

Anticipating, interpersonally, as it were, Freud's formula (70C) for the intrapersonal superego-ego relation "If I were the father and you the child I would treat you badly," Hans subjects (in fantasy and in exaggeration) the father to a punishment suffered originally by little Fritzl, a child. In so doing he identifies with the father. The question raised by the excess of his aggression is: does he not identify with an archaic father, an inherited father-imago? Freud thought so. "One may also say," he writes (70C), "that when a child reacts to the first great instinctual deprivations with an excessive aggressiveness on a corresponding strictness of his superego, it is thereby following a phylogenetic prototype, unheedful of what reaction would in reality be justified. For the father of primitive times was certainly terrifying, and one may safely attribute the utmost degree of aggressiveness to him."

It is certainly in response to this identification, whatever its nature, that Hans's father relinquishes under the impact of the fury of the parricidal incestuous "petit sauvage"—for a moment and at one point—reality, and counteridentifies with the superego, *in statu nascendi,* of his son. The response of the son to this counteridentification is a projection of the nucleus of his superego, as far as it has been formed, upon the father. The result of both counteridentification (19) and projection (20) is what it always is, a delusion: the father disregards reality by implying that he *"schimpft,"* and the son by maintaining that he *"eifert."* In other words, a delusion—for a brief moment one in a transient *folie à deux*—about the existence of a wrathfully scolding voice.

(ii) *The Voice of the Superego.*—In order to justify having called this voice the "voice of the superego" it is necessary to adduce several observations made by several observers; Freud himself and two of his students.

(1) Hans gives two different answers to the twice repeated, unrealistic question as to why he is scolded: "I don't know that" and: "because you do *eifern.*" In so doing he illustrates clinically Freud's observation, made many years later (70B), that "in the individual . . . the aggressions of the superego become, in the case of tension, *most clamorously perceptible as reproaches* whereas the demands themselves remain frequently *unconscious in the background.*" (Italics this writer's.) In other words, Hans experiences a vociferous scolding projected upon the father, but he is ignorant of its content. "If one brings them [i.e., the demands] to conscious recognition," Freud goes on to say in the place quoted above, "it becomes evident that they coincide with the prescriptions of the prevailing cultural superego" (i.e., the "superego of a cultural epoch"). This is illustrated by the father's concluding remark that the son had evidently remained "unimpressed" by the demand to relinquish the mother, i.e., by the incest prohibition, upon which civilizations are based.

(2) Isakower (26) has observed linguistic phenomena of a mixed motor and perceptory character in the process of falling asleep, that is, during the period before the superego has shrunk to whatever reappears, if it does, in the course of the redifferentiation of ego, as the "censor." He describes these phenomena as distinguished, at first, by "an almost exaggeratedly elaborate grammatical and syntactic structure," where "the speech flows along in complex phrases with strongly accentuated sentences of

animated and changing form." Subsequently, however, it "loses clarity" until at last "there remains only an impression of lively and complicated periods without any verbal elements which can be clearly grasped," and it finally ends in a murmur. He concludes, that it is here "not so much *content* that is characteristic of the superego but almost exclusively the *tone* and *shape* of a well-organized grammatical structure. . . ." In waking up these phenomena are "much briefer and more succinct" but have "often a superego-tinge, sometimes threatening, sometimes criticizing," and elicit "an inexplicable respect" from the individual, "although they are very often a quite unintelligible jargon."

The observation is confirmable, and equivalent to a clinical illustration of Freud's statement. In my experience, the phenomenon is not, however, confined to hypnagogic and hypnopompic conditions. I remember, for instance, a compulsive patient in whose daydreams it prevailed at times; he spoke and heard silently what he described as emphatic but senseless arguments, full of incisive oratory but void of all content. In a schizophrenic patient, the phenomenon appeared at first as a disturbing, often frightening, "noise," that became later identifiable as a "scolding"; violent, verbal, but again without signification.

The superego phenomenon here described is easily identifiable with the father's illusory *schimpfen,* incomprehensible to the son; and it is evidently the superego manifesting itself after the fashion of the phenomenon that compels the son to insist, projectively, that the father does *eifern.*

It is not so easy to reconcile the existence of the "phenomenon" with the fundamental remarks of Freud about the substratum of the superego. But I believe that it can be done. After raising the question (61B) as to whether the unconscious superego consists—as does the ego—in preconscious, originally acoustic, word images or in what else it does consist, Freud gives the "modest answer" that the superego "cannot possibly disown its origin from auditory perceptions; it is, after all part of the ego and remains by way of these word-images (concepts, abstractions) accessible to consciousness. Yet the cathectic energy of these contents of the superego is not supplied by auditory perception, instruction, reading, but by sources of the id."

The "phenomenon" contradicts this "answer" inasmuch as its nature is the opposite of that of "concepts" and "abstractions"; in the latter content prevails over form, in the former form over content. I would find the contradiction unresolvable, were it not for the fact that long clinical observation has convinced me of the correctness of a certain remark made by Freud about the constitution of the superego, although he made it but once (73A) and omitted it from his last summing up of the subject (77A). The superego, as far as it represents identifications with the parents, is "determined by the earliest parent-images" only; identifications with the later parents, however important for the formation of character, "concern . . . only the ego, are without influence upon the superego. . . ." If that is so, does it not imply that the parent, nuclear to the superego, is "preverbal"? The phenomenon would become understandable as a combination of auditory revival and motor imitation of the earliest parent's speech, perceived intensely but not, of course, understood. One could look upon it as symptomatic of a regressive re-identification, as it were, with this parent who spoke to the infant's ear merely in "lively and complicated periods" and "strongly accentuated sentences of animated and changing form." Thus the speech of the "earliest parent" would become the "voice of the superego."

This observation *complements* Freud's finding that the superego remains accessible to consciousness by way of word images denotative, singly or in combination, of concepts and abstractions; but it does not *contradict* it. After all, the child understands and speaks long before it forms a superego; and the "earliest parent," of a somewhat later phase, is therefore undoubtedly "verbal."

However, the voice of the superego is but incompletely understood if one does not add, in applying Freud's tenet, that the cathectic energy of this voice likewise is "supplied . . . by sources in the id." In fact without such supposition one could not explain either its intensity, its power and sometimes punitive nature, or how it ever became the voice of the superego. The conviction of "Little Hans," and for a moment that of his father, of the existence of a wrathfully paternal voice, is reactive to the preceding aggression against the father. Freud contends that the ultimate explanation for the feeling of guilt lies in the "primal ambivalence of the filial feeling" (*"uranfängliche Gefühlsambivalenz gegen den Vater"*), in other words, in a quality of the id. ". . . After the hatred," he writes (70C), "had been gratified through [the] aggression, [the] love became manifest in the remorse about the deed (of parricide), set up the superego by identification with the father, giving it the father's power *quasi* as punishment for the deed of aggression committed against him. . . ." While Freud presents here a reconstruction of the childhood of the human race, Little Hans illustrates it with an episode in his own personal childhood: for it is immediately after the violent—one is almost tempted to say Euripidean—fantasy of hurling the father to death, that he finds himself under the spell of the punitive "voice of the superego." That the remorse, linking crime and punishment, remains latent may be due to the precipitate interference of the counteridentifying analyst father with spontaneous self-expression.[23]

(3) As a third contribution toward justifying the term "voice of the superego," I may add the observation (20) that individuals characterized by a sadomasochistic relation between ego and superego, and the ability to produce autohypnotic states, prove themselves strangely dependent upon a voice. The characteristics of this voice, except for the prevalence of form to the exclusion of content, are antithetic to those of the wrathful scolding experienced by Little Hans. The voice—their own, or someone else's, the analyst's, the newscaster's on the radio—is monotonous, conversational, lacking all affect. It is experi-

---

[23] This is not, of course, the only possibility. The analyst witnesses almost daily the belated supply of missing links in a dream after the hour, in associations in the next hour, or even at a much later time.

enced as pleasant, not frightening; a libidinal, not an aggressive voice. Yet it is, nevertheless, the voice of the superego. Freud has taught us in his study on humor (68) that under certain conditions the superego manifests its origin, not from the "bad" and malevolent parent, but from the "good" and benevolent parent as well. It is the vocal representation of this parent that induces the individuals mentioned above to indulge in the hypnotic submission to an archaic father-imago. The concept of the nature of the hypnotic reaction as, in the last analysis, a phylogenetic remnant, is Freud's; I am merely distinguishing between the hypnotic *reaction* and the hypnotic *condition* because the case of what Ferenczi has called "mother-hypnosis" shows that the *reaction* can be induced by the voice of a libidinal parent while the *condition,* result of the reaction, constitutes, as Freud has showed, the submission to an aggressive parent. It is the latter that I have observed (20), as projected, by the patients mentioned above, upon the analyst. The projection of this archaic aggressive parent, nuclear to the superego, produces delusions about the analyst, and by so doing interferes with the illusion-producing transference of the individual parent. Most pertinent to the present subject is the fact that the archaic parent shows in projection the same unvarying traits: the intent of torturing and killing, mendacity and lack of humor.

These typical traits are not missing in the delusion of Little Hans; they are all present, if only—as is the case with some of them—in intimation. With regard to the first of the traits one must make the allowance that superego formation is being observed here *in statu nascendi:* the intent of killing the father cruelly is here still the son's; it has not yet been transferred permanently upon the superego, where it changes its object. The second trait, less intelligible but never absent, mendacity, is implied in Hans's protest: yes, it *is* true that the father does *eifern;* the father's denial is the equivalent of a lie. As far as the third trait is concerned, it is implied emphatically in the definition of *"eifern"* rendered above. (Cf. p. 32.) Consumed by ardent indignation, jealous, and in a wrathful state, Hans's father—or the archaic father projected upon him—is in a condition admitting of no benevolence, let alone humor. *"Yes, that is true . . . I know it. That must be true."*

It is hardly necessary to call attention to the fact that the child does not argue as he ordinarily would: yes, that is true, you scolded me only this morning, or last Sunday, when I did such and such and you got angry, etc. His argument is entirely *a priori;* he dispenses with observation and defends his position as one would in upholding a dogma. Yet the intensity of the argument and its formal qualities, tone and rhythm, supply the missing observation. It is really Little Hans himself who does *eifern.*

4. *Conclusion*

This is as far as I can possibly go in an attempt to persuade the reader to hear the speech as I hear it; and to doubt that the child was inspired to speak as he does under the impact of his personal experience alone. If my observations are incoherent, it is because I have followed an incoherent verbalization. If I have argued in a circle by adducing observations which Freud held to be phylogenetic as evidence of phylogenesis, I have done so only at certain points. At other points I have gone further and adduced typical manifestations, difficult to explain onto-genetically; and in one instance, that of the stone, I have tried to demonstrate that it may remain unexplained just because it is *pre*historic. I believe that I have removed incongruence and contradiction in the verbalization of Little Hans, both as to form and to content. That this can be done with the help of Freud's hypothesis, and cannot be done without it, is perhaps the strongest argument in that hypothesis' favor.

C. PHYLOGENETIC INHERITANCE: CONCLUDING ARGUMENT

"With the neurotic," Freud, grown old, jots down for himself in his *Posthumous Notes,* "one is as on a prehistoric landscape, e.g., in the Jura. The big Saurians are still at large, and the horsetails and rushes are as high as palms" (79); and with this metaphor completes the circle of thought that had found its first, almost casual, expression when almost forty years earlier he had spoken of childhood as a period "that had later become prehistoric."[24]

It is this thought that one must understand in order to profit from the hypothesis for the study of regressive conditions. In his own development the child traces that of the species; the acquisition of upright gait, continence, language, is psychogenetically speaking, repetition. The result: "The nucleus of the unconscious consists of man's archaic inheritance; and whatever part of that inheritance has to be left behind in the advance to later phases of development, because it is useless or incompatible with what is new and harmful to it, falls a victim to the process of repression" (56A).

1. Freud's Three Concepts of Repression

The foregoing formulation implies that we traverse an early period of our life where *im*pression and *ex*pression are, in part, phylogenetic; and that the "primal repression" (*Urverdrängung*) (49), successful or unsuccessful, through which we dispose or attempt to dispose of "archaic" experience is an individual repetition of what Freud has once termed "organic repression" in the development of the species (70D). One might call it a "following into organic repression" in analogy to all later repression, which Freud has called a "following into (primal) repression" (*Nachdrängen*), and in so doing recognize the central position of primal repression, intermediate between organic repression on one side and (following it to) repression on the other, that adds to the significance of this ontogenetically earliest form of defense. One does well, therefore, to bring the theory of it up to date.

2. An Addendum to the Theory of "Primal Repression"

Freud's definition of primal repression includes mechanism and object. The object is an unconscious idea—an idea that had

24 ". . . in der später prähistorisch gewordenen Kinderzeit" (31C).

never been conscious—and the mechanism is the establishment of a preconscious countercathexis. The result of the process: an unconscious idea remains unconscious, but is protected against ever becoming conscious. Primal repression is thus not only the earliest, but also the most primitive form of repression. The mechanism of following into repression, as Freud has described it, is a more complicated one; and the object of it is a conscious idea. The latter had been able to become conscious perhaps concomitant to its overcathexis with a preconscious verbal idea (*Wortvorstellung*) which, in the act of (following into) repression, must be relinquished and replaced by—perhaps transformed into—a countercathexis (49, 50).

This description implies that the beginning of primal repression precedes the existence of verbal ideas, that is the acquisition of language; but it raises the question as to the nature of the preconscious countercathexis. I believe that the latter is essentially that of a "primary identification." (Primary identifications were defined by Freud as the precursors of object relations; the latter, established later, are reconvertible into secondary identifications.) I believe, furthermore, that the objects of primary and secondary identifications, respectively, are what Freud, in describing one of their later vicissitudes termed respectively, the "earliest" and the "later" parents (73). The distinction between the two: the earliest parent is an ontogenetic elaboration upon a phylogenetic object; the later parent is purely ontogenetic, and fusible with those persons ("educators, teachers, ideal models") who will subsequently occupy his position. Primal repression, primary identification, and earliest parent have thus one characteristic in common: they are archaic. The description, however, of primal repression permits an addendum: the preconscious countercathexis preventing the unconscious idea from becoming conscious is erected in the course of a primary identification with an earliest parent.[25]

25 Hartmann (84), without distinguishing between the different forms of repression, had pondered the instinctual nature of the countercathexis. He believes it is "neutralized" aggression. Since, however, he does not adduce clinical observations necessitating the concept of "neutralization of instincts" I do not see

3. *On the Nature and Inhibition of Archaic Affect*

One benefit of such an assumption is that it permits an accounting, in primal repression, for the factor deciding upon success or failure of all repression: the inhibition of affect. An idea representative of an instinctual drive is, as Freud has explained, repressible only if the affect-quantum belonging to it is suppressible (49). In the case of primal repression the affect to be suppressed is archaic, its mastery is dependent upon the formation of ego and therefore, as is ego formation itself, upon primary identification. This means that Freud's classic description of the consequences of (following into) repression, which consist not only in a "withholding of an instinctual stirring [*Triebregung*] from consciousness but also from the development of affect and from the motivation of muscular activity" (50, 47) must be applied and adapted to the conditions under which primal repression occurs.

The first of these conditions is implied, I believe, in another of his posthumously published notations; "The assumption of inherited traces [*Erbspuren*] in the id changes, as it were, our opinions [*Ansichten*] of it" (79). One need not presume to know what was in the author's mind when he wrote this sentence in order to be aware that in describing the id in his comprehensive lecture on the "Anatomy of the Psychic Personality" (73A) as late as 1932 he made no mention of these inherited traces. They must therefore be added to this description; and their addition does indeed change our conception of the id to the extent that an indefinable number of "the instinctual needs [*Triebbedürfnisse*] . . . finding their psychic expression in it" must likewise be thought of as archaic.

The second condition specific for primal repression is that these archaic "instinct-cathexes [*Triebbesetzungen*] demanding discharge" must be denied it by an ego that is in the process of

---

any reason for following him. I prefer to confine myself to referring to the obvious fact that the primary identifications, mentioned above, begin in the oral-sadistic phase.

being formed. Thus the mastery of archaic affect can be successful only at the rate of the formation of ego. The ego, however,
concerned with "blocking the 'archaic' instinctual drive from
motivation of muscular activity" while acquiring articulation,
upright gait, continence, is primarily the body-ego. Its establishment is dependent upon primary identification with an articulate, upright and continent earliest parent; its "psychic quality"
is, throughout life, preconscious; and its role in the process of
primal repression is that of a countercathexis inhibiting the
liberation of archaic affect. Furthermore, in view of the function of dominant erotogenic zones in elaborating upon instinctual needs, one can hardly avoid the conviction that the
original discharge of archaic strivings is at first ingestive and
later excretory; and that continence is requisite to its inhibition. This is equivalent to regarding "sphincter morality"
(to borrow Ferenczi's term) as the precursor of morality; and
the developing ego, as far as the management of archaic affect
is concerned (to borrow Freud's term), principally a "body-ego."

All in all: the analyst must expect to find phylogenesis behind
ontogenesis, primary behind secondary identification, and primal repression behind repression. It is thus but a slight exaggeration to say that if we evaluate a therapeutic analysis
according to how much of the individual's prehistory it has
brought out of amnesia, we could by the same token evaluate
certain branches of analytic research according to how many
data pertaining to the ancestral prehistory they have been able
to add.

III. FREUD'S HYPOTHESIS OF THE LIBIDO: THREE DIFFERENT DEFINITIONS OF THE CONCEPT

With regard to the third hypothesis—that of the "libido"—
since it is controversial only among the dissenting schools, its
discussion could be omitted were it not so badly in need of
clarification. The concept "libido" has actually three different
definitions. The first is more definite than the second and third;

none has found in Freud's work a completely consistent application. The theoretician therefore is both compelled and entitled to define selectively for himself and to state his particular definitions.

In so doing, I shall not do too well; for I am unable either to abolish the ambiguity of the concept, to improve upon it or to replace it. It will remain in the end, as it is at the present time, defective—and indispensable.

A. *The First Definition*

The *first* definition: libido is the energy of the sexual instincts; not of all of Eros, but that from a group of instinctual drive whose origin is not only somatic, but systemic, and which supply, consequently, a particular, namely a sexual, kind of stimulation to the mental apparatus. "For the energy of the destructive instinct," Freud has stated, "we lack a term analogous to the libido" (77B). This is not, of course, to be understood literally, although it has so been understood. I believe that it means that within the death instinct, counterpart of Eros, there is one or a group of instinctual drives—the destructive (aggressive) instinct(s)—that is, or are, the counterpart of the sexual ones, but whose origin, although somatic, is not systemic. The difference becomes clear when the systems of origin and discharge are distinguished.

The system of origin for the sexual instincts is what might for want of a better name be called a "hormonal-metabolic entity"[26] in the body from which the id, open at one end (as it were) toward somatic (processes) absorbs the instinctual needs which acquire in it their psychic expression (73A). The system of discharge is the erogenic zone, without which what Freud has termed the "transformation of the instinctual need into affective expression" (48) could not occur. The system of discharge for the destructive instinct is the musculature, indispensable for a

[26] Cf. Freud (36): "In . . . distinguishing between libidinal and other forms of psychic energy we express the presumption that the sexual processes in the organism are distinguished from the nutritive processes by a special chemistry."

discharge upon the object, and often demonstrably active in instances of a "retroversion onto the subject." A specific system of origin is not, however, discernible at the present time. If the id, as it must be imagined as doing, "absorbs" destructive instinctual needs engendered by somatic processes, one cannot at present hold any particular system or process responsible for the production of what is absorbed.

It is, furthermore, undecided whether or not "pure destruction without libidinal addition occurs" (77C), and if it did, whether it could yield pleasure. We cannot, therefore, at the present time know whether the variety of destructive aims should be ascribed to the destructive instinct itself, or to the admixture of libido without which it has not yet been observed.

One can, of course, argue: be all that as it may, there is surely an energy to be postulated for the destructive instinct; why then not give it a name? I believe the abstention is wise. Any term would imply analogies with the libido of which we are ignorant and would permit us to forget how few properties of the destructive instinct are known. I cannot, therefore, go along with those authors who speak of a "destrudo," or of a "desaggressivization." They do not advance a single new clinical datum that would render these concepts necessary. I must therefore suspect that they simply do what Freud deliberately has avoided: make formal analogies concerning the nature and the vicissitudes of the destructive instinct to those of the libido, concerning which the original terms (such as, e.g., "desexualization") *had been necessitated by Freud's clinical observations.*

B. *The Second Definition*

As for the *second* definition of the libido, it is easy to show the need for it, but difficult to supply it, even by circumlocution. We speak unhesitatingly, following Freud, of a partial libido, of libido regression, of a desexualization of the libido. Do we imply a partial energy as distinct from an energy? Do we suppose that an energy undergoes a desexualization? The very questions are absurd.

The confusion made explicit here is, of course, implied in Freud's original introduction of the concept (36): "We have defined the concept of libido as a quantitatively variable force which could serve as a measure of processes and transformations occurring in the field of sexual excitation. We distinguish this libido in respect of its special origin from the energy which must be supposed to underlie mental processes in general, and we thus also attribute a *qualitative* character to it" (36A).

"Psychoanalysis," wrote Schilder in 1924, astutely but rather loosely, "means by the expression libido not only the energy (of the sexual instincts) but also the experience" (114). This records the need for a second definition, but it does not even attempt to supply the material for it: the libido is not definable as experience. Freud has once furnished a comparatively successful, if obscure, second definition himself: "The sexual instinct, whose dynamic expressions in the psychic life may be called 'libido,' is composed of partial instincts, into which it can also be decomposed again, and which compose themselves into certain organizations" (60). A "dynamic expression" can indeed be that of a partial instinct; it can be regressive and it can tend toward discharge of a nonsexual nature.

A well-known example may take the place of an improvement upon Freud's definition. The "second beating-phantasy" is described by Freud as dependent upon a "reverting" from the genital (i.e., phallic) "to the pregenital, sadistic-anal organization of the sexual life," due to which "the genital organization itself undergoes a regressive debasement to a lower level. 'My father loves me' was meant in a genital sense; owing to the regression it is turned into 'Father beats me (I am beaten by father).' Thus this being beaten is . . . *not only the punishment for the forbidden genital relation, but also the regressive substitute for it,* and it is from this latter source that it derives the libidinal excitation which is from this time on attached to it, and which finds its outlet in onanistic acts" (56B).

This example concerning an "infantile neurosis" contains Freud's description of a regression of the libido in the sense of its second, unfurnishable definition. Its application to certain clinical observations of adults may demonstrate the indispensability of the concept.

Juxtapose, for instance, two females, one in whom this fantasy, only slightly altered, is conscious and accompanies clitoral masturbation; and another who, without such assistance, responds orgastically to severe actual beatings. You will wish to say that in both the libido has regressed to the anal-sadistic stage. But you will want to say it without prejudice to whatever you may furthermore want to say about their egos. It is self-evident that the sexual constitution of the ego, as far as its erotogeneity is concerned, is a different one in each case; but if I add that the first suffered from an extremely severe depression, while the second did not, but had made an avocation of her perversion, it becomes equally evident that the ego, in other respects, the superego, and their interrelation, were also different in the two women.

C. *The Distinction Between Erogeneity and Libido*

The libido in the second, unformulable sense of its definition cannot be done without. The concept is indispensable; it particularly is so where the pursuance of the vicissitudes of a partial instinct makes it necessary to discriminate between its "dynamic expression in the psychic life," the "libido," and the elaboration upon the latter through the erotogenic apparatus reflected in the "body-ego." Libido, in other words, must be radically distinguished from erotogeneity, which denotes the function of an erogenic zone—part of the body and hence of the body-ego —that elaborates upon the libido with which it is being charged by discharging it or by inhibiting the discharge either partly or altogether. Schematically speaking the two are "consonant" at the time of the original dominance of a zone, and often "dissonant" in the case of later regression. Thus an erotogenic zone, consequent to its regressive revival, may be charged with elaborating upon a libido either more or less regressive than the zone itself in terms of its dominance, regained in the course of the regressive process. In either case, we need the hypothesis of the libido as an instinct-derivative product—topographically perhaps no longer id but certainly not yet ego—for the purposes of investigation.

D. *The Third Definition*

There is, finally a third usage, if not a third definition, for the term: the observable mixture of sexual and aggressive instinct derivatives, or the demand for elaboration made by them upon the ego, is frequently called libido. "We justify," Freud explains, "our inclusion of aggressive impulses in the libido by supposing that sadism is an instinctual fusion of purely libidinal and purely destructive impulses, a fusion which thence forward persists without interruption" (77C).

One might add that the inclusion makes it possible to defer judgment upon the plasticity of aggressive instincts. Do their aims vary, in analogy with the aim of the partial libido? Or is the apparent variety of aggressive aims (such as, e.g., Abraham's anal-sadistic *perdere* and *amittere*) a consequence of the degree of fusion and therefore really a variety of the partial libidinal aim, whose attainment depends merely upon the admixture of varying quantities of aggression? We cannot answer this question. But we cannot even ask it without employing the concept of the libido, in spite of the ambiguity of its definition.

PART TWO

PRELIMINARY REMARKS

In Part Two, the main part of the present volume, I have followed Freud in adopting Abraham's tabulation of the development of the libido; not only to achieve a semblance of order but at the same time, a progression, allowing me to "put stone upon stone" by adducing observations of relatively simple phenomena toward the explanation of more complicated conditions.

The extensive *overlapping* of the various phases in the development of the child is well known to his direct observer. "The oral phase, for instance," writes Anna Freud (23), "persists for months after the anal-sadistic organization has come into being; anal-sadistic manifestations do not disappear with the beginning of the phallic phase. The latency period is usually in existence for one or two years before the tendencies of the first infantile period fade into the background. It would, for instance, be erroneous to conclude from a persistence of oral or anal forms of autoerotic gratification into the fourth or fifth year, that the child has failed to reach the phallic level. It never happens that the libido expresses itself wholly in the manifestations of the latest phase of development; some part of it invariably remains attached to earlier modes of expression." And W. Hoffer (88) adds: "The process of development is not a straightforward one; it is rather in fact, as observation and child analysis have shown, an alternating forward and backward movement whereby many impulses do not undergo a forward transformation but remain in a latent state, to become regressively reactivated should an inner necessity arise for them to be so."

This "inner necessity" corresponds in the observation of the adult to the clinical *onset* of the neurosis. In certain instances such an onset is barely observable; there are at best a few short years, for example in early puberty, when the patient was clinically normal. In others, the infantile neurosis had, even under conditions of a disturbed latency, been overcome, and the patient-to-be was able, as Freud expresses it, "to perform and enjoy." It is only in his twenties or thirties that suddenly all achievement breaks down; and the neurosis has, as have most other diseases, an inception. It is extremely instructive to learn how at this point the individual's childhood, which for a decade or two had apparently been outgrown, in each and everyone of its damaging aspects becomes traumatic.

One may, with all this in mind, imagine how complicated a picture presents itself to the observer of regressive conditions.

In order to clarify this picture, at least in a measure, I have devoted the initial section of Chapters IV, V, and VI to clinical observations enlarging upon the *persistence* of characteristics of earlier phases of both erogeneity and libido in the later phase under consideration, notwithstanding their partly altered manifestations. This has made it necessary to show in much detail how a zone is compelled to elaborate upon a partial libido dissonant with it, and in so doing often to emulate earlier dominant zones. The rest includes a variety of observations, and portions of theory more or less increasing in number with each subsequent chapter. Yet the framework for all of them is Freud's and Ábraham's writing, which I cannot but expect the reader to have absorbed.

2

THE FIRST ORAL PHASE

The first oral phase requires a brief chapter, although little in it is original, because, as the French proverb has it, one should begin with the beginning. But I must ask the reader to appreciate my position. It is a different one with regard to this phase than it is with regard to all others. The analysis of adults is not the appropriate method for the study of the first oral phase, because the first six months of life are out of reach for the removal of amnesias. One does obtain, occasionally, reliable memories from the first year of life; but I have never found them to go back any further than to the ninth or tenth month. The evidence for anything prior to this time is circumstantial: re-enactment inside or outside of the transference, stories told to the patient by his family, etc. The method for the investigation of the oral-erotic and the inception of the oral-sadistic phase is the direct analytic observation of infants. It is here that, as far as I can judge, the most original work in all analysis in recent years has been done by such investigators as Hoffer, Margaret Mahler, Spitz, and next to them Anna Freud and Ernst Kris. I shall therefore lean heavily on their publications, selecting what appears as of particular relevance to the analysis of adults.

I. THE UNIT OF MOUTH AND EYE

Voltaire, in his *Dictionnaire Philosophique,* has Saint Clement report that the Lord, asked when His kingdom would come, gave the answer: "Ça sera quand deux ne feront qu'un, quand le dehors ressemblera au dedans, et quand il n'y aura ni male ni femelle."[1] Here the earliest individual past, where there was no aggression, no outside distinguishable from an inside, and no ego opposable to an object, is projected collectively into the remotest future. A world, at last at peace, is described as that of the nurseling at one with the maternal breast.

At first there is not, of course, a breast—only a nipple; but if the child is "all mouth," the nipple is merely the mouth in the state of gratification.[2] (Hoffer [87] remarks that the mouth sucks and swallows already inside the womb!) Of the sensory organs it is the eye that first becomes an accessory to the mouth; milk, for instance, felt and tasted initially inside the mouth, is later, when overflowing, seen on the breast and felt "outside" on the skin.

Spitz (137) has noted that at an earlier time the baby while nursing at the breast stares unwaveringly, from the beginning of feeding to the end of it, *at the mother's face;* and his observation has convinced him that "breast and face are experienced as one and indivisible." Mouth and eye would thus, almost from birth on, be a perceptory unit; the mouth can be observed as early as the later part of the first oral phase, at first sharing with, subsequently relinquishing to, the eye some of its functions.

As a sensory sphere, the eye appears well equipped for the role of an adjunct to the mouth in the oral stage: it is an organ of intake, and its subjective existence is identical with what it perceives. (Cf. p. 131.) As the eye begins to exist sensorily so does

[1] "When two make but one, when 'without' has the semblance of 'within,' and when there is neither male nor female."

[2] Anna Freud (28) is right when she takes exception to formulations stressing the importance of *objects* in early infancy when the child is actually dominated exclusively by *need*. "It is true," she writes, "that the mother's breast, or the bottle, have to be present so that the child can drink. But what is cathected with libidinal interest at that stage is *the moment of blissful satiation,* not the *object* which enables satiation to be obtained. I believe that we neglect the differences which exist between the object of a need, or a drive, and a love object. We should speak of the latter only after libido cathexis has been transferred from the experience of wish fulfillment to the (material or human) object by means of which satisfaction comes about." [Italics mine.]

the visual world; and this earliest "sensory mouth" is perhaps the first to establish a "without," although one not as yet opposable to a "within." (Cf. p. 71.) Small quantities of desexualized oral libido very early become employable for a reaction, the smile, which combines eye and mouth. The reaction is imitative; an incipient ego reacts to an incipient object by shaping itself after it, and thus consummating the first "affirmation." Freud's formula for this act (64) is applicable as far as affirmation is characterized as "belonging to Eros," and transforming a "without" into a "within"; but it is the eye, the sensory relative of the mouth, that negotiates this transformation on its own terms with the result that incorporation leads to imitation.

If one looks affectionately at a baby able to focus, he looks back at one; and if one smiles, he smiles back. This is so whether the child is contented, or in distress, as for example due to the absence of the mother—provided one likes babies, takes one's time, begins by standing still at a distance, is silent, and approaches by degrees. When one is near him he will then look unblinkingly at one, and given the chance, will close his little hand (see below) around one's finger.

This kinship of mouth and eye, observable in the baby "kept in," and "put out of countenance," persists throughout life: in crying as well as in laughter, in smiling and in the facial expression of disappointment. In amazement the jaw may drop as if, conversely, the eye, overburdened with intake, sought the assistance of the mouth. In look and kiss, finally exchange between individuals loving each other, eye and mouth of the subject persist in affording an exchange, erotic and at the same time mimetic, with the identical part of the object.

¶ LEO. I might have looked upon my Queene's full eyes,
Have taken Treasure from her Lippes.
¶ PAUL. And left them
More rich, for what they yielded [116].

Mine are, as far as the infant is concerned, naturally but a few chance observations; Spitz and Hoffer, however, have observed systematically and with great devotion. Their papers are therefore replete with the most instructive detail, and I emphatically recommend their study to the analyst of adults. With regard to the point under consideration Spitz (136), for example, has found that the smiling response develops in the third month of life.

Returning to my own field of observation I shall illustrate the unit of mouth and eye, and the substitution of one for the other, with some selected analytic material from a woman patient, who had repressed a strong homosexuality with all her might. She remembered, nevertheless, her visual fascination, in latency, with her adolescent sister's pretty breasts when the sister was primping before going out on a date. Later, during her analysis, an old friend of the family, whom we may charitably call a "character," paid her a compliment in rather idiomatic language, which expressed his wish for cunnilingus. She took this good-naturedly, in stride. But a short while after, when the man flaunted a youthful mistress, bragging in the same terms about her, the patient overreacted with outrage and disgust. This eventually became interpretable as an outbreak of unconscious envy; and the patient was able to supply spontaneously the data that the girl's age and certain outstanding physical characteristics, not concerning the breasts, were the sister's. Then came a short period in which she expressed perhaps the strongest devaluation of the female genital that I have ever encountered. It is not necessary to present the details because every analyst is familiar with them. In the analysis of the delusion I have found it generally most helpful if one is able to show to the patient, on the basis of historic material, that, while she means to talk about her genital as of today, she is actually and unwittingly talking about it when she was an undeveloped, "castrated" little girl. In the present instance this led to vivid and painful memories from the age of ten when the children urinated in an alley-way, the boys flaunting their organs and its performance and mocking the squatting girls, rendering, as it were, the castration final. Soon afterwards the strong-willed and intelligent woman decided to abstain from a certain alcoholic drink which she had been taking in excess and of which we had come to know that the addiction to it covered the origin of the sexual wish, mentioned above, for the sister. We were not disappointed in our search for this origin; but it is unnecessary to describe the memory, which contained in detail the mobilization of the wish for cunnilingus by a psychotic adult who had been transferred upon the sister. I shall instead present some material from the hour that brought the excessively strong, but frustrated, wish for the use of the mouth on the sister to the fore.

The patient reported one of her frequent, and now that she drank no longer, torturous episodes of compulsive rumination following certain women's meetings. What did Miss So and So say, and Mrs. So and So answer; and could Mrs. So and So, or the patient herself, not have interjected such and such at this or that point, etc.? She associated, following previous interpretations, a sexual curiosity about these women, interrupting herself with a *cri de coeur*: "I am afraid to let myself know how interested I really am!" and produced subsequently a fantasy that had all of these women undressed from the waist down and her look at them with great interest particularly in individual variations. "Here is a dumpy brunette, here a tall blonde with long legs, etc."

The fantasy allowed for a convincing reconstruction: I have found the displacement onto acoustic perception—in this instance, the conversations mentioned above—generally characteristic for originally visual observations on the occasion of toilet functions. (In the present case the latter were alluded to further by the particular partial undress with which the fantasy was concerned.) The representation of frequency through multiplicity (Freud) is obvious and the interest in variations of build reflects the erstwhile search for the phallus, which for technical reasons I left uninterpreted at this time. Thus the past was at first elucidated and subsequently remembered in a fashion befitting circumstances and personalities as they had become known from other sources: the traumatic mobilization of the wish through the seduction had abolished all latency; the practically daily observations of the adolescent sister in the situation mentioned above aroused perpetually the desire to use the mouth, but gratified only the use of the eye. It is in perfect accord with this fact from the patient's past that the removal

of the amnesia for it began with a fantasy that employed the
same substitution of a visual for an oral gratification, i.e., of
the eye for the mouth.

The hand, also, is a very early associate of the mouth: it is
sucked, even during the feeding process; its fingers "clutch,
stroke, claw and scratch on the breast" (Spitz, 137), it is often
preferred to the breast (Hoffer) and eventually grasps the bottle.
Hoffer (86) believes "that the hands, after being libidinized during the intensive sucking period . . . function more independently of the oral zone and are more under the influence of the
eyes, playing the part of an intermediary between eyes and
mouth." Spitz (137), who speaks of a "modality of primal perception and its three subsidiary organs," adds the perceptions
of labyrinth and of the outer skin surface to those of the hand,
and contends that originally the sensations obtained from them
"combine and unite with the intraoral sensations to a unified
situational experience in which no part is distinguishable from
the other."

II. THE PROBLEM OF ACTIVITY

The question as to whether or not passivity dominates in the
first oral stage appears controversial. The answer depends upon
method: direct observation of infants, the study of regressive
conditions, theoretical speculation. The result of the first of
these was summed up by Freud (71) in the statement: "At the
maternal breast being suckled is first replaced by active suckling," which means that the stage has an earlier passive and a
later active phase.

With regard to the former I believe that Spitz's observations
assist in the understanding of Ribble's earlier observations
(111): the handling and rocking that must accompany feedings
lest the baby dwindle and die in spite of sufficient caloric intake, stimulate precisely the sensory spheres constituting the
"modality of primal perception" (see above), i.e., skin and
labyrinths, while the hand is allowed to touch breast or bottle.

With regard to the change from passivity to activity toward "objects," Spitz (135) observes: "Before the sixth month the social contact manifestation is initiated by the adult and the child follows him; whereas after six months the infant takes the initiative and seeks for the adult."

A less drastic consequence of the baby's deprivation in regard to handling and fondling, but one of particular interest for the analyst of adults, has been suggested by Ernst Kris (96), in a study on autoerotism. The baby who is not sufficiently rocked, stroked and fondled, and whose feeding may be terminated abruptly and prematurely by an unloving mother, may later become the passive man who himself cannot love and for whom women are exclusively sexual objects.

To the patient, whom I consider paradigmatic, two ideas were utterly foreign: one was that a woman is a human being to whom one could talk, e.g., socially, and even enjoy it; and the other that one could decline the sexual advances of women. It made no sense to him whatsoever to converse with a woman unless he was trying to "make" her; and when a woman wanted him sexually she thereby became irresistible and could not be refused, although he was almost invariably premature. The latter bears out the passivity toward women mentioned by Kris; the exhibitionistic nature of the masturbation fantasies of these men, which Kris also considers as characteristic, is described in the parenthesis in the next clinical illustration further below. (Cf. p. 64.)

The physically very healthy patient produced for years severe conversion symptoms, mostly involving the gastrointestinal tract, which he ascribed, delusorily, to the eating of spoiled food;[3] and recounted ever so often that his mother had told him that her "milk did not agree" with him during a breast feeding of

[3] Mahler and Gosliner (102) write: "Since hunger is the most imperative biological need, the . . . qualities of 'good' and 'bad' seem to become equated with 'edible' and 'inedible' substances." They could, of course hardly have written this without applying Freud's classic on *Negation* (64). In my patient the application was a strange one: he acknowledged every major insight I was able to gain and communicate to him by saying "No." He was shown this many times until I finally got the habit of simply answering: "When you say no it means yes," which never failed subsequently to prove correct.

nine months. For a long time I could not make anything of this story which, in view of all known circumstances, sounded fantastic. After much analytic work its meaning became finally clear: the mother, who had affection for an older and a younger sibling, disliked him. Kris, whose article I had not read at the time, mentions this as one of "the factors which tend to be neglected." I had not neglected it, but when I became acquainted with his idea, quoted above, I was able to reconstruct, supported by the previous removal of certain amnesias, that the mother had indeed fed the patient without love and had terminated his feeding abruptly. I communicated the reconstruction in detail with the following twofold result: for one thing the patient's thinking—he was currently involved in a rather extensive business transaction—bogged down completely, and he gave up, as it were, with the words: "I've got a thing so big there, I don't know what to do with it," which could only mean the maternal breast from an early period where activity is as yet not possible and should have been supplied by the mother. The second result: the relatively stagnant analysis went much better after this reconstruction; and it became evident that the excessive libido regression to the anal-sadistic stage which the man, beset as he was with the most painful passive beating fantasies, would not relinquish, served as defense against certain specific oral conflicts.

This again, bears out Kris who, when queried for amplification, wrote me: "Naturally, in all such instances the preserved imprints do not only refer to the earliest situations experienced during the infantile period but are overlaid by later experiences, in which the same proclivity of the mother may find somewhat different, but in principle identical expression. But in my experience the imprints of these later experiences tend to appear in analytic material with preference in relation to oral material and early breast-contacts."

It is a strange fact—and demonstrative of the unexplainable variety of elaboration—that this patient had an unusual and completely natural grace in posture and movement, and a kinesthetic ability far above that of the average man of his age, whereas Kris has observed jerky motions in some of the individuals under consideration.

The *observation of the adult* seems, quite generally, to corroborate that of the *infant*: the analysis of regressive conditions in which the libido of the first oral stage has again become dominant, shows the patient so dominated as passive.

A clinical illustration presents itself in the sexual disturbance of ejaculatio praecox. Here the libido has acquired, regressively, characteristics of both oral stages, regardless of either degree or manifestations of the regression of ego. Behind the passive sexual aim described by Abraham (2) "to have his genitals touched by the woman and then to ejaculate as though he were passing urine" is the equally passive, but more regressive, oral-libidinal aim of being nursed. It is difficult to record this succinctly without anticipating Freud's formulation of the mentality of the young infant to be discussed further below (cf. pp. 71 f.): "The breast is part of me, I am the breast." The term "ejaculatio praecox" is, in the last analysis, a misnomer. The ejaculation is not "premature"; it does not "interrupt" a coitus (a coitus that actually was not intended), but it terminates an erection that is representative of the "breast-that-is-part-of-me" in the act of having it flow. It is thus that the ejaculation occurs in dreaming, upon arousal, or while fantasying with hardly any physical stimulation. A partner to the performance is not an individual but a convenience;[4] the interest in her is purely in her "body," particularly in her breasts which sometimes have relinquished priority to the buttocks. The relation to her, if any, is spurious; it is her willingness that makes her resemble the mother, who had seduced the child either actually or in his imagination. She represents, in the typical case, predominantly the preoedipal mother-object; and the activity with her consummates, consequently, an identification. (Cf. p. 76.) (This is most easily recognizable in those instances where the man's erection is dependent upon clitoral stimulation.) I have never analyzed a female partner to the performance, but it has struck me that the disappointment of which Abraham speaks is, in many instances, lacking. I have thus been led to assume that what they wanted was not coitus either, but rather the touch of the maternal breast, and the making it flow.

[4] See footnote 2, above.

The passivity of the man so afflicted is too well known to require description. (A patient who finally became active enough
to masturbate frictionally, did so still with the passive fantasy
of two women—symbolically, the mother; historically, a psychotic mother and an older sister—one of whom stroked and
admired his penis while showing it to the other.) The relation
to the analyst is not less narcissistic and no less passive: the
typical patient of this kind stays in an analysis because he transfers upon it a breast to cling to, but he is loathe to associate
freely; it is the "I am the breast" that makes him afraid of being emptied out of existence.

In other words, I have found it practically axiomatic that
wherever the wish to suck predominates, as e.g., in the wish for
fellatio, it is a wish with a passive instinctual aim. I am uncertain as to the correct explanation. Does psychology divorce
itself here from physiology? Is the libido regression always one
to the earlier oral-erotic phase? One would, in either case, like
to know: why?

The third method is *theoretical speculation*. Drives, one reminds oneself, are per se active; it is the aim that is either
active or passive; and activity, the performance of action, is
primarily muscular action. The musculature is, however, the
executant of the aggressive instincts, and one is consequently
accustomed to regard activity as their derivative by implication. Yet Freud has maintained that the death instinct, during
the first oral phase, is "neutralized by the libido within [*im
Inneren*]"; and that its earliest manifestations coincide with
the onset of the second. How does one then explain not only
the "active suckling," but also the undoubtedly "active" crying
of the older baby accompanied as it is by a vocalization so clearly
distinguishable from squealing? I am indebted to Dr. Edward
Bibring for referring me, in a personal discussion of the subject,
to one particular speculation of Freud's. Freud (61C) found it
indispensable to assume that "in the mind [*Seelenleben*]—
whether in ego or id—a displaceable energy, which, in itself
neutral [*indifferent*], can add itself to a qualitatively differenti-

ated erotic or destructive impulse and augment the total cathexis of the latter." And he thought it "plausible that this displaceable and neutral energy, which is probably active in both ego and id, stems from the narcissistic reservoir of libido, that is, that it is desexualized Eros." Bibring expressed the opinion that this neutral energy is responsible for the activity of the baby. The hypothesis is original, and the gain from it evident: one can abide by Freud's idea of neutralization of the death instinct in the first oral phase and regard all manifestations of this phase as manifestations of Eros. And one may look upon the activity of the first oral phase as a contribution of Eros to a libido whose aim is at certain times and in certain instances active while it is passive in others.

III. ON THE ROLE OF THE FIRST ORAL PHASE IN REGRESSIVE CONDITIONS

Every analyst, studying regressive conditions intensively over a long period of time, finds it necessary to amend Freud's statement that the fixation point determines the degree of regression, to the extent that the regression goes further. While many dominant traits in the clinical picture are explainable as effects of regression to the fixation point, there are other traits that are not; their understanding depends upon the acknowledgment that the regression, in certain respects, is complete. Without this acknowledgment it is not possible to abolish a morbid condition. Behind the oedipal aim is, in other words, a preoedipal one, and behind the desire to possess the mother as a man is, in the last analysis, the desire to own her breast as a nurseling.[5]

The oedipus complex contains thus, as its deepest layer, the conflict about usurping the mamma after the fashion of the first oral stage. Illustrating this is equivalent to the impossible task

[5] The Christ child on Mary's lap, in e.g., Renaissance art, has, conversely, often been inconspicuously given features not belonging to an infant but to a mature, sometimes even elderly man. It is thus that he is, unwittingly, made to resemble as it were his apparent forebear, the child consort of the mother-goddess of the Minoans.

of recording a whole analysis. I shall therefore employ a literary example, indicating the depth of the matter by the number of analysts that it takes to fathom it, as one might show the depth of a valley, e.g., the Grand Canyon, by the number of successive explorers that it finally took to reach bottom.

Martin Wangh closes an instructive study on *Othello: the Tragedy of Iago* (141) with an analysis of the famous handkerchief of Desdemona. Introductorily, he cites four writers (Sterba, Brunswick, Riviere, and Fenichel) as demonstrating the "oral envy" of which jealousy is the "outgrowth." He applies their findings correctly to the "oral imagery of Iago's dream-invention in Shakespeare's play" (127) (by his "raging tooth" and his tale that Cassio "plucked up kisses by the roots that grew upon" his lips) and to Cinthio's novella, Shakespeare's source. "Here," he points out, "it is not Emilia but Iago who steals the handkerchief from Desdemona and, significantly, he does this while Desdemona is holding his child in her lap, which is the classic situation of the curious older child." With regard to the handkerchief proper, Wangh cites a fifth author (Wulff, who himself employs the material of several other writers) for its identification "as a fetish," the child's substitute for the breast; and a sixth (Arlow) with the remark that "the handkerchief is embroidered with strawberries, easily recognizable symbols of the nipples."

The handkerchief, then, is the breast. Wangh fails to mention that Cassio, Iago's rival, to whom Desdemona supposedly gave it, had before been made drunk by Iago (while on duty, losing his commission); and that he is now alleged to have wiped his beard with the handkerchief (several times called "napkin"), i.e., again to have drunk.

Even so, the analysis remains incomplete: it does not show that the breast is preoedipal and that the rival drinking from it is the nurseling. To complete the analysis, one would have to adduce a seventh author (Isakower), who has described a sensation of one of his patients before falling asleep as follows (90): it is "as though I lay on something *crumpled*; but this crumpled something is at the same time in the mouth, and the whole of it issues from the palate . . . I seem to lie on a cloth that is crumpled . . . this something is not under me, like a *crumpled linen sheet,* but around me and it is unpleasant." This inside-outside "something," which is described in the report of another patient as "big," "round," "doughy," "issuing from the palate," and "lying on" the patient, is interpreted by the author convincingly, as the breast; and the quality "crumpled" no less convincingly, as reflective of the sensation of dryness in the nurseling's mouth.[6]

This enables one to appreciate the fact that the handkerchief of Desdemona is *crumpled.* It is elaborately introduced as such, although allusively and by implication. It is small (III:iii), light (III:iii), and of silk (III:iv); the embroidery (III:iii, iv; IV:i) is assumed likewise to be of silk—material that does not readily muss. But its owner was told by her husband to

> take heed on't
> Make it a Darling, like your precious eye:
> To loose't, or give't away, were such perdition,
> As nothing else could match, ... [III:iv].

and in response to this admonition is reported

> so loves the Token,
> That she reserves it everymore about her,
> To kisse, and talke to . . . . [III:iii].

It is in this much-used condition, in other words, crumpled indeed, that "she did let it drop by negligence" and that Emilia "took't up" and that Iago snatched it from her in order to "loose" it at Cassio's who finds it, much traveled and having changed several hands, in other words, more crumpled still.

The psychic stratification (mentioned above) that this is to illustrate becomes transparent if the dialogue preceding the italicized line, that convinces Othello is scanned. (Cf. p. 68.)

6 The same meaning may be that of an overdetermination of the "crumpled giraffe" in the hypnopompic fantasy of "Little Hans" (38B). It is the seizing upon it (Freud) that makes the child, although he is not afraid, seek the bed of his parents; he does not know why. But the next day, asked to say quickly what comes to his mind, he associates: "raspberry juice," and "a rifle to shoot to kill"—a combination of ideas, obviously indicative of an oedipal coveting of the breast.

Othello asks Iago for proof. Iago first conjures up a *genital* primal scene, recommending its scoptophilic consummation,

> ....Where's satisfaction?
> It is impossible you should see this,
> Were they as prime as Goates, as hot as Monkeys' eyes,
> As salt as Wolves in pride, and Fooles as grosse
> As Ignorance, made drunke . . . [II:iii].

He follows this by a *phallic* version, the counterfeit dream, which becomes briefly *sadistic* and ends with an oral-*sadistic* image:

> ....I lay with Cassio lately,
> And being troubled with a raging tooth,
> I could not sleepe. There are a kinde of men,
> So loose of Soule, that in their sleepes will mutter
> Their affayres: one of this kinde is Cassio:
> In sleepe I heard him say, sweet Desdemona,
> Let us be wary, let us hide our loves,
> And then (Sir) would he gripe, and wring my hand:
> Cry, oh sweet Creature: then kisse me hard,
> As if he pluckt up kisses by the rootes,
> That grew upon my lippse, laid his leg ore my Thigh,
> And sigh, and kisse, and then cry cursed Fate,
> That gave thee to the Moore [III:iii].

And he descends eventually to the deepest and earliest oral-erotic layer which the thirsty man-nurseling drinks from the breast of the motherly virgin,[7] whose marriage to an impotent husband had wanted its consummation:

> IAGO.   Tell me but this,
> Have you not sometimes seene a Handkerchiefe
> Spotted with Strawberries, in your wives hand?
> OTH. I gave her such a one: 'twas my first gift.
> IAGO. I know not that: but such a Handkerchiefe
> (I am sure it was your wives) did I today
> *See Cassio wipe his beard with* [III:iii].

---

7 See footnote 3, above.

It is thus, and thus only, that he succeeds in establishing the delusion.[8]

IV. ON THE INCEPTION OF EGO

With regard to the much-discussed problem of incipient ego formation a brief remark may conclude the present and introduce the following section.

The formation of ego is, in one respect, comparable to the settlement of a new continent: once the port of entry is gained, one group of colonists may progress to the fertile mouth of a river, another settle in a forest with game, etc. Food is the prime determinant of their choice. For a while the settlements remain isolated; only gradually do they establish connection, and it takes a long time until they organize into "colonies," and eventually into a nation. With regard to the infantile ego in the process of its being established, one is tempted to speak at first of ego- or pre-ego nuclei; but one is hesitant because one prefers to save the term "nucleus" for the mature ego organization. Yet one is justified in admitting that when the autoerotic instinctual discharge becomes narcissistic, the strivings demanding the discharge stimulate, at least temporarily, a formation of ego sufficient to be their subject.

It is thus far and no further that I would go in accepting the term "ego nuclei," suggested by Glover (82) who imagines a "multi-nuclear or multi-locular primitive ego-structure," and makes much of the fact that these nuclei are "dissociated," although that should really follow from their definition. The better part of the oral phase of development is, after all, dedicated to the transition from autoerotism to narcissism; and wherever an "ego nucleus" becomes established, it is at first observable in a quasi-autoerotic isolation. (Chapter III contains sufficient examples for this and for its repetition in the inception of speech.) To distinguish, as does Glover, "the concept of

---

8 The breast of the first oral stage is, of course, single. It is therefore only in Othello's absence and for the benefit of the audience that the two persons, Emilia (III:iii), and Cassio (III:iv; IV:i), confronted suddenly with the handkerchief react independently with the same idea: the "work" (the embroidery) shall be "taken out" (copied); in other words, it should be made into a pair.

nuclear autonomy clearly from concepts such as autoerotism where instincts or their components are gratified without the interposition of an external object," is confusing. Besides denying that the transition is gradual, the formula fails to qualify both "external" and "object." Instead of "external" it should read: "subjectively external" because nipple and breast are objectively external from the (autoerotic) beginning; and "object" requires quotation marks because its cathexis is not object-libidinal, but narcissistic; it is originally identical with "ego nucleus" in the formation of which it assists. One should, furthermore, confine the existence of "ego nuclei" to the oral and perhaps the first anal phases lest one suggest the erroneous conception that it is simply their confluence that forms eventually an ego. It is not. The establishment of an ego organization requires a much more complicated procedure (cf. p. 123), a contribution to which shall be attempted in the next volume. It is there that the work of Margaret Mahler and that of others on the original "symbiotic" relation between mother and child, and the work of Hoffer on the development of the body-ego shall be summarized by way of an introduction.

In concluding the present section I should like to refer again to Anna Freud's remark (cf. p. 56) that the early cathexes do not concern the *objects* but the needs and their fulfillment. My reason for repeating this reference is its importance for the analysis of adults. The cathexis of the need instead of the object here is not only revived, as the author points out, in the dreams fulfilling a bodily need (*Leibreizträume*) but it persists in some individuals as a character trait or, if they suffer from the ensuing lack of object relations, as a *character defect*. It explains, furthermore, why the pervert reminds one so frequently of the addict, whose interest in people is not even pretended and who generally admits to be after nothing but the need-fulfilling drug. The analysis of the character defects mentioned above cannot be accomplished if the cathexis of the need instead of that of the object is not clearly perceived and subsequently exchanged.

3

THE SECOND ORAL PHASE

"Having and Being in the Child" is the heading of one of Freud's posthumously published notes, dated June 1938: "The child likes to express the object relation through the identification. The Having is the later one, it reverts after the loss of the object to Being. Model: breast. The breast is a part of me, I am the breast. Later only: I have it, that is, I am not it" (79).

The note intimates a focal point, as it were, for viewing the second oral phase. Yet the view is difficult to record: it is fragmentary and must be patched together from glimpses. The picture, even while being described, falls apart into particulars of enumeration.

I. NASCENT EGO AND OBJECT: THEIR IDENTITY AND THEIR DELIMITATION

Whatever of ego is formed in the beginning of the second oral stage, Freud has taught us, is still identical with the object: "I am the breast." The breast is now, with the help of the hand and the eye, experienced as breast, not merely as nipple. But the experience includes withdrawal as well as obtainment; one might add therefore that I "am" only as far as I have become "the breast"; or that it *is* only as far as it has become me: my existence depends upon its existence and its existence on mine. Subsequently there occurs subjectively mutual delimitation of ego from object; but every bit of the latter, an intolerable "without," must be destroyed in order to become a "within." It is here that the destructive instinct makes its first appearance,

as do the teeth, and that the incipient ego discharges cannibalistic libido through the powerful musculature of the jaw.[1]

I have elsewhere described the regressive re-enactment, in
analysis, of this oral incorporation as "oral-erotic silence":
characterized by complete failure of speech, absence of recountable thought, and lapse of transference (18). This form of silence
(cf. pp. 293 ff.), distinguishable from others, is symptomatic of a
transient regression in the analytic situation to the second oral
phase. Since the phase is preverbal and cannibalistic, the function of speech, either silent or vocal, is suspended and the
mouth is regressively re-employed for the incorporation of the
analyst who, consequently, is no longer an object. The pre-
clusion of speech by such a regressively incorporative employment of the mouth suggests that originally the mouth has
employed incorporative tendencies for the subsequent development of the function of speech. (Cf. pp. 104-107.)

Spitz (135) has described at least one child, in whom this
became observable in almost experimental form. The seven-
months-old girl, in response to the separation from her mother
gradually goes into a severe anaclitic depression. She suffers

[1] The most detailed observation of the activity of the jaws in this phase is
Hoffer's, who wishes that we "differentiate three functions: *firstly*, an aggressive
use of the jaws, by which is meant biting the breast, chewing it, cracking the
nipple by actively working on it; *secondly*, a merely active grasping and holding
of the nipple which is arrested between the jaws and actively prevented from
being withdrawn so that the feeling of contact with the breasts will not be
interrupted. *Thirdly*, there is found in some infants a hostile snapping or closing
of the jaws. This is observed in certain babies who in this way resist being
forced to suck the breast, which for some reason they refuse, usually because
they prefer the more easily flowing bottle" (87A).
Much of this oral-sadistic activity can—since the musculature in general is, as
Freud has found, the organ for the discharge of aggression—and should—since
the child in this phase begins locomation—be discharged in motor and loco-
motor activity. Both Spitz and Anna Freud are emphatic in their plea for increased opportunities for the (institutionalized) child to move about; this of
course would necessitate much more spaciously-built institutions.
Spitz (135) reports, furthermore, that when an "anaclitic depression" with
which the child in the oral-sadistic phase reacts to a separation from his mother,
is terminated by the mother's return a tremendous (in part transient) increase
in his general motor performance occurs.
Also see Mahler and Gosliner (102): "The infant has the tendency to suck in,
to mouth, to incorporate, to devour as much of the outside object as possible.
Thus expulsive, ejective, ridding tendencies alternate with this tendency to
engulf."

from loss of weight, and insomnia, becomes unapproachable and "is mostly sitting in bed, her dress in her mouth, or sucking her hand." Later she lies dejectedly with averted face, "A pathetic picture of sorrow, helplessness, and demand for assistance." Subsequently she develops a stubbornly persistent cold.

Her "developmental quotient" has steadily dropped during this period. She has, in other words, in the course of her melancholic condition, regressed observably from the second to the first oral phase. In reaction to the therapy for anaclitic depression—the introduction of a loving mother substitute, when the mother herself is unavailable—the girl immediately accepts contact with other children, but only in an aggressive form. She is now, at the time of the report (about eleven months old) "biting, scratching, and pinching" these children "to the point of drawing blood"; and she "tries for a prolonged period to bite the observer's nose, chin, neck and hand"; she is, in other words, re-progressing again to the second oral phase. *"During these"* — cannibalistic — "attacks," the author reports, "she reaches out with her hands and *vocalizes different incoherent sounds, among which the word 'ma-ma' returns several times."*

"The breast is a part of me" describes a later phase of this stage. It is comparable in one point to the phallic "partial love with the exclusion of the genital" (Abraham) where a part of the ego retains narcissistic cathexis which cannot therefore be relinquished to a part of the object: here a part of the object retains narcissistic cathexis which is not therefore as yet employable for the formation of ego.

The patient cited above, whose inability to associate was paradigmatic of oral-erotic silence, proved subsequently also illustrative of this later phase. She explained her complete inability to feel anything for the analyst—i.e., to establish a positive mother transference—on the grounds that one cannot love anyone whom one has to leave after fifty minutes. This explanation satisfied her completely; it did not admit either of argument, or of modification on the strength of the regularity of her five weekly hours. Whenever one of these had to be canceled she reacted with sudden high fevers, orgastic dreams, or dreams that were not only transparent but manifestly emphatic about the very transference which she was unable to perform. None of this could, however, be shown her; she remained absolutely unimpressed: the fevers were "24-hour-virus," the orgasms coincidental, and the dreams confined to their manifest content in which someone else had of course taken my place.

When, eventually, after much improvement had depleted the motive power for the treatment, it became imperative that, as Freud has expressed it, "the transference furnishes the amounts of energy requisite to a continuation of the analysis," her experience on leaving the office was re-examined. The examination was a minute one; in reporting it one is apt to feel childish unless one remembers that one was actually speaking to a "child." No, she was not being "kicked out." Why did she act as though she were? Why did she bolt? Why did I find the hall empty as soon as she closed the office door? (I have previously reported her original dizziness upon leaving the office and how she collected herself only after reaching the street.) No, I do not stop abruptly after fifty minutes flat, in the middle of a sentence or thought, but conclude the session comfortably. There was always time for her to say something or to reply, etc., etc. The girl, who had been a partner to all this for years but had never known it, was deeply moved; and I began to understand my error.

I had been altogether unreasonable in expecting a transference of the mother upon me where I should have worked instead toward one of the breast. Consequently the breast remained "part of her"; severance from it was bound to cause mental and physical shock, postural disorientation. It was as though the end of the hour represented a mutilation, and I had expected love from someone for mutilating him five times a week. Of the fevers, orgasms and dreams I had to recognize that their appearance as transference phenomena had been a deceptive overdetermination: they were actually "withdrawal symptoms."

The patient's mother had alternately starved her by refusing to nurse, and choked her in order to get rid of excess milk. The second phase reflected itself in analysis through an irrational fright when I embarked upon lengthier explanations. The first was not, however, reproduced in the typical accusations that the analyst does not say what he knows, or refuses to answer questions, which would have meant that the breast had indeed been transferred upon him. It was instead, she, the patient, the regressive owner of the breast who starved me through extremely sparse associations, prefaced with "Do you know what I think?" as though she had to make sure that I did not know it already and that she would not be wasting a drop of information. It was only after all this had been understood that the breast, no longer owned, could be transferred, and in extension of the breast, eventually the mother.

Freud's "I have it (the breast), that is, I am not it" applies to the terminal phase of the second oral stage, where a rudimentary ego—subject of oral-libidinal and oral-aggressive strivings towards an object—is permanently established.

II. NARCISSISTIC IDENTITY AND REGRESSIVE IDENTIFICATION

The fact that the ego is fashioned through primary identifications, in other words, that the object in the beginning is merely ego, is of course of the greatest importance for the theory of identification.

(a) Even the fully established object retains, as Freud has shown, narcissistic cathexis. However, it would seem that the regressive process must be credited, at least under certain conditions, with increasing the narcissistic cathexis of the object as well as the *ego,* and with employing object libido retransformed into narcissistic libido for that increase. I believe such is the reason why many identifications appear as a "He is I" rather than as an "I am he," without really justifying the use of the term "projection." (Cf. p. 118.)

As one example of many one might adduce the case of a male who had fellatio practiced on him by certain women, recognizable as representing himself as a child. The question arose:

who was he? The removal of an amnesia gave the unambiguous answer: he impersonated a perverted adult who had seduced him to the same performance at the height of the phallic phase. The traumatic incident reinforced (under the exigencies of the oedipus complex) his passivity and his preoedipal mother identification to such a degree that one is tempted to say, in repeating it he *had* to be represented by women.

(b) Since the object is a preoedipal one, and the second oral phase that of the first full-fledged identifications, it is here that the problem of the preoedipal instinctual aim is first encountered. Freud's classic discussion of this problem bears no emendation (71). An addendum, however, may be sustained: preoedipal strivings—oral, anal-sadistic, and phallic—quite generally have the aim of consummating an identification.

This was the reason why in illustrating the passivity of the first oral stage with the example of an ejaculatio praecox, it was necessary to pre-empt Freud's formula pertaining to the second oral stage. "I am the breast—the breast is part of me" is also applicable to the patient afflicted with this disturbance because he has converted regressively that identity described by Freud into an identification. In the case of premature ejaculation that I was able to study most thoroughly, the psychotic mother had, for one thing, masturbated the little boy, "helping" him to urinate, with the result of making him passive (as described by Freud in the "Wolf Man") and having him, for the rest of his life, become her.

In presenting another example one may, possibly at the same time, contribute toward explaining the puzzling observation that in certain perversions—in contrast to others as well as to normal performance—the genital may respond with orgastic discharge, practically without any mechanical stimulation.

A male soon after entering treatment developed the compulsion to count the slats on a screen in the analyst's office. Summarizing the analysis of this symptom, one might say, not the slats, but the interstices, were the object of his interest; and it was not their number, but the number of women urinating who could, as it were, be watched through them. In his own place of work he kept a steady ear cocked for females using the bathroom. The evident promise held by the interpretative replacement of multiplicity through frequency was fulfilled by the analytic investigation. At the age of a little over four, the patient had been sick and had lived, under circumstances excluding the father, at close quarters with a mother with whom continence was a problem. She used the chamber in front of him; and she also slept at times in his bed. The observation of many women in the present had indeed in the past been the frequent observation of one. However, this was the *oedipal* mother. Severe attacks of precordial anxiety had one root in the terror of being later surprised by the father, gripped and yanked away from the keyhole of the bathroom door.

The *preoedipal* mother appeared in the patient's perversion. In the exercise of it, a sexual partner, coming home with him and about to go to the bathroom, was asked to sit instead on his lap and to urinate without either of them undressing. While this was being done, he himself experienced a most pleasurable urinary urge, accompanied by an erection that mounted and resolved itself finally in an ejaculation. A striking negative characteristic of the performance was the absence of any scoptophilic desire. Here the mouth of the oral phase had been revived regressively, and displaced up on the male genital which, in consequence of such transfer of function, became able to consummate orgastically an identification. Since all visual interest had been replaced by interest in a tactile stimulation through liquid (most of it displaced upon clothes, upholstery, carpet), it is probably more accurate to assume that the transfer concerned not the mouth alone but the functional unit of mouth and eye original with the first oral phase.

While suppressing a wealth of confirmatory material, and omitting all overdetermination belonging to the castration complex, I may add a further trait, unique in my observation. This patient was able to urinate under conditions of complete erection: the male genital that had become earliest mouth and eye could identify, sexually, with the flowing maternal breast.

The fact that to consummate an identification is the instinctual aim of all preoedipal strivings, originally as well as in the case of regression, is important. It will be referred to more than once in the present volume; the last time in the course of contributing to the theory of coition.

III. THE SUBJECTIVE REALITY OF THE CANNIBALISTIC ACT AND THE PERSISTENCE OF THE CANNIBALISTIC DESIRE IN THE INDIVIDUAL

A. ON THE RELATIVE ABSENCE OF CANNIBALISTIC MANIFESTATIONS IN THE CHILD

While the first oral phase admits of direct and complete instinctual gratification, the second does not: the nipple to be sucked is granted, the breast to be eaten is denied. This distinguishes, in fact, the second oral phase not only from the first, but from all other phases. "Sexual" defecation, phallic masturbation with urinary discharge and genital union are all actually performed, as is suckling; it is only the eating of human flesh (breast) that in historic times no one, with the exception of a very few psychotics, has ever done. It appears to me, that the analyst has not made enough of this *chose simple* which should lead him to expect that both the survival and the regressive revival of cannibalism will be found to be dominated by aim displacement and aim inhibition. Little biting and no devouring of the breast is permitted; teething toys, food,[2] are offered instead. It is therefore worth reflecting whether the analysis of the fear of being eaten by the mother—a fear observed by Freud only in men but actually observable in both sexes—does not require a step beyond those taken by Freud. "It would seem plausible to conjecture," Freud writes, "that this fear corresponds to the hostility which the child develops towards

---

2 Anna Freud (24) in the course of an instructive description of feeding disturbances from the second year onwards, writes: ". . . Much of the child's conflicting behavior towards food does . . . originate . . . from conflicting emotions towards the mother which are transferred onto the food which is a symbol for her." I am not certain whether it would not be more accurate to say that if food later becomes representative of the mother, it is originally *symbolic of the breast.*

her mother because of the manifold restrictions imposed by the latter in the process of training and physical care and that the immaturity of the child's psychical organization favours the mechanism of projection" (71A). Should not one, without invalidating a single word of this sentence, give it meaning pertinent to a historically earlier stage by simultaneously reading "mamma" for mother? The restrictions imposed upon the child by the mother in the process of bringing him up would then be reducible, in the last analysis, to the restriction against eating the breast.

René A. Spitz (136) describes clinically in a paper, whose study I recommend, the appearance of anxiety in the infant in the third quarter of the first year of life; and discusses theoretically why anxiety proper manifests itself for the first time no earlier than at eight months of age. His argument, as far as it goes, appears to be flawless: there must be enough of an ego, and enough of a mother-object *to be remembered* in order that her loss may be perceived. The mother, although already an object, is at the same time still a complementary part of the infant's immature ego; her loss is, consequently, a double threat. "It is the internal threat that the ego will be swamped by uncontrollable stimuli with which it cannot deal; it is the threat of a breakthrough of the protective shield against stimuli, in analogy to its prototype in the trauma of birth."

What the author does not consider is the fact that *the beginning of anxiety roughly coincides with the beginning of the oral-sadistic phase.* Thorough analyses of adults have left me with the impression that the normal affectionate mother assists most powerfully, in both of her aforementioned roles, in the control of the cannibalistic desires: as an object through her steady libidinal contact with the child, and as a complementary part of his nascent ego through stimulating *primary identifications.* Among the "uncontrollable stimuli" swamping the ego, and producing anxiety in the case of the loss (or the nonexistence) of such a mother, *oral-sadistic* ones should, I believe, be assigned a most prominent place.

In the analysis of adults one finds unambiguous evidence both for the conviction that the cannibalistic act was committed (sometimes repeated on the paternal phallus) and for its participation in producing the strongest feelings of guilt.[3] It would appear that here the fantastic incorporation renders intent equivalent to execution; but it would also appear that this is the first instance where a gap in individual truth is filled in with prehistoric truth. (Cf. p. 9.) The subjective reality of the cannibalistic performance should, in other words, have a phylogenetic[4] as well as an ontogenetic root. (For a further remark on the latter, cf. p. 161.)

B. PORTIA'S INJUNCTION AGAINST THE CANNIBALISM OF SHYLOCK

It is with consummate artifice that this fact from the past—the ontogenetic sequence of the *consummation of sucking* the breast, and the *non-consummation of eating*—has been projected onto the plane of a fictitious present.

In an imaginary courtroom in Venice Portia pronounces her (first) injunction[5] against the cannibalism of Shylock: he is permitted "to cut . . . flesh from off . . . [Antonio's] breast," but is forbidden to "shed one drop of blood," because the flesh is, and the blood is not, stipulated in his bond (125A).

Here one has the choice between either reconciling oneself to the fact that the peripety of one of the greatest plays ever written is brought about by a fatuous bit of sophistry, or developing the profound latent thought.

The impact of Shylock upon his environment is that of an atavist: he is therefore not quite believable to the men in whose midst he appears; and the scene is consequently introduced

---

[3] For a brief description of typical disturbances in the child's relation to food due to defective defenses against cannibalistic desires, see Anna Freud (24).

[4] One might perhaps appreciate in this context that, while only a small minority of us is crippled in general, we are all dental cripples. The X-ray of an average set of teeth reveals a condition that we would term deplorable if concerned with any other organ. Is it that this one has eventually deteriorated with the abandonment of its original use?

[5] For her second injunction, see Chapter IV, p. 125.

with the expectation that it will reverse himself in the end, and avert the danger to the Merchant in the manner, as it were, of an arousal dream:

¶ DUKE. . . . . . Shylocke, the world thinkes, and I thinke so to
That thou but ledest this fashion of thy mallice
To the last hour of act, and then 'tis thought
Thou'lt shew the mercy and remorse more strange,
Than is thy strange apparent cruelty . . . [IV:i].

However, Shylock forces them to believe him. He insists, and by so doing gradually convinces them, that his intent is actually cannibalistic. Gratiano finally speaks for all when, alternating between contemplation and curses, he verbalizes this recognition:

¶ GRATIANO. 'O be thou damn'd, inexecrable dogge,
And for they life let justice be accus'd:
Thou almost mak'st me waver in my faith;
To hold opinion with Pythagoras,
That *soules of Animals infuse themselves*
Into the trunkes of men. Thy currish spirit
Govern's a Wolfe, who hang'd for humane slaughter,
Even from the gallowes did his fell soule fleet;
And whil'st thou layest in thy unhallowed dam,
Infus'd it self in thee: For thy desires
Are *Wolvish, bloody, sterv'd, and ravenous* [IV:i].

In order to find the thought, hidden in Portia's pronouncement, it is necessary to acquaint oneself with Antonio, Shylock's victim. Antonio is a melancholic; he presents himself in the opening lines of the play:

¶ ANT. In sooth I know not why I am so sad,
It wearies me . . .
. . . and such a Want-wit sadnesse makes of mee, . . . [I:i].

He is indeed "to learne"; and if he does not know the lesson when it is taught him, we do. The basic make-up of the suicidal melancholic has been outlined further above. (Cf. pp. 4 f.) An-

tonio is not suicidal; but while his ego is being mauled by his
superego in consequence of a libido regression to the second
oral stage, he craves the peace of the first sufficiently to be
passive toward the killer. It is thus that, when Shylock is ready
to cut without benefit of a surgeon to stop the bleeding, he
addresses Bassanio with what supposedly were to be his last
words:

> Greeve not that I am falne to this for you:
> For heerein fortune shewes her selfe more kinde
> Then is her custome.................
> Repent not you that you shall loose your friend,
> And he repents not that he pays your debt.
> For if the Jew do cut but deepe enough,
> Ile pay it instantly, with all my heart [IV:i].

1. *Shylock's Suggestive Influence on Antonio*

Actually Shylock is to Antonio, in the last analysis, the per-
sonification of the archaic nucleus of his superego. I have tried
elsewhere (20) to describe the basic characteristics of the latter
and in this work to show (Ch. I) how "Little Hans" projects
them, transitorily, upon his father. (Cf. pp. 39 f.) Shylock is
"racially antithetic" (20) to Antonio; and his *"intent to torture
and kill" is,* in consequence of the regression to the second oral
stage, cannibalistic. The remaining two traits, however, *"mendacity"* and *"lack of humor"* have found their most ingenious
employment in the play. In order to get Antonio to sign the
bond, Shylock professes himself, *mendaciously,* his friend, and
calls his willingness to take flesh instead of money as interest,
a kindness, a *humorous* exercise:

> ¶ SHY. This *kindness* will I showe,
> Ge with me to a Notarie, seale methere
> Your single bond, and *in a merrie sport*
> If you repaie me not on such a day,
> In such a place, such sum or sums as are
> Exprest in the condition, let the forfeite

> Be nominated for an equall pound
> Of your faire flesh, to be cut off and taken
> In what part of your bodie it pleaseth me [I:iii].

Strangely enough—but not strange in view of the metapsychology of the melancholic—Antonio sees it Shylock's way:

> ¶ ANT. Content in faith, Ile seal to such a bond,
> And say there is much kindness in the Jew.

He rationalizes: his ships are homeward bound, he has ample time to repay the bond, there will be no cannibalistic execution. Actually, however, he has without knowing it, surrendered to Shylock's "suggestion."

To understand this surrender, one may first trace Shylock's influence upon Antonio, and attempt subsequently to explain it.

In discussing the influence of analysis on the patient, Freud, erstwhile physiologist that he was, once jokingly said he regretted (I have been told) that one could not split him in the middle and let one half go unanalyzed while analyzing the other. This is, however, almost literally what Shakespeare does: he has Shylock negotiate not with Antonio alone, but with Antonio and his friend Bassanio; and while Antonio submits, Bassanio remains critical and unmoved.

In the beginning Antonio, not as yet under Shylock's spell, sees Shylock exactly as does Bassanio, i.e., as

> ¶ ANT. ....A villaine with a smiling cheeke,
> A goodly apple rotten at the heart.
> O what a goodly outside falsehood hath [I:iii].

There the two—Jew and anti-Semite—face each other without pretense; Shylock's hate makes him sarcastic, Antonio's, spiteful:

> ¶ SHY. . . . . Faire sir, you spet on me on Wednesday last;
> You spurned me such a day; another time
> You cald me dog: and for these curtesies
> Ile lend you thus much moneys.

¶ ANT. I am as like to call thee so againe,
To spet on thee againe, to spurne thee too.
If thou will lend this money, lend it not
As to thy friends . . .
But lend it rather to thine enemie
Who if he breake, though maist with better face
Exact the penalties [I:iii].

But when shortly thereafter Shylock's suggestion is taking hold with Antonio, who is willing to "seale to such a bond" and to call Shylock "kind," Bassanio, uninfluenced, raises objection:

¶ BASS. You shall not seale to such a bond for me,
Ile rather dwell in my necessitie.

This causes Shylock once more to be mendacious about his cannibalistic intent (while admitting it, unwittingly, in his very protest as he compares man's flesh to that of comestible animals) and to simulate love:

¶ SHY. O father Abram, what these Christians are,
Whose owne hard dealings teaches them suspect
The thoughts of others: Praie you tell me this,
If he should breake his daie, what should I gaine
By the exaction of the forfeiture?
A pound of mans flesh taken from a man,
Is not so estimable, profitable neither
As flesh of Muttons, Beefes, or Goates, I say
To buy his favour. I extend this Friendship,
If he will take, so: if not adiew,
And for my love I praie you wrong me not [I:iii].

The differing effect on Antonio and Bassanio is the same as before, only stronger. With Antonio the suggestion has taken complete effect: Shylock, who had already been "kind" is now "gentle" and kind, and no longer really "racially antithetic":

¶ ANT. Hie thee gentle Jew. This Hebrew will turne
Christian, he grows kinde [I:iii].

To Bassanio, who remains uninfluenced and therefore, in response to Shylock's unwitting admission, even more critical than before, Shylock remains the villain:

¶ BASS. I like not faire termes, and a villaines minde [I:iii].

Antonio's transformation, abrupt and radical as it is, becomes understandable only when one assumes that what occurs on the stage is merely projected upon it and occurs actually within Antonio. Where we see Antonio submit to Shylock, it is truly the regressive ego that succumbs to the regressive superego of the melancholic.

2. *The True Shylock*

The submission is an abrupt one because of a sudden "cathectic displacement" from one topographical institution upon another, such as Freud (68) has assumed and exemplified in his study of "Humor." It is there that he illustrates the twofold origin of the superego from the good and bad earliest parent,[6] and showed that an overcathexis of the superego may render it dominant as the descendent of either. Shylock gains his suggestive influence over Antonio by feigning the "libidinal parent"; and it is in so doing that he appears protective and humorous and creates in Antonio, just as Freud has described it, an illusion.

In the courtroom scene Shylock eventually shows his true face, and it is the face of the "destructive parent." He is malign, and now he does crave revenge on his racially antithetic victim, whom he wants to torture by cutting, and to kill by bleeding.

---

6 In describing the nucleus of the superego one should, I believe, speak of a *libidinal* and of a *destructive* parent rather than of father and mother. Freud, in teaching us that (68) the superego, of whose nature "we still have quite a few things to learn," is capable of benignity toward the ego, did not either distinguish between father and mother. He formulates: ". . . when the superego . . . strives to console the ego and to protect it from suffering it has not thereby contradicted its descent from the parent-institution." The term "parent-institution" (*Elterninstanz*) is elusive. I am inclined to understand it as denoting the product of early identifications with the "earliest" (Freud)—i.e., partly archaic—parents.

He had been lying when he pretended to be benign and disavowed the intent of ever executing the "merrie bond"; he hungers for the cannibalistic act.

> ¶ POR. (To Antonio). Therefore lay bare your bosome.
> ¶ JEW. I, his brest,
> So says the bond, doth it not noble Judge? [IV:i].

3. The Meaning of Portia's Injunction

Portia's injunction, it will now be understood, conceals behind its sophistical wording a preconscious and an unconscious thought. The former: you may eat from your victim, but you may not kill him. The latter: if the phylogenetic subject, the atavist, must be allowed to reverse the ontogenetic antithesis between the first and the second oral stage, let the reversal be a complete one: if we permit him to eat the breast let us forbid him to suck it. If we award him the solid, let us deny him the liquid. In other words: let us give him the breast to devour, allusively; and by the same mode, allusion, refuse him the milk.

C. THE DEATH INSTINCT AND THE REGRESSIVE REVIVAL OF THE ORAL-SADISTIC MOUTH

The analytic investigation of regressive conditions leaves one quite generally with the impression that the death instinct is not only original with but *intrinsic to the second oral phase*. The mouth of this stage is transferable onto all subsequently dominant erogenic zones, and it is the degree to which it persists, or is revived regressively, that determines the manifestations of the instinct. In studying these latter, the two instinct components, the impulse to bite and the impulse to devour, should be traced *separately* for their vicissitudes need not be the same.

Chatting about Aufidius' fight with Coriolanus while waiting upon the general at his banquet, two the of Serving-Men muse:

¶ 1.   He was too hard for him directly to say the truth on't before Corioli; he scotched him and notched him like a carbonado.

¶ 2.   And had he been cannibalistically given, he might have boiled him and eaten him too [117B].

A "carbonado" is a "piece of meat, fowl or fish slashed for grilling"; "scotching" is cutting superficially, gashing; "notching" is "scoring," i.e., making furrows, indenting. Here the first waiter describes the biting whereby the teeth are displaced upon the sword, which is conceived as a kitchen knife; and the second waiter describes the devouring. However, the fantastic action is not continuous: in the first speech the hero grills this enemy, in the second he boils him. The devouring, in other words, although sequent to biting, is not consequent to it but to another preliminary in which the teeth do not appear directly but merely by implication.

In an ulcer patient attacks of abundant salivation seemed to reflect the first, and pylorospasms the second of the two instinct components. But the two symptoms never appeared in conjunction. When, in the course of a dream analysis, the biting impulse became conscious it did not fail to produce a "notching": in a fellatio fantasy the sulcus coronarius became literally an "indentation," that is an evidence for the patient's having sunk in his teeth. After this, briefly silent and mildly restless, he had lost all context and didn't "know what to say." The next hour demonstrated the continuing separation of the two impulses from each other in terms of the production of two different ego resistances: a repression resistance (*Verdrängungswiderstand*) had been opposed to the second, a transference resistance (*Übertragungswiderstand*) (66) to the first. Of the "devouring" which had remained unconscious in the previous hour, nothing was heard at all, nor were any derivatives of it perceptible in either form or content of the session. The "biting," however, appeared now in projection upon the analyst who was accused of being injuriously "sarcastic." (In other words, of an attitude defined by Webster as "cuttingly . . . reproachful" and derived from *sarkazein* = to tear flesh like dogs!)

As for pylorospasm and salivation, neither symptom occurred in either hour.

To those familiar with the peculiar grammar of the oral mentality where subject and object, at first identical, later become exchangeable, the following may be a clinical illustration. A female patient experienced, in the beginning of her analysis, the very first outbreak against a mother who had maltreated her to excess as a child. And the outbreak was oral-sadistic. She was asked for a certain—completely realistic—purpose to hold the tip of the mother's outstretched tongue and could barely resist the sudden urge to tear the tongue out.

The "Typical Re-enactment of the 'Weaning Trauma' in the Transference" described in Section IV of this Chapter is another clinical illustration of the same point.

D. CANNIBALISTIC AIM INHIBITION AND AIM DISPLACEMENT

I cannot conclude this section without being emphatic about my impression, gained from much analytic material, that many more different forms of violence than one is generally inclined to believe prove actually of a cannibalistic nature.

The pater familias from whom every penny of household money or allowance must be extracted with a major struggle is not simply an "anal character" who retains, but someone who wants to starve wife and children.

The mother, who plays such a prominent role in the material presented to illustrate the urethral-erotic discharge of cannibalistic libido (cf. pp. 155 ff.) did not, of course, either bite or eat her child; but among her cruel behavior traits were quite a few that impress one as oral-sadistic under conditions of aim inhibition and displacement: she took the child by the hair, washed it, hanging her head on the edge of the washbowl; rubbed "biting" soap into her eyes and scrubbed her back in such a way as practically to take the skin off. If the child ever complained she retorted that the more forcefully it was done the sooner it would be over—an answer, not only inane but indicative of a "cannibalistic impatience." (Cf. pp. 107 f.)

Far into the daughter's adulthood she kept the habit of calling her (whom we shall name "Mary"), "Miss Mary" in the presence of dinner (!) guests, and of pinching her arm, terminating the pinch in a most painful twist, obviously representative of the tearing off of flesh. The almost unbelievable fact that it would never have occurred to the patient, even when in her late twenties, to utter the slightest sound or remonstrance when the mother pinched her is symptomatic of the strength of their sadomasochistic relation.

Anna Freud (27) writes: *"Passive devotion to the doctor.—* It is the psychological meaning of pain which explains why doctors, and other inflictors of pain are not merely feared but in many cases highly regarded and loved by the child. The infliction of pain calls forth passive masochistic responses which hold an important place in the child's love life. Frequently the devotion of the child to doctor or nurse becomes very marked on the days after the distress caused by a painful medical procedure has been experienced."

The question arises: what is this "psychological" meaning of pain? I believe that the pain, in the last analysis, is subjectively symptomatic of a cannibalistic invasion of the child by the parent or parent-person. I do so because I observe not only that hate forges a bond equally strong, if not stronger than as that wrought by love but that it also causes the same, if not a higher, degree of identification.

To illustrate this convincingly with the case of the patient mentioned above (who, by the way, remarked more than once that as far back as she could recall she thought of herself as "a little old lady") would require an amount of detail, concerning both mother and daughter, incompatible with discretion. I have learned, however, that the inmates of the German torture and death camps, e.g., who had their flesh burned and their bones broken before their incineration in ovens strove eagerly for a cap or some other piece of their torturers' uniforms, which they wore with great pride; and that the "trusties" tried to outdo their captors in cruelty toward their comrades.

E. CANNIBALISTIC RE-INCORPORATION

A final clinical observation concerning morbid identification contradicts both logic and theory but is nevertheless valid and easily subject to confirmation. If, as theory has it, an identification occurs after the model of cannibalistic incorporation, its result is that the parent has become deposited in some part of the ego (in the wider sense of the term). One is consequently prepared to recognize him in the adult patient as a constituent part of a morbid ego and as the nucleus of a morbid superego. Yet what brought him there is, one would think, altogether a matter of the past. One expects, in other words, to find the deposit but to look upon the deposition as completed. Actually, however, the first is true but the second is not: the process of deposition continues. It is as though the incorporation, theoretically effected long ago, were maintainable, clinically, only with the assistance of constant re-incorporation.

I have observed this most clearly in the case of the psychotic parent with a neurotic daughter or son. If the parent is still alive the introjective contact is maintained with him directly; if not, with substitute persons. The re-introjection is, of course, always the result of a compulsion, observably mutual; but the parent appears in most instances as the invader and his child; the patient, as the invaded person. The forms that these re-incorporative performances take vary greatly, although mouth and eye play often a dominant role.

An agoraphobic woman, for instance, daily had an hour-long telephone conversation with a psychotic older sister who had, in puberty when the psychotic mother died, taken the mother's place. During these conversations she was berated and ordered about by the sister of whom no more need be mentioned here than that she was given to talking confusedly, and that she practiced prostitution. The patient, a rather intelligent woman who lived in a tightly-knit group, did not allow herself to be aware of either. Instead, she herself became subject to episodes of confusion, and developed the agoraphobia as a defense against her own wishes to be approached in the street. It is obvious that here the vehicle of identification is the mouth. The patient, besides, lives in a steady conflict over masturbation. She is just becoming aware of this conflict, which convinces me of the pertinence of the symbolic meaning of the telephone, or telephoning = (masturbation; cf. p. 225). The analysis has not, however, progressed far enough to enable me to support this conviction.[7]

The woman patient who, during latency, had been seduced by her psychotic and excessively exhibitionistic mother to suck her nipple to the point of orgasm (cf. pp. 112 f.) had to repeat this performance masturbatorily in front of a mirror, particularly before her menstrual period (cf. pp. 216 f.). Although in this patient whose mother had died long ago, and whose premenstrual dreams, fulfilling the same wish of incorporating her, shall be reported further below (cf. pp. 230, 254 f.), the masturbation was actual instead of symbolic and the eye was auxiliary to the mouth (cf. pp. 55 ff., 101 ff.), the need for periodic reincorporation was the same.

The patient who re-incorporated the maternal breast in the transference and in so doing, produced oral-erotic silence (cf. p. 294 and the page references given there) re-incorporated the mother by seeing her; one of her first "orgastic dreams" during analysis occurred after having had lunch (!) with her mother. In addition the mother, whose kisses were, she said quite spontaneously, "really bites," invaded her privacy with senseless telephone calls at odd hours. She remained for a long time defenseless against these attacks which before she became capable of resisting them, left her depressed. I need hardly point again to the prominence of mouth and eye in this material, from which I must omit all evidence corroborative of the telephone as a symbol.

The same is true in the case of another female whose mother, besides engaging in the same type of telephoning, was in the habit of buying all manner of clothes for herself which she could not possibly wear, and then forcing them upon the daughter.

[7] I am indebted for this material to Dr. Irvin Galin.

In the case of a male, who was almost completely identified with a psychotic father, the invasion took place under conditions of an extreme libido regression to the anal-sadistic phase: one could say that it was the cash register that was invaded. The father insisted upon injecting himself into all kinds of business transactions, squandered money and assets, and when the son became able to separate and protect himself from him, proceeded to take his own life.

The practical value of these observations for the technique of analysis is self-evident: one could not at the proper time subject these re-incorporative actings out to the abstinence rule if one did not recognize them as such. Theoretically one might, of course, say that the phenomenon is but one of many, caused by the repetition compulsion. I am not certain, however, that in saying so one has explained it.

IV. A TYPICAL RE-ENACTMENT OF THE "WEANING TRAUMA" IN THE TRANSFERENCE

Further evidence of the persistence of cannibalistic desire can be found in a typical re-enactment of the "weaning trauma," i.e., of the mobilization of excessive cannibalistic impulses upon *withdrawal,* which is occasionally observable in analysis as a typical transference resistance. The patient so engaged seizes upon the apperception and reproduction of speech as a means of expressing—"acting out"—regressive impulses original with the second oral stage. It is only natural that this should occur in a situation where verbal intercommunication is the only "physical" contact. The resistance is infrequent but typical; and the sudden precipitation of oral-sadistic desire of which it is symptomatic does not lack a concomitant disintegration of the ego. The patient engaged in it ceases abruptly hearing the analyst; the occasion is almost invariably one where the analyst merely repeats a word or words uttered previously by the patient. Re-iteration is of no avail; when repeated, even when twice repeated, the quotation has the same fate as it did the first time:

it is either not heard at all or is distorted. The distortion has constant characteristics: it is utterly senseless in itself, or at least in the context of the preceding conversation. When one is finally understood, it is always too late: the context is by now forgotten, and consequently, the words have lost their meaning. An example may precede the analysis of this form of defense.

Freud is said to have remarked on the widows who keep a daughter by them to the end of their days: "They feed on their daughters. That is why they live so long." The paradigmatic instance—the most violent and, in part, a unique one in my experience—was furnished by such a daughter, who would never have entered analysis had her mother not finally died. Many years previous to her treatment she had let herself be approached by a man whom she found "exciting" although he "did not even look human," and had eventually given him access to her room. Locking the door he had forced himself upon her, beating her black and blue in a struggle during which she had finally prayed. At the end of her strength she felt that God had inspired her with the proper words. She told the man: "The You that I liked has gone away."[8] Thereupon he ceased fighting, negotiated and proved amenable to an arrangement preclusive of penetration.

When I quoted her magic words later, in an attempt to apply them to other material, she abruptly ceased to hear me. The reaction repeated itself on several other occasions within a few days. Aware of its violence, I took pains to explain that it was typical, repetition fruitless, and that one must respect it as an admonition not to proceed prematurely; the unconscious could not be forced. She was unimpressed, remained angry, and assured me emphatically that she could not stand having questions go unanswered. Repeatedly she adduced an occasion where she had asked me whether or not she had spoken of a certain matter before. "But I did answer you; I said that I had no idea." "That is no answer. Of course you know. You just did not want to tell me, etc., etc."

The situation came to a head a few days later, when I made a

8 An only slightly altered version, it turned out later, of what her mother used to say to her as a child.

reference to the "Tennessee man,"[9] as we had come to call him. "*What* did you say? Did I see a man? . . . What do you mean by that? Did you say, 'Let us see what we can'? What *did* you say? . . . etc., etc." On the strength of the explanation mentioned above, as well as of others to the effect that questions are associations which we must try to understand instead of having them answered, I remained silent. The patient, exasperated, became increasingly restive. She could not support the silence; it felt to her as though the analyst standing over her "slashed" her with a "bayonet" taking bits out of her, as it were. Asked to say all that further came to her mind she was briefly silent, jumped up from the couch, stalked furiously out of the office, and slammed the door.

It is hardly necessary to add that in the evening she left a note in the mailbox, apologizing and asking that her hour remain reserved; nor is it necessary to state how the situation was dealt with. She was assured that the incident would repeat itself if the inflation of ego, prerequisite to it, and the demonstrable product of a twofold (secondary) parent identification, were not resolved; and she was shown that, although her experience was not hallucinatory, the reality of the analytic situation had, nevertheless, been emotionally relinquished. Character analysis of this kind, if successful, has the effect that the repetitions become less drastic. The next one consisted, as far as the transference was concerned, in a spiteful assertion that she could not be analyzed and had better not try, but it was accompanied, on the outside, by the sudden fear of a lover who had kissed her so violently that she had "felt his teeth."

A few days later, however, she experienced an agitation, almost as violent as the original one in the office, and accompanied by the same excessive impulse "to get out"; but she did so in a different and elucidative situation. The scene, a restaurant, the occasion a luncheon, the partner, a woman friend. She was host to this friend, and had been feeding her from early morning on, each time after question and answer: "Would you like such and such?"—"Yes, that would be lovely."—It was thus that the guest had obtained an "eye-opener," breakfast, a drink,

---

[9] The name and its distortions are, of course, substitutions.

the promise of more to come, and an invitation to stay again over night. In the further course of the morning she was subject to weakness, mounting anxiety, and irritation. Her description of these feelings, which I cannot quote, indicated without doubt the fear of a passively cannibalistic fate. Finally, upon settling down in the comfortable surroundings of the restaurant to have luncheon with her somewhat lethargic friend, she became suddenly nauseous, and, as described before, claustrophobic. She decided eventually that eating would abolish the nausea and ordered, as did her companion, a salad, which actually proved remedial.

It became now demonstrable that, as far as her unconscious fantasy was concerned it was she herself, not her food, that was being eaten; and that in the previous episode, where she had felt gashed by the analyst, she was being, to borrow the Serving-Man's words (cf. p. 87), "Scotched and notched like a carbonado." Simultaneously her particular fear of free associations, exhibited over a long period of time, became intelligible without further effort. It was the "all," in saying all that comes to mind, the infinitude of the analytic demand, that she feared as an insatiability of the analyst who would leave her collapsed and empty, skin and bones as it were, in the end.

In analyzing this typical form of resistance in the transference one does well—as in all analysis—to attempt to begin with the surface. It is obvious that the analyst is abruptly deprived by the patient of his means of influencing him, i.e.,[10] of penetrating his mind. A word or words—always significant, never indifferent—do not penetrate, or while entering lose its meaning. Thus the analyst is rendered impotent, his above-mentioned "physical" contact with the patient is broken off, he becomes subject to castration.

The castration complex, however, is not limited to the psychic surface; it reaches into the deepest strata; and its premise, the phallic organization, has the identity of subject and object—

10 The German *Einwirkung* would denote accurately what is vitiated by the patient.

although restricted to the dominant erotogenic zone—with the oral organization in common. It is consequently the patient's own word or words that are destroyed. But the abruptness of their destruction, the desperate attempts to retrieve them only to maul them further; and the inability of the patient, helplessly caught in a tragedy *en miniature*, to leave the incident and go on associating, suggest an extreme degree of regression. It is not, therefore, enough to say that the castration is one through biting, and that the phallus represented by the penis, which has, as Freud expresses it, "inherited from the nipple of the maternal organ" (73B), is overdetermined by the breast. One must, instead, realize that the "maternal organ" has been transferred upon the analyst's mouth and the infantile "oral" mouth of the patient, via ear and speech motor apparatus, upon her own. One is then able to recognize that quoting her had meant injuring her by withdrawing the narcissistically owned nipple and offering it at the same time as an "object" for the vehement cannibalistic impulses mobilized by the withdrawal. It is thus that the words are either "bitten" out of existence or mashed into a *salade de mots*. The reaction to this, the desperate search for the lost word or words through questions demanding answer, represents a frantic attempt to retrieve the lost nipple by a child in immediate danger of starvation. (See in the example where the salad the eating in common of which permitted the patient to discharge the strivings in question and in so doing abolished nausea and claustrophobic agitation. I could be still more convincing were I allowed to name the salad and its symbolic meaning.)

There is hardly a more primitive instance, a more direct acting out, a more drastically compulsive repetition of the interference of biting with suckling than this particular form of resistance.[11]

[11] For the erotic counterpart to this destructive performance see *Midsummer Night's Dream* (126) where Helena, jilted by Demetrius whom she loves but who loves Hermia, wants to win the beloved man by becoming the woman he loves. How to bring this about means to her—how to look and speak like her friend: it is the unit of mouth and eye that she describes as vehicular to the desired

V. ON THE COLLECTIVE PERSISTENCE OF THE CANNIBALISTIC DESIRE

To demonstrate the collective persistence of the cannibalistic desire is the task of the analytically competent sociologist, anthropologist and historian. I ought therefore omit the subject were it not so important. In compromising I shall confine myself to aphoristic remarks upon two rituals, practiced in our time: execution and communion.

(a) I have found myself for a long time bewildered by the intent of and the arrangement for execution. If the intent is a punitive one, why have the cruel methods used by the Inquisition and the inhuman procedures described by the Sansons, the family of executioners, been abolished? If the protection of society is intended, why does a beneficent, lethal hypnotic such as carbon monoxide remain generally unemployed? Why hanging, gas chamber, electric chair? The answer would seem to be that the philosophy of execution is impinged upon by the demands of the instincts. Once more philosophy stems, as Nietzsche has said it did, from the stomach; and the stomach is hungry. The confusing disarray of proceedings for the collective killing of a fellow man admits of an ordering principle if

---

identification. In the line that I have italicized it is directly the mouth of one that receives from the mouth of the other.

¶ HELENA.   Oh Happie Faire!
               Your eyes are loadstarres, and your tongues
                              sweet aire
More tuneable then Larke to shepheardes eare,
When wheat is greene, when hawthorn buds appeare,
Sickness is catching: O were favor so,
Your words I catch, faire Hermia ere I go,
My eare should catch your voice, my eye, your eye,
My tongue should catch your tongues sweet melodie,
Were the world mine, Demetrius being bated,
The rest Ile give to be to you translated.
O teach me how you looke, and with what art
You sway the motion of Demetrius heart.
   ¶ HER. I frowne upon him, yet he loves me still
   ¶ HEL. O that your frownes would teach my smiles such skill [126A].

it is looked upon as an arrested cannibalistic orgy: one need combine only a few of the measures codified in a few different states or countries in our time, in order to have the composite picture of beheading, neckbreaking and "frying."[12]

A *précis* of the matter can be found in the conversation between Posthumous, ordered executed, and his jailer

    ¶ GAOLER. Come sir, are you ready for death?
    ¶ POST. Over-roasted rather: ready long ago.
    ¶ GAOLER. Hanging is the word, Sir, if you be ready for that you are well cook'd
    ¶ POST. So if I prove a good repast to the spectators, the dish pays the shot [118].

(b) If the analysis of the individual is, as Freud has suggested, one source of information about the prehistory of mankind (cf. p. 9) it would appear that history is another. It is difficult to resist the impression that the impact of a certain prehistoric event has caused waves, as it were, in the distant past, which are discernible as ripples (to continue the analogy) in the recent past. These, repetitive of the event, are perceptible (like the agitation of the pool after the stone that caused it has sunk from view) where the event itself is obscured. Thus the comparison of a passage from each of two documents, written less than twenty-five hundred years apart, gives one a vivid picture of the struggle for the relinquishment of cannibalism which must have taken place in far earlier, undocumented periods. I am referring in the first case to Genesis, and secondly to the decisions at the Council of Trent (1545-63 A.D.).

(1) Genesis (redacted ca. 800 B.C. from earlier sources containing in part, prehistoric material) records (italics this writer's):

12 The above remarks were made in ignorance of Montaigne's, which later came to my attention: "I think there is more barbarity in eating a live then a dead man, in tearing on the rack and torturing the body of a man still full of feeling, in roasting him piecemeal and giving him to be bitten and mangled by dogs and swine (as we have not only read, but seen within fresh memory, not between old enemies, but between neighbors and fellow citizens, and, what is worse, under the cloak of piety and religion) than in roasting and eating him after he is dead" (103).

"That God did tempt Abraham and said unto him . . . : Take now thy son, thine only son Isaac, whom thou lovest, and get thee into the land of Moriah; and *offer him* there for a burnt offering upon one of the mountains which I will tell thee of. And Abraham rose up early in the morning and . . . . took the wood of the burnt offering, and laid it upon Isaac his son; and he took the fire in his hand and a *knife;* . . . laid the wood in order, and bound Isaac his son, and laid him on the altar upon the wood. And Abraham stretched forth his hand, and took the knife to slay his son. And the angel of the Lord called unto him out of heaven, and said . . . . *Lay not thine hand* upon the lad, neither do thou anything unto him: *for now I know* that thou fearest God, seeing thou has not withheld thy son, thine only son from me. And Abraham lifted up his eyes and looked, and behold behind him a ram caught in a thicket by his horns: and Abraham went and took the ram, and offered him up for a burnt offering in the stead of his son. . . ." (81).

I would assume that in the course of the formation of a "father religion" (Freud) cannibalism was first relinquished to the God as his prerogative, who in his turn relinquished it in favor of obedience—not however, without devouring an animal in compensation. And I would further believe that the injunction against speaking ("mouthing") the name of the God and the prohibition of making an image, are—in view of the unit of mouth and eye (cf. pp. 55 ff.)—in the last analysis, anticannibalistic.[13] Intercourse between man and god, once incorporative, had become introjective; or, to express it simply: since what is visible is also edible, the equipment of the object world with a human—or (totem?) animal figure—cannot, in view of

13 Cf. Leonardo's exhortation (99): "If you meet anyone who is virtuous and good, . . . do him honor, . . . for these are your Gods upon earth; these deserve statues from us and images; but remember that their images are not to be eaten by you as is still done in some parts of India: where when the images have, according to them, performed some miracle, the priests cut them in pieces, being of wood, and give them to all the people of the country, not without reward; and each one grates his portion very fine and puts it upon the first food he eats, and thus believes that by faith he has eaten his saint, who then preserves him from all perils. What do you think here, Man, of your own species? Are you as wise as you believe yourself to be? Are these things to be done by men?"

the strong temptation, be allowed. One regress in the course of the progress in spirituality, the re-erection of an esculent diety, is told in the famous episode of the Golden Calf.[14]

(2) Among the discisions of the Council of Trent, spread over the years 1545-63 A.D., there is once concerning the "Holy Sacrament of the Eucharist" and settling the controversial question of "Transsubstantiation" (16). It determines that "If anyone . . . shall deny that wonderful and singular conversion of the whole substance of the Bread into (His) Body and of the Wine into (His) Blood, the species only of the Bread and Wine remaining; let him be anathema!" "Substance," the experts ex-

---

[14] Rashi's Commentary (the reference to which I owe to the kindness of Dr. Matthew Brody) to the passage quoted above is peculiarly reflective of the struggle over the cannibalistic desire. It is as though the medieval rabbi had to defend the God first against having and then renouncing the desire, as evidenced by his change of mind. He imputes the desire to man. Here are the pertinent comments to the italicized fragments of the text (89):

"'And offer him' (God) did not say to him 'Slaughter him' because the Holy One Blessed be He did not desire to slaughter him, but only to bring him up to the mountain in order to prepare him as a burnt offering. But after (Abraham) had brought him up, He said to him, 'Take him down.'" (Note the "legal" character of the argument opposing the letter of the command to its spirit in order to abstract or construct a defense.)

The Knife: "'A knife' because it devours flesh as is stated (Deut. 32, 42) 'And my sword shall devour flesh,' and because it prepares meat for eating . . ." (It is Abraham, not God, who brings the knife because it is he who understands the command as one to "devour flesh.")

"'Lay not (thy hand)': [Abraham] said to him, 'If so for naught have I come here. I shall make him a wound and draw forth from him a small amount of blood.' . . . [The angel] said to him 'Do not do anything to him,' [that is] do not make in him a defect . . ." (It is Abraham who rebels against God's anti-cannibalistic injunction. If the son's flesh is not to be devoured, his blood at least should be drawn; and one must evidently add, be drunk.)

"'For now I know': Rabbi Abba said: Abraham said to him '(God), I shall declare before you my complaint. Yesterday you said to me, "for by Isaac will be called thy seed." Then you retracted and said "Take now thy son." Now You say. "Lay not thy hand upon the lad." The Holy One Blessed Be He said to him "I shall not profane my covenant and the utterance of my lips I shall not change." When I said to you "Take the utterance of my lips, I shall not change." I did not say to you, "Slay him," but "Bring him up." You have brought him up, bring him down.'" (Abraham protests further, because the angels command ". . . do not make in him a defect" forbids him to castrate his son. But the God will not change the utterance of his lips. Instead of eating man he commands him; yet the incisive command bears the traces of the erstwhile incisor action; one may be tempted to see in the "up" and "down" a displacement upon the victim of the movement of the jaw.)

plain, "means reality," "species" the outward appearance; the God is, in other words, *actually*—not figuratively—being eaten. Thus the transformation of the father religion into a son religion (78), and the reverting from monotheism to polytheism[15] is accompanied by the regression from an identification ("obedience") to a cannibalistic incorporation.[16] Once the mouth's prerogative is restored, the eye's is: pictures and sculptures of the god abound, as does the use of his name.

VI. THE EYE-MOUTH UNIT OF PRIMARY IDENTIFICATION. "EMPATHY" AND SCOPTOPHILIA

If one recalls that the future "object" is the material out of which the ego is carved; and that hatred, not love, is the "original affective relation between humans [*die ursprüngliche Gefühlsbeziehung der Menschen*]," one is almost tempted to say that the carving is done with the teeth.[17] One remembers, however, that neither the mouth nor the destructive instinct are observable in isolation: it is the functional unit of mouth and eye that, concerned with the discharge of aggression fused with libido, delegates motor impulses to the general musculature for their postural consummation. Much of the earliest primary

15 In the "E" source from which Genesis XXII: 1-14, containing the story quoted above is supposed to stem (Dr. Brody informs me), God is not called *Jahwe* (Jehova), as he is in the *earlier* "J" source, but *Elohim* (plural: gods). Is the story thus documentative of a polytheistic-cannibalistic relapse? If it is, it has the build of so many screen memories which deny a previous activity by *preserving* an instance of its subsequent discontinuation.

16 Cf. Freud (78B): ". . . more than one author has been struck by the close resemblance between the rite of Christian communion—where the believer symbolically incorporates the blood and flesh of his God—and the totem feast, whose inner meaning it reproduces." When Freud repeats this, abstracting it a few pages later, he omits the word "symbolically."

17 Cf. W. Hoffer's summing up of his careful and most instructive direct observation of oral-sadistic instinctual discharge in babies: "No doubt exists as to the aggressive and destructive character and aim of the infant's oral attack on the mother's breast or its substitute. But in the oral-sadistic phase the breast has already become an object; it is not 'me' for the baby any more. With this differentiation of an object in the outer world, a world of 'me' and 'not me' has appeared in the infant's primitive mind" (87).

identification seems to be postural imitation, and creative, at the same time, of body-ego.

> I remember the photograph of a little girl, less than nine months old, happily seated on the arm of her equally happy *adoptive* father, and actually looking his "spitten image" in countenance, gesture.

> How dependent the mouth remains on the eye was impressed upon me when I saw an infant on her mother's arm cry bitterly over the "loss" of a half-eaten zwieback, which she was holding all the while in her hand with the arm outstretched sideways, that is, out of sight. The tactile possession of the zwieback did not as yet make her own it: it was only after the mother had taken the hand with the zwieback and brought it back in front of mouth and eye, that she looked down on it, smiled while the tears were still wet, and resumed munching.

> The same dependence once caused another mother to complain about an older girl who insisted on climbing out of her playpen which stood in the living room next to the kitchen. It was not difficult to guess that the child, although she could *hear* the mother, felt abandoned because she could not *see* her, and to suggest moving the playpen into her line of vision, with the result that the child stayed happily put.

In regressive conditions the kinship of eye and mouth is sometimes no less distinctly expressed.

> To a female who had transferred the mouth of infancy upon the vagina, the partner's penis in its capacity as a nipple furnished abundant if inadequate gratification. It was only post-coitum that the eye, as a mouth of the second oral stage, raised its demand in a strong urge to observe the man in the act of urination. Eagerly doing so, she experienced a strange absorption, unaccompanied by a directly sexual feeling, but ending in complete satisfaction. Theory, as summed up above, would consequently demand that her body serve her as phallus and, since the ego is "above all [*vor allem*] a body-ego," that she had remained dependent upon this service. I am not free to describe the degree to which this was so. However, she observed in the

beginning of her analysis, spontaneously, that she had two personalities: one that she named after a certain sport which offers perhaps the closest realization, in wakefulness of the "dreams of flying." Here she excelled and felt free; in particular, as she expressed it, "free to show." And another, dominating the rest of her life, where she was inadequate, felt inhibited and depressed.

In this context, and on the strength of observations such as are epitomized in the last example, Freud's remark upon scoptophilia requires an emendation. "The drive to see the specifically sexual parts in the nude is one of the original components of our libido. It is itself perhaps already a substitute reducible to a pleasure, to be supposed as primary, in touching these sexual parts. Looking has here, as it has so frequently done, replaced 'feeling' " (35). The tactile pleasure, replaced by the pleasure in seeing is that accompanying the tactile cognizance, originally achieved by the mouth into which the small infant is apt to put anything within reach as if in order to know it. One might say that a little later, when the motor mastery requisite to coordination renders the objects three-dimensional and thereby, perhaps, provocative of ocular incorporation, he "puts" everything "into" his eyes. And one may regard the unblinking gaze of the infant as indicative of the eye's imitating the mouth of the first oral phase before imitating that of the second. The hand gradually supplements the percept gained by the eye, whose motor contribution, e.g., to the sublimated aesthetic enjoyment of the adult, has not always found proper appreciation. It is in this motor function of the unit of mouth and eye that the much discussed "empathic" consummation of art has its origin; and it is here that the name "taste" for aesthetic discrimination—a name that derives from "ME. *tasten* to feel, fr. OF. *taster,* to try by the touch" (Webster)—finds its justification.

The eye, then, is an adjunct to the mouth of both the first and second oral phase. Yet one gains the impression that in the course of normal development the eye ceases in certain instances being much of an auxiliary to the first oral mouth while it remains a subsidiary to the second. Ocular incorporation, in other words, is devouring rather than sucking. In the tender, sexual kiss, for example, the eye is closed as though its "biting" would interfere with, as well as deflect instinctual energy from, the "sucking" in which the mouth is engaged. In as far as going to sleep is interpretable as a regression to the first oral stage, one may note that it is likewise dependent upon closing the eyes.

VII. THE BEGINNING OF SPEECH: BISYLLABIC REDUPLICATION

The mouth itself gradually finds another, likewise imitative, mode of discharge in attempting a linguistic reproduction of acoustic word-images reactive to their apperception. It is thus instrumental in establishing, through the motor function of speech and, by now, in collaboration with the ear, an incipient "psychic ego," of which Freud has said that its core consisted of "word-remainders." In a study devoted to another but related subject, Hendrick (85) describes this process. "The infant," he writes, "is biologically endowed with an ability for and a pleasure in uttering sounds. He practices his phonetic repertory until his ability to control the utterance of consonants and vowels is fairly well developed. This provides him with an instrument which at first has no social utility. When verbal intercourse with others is possible and desired, it is by using the words of other people that it is achieved. . . .

"I recently observed," he goes on to report, ". . . the intimate relation of social need and language development in a child of two. One day she appeared unusually melancholy; she then uttered and kept 'verbigerating' the first full sentence of her life: 'Ma-ma go-go do-do' (Mama went out the door). Apparently her unusual emotion occurring at a time when her potentiality for the use of language had matured, had produced this rhetorical achievement."

The example—illustrative, in the author's words, of "the role of primitive [we would prefer, with Freud: "primary"] identification through the development of language"—is unusually instructive.

The child is melancholy in response to the mother's absence; she is introjecting, we must assume, the lost object and in so doing establishing ego. She identifies with the mother by speaking, that is by speaking as does the mother. But her speech is not like the mother's. It varies in three respects: it is *repetitive,* it is confined to the present tense, and it employs *reduplicative bisyllables* only. I believe that all three of these characteristics are symptomatic of the formation of ego.

To begin with the *repetition*: it is "verbigeration." The quotation marks, with which Hendrick surrounds the word, distinguish the formative process in the child from the restitutive process in the schizophrenic. It is informative to identify this process in the traumatic dream, where the attempt to re-establish ego employs the same means—repetition—which the child uses to establish ego; except that here the identification appears to be one with the individual's own ego previous to the trauma.

Of the confinement of the child's utterance to the *present tense* the traumatic dream is not in itself elucidative because all dreams appear, by virtue of being dreams, so confined. One may perhaps be inclined to dismiss it as a psychological problem by explaining it with the obvious lack of skill of the child who can only say "go" but not "went." I believe, however, that one may apply to it Freud's first discovery, concerning the nature of aphasic speech. There as here the speech expresses circumstance immediately previous to the trauma precipitating the verbigeration. "Ma-ma go-go do-do" does not mean: Mama went, but, means Mama *goes,* out the door; and its repetition perpetuates the last moment of her protective presence as against her traumatic disappearance.[18]

The *bisyllabic reduplication* requires the closest inspection.

[18] Cf. Freud: *On Aphasia* (29) and Fliess: *On the "Spoken Word" in the Dream* (21A). Needless to state that the superego, operative in the production of aphasic speech, is inoperative in the speech of the child, since it has not as yet been established.

In the course of it one feels prompted to enlarge upon an old bit of speculation. Speech, mimetically productive of ego, is expiratory, as are all the vocalizations and interjection from which it gradually develops. It begins with denotative sounds, which are externalized through the mouth after having been internalized through the ear. The first objects so designated are narcissistic: in addition to the parents ("products" of primary identification), the two excreta (at first parts, later products of the body) which by gradually becoming expendable become objects. (Cf. pp. 111 ff.) This transformation, concomitant to the formation of ego, is reflected linguistically in the ambiguous denotation which is a common one for both process and product of elimination.[19] The designations are all onomatopoetic; note in the case of the mother (mama) the expiratory imitation of suckling, in that of the stool (a-a) the stimulation of diaphragmatic assistance to expulsion, and in the case of urine (wee-wee) the mimicking of small aperture and high pitch. In the case of the father (papa, dada) the more energetic labial or gingival expulsion (the p or d sound) is perhaps facilitated by the circumstance that the object is unencumbered by association with the previous activity of these parts of the mouth in the intake through suckling; one has not been nursed from the father's nipple. That the nicknames for nurses, siblings, fetishes, etc., are often reduplicates after the pattern of the original ones is common knowledge. Hendrick's example, however, shows another extension of reduplicative elaboration. Not only the mother (mama) but the act of her disappearing (go-go) and the aperture that dismisses her (do-do) are treated by reduplication. It is thus as though these elements of the object world were in *statu nascendi* extensions of the mother-object, bore her imprint, and derived their original meaning from her and her disappearance.[20]

19 The adult term "bowel movement" has retained this ambiguity: it denotes the process of defecation as well as its product, the feces.

20 In the last analysis this is the same psychology that enables the Elizabethan stage to omit all scenery while employing elaborate costumes and props: a king on the throne in regalia and his retinue make the stage a hall in the palace,

I believe that the reduplication is, quite generally, symptomatic of the infant's "work of mastering the outside world" (*Bewältigungsarbeit*)—a work necessitating, as Freud has expressed it, the "endeavoring to repeat even such impressions which it would have good reason to avoid because of their painful content." Since the mastery is one of "transformation into activity" of a passive experience, it appears as though the first of the two syllables were indicative of a jolt, experienced passively and slightly shattering the rudimentary psychic organization, and the second of a recuperative mastery through active repetition. The effect of this sequence is not, however, a mere restitution, but an extension and solidification of ego.

It is thus that the mother (as does Miranda) tenders speech; and the infant (as does Caliban) employs it eventually for its own design:

¶ MIR. . . . . I endowed thy purposes
       With words that made them known . . . . [129].

VIII. THE CANNIBALISTIC AFFECT: IMPATIENCE

It is rare that an affect proves correlative to the discharge of one partial libido only. The "sexual affect" (*Sexualaffekt*) appears as an example, but the "genital" partial libido is actually a component; the anxiety affect leads, as it led Freud, into difficult, fundamentally inconclusive, investigations; sadness and joy have had little elucidation, and some affects have not even found their description.

Of impatience, however, one can say that it is engendered by the cannibalistic impulse and adherent, as affect quantum, to the instinctive idea (*Triebvorstellung*) of devouring. This is

---

the same king and his nobles in armor make it a battlefield; for a shepherd it is a heath. Entrances to the stage are to warriors the gates of a beleaguered city, to a noble lady the doors of her chamber, and to the exiles in the countryside apertures leading to caves. Although masques and pantomime in the poet's time used elaborate scenery, drama relied on the power of the *dramatis persona* to extend himself into environment and, in so doing, creating the illusion of a locale.

clinically important because the idea is often repressed while the affect is insuppressible; its presence is then indicative of the presence of the idea. Impatience may thus be the sole manifestation of a cannibalistic desire.

The division of a meal into courses, the fashion in which these are served, the delegation to knife and fork of certain functions of the teeth, and the observance of table manners all combine toward a delaying effect.

The patient with the cannibalistic impulses toward the maternal nipple (cf. pp. 112 ff.) could not stand the delay. She was able to attend dinner parties only when she was no longer hungry, having taken care to eat beforehand. At one period in her analysis, when coming home in the afternoon to her kitchen, she regularly had to eat bread, butter and cheese in great haste. At the same time, she recalled a detail of certain instances of breast sucking: she stuffed as much of the breast into her mouth as would go in, so that the mouth was kept open and she—these were her own words—was prevented from using her teeth. This gave me the opportunity to interpret the cannibalistic impatience in the "vegetarian" re-enactment mentioned above. The interpretation was confirmed by her telling me, with bursts of uncontrollable laughter, how, one day, she had bitten a hunk off a loaf of bread so voraciously that she bit her finger.

The patient, paradigmatic for the typical re-enactment of the "weaning trauma" in the transference (cf. pp. 93 ff.), got into the habit of having luncheon immediately before her analytic hour. Her analysis became relatively static; and the eating became recognizable as an acting out through which she discharged her oral-sadistic strivings, and in so doing allayed instead of transferring them. It was therefore necessary to apply the "abstinence rule" which she frequently broke. Once, when she had a late afternoon hour, circumstance brought her close to the office half an hour early; she promptly had coffee and cake. She announced this as usual with a measure of glee; and when it was discussed, broke out in an angry excitement: "This is absolutely impossible. I could not have sat there for half an hour just gnashing and gritting my teeth!" Fantasies first of chewing the bark off a tree, then of the flesh off the analyst's penis with her teeth followed the outbreak.

The ulcer patient (cf. p. 87) had the same habit, as did the first-mentioned patient. Besides, when he ate, he ate hastily, finishing before everyone; and when he drank he gulped. When he was delayed on the road by a slow driver or merely in the street, waiting for a change of lights, the otherwise thoughtful and courteous man responded with outbursts of impatience, swearing and getting into a rage.

Eventually the cannibalistic nature of his impatience became manifest. Caught in Christmas traffic he had had a milder attack of rage at the driver ahead of him who did not round the corner fast enough after the lights had changed. However, he was able to calm down, telling himself that the driver had to slow-up because there were pedestrians crossing the street. While telling me this he remembered suddenly that during his feeling of rage he had wished these people were run down by the driver ahead of him, and that he would have liked "to hear their bones crack. . ." The subsequent associations concerned his preference for soft or semi-soft foods, his dislike of raw steak, and his avoiding the use of the molars in chewing.[21]

---

[21] If one remembers that execution is cannibalistic (cf. pp. 97 ff.), one will not wonder why the Shakespearean "cannibal" is impatient and that the plea for mercy is first of all a plea for delay, table manners in execution, as it were. In *Measure for Measure,* Angelo, acting ruler of Vienna in the Duke's absence, has condemned young Claudio to death. It is in vain that Isabella, Claudio's sister intercedes:

¶ANG. Be you content. (faire Maid)
It is the Law, not I condemns your brother,
Were he my kinsman, brother, or my sonne,
It should be thus with him: *he must die tomorrow.*
¶ISAB. Tomorrow? Oh, that's sodaine, (sudden)
Spare him, spare him:
He's not prepar'd for death; even for our kitchins
We kill the fowle of season: shall we serve heaven
With lesse respect then we do minister
To our grosse-selves? [124A].

The affect has found its expression in the form as well as the content of these lines. The first of the latter is a preamble; its form in modern parlance: "free verse." (Unrecognizable as such in the modern editions where it complements a preceding half line, spoken by Isabella in order to add up to a iambic pentam-

The impatience, symptomatic of cannibalistic impulsion, appears not infrequently in projection. The individual—now the object instead of the subject of the impatience—feels "chased" by others, making demands on him, crowded by his schedule, and overwhelmed by his obligations, for which "there is simply not enough time," and beset with deadlines. The unawareness of the projection is usually assisted by a skillful exploitation of actually pressing situations, although these are exaggerated, if not arranged, by the patient.

This is not the place to attempt a theory of impatience. One need merely recall the haste with which the beast of prey pounces upon his victim; and remind oneself of the fact that the interpolation of "delay through thought" does not exist in orality, but is at first performed in the subsequent anal stage.

---

eter which, for reasons that have no place in the present context, I believe could not have been intended.)

The second, the third, and the first part of the fourth are iambic pentameters strictly conforming to stress. But the meter breaks down at the colon: the impatience flares out, changes the rhythm abruptly and ends the line with a presto of murderous strokes: ". . . he must die tomorrow." (The juxtaposition of different style elements such as blank verse and prose, is habitual with the poet and is a means of characterization. Here the criminal hypocrite becomes suddenly incapable of maintaining his pompous iambic "persona.")

Through coordination of rhythm and pitch the desired slaughter is portrayed in the manner of a recitative. Isabella is stunned. She repeats the "tomorrow," and begins her objection to the impatience with a half-line of her own, unanalyzable for the relative lack of knowledge of Elizabethan pronunciation. But the rhythm, the tempo, the phonetic spelling and the use of the mute "e" now extinct, suggest that she opposes the hammering *presto* with the calm of a reflective and mournful *adagio* before imploring the would-be murderer, in an *allegro appassionato* for mercy. For a brief moment, in the italicized line, it is as though the patient sufferance contended, poetically, with cannibalistic impatience.

4

THE ANAL-SADISTIC PHASES

It is not profitable to attempt a separate treatment of the two anal phases. With these phases there is no newly acquired organ (such as the teeth) and no new group of instincts (such as the death instinct) distinguishing one from the other. The distinction between the two anal phases can be epitomized, descriptively, as a change in the behavior of an erotogenic zone; but it must be remembered that the change is symptomatic both of a difference in the libido elaborated upon by the zone, and of the relative inhibition of discharge by a further developed ego.

I. ON THE PERSISTENCE OF ORALITY IN THE ANAL PHASES

A. ANAL-EROTIC ELABORATION UPON CANNIBALISTIC AND ORAL-EROTIC LIBIDO

One can sum up Freud's and Abraham's findings by saying that the first anal-sadistic phase inherits libido from the second oral phase, and that the second anal-sadistic phase inherits libido from the first oral phase. But one must add that the "object" inherited by the excrement does not follow this sequence. Thus, in the beginning, defecation discharges a cannibalistic affect, in spite of the "vector" antithesis between elimination and incorporation. This is why, as Abraham (7) has discovered, the fecal "object," "bitten off" by the anal sphincter, is destroyed. The object, naturally, is at first the nipple, later the breast; and if, as Freud (71) has suggested, the "preoedipal dependence upon the mother" contains the "germ of the later

111

paranoia in the female," the germination begins with the elaboration upon the oral-sadistic relation between infant and "mamma" (cf. pp. 78 ff.) in terms of the anal-sadistic phase.

In exemplification I shall adduce material from two sequent hours of a fractioned analysis of a female, that was resumed after the operative removal of an extensive *fistula recti*.

The first part of the analysis, during which (for reasons that I cannot report) the fistula was allowed to persist, had a partial therapeutic result; it reduced the patient's paranoid reactions but it did not abolish them, and it was ineffective against her compulsion to overeat. The transference had retained the ambivalence described by Freud as typical for the anal-sadistic mentality of the child; the analysis held no further promise and was *discontinued*.

The progressive growth of the fistula brought the patient eventually to a competent surgeon, who was completely *successful in a major surgical operation*. A short while after her full recovery, she engaged, altogether gratuitously, in a parapraxia, hurling herself down a cement cellar stairway; but sustaining, miraculously, no more than relatively minor damage.

After this the analysis was *resumed*. I had now, over a period of months, the almost unique experience of working with a purely positive transference, lacking all paranoid manifestations and affording an unobstructed access to the traumatic past. The patient remembered readily how her mother, a deteriorated psychotic, had, in a state of premenstrual agitation, periodically seduced the child to suck her breast forcefully, and in so doing produced an orgastic response. This performance, begun at a late phallic age, was in late "latency" (after an interruption?) varied to the extent that the mother, no longer lying in bed, busied herself in the kitchen, and pretended to be unaware of the child's sucking her breast off and on; it was not remembered with what effect. The authenticity of these memories, which were full of detail, did not permit any doubt.

So much for the background of the two hours.

First Hour: The patient amends previous reports that breast sucking, vigorous and often painful, had always been an elaborate prelude to intercourse, to the extent of a playful pulling away of the breast and the partner's reaching for it with his mouth; in imitation, obviously, of the latency play with the mother. She associates the eating of clams and likens it to a "biting off without biting" of the nipple and of the area surrounding it, to which I add: in other words, as though it were detachable and could be swallowed like milk. This brings to mind her favorite Italian dinner—spaghetti, tomato sauce and cheese—which she now calls "eating a menstruation." I fit this association into other material, obtained previously and pertaining to the distant as well as to the recent past.

Second Hour: The fistula symptoms have suddenly reappeared: rectal discomfort, soreness around the anus, slight discharge. (All this was now pure conversion; the surgeon, promptly asked for a re-examination, found the region in perfect order.) The patient associates to these complaints the beginning of the previous hour and calls the playful pull on the nipple, as akin to the eating of clams, a "mmm-ing it off." I remark that this expression is indeed a fitting one for the "toothless" separation of a bowel movement in defecation. (I had previously, in the first part of her analysis, commented that the fistula circumvented a sphincter problem by supplying "incontinence without being incontinent," as it were.) The patient associates next her husband's walking around with the fly to his trousers open because of a broken zipper, and how he makes out of that "a big production. . . That's how much he wants to show a penis." I correct this interpretation on the basis of much previous material: No, that's how much he must show himself as a woman. Whereupon she remembers suddenly the open flap of the mother's drawers in the act of defecating into a bucket in the kitchen. The woman was moaning, blowing out air, wiping herself with rags, and fascinating the child who could be recognized as the intended object of this psychotic and evidently pleasurable exhibition. The patient responds to the awareness of this with a mild clitoral excitation, and, simultaneously, the *complete cessation of all rectal and perineal discomfort.*

I think that this record can be left to speak for itself. In the first hour the cannibalistic intent toward the nipple becomes conscious (the foreplay) and its two phases are, in typical fashion (cf. pp. 86 ff.) subjected to separate elaborations: the oral-sadistic biting is attenuated through oral-erotic sucking (the clams: "biting *without* biting"), the devouring is displaced (the Italian dinner: "eating a menstruation"). The response to this, in between the two hours, is a conversional imitation of a past proctological pathology on the basis of an identification with the preoedipal mother, and the renewed acquisition of her "cloaca." In the second hour the separatory sphincter function is associatively *transferred upon and imitated with the lips,* assisted by vocalization (the "mmm-ing it off"), and the historical mother-object ("proctologically" active) is remembered. The reaction: the rectal conversion syndrome, symptomatic of the mother identification, disappears.

The "preoedipal dependence upon the mother"—the dependence of the early mouth upon the nipple—had here indeed been elaborated upon by the anal-erotic zone. Severe rectal pathology had perpetuated the dependence internalized with the assistance of an identification. The results, descriptively, were paranoid reactions in a female who was not paranoid. A transient imitation of the proctologic symptomatology through conversion occurred in consequence of an associative re-experiencing of the breast experience, and disappeared in consequence of an associative removal of the amnesia for the mother's cloacal exhibitions.

The well-known rage reaction to enema application (Brunswick, Freud) is, in the last analysis, likewise a cannibalistic response to—*mutatis mutandis*—a passive cannibalistic experience which makes the child feel devoured.

The two patients (cf. pp. 73 ff., 93 ff.) who as children had both been maltreated with excessive enemas by their mothers, both experienced the identical feeling in the transference in response to the analytic demand for unlimited free association: they felt eaten into from the anus, "hollowed out," and left weak and empty, "without guts."

Of the two, the *second* case was the most instructive, because the analysis of the oral-sadistic question-and-answer game (cf. p. 94) had to be complemented in anal-sadistic terms. The perverse mother had insisted on learning everything about the state of her daughter's bowels, and the properties of their products by asking questions. In response to what she considered "constipation," she would put the child in the bathtub with a pillow to rest her head on, and apply interminably a hot soap and water enema, while telling stories and asking ever so often "Couldn't you take a little more?" . . . "Still a little more?" . . . etc., to which the daughter submitted at first with pleasure, then with agony until she felt she would burst. It was upon termination of this performance that she was left with the feeling, described above. The reproduction of both—the question-and-answer game, and the feeding—the former while feeding her friend, and the latter in part at least in the attack of weakness on this occasion, were reported above. (Cf. pp. 94 f.)

As far as the question-and-answer conflict and the rage reaction in the transference situation are concerned, the re-enactment of the former by the patient's furiously stamping out of the office and slamming the door has likewise been previously reported. (Cf. p. 94.) The "cannibalistic impatience" (see Chapter II, Section VIII) displayed in this performance need hardly be pointed out.

In the *first* case the revival of the rage reaction in the analysis preceded that of the localized feeling by several years and was therefore unununderstandable when it occurred. The patient had entered analysis with a severe inhibition of speaking as well as of eating, and had characterized her mother as her best friend "to whom I tell everything." However, in the first year of analysis, she was, upon meeting her, suddenly overcome without any apparent provocation by a violent impulse to throw her down the stairs. This was followed by an attack of dizziness lasting eleven days.

Note again the "cannibalistic impatience" in the precipitate nature of this violent impulse toward destructive elimination and apply to it the remark on proneness to accidents involving a fall. (Cf. p. 117.) Dominant in the instance reported here is obviously an object relation; in the case of accident proneness it is an identification.

That the sucking function of the sphincter—which, as Abraham taught us, prevails in the second anal phase over the biting characterizing the first—is, in the last analysis, that of the mouth can be recognized in the common delusion that constipation poisons the system. "It is probable," Freud (71) writes, ". . . that the fear of poisoning is connected with weaning. Poison is the nourishment that makes one ill. Perhaps, moreover, the child traces his early illnesses back to this frustration." If the eliminatory biting impulse requires excessive counter-action through retentive sucking, constipation ensues: not, however, without revealing the oral-erotic origin of the anal-erotic performance: "food" becomes poison again, the libidinal "nipple" destructive, and the individual subject to "toxinosis."

> Of the two patients, mentioned above, only the first is illustrative of the delusion. She had great difficulty in analyzing instead of medicating her constipation. One late relapse in breaking the abstinence rule occurred on a Friday and would, she said, have been avoidable had she been able to see me, i.e., have her enema by submitting to the analytic rule. She settled finally for eating the breast symbolically, at bedtime, in the form of an orange.

B. ORAL QUALITIES OF THE ANAL-EROTIC OBJECT

With regard to the object, in the beginning of anal-sadistic behavior it is—as it had been throughout most of orality—still identical, wholly or partly, with the subject: feces are both an object and a part of the individual, who is prone to identify with them as it were. It is thus that young children exhibit a fear of defecating because the act is equivalent to the relinquishment of a part of themselves, in other words, in the last analysis one of self-mutilation.

> Among observations to this point I remember how a little boy in a certain phase of his toilet training was afraid of using the toilet, although it had a seat fitted for him, but was perfectly willing to use the chamber and have it subsequently emptied into the bowl. It was the fractioned procedure, during which the stool outside of him was still visible and was "handled,"—i.e., remained extant although he had given it up—that protected him against the injury of sudden loss.

In adults one observes not infrequently that this fear has persisted and merely led to a modification of the procedure, attenuating the loss through delay: they inspect excrement before flushing it down.

A symptom of the regressive *identification* of the adult with his excrement as a hated object (Abraham) is "accident proneness" wherever it has to do with a fall. The symbolic meaning of "falling" (*niederkommen*)—"to give birth"—is an overdetermination, based on the feces=child equation and the infantile sexual theory of anal birth; it does not imply the destructiveness of the act, which derives from the first anal-sadistic phase.

The "cannibalistic impatience" is frequently traceable in the accident; for it can often be shown that the latter was the result, in the first place, of an undelayed action which should have been a delayed one.

> On the street people rush gratuitously into vehicular traffic, at home they do things simultaneously instead of in sequence; they proceed into a dark room without stopping to turn on the light, or act at once, where they should have waited for someone to lend them assistance. In most cases they have not even a rationalization for their hurry.

There is another characteristic of the *incipient anal-sadistic object*. It appears that feces are at first animate:[1] their narcis-

---

[1] It is upon this particular point in the present description—the originally animate nature of feces, at first implied by Freud in his description of the fantasy of anal birth (*"Lumpf"*) and later made explicit by Nunberg (cf. footnote 2, below)—that analysts have enlarged through the direct observation of children. The following quotation is taken from a discussion of *Problems of Infantile Neurosis,* in which Anna Freud said: ". . . Dr. Bychowski . . . describes a rhythmic, autoerotic play activity which some of his patients had carried on with their feces, creating out of their own body a pseudo object with which they could enter into some sort of pseudo object relationship. I want to confirm Dr. Bychowski's remarks by referring to the case history of a two-and-a-half-year-old child. This boy had a series of traumatic experiences at the end of his second year. There was a complete upheaval in the external conditions of his life; there was a sudden short separation from the mother due to illness on her part; and finally, there was a period of mourning and depression on the part of the mother, caused by the loss of her relatives. The boy reacted to the accumulated strain by soiling, and investigation proved that this was more than a regression in toilet habits. He called the stool out of his body quite deliberately, to have company at a time when he felt abandoned by his mother, and, in reaction to her mood, withdrew his own feelings from her . . ." (28).

sistic nature equips them with the motor characteristics of the peristaltic process and the retroperistaltic response to expulsion endows them with a tendency to re-enter the anus. This is the nature of "material projection" (106) which is the model for projection by the same token by which incorporation is the model for identification.[2] The projection can thus become one upon animate objects, from whom persecution can be feared and whose destruction can become an instinctual aim. Whether or not the child's fear of "small animals, issuing from and disappearing into holes" (Freud) finds an ontogenetic explanation, or a contribution toward it, in a transfer upon them of the peristaltic qualities of the feces of the first anal stage is a question that child analysts may at some time be able to answer. However, in extension of peristaltic characteristics other qualities of the subject can adhere, as it were, to the "object" of the projection; who, consequently shares them with the subject.

A classic example is the fetish *"Glanz* [shine] on the nose" described by Freud (67) and understood as a "glance [look] at the nose." The glance is the subject's, not the object's; and the subject, who keeps on glancing, retains the glance while equipping the object (the nose of certain persons) delusorily with it as a *"Glanz"* that the others cannot see. Since a shiny nose is by social standards an unclean nose, the "project" still bears the hallmark of the original object of the "material projection."[3]

Another example is the relatively frequent representation of the "man (the father) in the dark," particularly in dreams of the primal scene, through the negro. Here again it is as though

[2] Nunberg, who has coined the term, describes feces as animate, but does not describe the peristaltic and retroperistaltic nature of excrement; and, instead of naming (material) incorporation as analogous to material projection, names identification.

In the revised English edition of his book (106A) I could not find the term and its definition; I therefore questioned the author who told me that he had left it out because he found it too definite a concept. I do not and propose that we restore it and expand it in the sense of the addenda suggested above in the text.

[3] Symptomatic of the persistence of orality, is, in fetishism at large, the incorporative employment of the fetish. The latter is looked at, wrapped around membrum or person, inhaled. In the last instance, that of olfactory introjection, the fetishist uses directly a phase of eating: the (gustatorial) "tasting" of food.

the darkness, a quality of the subject's scoptophilic experience, had "come off" on the object who is consequently a dark man. And again—the "hallmark" mentioned above, which in this case is the object's odor.

Instances where a child refuses to defecate upon the unbearable loss of an object—in other words, where excrement is "possessed" regressively as an object—are almost too well known to require exemplification.

A patient became "constipated" as a child of about two when her nurse was dismissed and stayed so until the nurse was re-hired.

Dr. Editha Sterba (138), in the analysis of a *Psychogenic Constipation in a Two-Year-Old,* shows how the little boy had a relapse when he was angry at his mother and believed that she would not let him come any longer to see the analyst. He was constipated again, she writes, "on the one hand out of obstinacy and, on the other, he identifies me with his stool and would not give up the loved object."

It is noteworthy, however, that when this is re-enacted in analysis the object, now to be given up, is invariably one of an intense pathogenic identification.

In the patient mentioned above (cf. pp. 114-116) the constipation could be called a "pilot" symptom, since it was obviously a model for other and no less "pathogenic" forms of retention of the lost object, e.g., through identification. She reproduced in the beginning of her analysis the incipient symptoms of a heart disease, from whose terminal consequences the mother had finally died; and she did it so faithfully that one had to insist on a (completely negative) cardiological examination. The constipation disappeared gradually and at the rate at which the patient became demonstrably a person in her own right.

In the course of the rectal "possession" of the fecal "object"—both originally and in its regressive re-enactment—the tactile cognizance originally achieved by the mouth (and the eye) (cf.

pp. 102 f.) is resumed in terms, as it were, of the anal-sadistic erotogenic zone. In the case of the mouth and the eye it was the object that dictated motor performance and molded the kinesthetic impressions; in the case of the rectum it is the peristaltic motor intent that molds the object, while the ensuing kinesthetic impressions find an employment, the description of which must be reserved for a different context.

This "sadistic" treatment of the stool is the model for the later sadistic treatment of objects. It is then that at first the hand becomes an adjunct to the anal-sadistic zone and the child exhibits the impulse to dirty, disfigure and destroy whatever he is able to reach.

Abraham has described the pertinent manifestations so exhaustively that one can dispense with all exemplification and refer the reader to his work. There, besides the *Anal Character* (4), and the *Development of the Libido* (7), the short study of *The Narcissistic Evaluation of Excretory Process in Dreams and Neurosis* (3) should not be overlooked. In his *Transformation of Scoptophilia* (1), Abraham, by the way, describes at least one psychotic girl who had re-transferred, regressively, the destructiveness of the rectum upon the eye.

There is, finally, a fantasy which supplements that of anal birth, discovered by Freud, with the idea of rectal procreation. It appears as though the child (the *"Lumpf"*), to be expelled through the anus, originated in the rectum by the apposition of feces. Actually, the imaginary process must be much more complicated and employ the fact that stool is the product of eating as well as the "animate" nature of the resultant bowel movement. Theoretically the fantasy is understandable only if the orality of procreation (cf. pp. 238 f.) is taken into consideration; clinically I have never been able to trace it clearly enough to produce an example.

The fantasy becomes traceable and overt when, while unconsciously concerning feces, it consciously concerns money.

When Viola, for instance, gives a coin to the Clown as reward for his information, he begs for another:

¶ CLO. Would not a paire of these have bred sir?

¶ VIO. Yes being kept together, and put to use.

¶ CLO. I would play Lord Pandarus of Phrygia sir, to bring a cressida to this Troylus.

¶ VIO. I understand you sir, tis well begg'd [131].

The significance of the fantasy is a considerable one for the psychology of interest, where money begets money. Charging interest has, in many ages and places, been considered a dirty business relegated to the Jew, and has served as excuse for holding him in contempt.[4] Without knowing the fantasy one cannot possibly understand how a necessary phase of economy can become subject to disrepute, since there is, of course, no rational reason why money, a commodity like any other, should not have its price.

> In discussing interest with Antonio, Shylock adduces the Biblical story of Jacob's breeding of Laban's sheep to his advantage. Antonio doubts that the illustration is to the point.

> ¶ ANT. This was venture sir that Jacob serv'd for,
> A thing not in his power to bring to passe,
> But sway'd and fashioned by the hand of heaven.
> Or is your gold and silver Ewes and Rams?
> ¶ SHY. *I cannot tell, I make it breed as fast* [125B].

Most questions concerning the fantasy—e.g., its connection, if there is one, with the fantasy of anal (cloacal) intercourse— must at present remain unanswered for lack of knowledge. But that did not seem reason enough to exclude it from mention.

II. SPHINCTER CONTROL AND THE CONTROL OF ARCHAIC AFFECT

A. THE FIRST "MORALITY": THAT OF THE SPHINCTER

The most significant of the distinctive characteristics of the anal-sadistic phase is derived from the physiological fact that the

---

4 Only lately, in our own lifetime, Hitler promised the Germans liberation from "servitude of interest" (*Zinsknechtschaft*) by "purging" their country of Jews.

instinctual impulses, germaine to it and opposed by what Freud termed "the influence of civilization," must be mastered through sphincter action. "The little primitive," Freud has summarized, "must in a few years have become a civilized human being, and have passed through an immensely long stretch of human cultural development in an almost uncanny abbreviation. This is made possible by hereditary disposition; but it can scarcely ever be achieved without the additional help of education, of parental influence, which as a precursor of the superego,[5] restricts the activity of the ego by means of prohibitions and punishments, and facilitates or compels the setting-up of repressions" (77D). The first morality due to this influence is therefore sphincter morality, to be acquired by an ego comprised of primary identifications that enable it to defend itself against archaic instinctual impulses by means of primal repressions. (Cf. pp. 41-44.) The instinctual aim of these impulses has been treated in the previous sections; an indefinable part of them need not ever be conscious, yet it is nevertheless their discharge that begins to transform defecation from a reflex into a primitive action.

One could say, at the risk of sounding absurd, that it is here that the child's development follows the blueprint begun by Freud in the famous Chapter VII of *The Interpretation of Dreams*. A psychic organization deserving the name of an ego is interpolated into the reflex arc; and the core of this organization is, as Freud later determined, the system Pcpt.-Cs. Now the striped musculature is no longer drafted by the smooth musculature as an auxiliary to its reflex response but becomes the executive of "motility," and as such allegiant to the ego. After language and upright gait are developed, toilet-training trans-

5 The similarities and the dissimilarities between this "precursor" and the superego itself are not always remembered, although Freud has outlined them clearly, and it is not difficult to observe them. A similarity between precursor and superego is that the pre-stage of the conscience exists, as does the superego, from the time of its establishment to the end of life. In other words, it persists, as Freud has expressed it, "beside" and "behind" the superego. A dissimilarity: —the "original infantile pre-stage of the conscience" is expressive of an interpersonal relation to the parent who has not as yet been introjected, the "guilt" feeling is at that stage consequently a social fear: the fear of the loss of love.

forms this primitive action at the time of the gradual prevalence of the sucking function of the sphincter (cf. p. 115), into a full-fledged psychic act. Thus the first *Denkaufschub* (Freud)— i.e., the delay of instinctual gratification through the interpolation of thought-yielding judgment—assists the achievement of continence in the child. This is possible for two reasons. Firstly, primary identifications have established an ego which has relegated certain archaic impulses to primal repression and, in so doing, has counteracted their impact upon both smooth and striped sphincter. In the second place, the ego has become capable of observing and opposing itself to that part of itself which can be considered the subject of the instinctual strivings demanding discharge. This amounts to a structurization of ego, so different from a mere fusion of ego nuclei (cf. pp. 69 f.) and of such import, that the present context cannot contain its description.

Abraham's classic observation of the little Hungarian boy who threatens his nurse with the words: "If you anger me I'll shit you from Buda (across the Danube) to Ofen!" (7) contains almost all these circumstances in condensation. It is obvious that the child saying this is already angry. Yet the affect, whose bodily symptoms Abraham was the first to equate with those of defecation, is controlled. It has become, as does anxiety (Freud), a "signal-affect" observed by an ego, capable in a measure of deciding whether to discharge or to suppress it. The *Denkaufschub* (see above) yields a twofold result: the imminent defecatory discharge is suspended while a relatively small quantity of the affect is discharged in a verbal threat; and the ensuing verbalization describes therefore the sequence of stimulus and response in the cognitive form of a conditional clause. (If you . . . [then] I will . . .) It may appear inconceivable that such a high degree of mastery and employment of intellect be compatible with a mentality primitively conceiving of feces as object until one remembers that the impact of affect shatters the immature ego and causes a partial regression.

It must here suffice to remember that the anal sphincter is

both the first to become executive of an ego and the most powerful of its kind; and that the dividing line between the fixation
points reached by the regressive process in a narcissistic and
transference neurosis, respectively, is that separating the incontinent first anal phase from the continent second. If one adds
to this the persistence of orality in the anal-sadistic phase described previously (cf. pp. 111 ff.) and the persistence of characteristics of the latter in the phallic phase to be described subsequently (cf. pp. 145 ff.), one will understand the quasi-
central position frequently occupied by the anal-erotic zone
in regressive conditions. *It is often as though the anal sphincter
were charged with the mastery of regressive and archaic affect,
intrinsic to whatever phase of development, because it is strongest;* and as though the ego chose anal-erotic elaboration upon
instinctual strivings of whatever nature as the most reliable
means of preserving its organization.

Best illustrative are the cases presenting the deceptive clinical
picture of a severe compulsion neurosis, which becomes recognizable as a system of successful reaction formations against a
further dissolution of ego through the impact of the psychotic
process. This is the nature of the compulsive interval, described
by Abraham in the melancholic. But it is likewise present in
schizophrenics where one can sometimes observe how a threatening aggravation is arrested by grotesquely exaggerated compulsion.

As an example of failure of such elaboration I remember a
melancholic who, during a consultation, pulled folded currency
amounting to several thousand dollars out of his pocket. "Here,
doctor," he said sadly, "I always carry this stuff around; my
wife tells me I shouldn't because I might lose it." And with tears
in his eyes: "I don't know why I do it." The anal-erotic incontinence manifested here need not be pointed out.

Those familiar, furthermore, with the frequent attenuation of
the mutual to the common meal, i.e., with the substitution of
eating together for eating each other,[6] will penetrate Abraham's

---

[6] Applicable, of course, to the episode of the two women friends in the restaurant, described on pp. 94 f.

classic report (4) on the "two unmarried brothers who kept
house together" during the first World War. "When rationed
meat for both was put on the table they divided it by weighing
each portion on a pair of letter scales. Both were anxious lest
the other should go short or feel himself unfairly treated." What
is described here is in the last analysis an unconscious cannibalistic desire, against which the two anal character traits, "need
for symmetry," and the "need to 'be quits' with the other" (described by Abraham in the same chapter) are brought to bear.
One need not therefore, finally, be surprised to encounter the
same abuse of the scales toward the same irrationally exaggerated exactness in Portia's second injunction against the cannibalism of Shylock:

¶ PORTIA. . . . . if thou tak'st more
Or less than a just pound, be it so much
As makes it light or heavy in the substance,
Or the devision of the twentieth part of one poor
Of one poore scruple, nay if the scale doe turne
But in the estimation of a hayre,
Thou diest, ... [125C].

B. THE ANAL REVERSAL

Prerequisite to such employment of the anal sphincter for
the control of instinctual discharge is its overcathexis. Cathectic
quantities, adherent to the oral-erotic or phallic zone threatening discharge, must be displaced to the anal-erotic zone promising to inhibit the discharge. This displacement is therefore
one from the front to the back. Clinically, however, it does not
always appear as an exchange of the back for the front but also
as an exchange, a confusion, between right and left. Freud was
the first to observe such reversals (e.g., of front and back) and
to conceive vaguely, of their meaning. Jones (92) followed with
more observations (e.g., right and left, east and west, etc.) and
Abraham (4) gave the theory: the reversal is symptomatic of a
libido displacement from the genital to the anal zone.

To these observations one must add the reversal in time,
where the "fore" and "aft" becomes a "before" and "afterwards,"

of which Freud's work contains more than one example; and to the theory, that it need not be the genital but can also be the oral-erotic zone from which the libido is displaced. Yet the displacement is always one onto the anal-erotic zone; and the reversal indicative of it is so typical and so frequent that it deserves the name "anal reversal." This in particular since it is the reversal, as such, that matters; so that if it occasionally appears as an exchange of the front for the back it may still be indicative of the same shift of cathexis.

Needless to add that the cathectic displacement need not always be a preliminary to sphincter control. In the very first example, for instance, mentioned by Freud (33)—the deliberate, jocular reversal of syllables in the German word *Eiweissscheibchen* to *Eischeissweibchen,* which transforms "little slices of egg-white" into "little women shitting eggs"—it obviously initiates not inhibition but action of the sphincter.

An instructive example of indeliberate reversal of letters stems from clinical observation. A schizophrenic female, who had been sent to the gynecologist, Dr. Kulka,[7] became uncertain about his name and kept calling him "Dr. Kulak." When the correct name and the fact that she reverses only the letters of its second syllable, leaving the first intact, is pointed out to her, she confesses that she did not listen attentively but that it "reminded her of" or "sounded like" a French word. This word, the knowledge of which she denies, is obviously the French slang word *"cul"*; and of the letters "k-a" it becomes clear that they had to be reversed because they connoted a German-Jewish slang expression for feces.[8] During the analysis of the reversal the patient expressed a transient need "to pass gas"; but "felt," otherwise, for the first time in years, "sweet," because the doctor and his nurse, whom

[7] I am indebted to Dr. Kulka for the permission to use his name.

[8] How appropriate Socrates' formulation in "Cratylus"! ". . . the offspring of every kind, in the regular course of nature, is like the parent, and therefore has the same name. Yet the *syllables may be disguised* until they appear different to the ignorant person, and he may not recognize them, although they are the same, just as any one of us would not recognize the same drugs under *different disguises of color and smell,* although to the physician, who regards the power of them, they are the same, and he is not put out by the addition or *transposition* or subtraction *of a letter or two,* or indeed by the change of all the letters, for this need not interfere with the meaning." (Italics mine.)

she fantasied as being my wife, had been "so very nice" to her. Here the control of anal-erotic discharge is directly experienced; it appears stimulated by a regressive fantasy about the gynecologist's ministrations, evidently allusive to the primal scene.

For still another clinical illustration it will be remembered that of all of Freud's classic patients, the "Rat Man" experiences the "command" to cut his throat with the razor blade *followed* by the idea of traveling to the sick grandmother, who keeps his lady from him, and of killing her. The interpreter rectifies the reversal: his patient wants to kill the old woman, and, by committing suicide, to punish himself. Freud's analysis of this "unconscious attack of rage" closes with the recognition that ". . . the whole process passed into the obsessional patient's consciousness accompanied by the most violent affect and *in a reverse order* [Italics Freud's]—the punitive command coming first, and the mention of the guilty outburst afterwards" (39A). Since this patient is, as the "rat-punishment" shows, dominated by a passive cannibalistic fantasy concerning the anal-erotic zone, I would not hesitate to suspect that the "most violent affect" with its concomitant fantasy of the knife (cf. p. 100) is cannibalistic. The reversal would, then, again be indicative of a simultaneous overcathexis of the anal sphincter for the purposes of control.

The cannibalistic "communion" (cf. pp. 98-101), finally, does not fail to allude to the same anal-erotic control of archaic affect, because it, too, contains a reversal. In the case of the cannibal, animal matter is eaten and transformed, digestively, into vegetable matter (dung, a bacterial product); in the case of communion, vegetable matter (bread, wine) is eaten and transformed transsubstantively, into animal matter (flesh and blood).

The cathectic displacement, reflecting itself in the "anal reversal," can, of course, also produce other manifestations. Yet this one is so typical, and so frequent, and in spite of that so relatively little known, that it seemed to deserve special mention and at least some exemplification.

Clinically I have found my erstwhile ignorance of the reversal in time most confusing because it leads not infrequently to a reversal of cause and effect. Once one knows this, it is easy to free oneself from the prejudice that the cause (a transgression, for instance) must precede the effect (the punishment for it) and to reconcile oneself to the former's following the latter. It is not difficult to observe that this occurs—in fantasies, symptoms and associations—exclusively in such individuals where, and at such times when the prevailing libido is anal-sadistic.

III. ON THE MOTOR CHARACTERISTICS OF THOUGHT

It is during the anal-sadistic phase that the ego becomes fully opposable to what Freud has characterized as a double environment: the object world, and the body. The reaction of the ego's nuclear system Pcpt.-Cs. to this twofold external world is "external perception"; its effect: the establishment of psychic representations. The environment proper becomes reflected in "object representations" to which the ego opposes itself; and the body in organ representations," elemental to a body-ego, from which the rest of the ego is distinguishable as psychic ego. Yet there is, in addition, a newly acquired internal world, the reaction to which is "internal perception": the world of thought. Its elements, according to Freud, are memory traces of (originally acoustic) word-images; so-called "word-remainders" which are subjected to a process, the thought process, described by Freud as essentially of the nature of action. Hence his profound proposition: "Thinking is trial-acting with smallest quantities of cathexis" (42). I believe that one may understand this to mean that thought has latent characteristics which become manifest when it stimulates motor phenomena: facial expression and gesture, vocalization and verbalization. Needless to state that all these manifestations require an increase in cathexis.

> One of the secrets of Shakespearean thought is that its latent characteristics have a tendency to become manifest; it is, in other words, so conceived as to engender these manifestations. One of countless examples: Hamlet inquires about a military expedition which he sees drawing up, and wants to know its objective.

¶ CAPTAIN. Truly to speake, and with no addition,
We goe to gain a little patch of ground
That hath in it no profit but the name:
To pay five duckets, five, I would not farm it;
Nor will it yield to Norway or the Pole
A rancker rate, should it be sold in fee [120A].

The thought expressed in the first line is abstract and the line is in prose. The second and third lines convey concrete thought and with it its motor characteristics: their strict iambic stresses compliance, their alliterative and half-alliterative scanning and their masculine endings, dividing sentence from clause without carry-over into the next line, sound the footsteps of the marching column of men as a background. In the fourth, the italicized line, the human figure rises against this background as it does in so many paintings of the Renaissance. Yet again it is virtually impossible to speak this line—an emphatic aside in which the anonymous captain draws upon his own rural background—without a certain inflection, facial expression, and where the "five" is repeated, a gesture. One feels compelled to extend one's arm halfway, showing the hand, palm toward the face, and with the thumb abducted, in approximation of the shape from which the Roman numeral "V" has been derived.[9]

Later it becomes possible to overcathect thought without provoking overt motor action. But the mental process will then employ the inaudible speech more exhaustively, searching for word-combinations in order to formulate; while a pose, symp-

[9] Conversely, Shakespeare describes motor performance in terms of thought, e.g., when he has Cassius tell of his swim in the Tiber with Caesar:

The Torrent roar'd, and we did buffet it
With lusty Sinewes, throwing it aside,
And stemming it with hearts of *Controversie* [122].

Or in terms of musical thought (cf. pp. 139-143), as in the report on Macbeth's fight with Norway:

Point against Point, rebellious Arme 'gainste Arme,
Curbing his lavish spirit. . . . [123B].

The listener to counterpoint, played expertly, can actually discern, besides its horizontal (melodic) and vertical (harmonic) properties, its dynamics: literally a clash, most enjoyable, of "punctus contra punctum."

tomatic of motor restraint is assumed (unless the motor energy is discharged otherwise, as for example, in walking).

> Rodin's famous "thinker," a naturalistic product of a "free" period in art, may suffice as an obvious illustration. The motor restraint is in evidence throughout; most conspicuously in the support of the head by the captive arm, with the torso in a forward slump. Offensive aesthetically, but illustrative of the relation between motility and peristalsis, is the fact that the man looks as though he sat on the toilet.

Eventually, however, thought can be further refined. It then forms "unimaginable" ideas, and employs elements other than words for their representation. Freud, in formulating that "thinking takes place on word-ideas" (*spielt sich an Wortvorstellungen ab*) has omitted mathematical as well as musical thought. Mathematical thought does not take place on word-remainders but on elements of a different kind and, from the standpoint of thinking, of a much higher order. Mathematical symbols such as are employed, e.g., in calculus, imply complicated yet typical thought processes that cannot be performed without them; and by virtue of such implication spare, at the same time, the thinker their repetition. Thinking becomes thus both more economical and more abstract.[10]

It is instructive to apply, however cursorily, what has been said in this subsection to the case of man's satisfying his curiosity about the world. He has gradually delegated, as it were, his most sublimated scoptophilic interests to a small number of individuals who alone are equipped to perform. They elaborate naturally in the last analysis, as he does, through thought processes upon perceptory data, and employ motility for reality testing. In former times such elaboration was often immediate: when a ball rolled a stretch and arrived as the same ball at the end one found matter in motion during a certain period of time. Everyone knows today that this seems so but is not: physics now has it that the ball is altered, the distinction of time from space

---

[10] Certain stereotyped phases of it may even be "canned" and imitated by machines which do not, of course, fail to manifest the motor characteristics of thinking in the movement of their parts.

in the last analysis untenable, and that the occurrence requires an altogether different description (115). The obsolete concepts and their relations had suggested themselves because the old observer had simply trusted his senses. The modern observer works under conditions not only of the refinement of thought mentioned above, but of a prosthetic alteration as it were of his body-ego.

In order to understand this alteration one must be aware of the fact that the sensory spheres furnishing the perceptory data are points of fusion between the two environments distinguished by Freud. They are interstices in the system of organ representations, occupiable only with object representation; in other words, gaps in the body-ego filled with the outside world.[11] Modern man has become increasingly able to exploit these fusion-points for the extension of one environment through the other, of the body through the object world, while at the same time borrowing energy from the latter that he cannot generate in the former. Thus the observer has been equipped, prosthetically,[12] with a perceptive and motor power furnishing him with data representative of a reality that has not previously been within reach. However, in order to form ideas about this naturally unimaginable reality a grandiose "delay through [refined] thought" (42) is required: an elaboration upon the data through the highest mathematical thinking. Only then can reality testing be performed conclusively; and it requires expenditure of enormous amounts of "borrowed" motor energy which is, of course, as is motility, potentially destructive.

IV. ANAL-SADISTIC DEVELOPMENT AND THE EAR

Concomitant with the entry of the anal-erotic zone into the incipient body-ego and with the domination of instinctual life

11 My visual sphere is represented only by the objects I see; in total darkness it is not represented at all. In complete quiet the auditory sphere lacks representation, etc., and if my arm hangs relaxed by my side in the dark I do not know that I have a hand unless, e.g., attention directs an increased flow of blood to it, precipitating kinesthetic impressions.

12 Cf. Freud's "prosthetic god."

by anal-sadistic libido—the sensory sphere that acquires prominence is the ear. The structure of language entering through it is apperceived; the emulation through speech motility of these acoustic percepts is perfected; and a psychic ego, consisting of "word ideas" is wrought.[13] To speak of a unit of ear and anal-erotic zone analogous to the unit of mouth and eye would, of course, be absurd. But the ear maintains, and persists in maintaining, functions and characteristics, derivative of and concurrent with those established or perfected in the anal phase. Some of what has been said of the anal-erotic zone, its product and the achievements dependent upon its dominance, can be modified and applied to the ear. Pending future research—in particular on the part of a psychoanalytically motivated analysis of the senses—I shall confine myself to a few brief observations.

A. THE PERSISTENCE OF ORALITY (MOUTH, EYE, HAND) IN LANGUAGE

Such persistence is conspicuous both in terms of the *eye* and of the *hand*: We treat auditory perception as though it were visual, thought as though it were object. We induce someone to lend us his ear by the imperative *"Look . . .,"* and after having explained we ask: "Do you *see* what I mean?" He is supposed to "grasp" what he hears, and to "comprehend" what is spoken as though it were concrete material and within the reach of his hand. Of the word "understand" (lit.: "to stand under" = to apprehend the meaning, to grasp the idea, to comprehend) Webster notes: "The development of sense is not clear." Yet it would be if it described the original position of the upright and sexually curious child of the second anal phase relative to the object of his curiosity: the maternal cloaca.

[13] Anna Freud stresses this original tie between speech and the anal-sadistic phase of development by describing, on the basis of direct observation of children, how a regression from this phase undoes the newly acquired speaking: "When, for instance, infants regress from the anal to the oral level while they are beginning to speak, they lose their speech almost regularly. The same is true for the beginning of walking which may regress to crawling under the influence of instinctual regression. The same is true also for the loss of bowel and bladder control . . ." (26).

The analysis of "affective" disturbance of comprehension furnishes every analyst with material supporting this speculation. Here it might be recalled that the first observation of the substitution of the ear for the eye was Freud's when he recognizes that a man, who tells a "dirty," i.e., cloacal, joke in front of or to a woman, imaginarily disrobes her or himself or both, for the purposes of an active and passive scoptophilic enjoyment (35).

The persistence psychologically of the *mouth* proper in the ear, although not as obvious, is nevertheless observable clinically and has more than once found its poetic description.

For a *clinical observation* cf. p. 96, where the *sudden cessation of hearing* is shown to be, in the last analysis, an *abrupt biting off* of the nipple.

For *poetry,* there is Mephistopheles consoling the freshman, who feels claustrophobic in the bare and narrow halls of the university, by telling him that listening is merely a matter of getting used to the *breast:*

> ¶ MEPHISTOPHELES. Das kommt nur auf Gewohnheit an.
> So nimmt ein Kind der Mutter Brust
> Nicht gleich im Anfang willig an,
> Doch bald ernährt es sich mit Lust.
> So wirds Euch an der Weisheit Brüsten
> Mit jedem Tage mehr gelüsten. . . .

> This depends only on being used to it. Thus a child does not willingly take to the mother's breast right from the beginning, but it will soon feed with pleasure. Thus though, you will crave the breasts of wisdom more and more day by day! (83).[14]

14 The most intricate poetic account of the survival of the mouth in the ear describes the audience listening rapturously to young Henry V: I have relegated it to a footnote because the verse itself and its analysis may appear precious to many a reader.

> ....when he speakes,
> The Ayre, A chartered Libertine, is still,
> And the mute Wonder lurketh in men's eares,
> To steale his sweet and honeyed Sentences [121].

Whether, as the disagreeing etymological experts would have it, a "Libertine" is a freeman, or a licentious person; and whether "chartered" means "hired" or

It is in *training analyses* that the ear as an eye seems to come not infrequently under observation. There are instances where the student is emotionally overwhelmed to the point of a block in his work or is simply unable to listen to his patient's associations, and where this is reducible, through amnesia removal, to traumatic childhood experiences of a scoptophilic nature. Psychologically speaking, the patient does not *tell* him but *"shows"* him and, in so doing, presents him with an unbearable re-enactment of his past.

Needless to add, that in merely therapeutic analyses one finds the complementary exhibitionistic conflict ever so often at the bottom of the patient's difficulties in following the analytic rule.

B. THE SPOKEN WORD AS A PART OF THE BODY, WHOSE LOSS AND WHOSE (AUDITORY) RE-ENTRY IS FEARED

The spoken word under certain conditions is—as are feces in the anal phase—conceived of as part of the speaker (= the speaker's body). Its loss is feared—as is its re-entry—and it must therefore—as must excrement—be inspected. Both inspection and defense against re-entry takes the form of the transformation of the "animate" or spoken into the inanimate or written word.

> In illustrating this one may turn to a myth of our time. The analytic session has caught the public's fancy: it is drawn and caricatured; even a show window on Fifth Avenue at Christmastime was once dressed with analyst, couch and lady patient. But whatever the medium, the analyst is invariably represented as *writing* down his patient's associations. The idea that the an-

---

"licensed," air is likened to someone who, committed to, or permitted much activity, has subsequently either contracted to be, or been allowed to be still.

In the next line it has become a "mute wonder," a something that does not speak but conveys admiration, and that hides in the listener's ears. In the third line it steals, as does the child in his regressive quest for the breast, what is sweet. Sentences thus taken in are "honeyed"; listening to them is sucking food, representative of the food from the breast.

It is the earliest "passive" and sucking mouth that these lines develop, regressively and by means of allusion, out of the later active one, while transferring it onto the ear.

alyst makes notes, tape-records, keeps records, occurs, furthermore, at one time or another, in almost every analysis. (One
patient, too familiar with the facts to indulge in such precon-
ceptions, varied it to the extent of believing that identifiable
material containing mutilative information would be published.)

I believe that the relative incorrigibility of this public prejudice, in spite of much information, and the frequency of its
appearance in patients, are indicative of a fear of the spoken
word. By transforming what is spoken and heard into what is
written and read, it is preserved, inspectable, and incapable of
directly re-entering the ear.

To appreciate the significance of this fully one must remember that one learns reading and writing only after one has
acquired a superego. It is often the voice of the latter (cf.
pp. 35-40) that the auditory re-entry of the patient's own speech
represents at certain times and under certain conditions.

An extremely difficult patient, of whom I have elsewhere (20)
described how he projected the archaic nucleus of his superego
upon me with the result of abundant hypnotic evasions, experienced, for years, the greatest difficulty in telling me of improve-
ments. He had had a good day, things had gone well and he had
enjoyed them; but when it came to verbalizing this he could
hardly do it, and as he put it, it "felt like a lie." He ought to come
in and report how miserable he was and how badly things had
gone. It became quite clear, finally, that this strange impulsion
was but another consequence of the projection mentioned
above. By virtue of this projection I had become the wrathful
archaic parent, who occupied, as it were, the core of his superego superimposed by the excessively punitive internalized father
from childhood. Anything enjoyable was an oedipal crime for
which one part of him, projected upon the analyst, had to
punish the other. The urge to tell me the opposite of the truth
was self-preservative; it meant: do not think I have enjoyed
myself and do not, therefore, punish me for it; look what a
miserable creature I already am, you do not have to punish me
in addition.

He was always very emphatic about the fact that "saying it out loud" was the trouble, in other words, that his problem lay in the act of verbalization.

At last, after many years, the picture changed abruptly at the beginning of an analytic hour. The latter had been preceded by a week of successful days, each of which had left him in the evening with a "cranky feeling," as though everything that had been good had been bad. Starting the hour, he observed that it was still difficult to verbalize his success but that this had no longer anything to do with the analyst; it was not telling me, but telling himself that constituted the problem. In other words, what disturbed him now was the auditory re-entry of his own speech, which in this instance need not have represented the voice of the superego but the voice of the ego (the child) directed at the superego (the father).[15] Needless to add, this showed that he had relinquished the projection.

What amazed me, and what I found so instructive, was that his superego, although no longer projected, had nevertheless—at least in the analytic situation—retained a quality of the historical father: it was reachable not from the inside through thought but from the outside through verbalization, in other words, through the ear.

The idea of writing can then become equivalent to a rendering inanimate of that voice of the superego; in the last analysis to the intent of killing the father.

In this fashion, Hamlet elaborates, I believe, upon the voice of the paternal ghost. It shall "live," he soliloquizes, but in "book" and "volume":

¶ HAM. . . . . . . Remember thee?
Yea, from the Table of my Memory,
I'le wipe away all triviall fond Records,
All sawes of Bookes, all formes, all pressures past,
That youth and observation copies there;
And thy *Commandment all alone shall live*
Within the *Book* and *Volume* of my Braine . . . [120B].

[15] In an article on the "spoken word" in the dream (21) I have dealt with this double role of the spoken word as representative of the ego and superego, respectively.

It is upon this rumination that an abstract containing the uncle's portrait, as the voice had conveyed it, is written down and that the act of "parricide," subsequently to be postponed for the better part of five acts, is—in displacement—committed.

¶ My Tables, meet it is I *set it downe,*
That one may smile, and smile and be a Villaine;
At least I am sure it may be so in Denmarke;
So Unckle there you are: . . . . . . [120B].

It appears to me that the last line, referring to the erstwhile auditory percept of the paternal voice as a visible one by virtue of its transformation into script, addresses the oedipal father-object as killed.

C. THE WORD AN OBJECT TO THE UNCONSCIOUS
    IN THE CASE OF THE NAME

A frequent instance in which the word represents an object, often a narcissistic one, is that of the name. The identification by the unconscious, of a name with its owner, is so well known to the analyst that it requires no clinical illustration. Nor is it necessary to mention Freud's and Abraham's work. To a colleague I owe the astute remark that persons who habitually forget other's names are likely to be dissatisfied with their own.[16]

The equation of name and object is epitomized by the Clown in his chat with Viola:

¶ VIOLA. . . . . . . they that dally nicely with words, may quickely make them wanton.
¶ CLO. I would therefore my sister had had no name Sir.
¶ VIO. Why man?
¶ CLO. Why sir, her names a word, and to dallie with that word, might make my sister wanton [131].

D. THE CONTROL OF SPEECH AND POSTURE (UPRIGHT GAIT)
    BY THE EAR

It is noteworthy that the control of both posture and speech is exercised by the ear. Maintenance of upright gait is as de-

16 Personal communication: Dr. Franz Cohn.

pendent upon imperceptible trial action as is thought upon imperceptible speech; and an impairment of the organ of equilibrium impairs posture, an impairment of hearing impairs speech. It is, therefore, as though the ear had to insure certain accomplishments of the anal-sadistic phase of development (cf. footnote 13, above) throughout life. When the ear fails in this function, the ensuing disturbances present distinctly traits that are further regressive.

Certain disturbances of the organ of *equilibrium,* of which seasickness is paradigmatic, while not affecting the sphincter, combine the collapse of upright gait and of much motor action with some of the symptoms of severe feeding disturbances in the infant. The enforced regression, whose onset as well as recovery can be either gradual or abrupt, causes the strangest feeling of illness coupled with complete physical health. At the height of it the individual finds himself utterly helpless and extremely averse to being either rocked or fed; a baby, as it were, in reverse. However, his retroperistaltic preoccupation and his disgust reaction to food permit the question as to whether certain characteristics of the second anal phase have not been imposed, in the course of the regression, upon those of the first oral phase dominating the clinical picture.

Disturbances of the organ of *hearing,* causing deafness, impair the motor action of speech. Speech, uncontrolled by the ear, i.e., no longer under the supervision of hearing, gains volume, loses inflection, and grows defective in enunciation. These qualities are, again, regressive; they bear a distinct resemblance to those of the speech of the child. In the child, volume is uncontrolled, enunciation only gradually perfected, and his speech retains for a long time deficiencies of inflection, which become particularly apparent when he is made to recite prose or poetry not conceived for his age. The proverbial distrust of the deaf, however, a characterological concomitant of the affliction, is sufficiently paranoid to be looked upon as indicative of a regressive influence upon thought traceable to the first anal phase.

E. THOUGHT AND MUSICAL THOUGHT

There is another auditory perceptum directly stimulating motility (dance), postural rearrangement (the physical transfiguration observable in a concert audience), and affect (feeling, emotion) via the ear. It is music. The appearance of music as a pure "affect language" is deceptive; music is actually a language in which the ratio of idea and affect is, as compared to language, reversed. It is the expression, in music, of ideas as well as of affect that justifies our speaking of "musical thought." Thought and musical thought have in common that they are both "trial-acting," performed on acoustic (or originally acoustic) ideas. But they differ in that the word-ideas of thought are replaced in music by ideas of a different kind, *sui generis,* subject to their own notation, and untranslatable into words.[17] One cannot, therefore, describe an idea in music through language, except for certain properties of its form. With regard to its content, experience must take the place of description.

In illustration I quote one of the best descriptions of a piece of music that I know. It comes from the pen of a master musician who combines profundity in scholarship with genius in execution. Wanda Landowska—who rediscovered the harpsichord, and had it rebuilt for herself after the models of its greatest period, including apparently Bach's own specifications —introduces a recording of Mozart's *Rondo in D Major* (K. 485) with a detailed account. To appreciate her text one must remember that she hears every phrase not only in terms of that "stop" of her keyboard instrument most appropriate to it, but also in terms of those of the most appropriate instruments in an imaginary orchestration: "The form of this *Rondo,* which makes

17 I have more than once heard Mme. Landowska, the harpsichordist, explain, while inflecting the words toward a colon: "Bach he *says*": and then play the phrase.

Conversely, the Bishop of Canterbury praises Henry V as a speaker (cf. pp. 133 f.).

List his *discourse* of Warre; and you shall heare
A fearefull Battaile rendered you in *Musique* [121].

us think of the movement of a sonata, with reprise, development, and coda, its perfection, its balance, give this piece a place by itself. And what surprises it holds for us! In the last movement of the *Quartet in G Minor* (K. 476), a theme in D. Major appears and disappears like a flash. It is playful and tender, Mozart does not forget it and three months later he will take it up again and on it he will build the *Rondo in D Major.* It is of no importance that this theme is not Mozart's but Johann Christian Bach's (the eleventh and youngest son of Johann Sebastian). Plagiarism? Irreverence? No! On the contrary, homage to an admired master. It is the oboe which plays the theme in the first movement in Johann Christian's *Quintet Op. XI.* No. 6, the pastoral and joyful oboe.

"Mozart, after having stated and extended Johann Christian's theme, will follow it, in the *Rondo,* by an adorable motive, light and vivacious, which he will use twenty months later. It is the first violin which plays it in the *Allegro* of the *Kleine Nachtmusik* (35th measure). So we are happy in the midst of themes and motives which are familiar and dear to us; and also, we are able to understand the instrumental character of this piece which evokes the smooth strings, the swift and gentle flute or oboe and the bassoon with its roguish smile. Scales cascade and rush along exuberantly. After the adventures of the development, after many modulations, Mozart reaches the dominant where he leaves the interpreter free to improvise a short cadence, very short, because one must not go beyond the limits of the piece.

"And here comes our theme again, slightly ornamented according to the fashion of the period. A brilliant passage runs from one end of the keyboard to the other and flows into a little *tutti* which, after a lull, suddenly stops on a deceptive cadence. But Mozart, this time, decides irrevocably to come to an end and says farewell in a little *coda* adorably graceful in its innocent simplicity" (97).

This is not a transcription of musical thought from notes into words. It concerns merely the affect collateral to the thought, and the form of the latter; and it will, at that, probably be meaningless to anyone ignorant of the form elements mentioned, and inexperienced in responding to Mozart. For the content of the musical thought one must listen to or, if sufficiently literate, read the music.

The relation between the two kinds of thought—"thought" and "musical thought"—is, in view of the indescribable nature of the latter, much closer than can be set forth. It is not enough to remind oneself of their common origin, of the dependence, in certain languages (such as, e.g., Chinese), of the word's meaning upon pitch alone, and in all poetic language upon pitch, modulation, beat, rhythm and upon the various kinds of musical pauses, or to remember what language can do for music and music for language. To establish particulars of the relation one would have to engage in a comparative study of language and music, thought and musical thought—a collaborative task for the semanticist and the musician.

An example of what language can do to *music* is "program music." Here a thought, expressible through a thought fragment in language, influences the understanding of musical thought even where the latter dispenses with all acoustic imitation. *Soeur Monique,* for instance, the title of Couperin's *Piece de Clavecin* (15), is a concept, representing the thought: "The following is a tone portrait of Sister Monica"; and equipped with this preconception one listens to the three-part rondeau played "doucement sans lenteur," with the result that it creates an image before the mind, drawn and colored with the finesse, the luminosity, the intensity of a Clouet.

As an example of *what music can do to language* one may recall what becomes of a linguistic atrocity such as, e.g., the couplet:

¶ Blut und Reu
Bricht das Sündenband entzwei! [St. Matthew Passion]

under the hands of Bach; or the miraculous transformation by him of the awkward monkish Latin such as

Et in spiritum sanctum, dominem et vivificantem . . . .
qui cum patre et filio simul adoratur et conglorificatur . . .
Et unam sanctam catholican et apostolican ecclesiam [8]

into a language commanding the ear and transporting the lis-

tener with its force, its profundity, and the ineffable beauty of
its inflection.

As far as a *comparative study of thought and musical thought*
is concerned, I am not qualified to supply illustration. I can
merely imagine that such a study might attempt, for one thing,
to analyze language in terms of musical elements, and music in
terms of linguistic structure. When, e.g., Pascal fashions the
timeless portrait of certain individuals in an academic com-
munity,

> *qui intriguent beaucoup, parlent peu,*
> *et ne publient jamais* [107]

one could perhaps investigate how far melody, contrast of pitch,
modulation, etc., are requisite to such perfect expression of
thought. And when Mozart, to mention but the very simplest of
instances, introduces a phrase and its accompaniment conceived
within the confines of one octave of a G-Major chord, with a
chromatic preparation of the accompaniment (104):

one could try grammar and syntax, understanding the introduction as the equivalent of a qualifying clause that "defines" the
"D" for the particular purpose of being an element of the
thought expressed in the phrase:

I have mentioned musical thought in addition to thought proper, and compared the two, mainly as a specific instance supporting the general formulation that what Freud has called the "affect-quantum adherent to an idea" (49) [18] can become *an idea adherent to the affect-quantum.* This is of interest to the student of pathological thought. Here affective processes or their suppression interfere with thinking in such fashion that the thought becomes dependent upon the process or its inhibition. The comprehension of thought is then dependent upon that of the affect mechanism of which, or of certain parts of which, the thought has become what (borrowing the mathematical term) might be called a "function." The relation to the particular "affectivity" (Freud) here concerned, i.e., to the erogeneity of the anal zone, is, of course, variable; in compulsive and in paranoic thought it is close, in manic or phobic thought it is distant if it exists at all.[19] But the thought process as such has, by way of its origin, a relation to erogeneity, which may be lost in the course of normal development but which, in morbid thought, may be resumed.

[18] My quotation is summatory rather than verbatim. Freud speaks of "instinctual energy" adherent to the idea. But he does so, after having explained that the affect-quantum (*Affektbetrag*) "corresponds to the instincts inasmuch as it has detached itself from the idea and finds expression, proportionate to its quantity, in processes which become perceptible as affects."

[19] Cf. Freud's remark on schizophrenic speech, the expression of schizophrenic thought: "In the content of these utterances a relation to bodily organs or bodily innervations becomes often prominent" (50).

5

THE PHALLIC PHASE

I. INTRODUCTION

The study of the phallic phase—that phase characterized by an "infantile" ego organization, by the dominance of the antithesis phallic-castrated, by its applicability to both sexes, and by the operation of urethral-erotic discharge as precursor of ejaculation—has particular difficulties of its own. In most instances it is the female, who offers herself as a comparatively more suitable subject; the man's inferiority is predominantly based on female identification. Yet in all instances one must "locate" the phallus, i.e., determine its relation, sometimes simple, sometimes complicated, to the anatomy and physiology of the person. In the study of regressive conditions, this amounts to distinguishing between a phallic and genital penis in the male—a distinction, comparable after a fashion to that of discriminating between a preoedipal and an oedipal mother. In the case of the female it is not enough to pursue the original substratum of the phallus, the clitoris, into its displacements; one must acknowledge the existence of an imaginary phallus, a psychic formation erected subsequent to the acknowledgment of castration, and trace its manifold anatomical and physiological manifestations. An attempt to do this shall be made in both the main sections of this chapter; one devoted to the persistence of earlier phases in the phallic phase and the other to some primal fantasies concerning the phallic phase.

II. ON THE PERSISTENCE OF EARLIER PHASES
IN THE PHALLIC PHASE

A. ANAL-SADISTIC PHASES

1. *The Second Anal Phase*

a. A Phallic Pleasure-Physiological Copy of the Rectum

It is expedient to describe the persistence of earlier phases in the phallic phase in reverse order.

The suitability of the clitoris for an employment modeled after the fashion of the *second anal phase* becomes evident when one adds to the fact that it is embedded in the vulva and excitable through muscular pressure, the observation that the pleasure organ so employed includes the distal third of the vagina. This part of the vagina is, pleasure-anatomically, part of the vulva-clitoris combination and, pleasure-physiologically, "castrated" in the sense of the mentality of the phallic phase. The sexual use of the "organ," consisting of vulva, clitoris, introitus, and initial third of the vagina, bears much similarity to that of the rectum: it is covert, need not be conscious, dispenses with adhibition of the hand, and by means of a rhythmic application of pressure, yields pleasure lacking a climax, which remains almost invariably unperceived. The complete action requires crossed legs and femoral cooperation; but the execution is often abortive, static rather than rhythmic, and restricted to pelvic muscular action. It is then unobservable except for a motionless, sometimes rigid position, retained throughout a part or a whole of the session, accompanied by various facilitating positions, particularly of the legs. The resemblance to rectal stimulation continues, likewise, in the promotion of continence by means of pressure; sphincter closure—there anal, here urethral—is muscularly assisted; and the female so engaged will experience sooner or later, a strong, rarely painful urinary urge during the analytic session. She remains, however, unaware of its sexual nature and of its stimulation through a transference.[1]

The sexual constitution of these individuals is, in other words, distinguished not only by a regressive revival of the anal-erotic zone proper, but also by that of its phallic copy. Yet it is further complicated by a fusion of the two in the service of a regressive revival of the cloaca to the extent that the perineum, separating them, is practically not owned. It is instructive to observe in detail how the regressive pleasure-physiological practices of these patients consummate, as it were, the existence of such fantastic regressive pleasure-anatomical organs.

An engaging and frank young girl, crisp and immaculate in appearance, begins her analysis with the description of taking a bath. Lying down in the tub she urinates copiously into the bathwater, and then soaps and dries herself without benefit of a shower. She "could urinate all day long" and does so in intervals just long enough to avoid attracting attention. After urination as well as after defecation, which is also extremely frequent, she wipes herself from the anus toward the vulva, and supports, in so doing, the fantasy of a cloaca. The only conscious representation of this fantasy is contained in the fear of having to offer a genital, sullied with excrement, to the male whom she expects to react with disgust. The "masturbatory" exercise of the pleasure-physiological "organ," described further above, is in her case conscious, but again complicated by a muscular consummation of the cloaca in homology with the dermal one in the wiping: she begins by squeezing buttocks and anus and

1 Annie Reich (110), without furnishing much detail, speaks of "masked masturbation," which "consists of activities which are accompanied by sexual excitement, but where the sexual character of the feelings as well as of the activity is not recognized." As an instance she mentions "the masturbation of girls which is done by thigh pressure without the use of the hands and without any awareness of the sexual character of the sensations and of what is going on. This lack of awareness," she remarks, "does not prevent the development of guilt feelings, which then are usually connected with a secondary reason."

Very true. But I think that one applies Freud's description of the vicissitudes of the affect (50) more closely to the observable facts if one says that the sexual feelings, precursor to the sexual affect, is in some instances wholly suppressed (as, e.g., in the patient described on p. 149), while in others (such, e.g., as the one described below) it is "transformed into a qualitatively different" feeling.

works forward until the pressure reaches eventually the vulva. Pleasure is not obtained by this performance which, when assisted mornings in bed by a manual squeezing of the labia, yields merely an extreme urinary urge; nor is the act initiated by anything but an unqualifiable need. The clitoris is only theoretically known to the patient, and it cannot, in practice, be manipulated except through pressure upon the part of the labia in which it is embedded. The necessity to do so arises abruptly and is by so doing abolished; yet neither phase is distinguished by even the faintest sexual feeling. "I do not know why, but I have to do it"; or, "I suddenly felt that I would go crazy unless I did it" is all the obtainable information.

b. On Some Typical Ideas of Inferiority

The peculiarities of the pleasure-anatomical constitution described above explain same of the particular characteristics of the inferiority feeling of their owners. They experience, anatomically, their body or the unclothed parts of it, in identification[2] with these different "organs." The physiology of the latter reappears in their relation to objects which is as coercive, either actively or passively, and as inhibited as is their relation to themselves. It is symptomatic of the persisting erogenic employment of the rectum, that the "inferiority feeling" has here actually become a *conviction* of inferiority, and as such, a delusion: hence its incorrigibility through experience. If the environment flatters these individuals, if they are liked or loved, if a man wooes them, or a husband embraces them, such will not shake their conviction.

It is as difficult to delineate the different ideas of inferiority against each other as it is to dissociate the pleasure-physiology of the different erogenic combinations. The very persistence of anality makes it so. Yet one can, nevertheless, contribute to

[2] I prefer this description to speaking simply of a "displacement." An old joke expresses the matter succinctly. Mr. Engel, a noted comic and wit, had an enemy, Mr. Gumpert, who once said to him: "Engel, if I had your face I would carry it in my pants pocket; and instead, my behind on my collar." Engel answered: "Tried that long ago. Didn't work. Everyone said to me: 'Hello Gumpert.'"

the explanation of some of the typical manifestations of inferiority by tracing some of these typical identifications. In so doing one lends additional weight to the finding of Freud that "the ego is predominantly a body-ego."

The "I am just no good," for example, is based upon an identification of the person with the clitoris, called by Freud "the inferior organ, the real little penis of the woman" (67).

> An epitome of this presents itself in a particular pairing in Latin of the masculine and feminine genders, e.g., *campus*= a field; *campa* = a *small*, or a *bad* field; *hastus* = a *good*, or a *big* lance or pike; *hasta* = an (ordinary) lance or pike (134).

With it goes the complaint "I can't do it, can't finish it," often in reference to the analysis, in particular to the producing of free associations. The idea expressed here is the same as that formulated by Freud for the case of the woman "who has not overcome the wish to be a man [and] dreams so frequently of bridges which are too short to reach the other side" (73C), but it is overdetermined by the continence problem manifested in the use of the phallic "organ" (cf. p. 145) of which the clitoris is a part.

> The female so afflicted will occasionally complain that she cannot finish urination because the very act of wiping herself causes the urge to recur.

"I am ugly, unattractive" is supported by an identification of the individual with the external female genital as a whole; but the companion complaint "I am a mess" shows the excremental interpretation of the genital under the influence of the fantasy of the cloaca. The identification of person and personality with the anatomy and pleasure-physiology of the phallic "organ" seems to account for behavior: the fear of exhibiting oneself socially or professionally, and the painful "not knowing what to say," i.e., what to express, appear to emulate, as it were, the covert physiology of the erogenic combination. The expectation, however, that one will go unnoticed, or not be recognized at the next time of meeting corresponds to the projection of the lack of recognition of the "organ," by the individual, onto others. Such is, of course, only one determinant of these symptoms; but an important one. Not infrequently, ignorance of it accounts for a lack of therapeutic success in the analysis.

> The connection established here is demonstrable in analysis when the changes in sexual and social behavior correspond. The experienced analyst will not, of course, conclude from the obviousness of behavior at its being conscious: a particular female, for instance, who performed the most excessive swaying motions with her crossed legs proved nevertheless completely unaware of her constant employment of the "organ" when it was finally pointed out to her after a year. When the abstinence rule was enforced and no partner was available, further progress became manifest in her masturbation. The latter, which had essentially been of the pressing type and confined to vulva and clitoris, became more and more vaginal, imitating the male frictions, while the patient changed her position from an abdominal to a dorsal one with spread instead of closed legs. It was most instructive to observe how at the pace at which the vagina, replacing the phallic "organ," contracted and yielded orgastic pleasure, its owner discovered her "grasp" on subjects of thought, and began to "take hold" of people in the exercise of her duties.
>
> In another patient vaginal masturbation with objects had to be performed in front of the mirror, before her excessive fear of not being recognized by people she had met before, disappeared.

Sometimes it seems as though the physical pressure requisite to the exercise of the phallic "organ" transformed itself, psychologically, into depression; and the urinary discharge provoked by it, physiologically, into tears.[3]

Clinically the occurrence of sadness and of crying in this type is, in most instances, characterized by its sudden onset and by the fact that it is often ununderstandable to the patient as well as the analyst, who cannot relate it to the material. The patient is apt to say: "Here I go crying again," or "I don't know why

---

[3] This would, in part at least, be equivalent to an *"aktual*-neurotic" contribution to the feeling of depression.

that should make me cry"; and the analyst wonders whether or not the incongruity between ideation and affect is brought about by a displacement of the former against the latter, in the context of an analytic hour, such as Freud has found in the manifest content of the dream.

Needless to add that some of the same manifestations of inferiority, and occasionally the same urinary urge, are observable in the male patient who, besides having regressed, has identified with the female. Crying, however, here is rare and usually abortive; and the feeling of physical inferiority does not, ordinarily, find the "cosmetic" expression that it does in the woman.

2. *Both Anal Phases*

A persistence of *both* anal-sadistic phases in the phallic phase is recorded by Freud in his supplementary interpretation of the fantasy of *"A Child is Being Beaten"* (56) presented six years after the original publication: "The child," Freud writes, "who is being beaten (or caressed) may ultimately be nothing more nor less than the clitoris itself, so that at its very lowest level the statement will contain a confession of masturbation, which has remained attached to the content of the formula from its beginning in the phallic phase up to the present time" (65). The alternative "beaten-fondled" corresponds to the first and second anal phase, respectively, for it reflects the antithesis between destroying and sparing the object (Abraham); and the whole touches upon a clinical problem. I have seen a number of patients of both sexes persist in refusing to remember being beaten (or being beaten more than once) by a cruel (usually psychotic) parent, although the material permitted absolutely no doubt. Is the amnesia so persistent here because its relinquishment would amount—as does the fantasy—to the confession of (phallic) masturbation?

3. *First Anal Phase*

Evidence for a persistence of the incontinent *first anal phase* in the phallic organization is rare. It appears occasionally in the form of abrupt, explosive orgasms, devoid of fantasy and, as far as the individual is concerned, unprepared for and unexpected.

A male insomniac—who preceded nocturnal sedation with a bowel movement set off by the insertion of a piece of soap in the rectum—experienced, after he had relinquished both habits, a maximal erection before going to sleep. Upon manual pressure of the area surrounding the penis he had a violent ejaculation. His description in the analytic hour of how the semen had shot out and backward over his shoulder left no doubt in either tone or gesture that the target of an excremental outburst of rage had, in an unconscious fantasy, been the analyst.

A female patient, who as a child used to tell her father when he came home at night how bad she had been in order to be taken into a closet where, in trying to get out, she hit, kicked and bit him until both were spent, one day busied herself with housework. During many hours of unremitting chores she played off and on with one nipple, had it fall back, then pressed it out again in endless repetition. When she finally dropped exhausted into a chair the sexually very inhibited girl was suddenly, without any foreboding, seized and shaken by the most violent orgasm of her life.

A male patient with a history of overt, if abortive, anal practices with male partners, experienced while walking to an analytic hour strong sexual excitation, a full erection and a feeling of imminence of ejaculation. To avoid the latter he had to diminish the friction of his clothes by slowing down his pace.

B. ORAL PHASES

1. *Second Oral Phase*

In studying the persistence of orality, in particular of the *second oral phase*, in phallic sexuality, one faces a situation essentially different from all previous investigation of persistence. Heretofore, when an earlier libido was discharged, when its discharge was inhibited by a subsequently dominant erogenic zone, or when organs auxiliary to either took over their functions, it was their erogenic *resemblances* that enabled them to perform the discharge. Consequently, one could not always discriminate between erogeneity and libido, and so separate the transfer of the former from the elaboration upon the latter. Even the phallic pleasure organ of the female described above resembles the anal-erotic zone retentively, and the male penis excretorily, in a measure sufficient to copy some of its pleasure-physiological habits.

In the case of the phallic elaboration upon cannibalistic desire such resemblance is *lacking*: the phallus engages in the urethral-erotic discharge of oral-sadistic libido, but it does not, in so doing, either imitate or resemble the mouth.

It is here that erogeneity becomes clinically distinguishable from libido.

a. On the Urethral-Erotic Discharge of Cannibalistic Libido

(i) *Ambition*. This distinction between erogeneity and libido both Abraham and Freud have omitted in their analysis of the *character trait* of ambition. It will be remembered that Freud's derivation of the latter from urethral erotism (37) did not, to Abraham, appear "to have penetrated to the deepest sources." He felt ambition rather to be "a character-trait of oral origin . . . later reinforced from other sources, among which the urethral one should be particularly mentioned" (6).

Actually, if Freud has supplied the nature of the erogeneity, Abraham supplied that of the libido. There is no doubt: *ambition derives from urethral-erotic elaboration upon libido of the second oral stage.*

Once, when a patient entered the office, I excused myself while finishing clipping some manuscript pages together, and was seated only a moment after she had lain down on the couch. Her response was that of extreme impatience. (Cf. pp. 107-110.) Bursting out against my tardiness, she reported having felt so tense during the short period of waiting that she had had to hold onto herself and, in order to do so, had dug the nails of her right hand into the palm.

The patient, an intelligent and ambitious career woman, had lately received a substantial promotion—an exterior circumstance which had assisted us, in subjecting her strong biting impulses to an elaborate working through. The latter, at that time in progress, made it obvious that the hand, in the gesture described by her, had been simulating the mouth, and that the impulse discharged in this fashion was that of biting. Her answer, however, to my question as to the meaning of the gesture was, surprisingly, that she had no idea of what I "had in mind," and could only report what she felt: an almost overwhelming urge for urination. (The urge was described as located in the clitoris, and as having a sexual quality.) Only after her own words, "digging my nails into my flesh" had been repeated to her, was she able to recognize the displacement of the biting impulse onto the hand. Following this, she likened her acute general tenseness to that observed a few days before, in her four-year-old nephew who, while kissing her in a peculiar state of excitement, suddenly bit her cheek.

(ii) *The Urge to Talk*. Proceeding from a character trait to a *symptom*, Abraham's description of the coexistence, in some individuals of an *excessive* urge to talk and to urinate, must be amended in one particular point. The author mentions the urethral-erotic companion-discharge in those who give by way of the mouth, and omits it in those who destroy in the same way. In other words, where "in place of biting and devouring the object a milder form of aggression has appeared, though the mouth is still utilized as the organ of it" (6), we read neither of pollakisuria, nor of acute urges for urination. Yet the disorder exists there as well, and testifies to the phallic-urethral-erotic elaboration, or assistance in elaboration, upon the libido of the second oral stage.

A teacher, who forced upon his pupils lessons lasting two and three hours instead of one, afterwards had to urinate copiously in a state of nervous exhaustion. In analysis, he talked incessantly, and in so strident a tone that the soundproofing of the office could not contain it. The dilution of thought corresponded to the dilution of urine; he took thirty minutes of largely empty talk for what could have been said in three. When one made a remark, he talked on; when one repeated what one had said, finally matching his loudness, he responded with an explosive "Pardon me?" It is evident, at this very point, that such talkers delete the listener. The analyst, unable to "get a word in edgewise," as far as the patient is concerned, does not exist.[4]

After sufficient progress, we could examine his teaching. What we could observe was complicated; but it showed an extreme impatience, and left no doubt that the pupil was being attacked by the teacher who, at the same time, identified with him, and was himself afraid of attack. After the excessive talking, inside and outside the hour, had subsided the patient was terrified at the demand for free association, which appeared to him to represent urethral incontinence. He did not know what he feared but he had to report both an increasingly frequent urination outside the analysis, and strong urinary urges during the sessions. In other words: after the analyst was no longer annihilated with the mouth, the original discharge through mouth *and* urethra of oral-sadistic libido had become *altogether* urethral-erotic.

(iii) *The "Preservation of Fire."* Proceeding further from a symptom to a *myth,* one may point to another illustration of *urethral-erotic discharge of oral-sadistic libido.*

Freud has shown that the collective renunciation of urethral-erotic instinctual discharge made it possible for man to "preserve" fire. The method enabling Freud to arrive at this conclusion was the translation of symbols, and the interpretation of mythological elaboration. The same method applied to the same material, however, shows unmistakably that the libido involved in the discharge is oral-sadistic. One need merely study *The Acquisition of Power over Fire* (72): the phallus is picturized by a stalk of fennel, a *culinary herb.* The symbols for it are the flame, that *devours* and is compared to a *tongue;* the snake, an animal feared for its deadly *bite;* and the vulture, a bird of prey *eating* Prometheus' liver. The hero's crime is the favoring of man to the disadvantage of the god on the occasion of *sacrifice,* an originally cannibalistic performance; and foremost among

---

4 The German idiom for "talking someone deaf and dumb" is *"Jemanden totreden"*= talking someone to death.

the benefits gained from the taming of fire is the invention of *cooking*, the inception of cuisine.

(iv) *Further Clinical Material.* To illustrate the urethral-erotic discharge of cannibalistic libido—the cannibalistic provocation of urination—with analytic material is not easy because the two, the cannibalistic and the urinary urge, are much more apt to appear separately than in combination.

(1) The following are excerpts from four analytic hours of one patient, distributed over about nine weeks:

January 24. The patient had found herself unable to use a certain bathroom because her father, present in the adjoining room, would hear her. The analyst refers (in nontechnical language) to the fact that, conversely, for a year or more, primal-scene material had been confined to memories of listening to noises in the parents' bathroom at night, to speculations about them, and, subsequently, to direct observations of the mother's toilet functions. At this point, the patient experiences an urge to rub her clitoris and remembers the same experience several weeks ago at home. Muscular squeezing, she explains spontaneously, cancels the urge. Had she followed it out, she further explains, it would have become an urge to urinate. The next aggregate of associations concerns the mother's greed; she eats from everyone's plate, "drools," loves to "suck on" large quantities of "red steak"; and the patient's inability, as a child, to eat any meat whatsoever.

February 17. The hour begins with the complaint that the patient who is subject to sudden urinary urges, had tried to use the toilet prophylactically after the preceding session because she was going out, and had failed. There was but little urine, while in the course of the evening, she was plagued with strong urges and abundant urination. In the ensuing general discussion of her troubles in this respect she mentions that if she has no such urge, and practices no such prophylaxis after the session, she will suddenly be disturbed by it when the bus comes; and if she then uses the toilet the bladder may actually be found full. I interpret being in the bus as a situation where, from the child's standpoint, there is no possibility of going to the toilet;

and state that the whole confused picture (the details of which need not here be reported) impresses me as a repetition, or rather, a perpetuation, of the lack of understanding for the needs of the child by a confused mother. I express the hope that she will get to specific instances of such kind.

This produces the following memory: at the age of seven or eight she eats in a restaurant with her mother. She has a strong urge to urinate, and starts squeezing and wiggling, as children will; but the mother instead of taking her to the toilet, shouts at her to sit still. She suppresses the urge but becomes at once incapable of eating her meat. For many years after this she still could not eat meat. When she attempted it, she found herself absolutely unable to swallow.

At this point I must have made some noncommittal remark, which I could not remember when I recorded the session the next day. It may merely have been an admonition to go on saying what came to mind; I am certain that it contained no information, because, aware of my interest in the subject, I made it a point not to influence the material. Her immediate and spontaneous response: "Yes, but this all belongs together. The urge to urinate and the not eating meat feels somehow the same. . . ."

March 7. In the course of the hour the patient refers to an observation of parental intercourse at the age of seven, which had previously in analysis been recalled from repression, with the words: ". . . when my father swallowed my mother." From there on she alternates between commenting upon this experience and that of a sexual intercourse during which she had been anesthetic. She recalls, as she had done before, that "it was better" the second time when she lay on top of the man because, able to remove herself at will, she did not feel victimized and had stopped, indeed, prematurely. Asked what she meant by "better" since it was known that she had remained anesthetic, she answers that she had had "more feeling in the mouth," kissed the man harder and had, in fact, bitten his lip. Upon saying this she experienced suddenly an acute urinary urge. It is only now that I mention to her that the two, the urge to bite, and to urinate, belong together; and remind her that she had said so herself in reference to the incident in the restaurant with her mother.

April 1. The hour begins with one of the typical disappoint-ments of the patient in her mother: she had taken the mother and an acquaintance of the mother for luncheon to a certain place, which she knew, and recommended their hamburger as particularly good. Whereupon the mother ordered a grilled cheese sandwich. Patient and acquaintance had hamburger, mother and acquaintance talked incessantly, patient had noth-ing to say since the conversation was topical and people and circumstances unknown to her. Twice in short succession, before the meal and once afterwards, copious urination.

In discussing the incident and the fact that the childhood inhibition of swallowing meat, which had disappeared long ago, had reappeared in analysis although confined to the mother's presence:
Patient: But I could get my food down!
Analyst: Yes, I knew that.
Patient: Why?
Analyst: Because you did not have to defend yourself against the eating; all of the urge had been taken care of by urina-tion, etc.

The rest of the hour is filled with the subject of the mother, cooking and eating. On this occasion, the unusually accurate and sharp-minded patient gives a completely fantastic descrip-tion of the masticability of vegetables vs. meat. Vegetables, all of which she treats alike, disregarding their different consisten-cies, "become mush with one bite"; whereas meat will not yield even to endless chewing. In the course of her associations it becomes clear that what she describes as meat is actually gristle which her mother has the habit of chewing and finally spitting out (patient, agitatedly: "And I really mean spits, without put-ting it on the fork or anything. . . .") with her teeth marks on it.

I doubt that these excerpts require much comment. In the first the experience of a phallic sexual urge in response to primal scene fantasies and the envisaging of its urethral-erotic consum-mation precipitates cannibalistic material. In the second the discussion of urinary symptomatology produces a memory from the latency period where the enforced suppression of the need to urinate during a meal creates a lasting inhibition of eating meat. The memory, in its turn, brings about the spontaneous realization that the urethral-erotic desire and the defense against cannibalistic impulses, mobilized by a coercive mother, belong together. In the third the memory of the oral-sadistic interpretation of a primal-scene observation fuses with that of a recent oral-sadistic behavior in intercourse and precipitates an acute desire for urination. In the fourth, urethral-erotic performance around a meal with the mother restores the previously sexualized and therefore inhibited eating of meat; and the analysis shows that vegetables and meat, respectively, have become, via the mother's mouth and its activities, representatives of a regressively oral-erotic and oral-sadistic mother object.

(2) I append, finally, a few words on a case of infantile enuresis. Anny Katan (94) presents an expertly and successfully performed analysis of a three-and-a-half-year-old enuretic girl, whose disturbance was of recent origin, and whose treatment required therefore only six weeks.

Toward the end, the child became dry, first for three and subsequently for eight nights until three weeks later she had once more a final relapse after which she was cured. It is most instructive to study the analytic material of this terminal phase: it is all oral-sadistic. Some of it is veiled, some startlingly direct; some actively, and some passively cannibalistic. "Anxieties and dreams appeared," in the period before the eight continent nights; "they disappeared when her oral-aggressive wishes were interpreted," writes the author, without being aware of the urethral-erotic discharge of cannibalistic libido. The closing clinical observation quotes the child as saying "Sometimes I think that I eat you all up and swallow you, but you have a knife and cut my tummy and you jump out again"; and has the author reporting: "Now Grete remained dry . . ."

b. Consequences of the Discharge for the Ego Organization

In order to appreciate the clinical significance of urethral-erotic discharge of cannibalistic libido one must consider the prevailing ego organization. Freud, although seemingly unaware of the nature of the libido involved and the consequence of its discharge for the ego, was nevertheless the first to remark

upon the archaic character of the reaction, accompanying urethral incontinence in the phallic child: the reaction of shame. "It
is very remarkable," he writes, "that the reaction of shame
should be so intimately connected with involuntary emptying
of the bladder (whether in the daytime or at night) and not
equally so, as one would have expected, with incontinence of the
bowels. Experience leaves no room for doubt upon the point.
The regular relation that is found to exist between incontinence
of the bladder and fire also provides food for reflection. It is
possible that these reactions and relations represent precipitates
from the history of human civilization derived from a lower
stratum than anything that is preserved for us in the traces sur-
viving in myths or folklore" (55C).

Having learned from Freud's later work (62) that the ego
organization dependent upon urethral-erotic instinctual discharge and reacting with shame to it, is "phallic," and from my
own clinical observation (cf. pp. 152 ff.) that the libido so
discharged is cannibalistic, I may extend this remark by the
following considerations: urethral sphincter control is indicant
of the establishment of a phallic ("infantile") ego organization;
sphincter failure is symptomatic of its dissolution. It is thus that
one finds urethral incontinence so frequently equated with
castration, and castration with death. One important characteristic of the infantile ego organization in the phallic phase is its
ecology: the child's existence, originally dependent upon the
mother, becomes gradually dependent upon the group. The
dissolution of ego, consequent to the breakthrough of cannibalistic libido enforcing urethral discharge, therefore involves him
in an archaic reaction that is incompatible with his position in
the contemporary social context. In the case of incontinence he
cannot, in other words, maintain himself either individually or
ecologically, but

> Must instead yeeld to such inevitable *shame*
> As to offende, himselfe being offended [125A].

i.e., temporarily suffer a relative dissolution of his psychic organization simultaneous with a sudden, if transient, suspension of his membership in the group.

This makes one wonder whether one should not look upon the physiological manifestation of shame, namely blushing, as a regressive phenomenon, and consider it symptomatic of an overcathexis of the integument, indicative of a rudimentary self-introjection, as it were, in lieu of a "return to the womb." The idiomatic description of the feeling of the adult in a situation evoking shame: "I could have sunk into the earth" seems to lend symbolic support to this speculation.[5] It would, in view of the development of the ego from dependence upon the mother to that on the group, be understandable if the reaction to the threat of a disintegration of ego, both individually and ecologically, were a sudden impulse to return regressively to the mother, the womb.

I have never had the occasion to study a case of erythrophobia; but I have analyzed several individuals of both sexes with pronounced *social fear*. These, I have found, are apt to live in a state of "pseudo continence," using striped musculature as an auxiliary to the smooth sphincter. A good deal of what is generally called their "tenseness" is actually an extension of this permanent muscular spasm, further and further removed from the sphincter yet intended to insure its control. The situation, although it concerns the body (and consequently the body-ego), in one point is homologous to that of the phobic, in whom it concerns the environment: suppression of the anxiety-affect requires an ever-increasing expansion of the suppressive measures at the cost of motor restriction; in the individuals under consideration, affect motility, and locomotility in the phobic. The homology is significant because the attitude of these individuals toward sphincter failure is phobic: They mistrust their sphincter urethrae and are afraid that, if they relax enough to

---

[5] Arthur Schnitzler, in one of the humorous dialogues of his *Reigen*, hints at the orality involved in this reaction when he has the young married woman at her first tryst expect to be too ashamed to meet her lover the following day at a party: ". . . *The young woman* (from the bedroom): O, I shall not go. What do you think?—I would actually . . . (she enters the drawing-room fully dressed, eats a chocolate cookie) . . . sink into the ground. . . ."

associate freely, urine will escape. An enormous and, to the analyst, otherwise enigmatic resistance to free association in some individuals has one of its sources in this phobic expectation.

> Both patients, mentioned in this section (cf. pp. 155 f., 152 f.) are paradigmatic for this symptomatic fear. Having relinquished the fantasy of the cloaca, and the resultant abuse of the anal sphincter, and having become aware of their tenseness and its interference with free association, declared themselves convinced that if they relaxed they would immediately urinate against their will.
>
> In the male patient, mentioned on pp. 153 f., this fear became never really conscious; but the analysis, after having cured him of his pronounced social fear, had to be discontinued because he could not enter sufficiently into free association.

One may furthermore ask oneself whether the enuretic discharge of cannibalistic strivings in childhood, an objective reality, does not furnish an ontogenetic root (cf. p. 80) for the subjective reality of the cannibalistic act? In other words, while the child has not discharged his cannibalistic impulse directly by eating flesh from the breast in the oral-sadistic phase, he has however later been enuretic.

In concluding I must resume and complete the fractioned discussion of a symptom complex remarked upon several times before (cf. pp. 61-64, 76-77): *ejaculatio praecox*. It is now possible to name the chief determinant of this disturbance. The logic, requisite to its deduction, is easy to come by. Abraham has discovered that the erogeneity is urethral-erotic; I have observed that urethral-erotic discharge is one of cannibalistic instinctual strivings; ergo: the individual in the act of premature ejaculation *discharges cannibalistic libido*.

The inductive nature of natural science demands, however, that it be shown that this is really so, although a clinical illustration is not easy to obtain. For one thing, the man afflicted with the disturbance is passive and one rarely gets far enough with the analytic work. For another, he has transferred most of his conflict upon the anal-erotic zone; which not only makes him a severe compulsive, beset with doubt, dominated by inhibition and unconscious of his fantasies, but also apt to harbor (and conceal) full-fledged delusions inside and outside of the transference situation.

I have nevertheless one example. It stems from the analysis of a man who had originally been forced to go through a strange ritual. He was compelled to date some woman over the phone. Her acceptance induced a bowel movement and an unwillingness to see her which he nevertheless had to do. Ejaculating ante portas, often after a foreplay of an hour's duration or more, he felt extremely disgusted and could not get rid fast enough of his partner whom he berated silently as a "piece of shit." It was, of course, easy to see (cf. Abraham) that the curse expressed the belated and unconscious recognition of the partner's identity with the original bowel movement through which he had had to expel her in the first place. Ecologically the performance was self-destructive. It left him a beaten man, "cringing" before the people with whom he had to deal in the exercise of his profession, and with the feeling in any gathering that "everyone was against him," very much in the manner of the paranoiac yet with only occasional and abortive systematization. In addition he suffered from almost constant gastrointestinal trouble without any organic basis, and from an agonizing expectation of losses brought about either through oversight, or through errors in judgment, and invariably concerning money. As to the cause for his conversional symptomatology, he insisted delusorily on having eaten something that did not agree with him; although he ate only in restaurants of a high order.

The analysis convinced us both that he perpetually re-enacted a phallic-oedipal cycle of possessing the mother with the effect of a urethral-erotic discharge (he himself came to call his performance "pissing down his leg") and then of being beaten for it by the father. Yet it convinced me above and beyond that of the oral-sadistic nature of his conflict. I felt that there could be no cure for him unless this conflict became conscious.

One hour, eventually, gave me hope but only in the end to disappoint me: the patient had experienced the ordinarily mild disgust reaction that anyone might feel in a restaurant upon seeing one's meal served all over again to someone else, but in gross exaggeration and accompanied by an illusion. He not only felt revulsion at the food, but the people handling it (waiters, cooks) "looked different" to him upon satiety. This, however, led nowhere.

It took another of many years of arduous analytic work under conditions of relative abstinence until the analysis of a short dream in which he saw his mother "ripped to pieces" made him suddenly conscious of the fact *that he was under the unbearable impulsion to eat women and could rid himself of it only through premature ejaculation*. After the act, women "looked different," i.e., "like something eaten and thrown up." On the day before, a medium-done steak did not agree with him, and he realized in thinking it over that *all meat to him becomes human flesh*. (The realization produced nausea and a headache resembling migraine.) The historic truth in his delusions of having eaten something that did not agree with him, became thus apparent.

On the day after this hour he had to walk out of two (!) restaurants, unable to order dinner; and finally prepared himself a vegetarian supper at home. In so doing he duplicated the frequent experience of another patient from whom the material reported on pp. 155-158 was taken; for she too could at times not eat any food except such as she prepared herself. In one subsequent hour the man, who had often described the aftermath of his performance as "going down the drain," said: "I want to eat the woman and I end by being eaten." In still another session he divided attractive and unattractive women into such as he could eat or would be eaten by.

The deduction is after all verifiable, as it should be, by clinical observation. Ejaculatio praecox, where the erogeneity of the phallus is transferred regressively upon the genital with the result of a quasi-urethral-erotic discharge, elaborates actually upon cannibalistic libido.

c. Résumé: The Analysis of Shylock's Speech

Much of what has been abstracted from clinical observation on the preceding pages can, in this section, be summarized by the analysis of a literary document: Shylock's speech in the *Merchant*. It is a great argument in which the atavistic cannibal (cf. pp. 80 ff.) searches his soul to account to the judge for his inhuman impulsion. As the reader of the preceding section might have been led to expect, he compares his predicament at first to that of the phobic and, eventually, to that of the enuretic: he must cut flesh from the breast as the incontinent must pass urine. The speech, extremely condensed, is profound, and its detailed study rewarding. To undo the condensation one is in this instance obliged to comment upon each new image, and to examine its symbolic content. The method used here resembles that employed in Chapter I, in the study of Little Hans's speech with his father.

(i) *The Speech:*

¶ JEW. . . . . You'l aske me why I rather choose to have a
weight of carrion flesh, then to receive
Three thousand Ducats? Ile not answer that:
But say it is my humor; Is it answered?
What if my house be troubled with a Rat,
And I be pleas'd to give ten thousand Ducates
To have it bain'd? What, are you answere'd yet?
Some men there are love not a gaping Pigge:
Some there are are mad, if they behold a Cat:
And others, when the bag-pipe sings i'the nose,
Cannot containe their Urine; for affection,
Masters of passion, swayes it to the moode
Of what it likes or loaths. Now for your answer:
As there is no firme reason to be rendred
Why he cannot abide a gaping Pigge?
Why he a harmlesse necessarie Cat?
Why he a woolen bag-pipe: but of force
Must yeeld to such inevitable shame,
As to offende himselfe being offended:
So can I give not reason, nor I will not,
More than a lodg'd hate, and a certaine loathing
I beare Anthonio, that I follow thus
A loosing suite against him? Are you answered? [125A].

(ii) *The Analysis of the Speech:*

"You'l aske me, etc.": The speech begins by imputing a question to the judge and pretending to refuse the answer, although Shylock is, on the one hand, nowhere questioned, and his speech, on the other, is but one ever more exhaustive reply. One is reminded of the female patient's cannibalistic question-and-(refusal of) answer game referred to on pp. 93 ff.

"But say it is my humor": His humor? That is an affect or a derivative of an affect, called a mood; and, in its turn, derivative of a pleasure-physiological process. Thus the search becomes one for erogeneity and libido. It must pursue the cathectic changes—represented in part directly, in part indirectly—observable through their representations. The cannibalistic struggle is at first anal-sadistic, then oral, then "infantile genital," i.e., castrative, and finally phallic. It ends climactically in what Freud has described, for the case of extinguishing fire through urine, as "the pleasurable wrestling (of the phallus) with another phallus." The outcome of it is in the present instance urethral-erotic incontinence in the loser.

"What if my house be troubled with a Rat, etc.": Cf. Freud's analysis (39) of the "rat punishment"= a rectal attack by a rodent. Here oral-sadistic libido, with a passive instinctual aim, is discharged through the erogeneity of the rectum in terms of the first anal phase, symbolized by the rat eating the insides. It is a perfect example of anal-erotic elaboration upon cannibalistic libido, described and illustrated above (pp. 111 f.). The individual so attacked is passive, a "woman" in regressively anal-erotic terms; hence the female symbol of the "house." The object eaten by the rat is, in the language of the anal-sadistic phase, feces. Its symbolization is money. Much money, expressive of the child's narcissistic appreciation of its excretory product, and money, qualified symbolically by a "3," so as to render its loss interpretable as a regressive form of castration.

If this symbolization is understood and compared to the subsequent symbolizations it appears, in addition, as one example of the attempt (described on pp. 124 f.) to master the impact of archaic oral-sadistic libido by employing the anal-erotic zone, to which it is extrinsic, and to rely, in so doing, upon the powerful anal sphincter.

"Some men there are love not a gaping Pigge": It is in this and the following line that Shylock compares himself to the phobic. But the phobic attitude changes its object with the change in erogenic cathexis. The cathectic changes are necessitated by the attempt, in the end unsuccessful, to control an instinctual impact that remains oral-sadistic throughout.

The pig still dirty, but delicious as a food, itself is gaping, i.e., opening its mouth, desiring food (= the first meaning of "gaping" listed by Webster). Through the choice of this animal, which is taboo to the Jews, the individual phobic attitude is made to imply a collective one, setting not only Shylock but the Jews of whom he is one apart from the Venetians.[6] Thus the problem of ecology (cf. p. 159) is at first allusively introduced.

"Some there are are mad, if they behold a Cat": The frequent symbolization of the female genital through the cat (*le chat*) is known to everyone; but not all may have given thought to the fact that the hair, representative of the denial of castration, is as prominent in it ("pussy") as is the eating of a synonymous symbol: the mouse. The cat is a qualified symbol; it denotes the genital of the female, and connotes devouring as well as a reparative displacement, so frequent of the phallus, upon her hair.

For a description of the "fright of castration [*Kastrationsschreck*] as tied to a sight," a beholding, see Freud's *Medusa's Head* (59); for incontinence as a fantastic consequence of castration cf. p. 171.

"And others, when the bag-pipe sings i'the nose,
Cannot containe their Urine, etc.": Here the phallus, the bagpipe, equipped as it were with a lung, invades another phallus,

---

6 ¶BASS. If it please you to dine with us.
¶JEW. Yes, to smell porke, to eate of the habitation
which your Prophet the Nazarite conjured the divell into:
I will buy with you, sell with you, talke with you,
walke with you, and so following: but I will not eate
with you, drinke with you, nor praye with you [I:iii].

the nose, similarly equipped, and produces incontinence. The irresistible stimulus is acoustic, the receiving sensory sphere is olfactory, and the response is urethral-erotic—transformations traceable but not comprehensible, perhaps because they "reach" (as does the companion reaction, shame) "deeper than anything preserved through its traces in myth and folk-lore." (Cf. p. 159.)

Clinically one can only remind oneself, in the first place, that the upper respiratory tract is an extension of the oral-erotic zone;[7] a fact that enables the fetishist, e.g., to assure himself of the phallus through its olfactory incorporation; and in the second place, that organs, in fantasy and under certain conditions, are with respect to their pleasure-physiological functions interchangeable; so that, e.g., speech, as had been shown further above (cf. p. 96) is subjectively received by the mouth instead of the ear. Finally, everyone has observed individuals who react to certain sounds (of a knife scraping, chalk on the blackboard, etc.) as though they were under the threat of castration.

The irresistibility of the bagpipe in provoking incontinence is obviously that of the flame (cf. *The Acquisition of Power over Fire*); its attenuating qualification as "woolen," allusive to hair, i.e., as "phallic" and therefore representative of continence (cf. p. 171), comes too late; it appears in the summary only, not in the exposition.

"Must yeeld to such inevitable shame,
As to offende himselfe being offended": See the comment on the phallic ecology (pp. 159 f.) where the two lines are quoted.

Of the speech in general one can say, for one thing, what Tausk was the first to say about a certain kind of dream: that it "reacts to the repudiated wish for discharge with a successive alteration of symbols" (139). But the symbols are all equipped with a mouth, and all allude to eating except the last pair, nose and bagpipe, which, although still oral and phallic, have neither mouth nor sphincter, and are employed in explaining, con-

---

[7] W. Hoffer, in an instructive paper based entirely on direct observation of infants, speaks of the "mouth respiratory tract" as one of the "three oral-organ systems" (87).

versely, cannibalistic incontinence with the loss of urinary control.

For another thing, one should not overlook the reduplicate character of the speech. It is true that the Elizabethans studied Cicero eagerly and that rhetoric was *en vogue;* it has even been surmised (93) that Shakespeare was acquainted with the newest books on the subject. One could therefore dismiss the repetition by Shylock of his argument as the orator's summing up. But so doing is denying the unconscious. I believe that, while conforming to forensic custom, the reduplication is at the same time derivative of the original bisyllabic reduplication of the child, discussed on pp. 104-107, and that the theory developed there is applicable to it. I believe so because Shylock is engrossed in the fantasy of an ego overwhelmed by archaic impulse and destroyed by incontinence—an exigency compelling him, after the fashion of the traumatic dream (cf. p. 105), to attempt restitution through repetition.

To know that *urethral-erotism* discharges *cannibalistic* libido is clinically important because it is rare that cannibalistic and urinary symptomatology coincide. One is—as has been said above—much more apt to encounter them separately; and for a long time only one without the other. Ignorance of their connection has deprived me for many years of the understanding of essential material.

2. *First Oral Phase*

Evidence for a persistence of the *first oral phase* in the phallic phase is ambiguous, and its evaluation uncertain.

I do not, therefore, feel entitled to state that the characteristics of the first oral phase persist in the phallic. (It is possible that the child analyst may eventually settle the question as to whether or not they do, through direct observation of the phallic child). I shall therefore conclude this chapter with a description of some primal fantasies of a phallic nature; and observations on a typical delusion in the transference concerning the castration complex.

III. SOME PRIMAL FANTASIES CONCERNING THE PHALLIC PHASE

There are a few fantasies concerning the phallic organization, not known generally, or not known at all; and if known, not sufficiently understood. Some of them appear mutually exclusive but that does not, of course, prevent them from existing in the same person. It is these fantasies that shall hereinafter be described, illustrated and discussed.

A. THE FANTASY OF PREGNANCY THROUGH A FILLING OF THE "MOTHER'S BELLY" WITH URINE, AND OF ERECTION THROUGH A FILLING OF THE PENIS WITH URINE

These two fantasies have probably been observed by many; their explanation appears to be that the child, in the course of his "sexual research," deduces with incontestable logic that what comes out was once within.

> This explanation was sufficient to convince a father that a newly acquired phobia of his three-year-old boy was meaningful, and to induce him to remedial action. The boy had refused suddenly to go bathing in the sea with the father, and it was obvious that this had to do with his having observed the pregnant mother in the act of urination. When he was enlightened about the nature of pregnancy his phobia disappeared; not, however, before at first being displaced upon a puddle (!) left by the receding tide on the beach. Stepping fearfully, although hand-in-hand with his father, around this puddle, he was able again to walk with him into the sea.

Actually, the little "primitive," who, as Freud (72) said, has "to grasp the external world with the help of his own bodily sensations and states," forms this fantasy in the phallic phase because, as Freud has discovered, phallic instinctual discharge is urethral-erotic. The second fantasy in particular satisfies a retentive tendency, stemming from the second anal phase. (Cf. pp. 115 f.) In so doing it counteracts cannibalistic impatience (cf. pp. 107-110) and presages, as it were, the adult's erective insurance against incontinence during sleep.

A four-and-a-half-year-old boy of Berta Bornstein's observation (9) retained his urine and subsequently developed an elevator [!] phobia. He "confessed with *shame* [!] that he refused to use strange bathrooms because he thought they were inhabited by giants who might *bite off* [!] one's penis" (my italics). In his analysis he told, when he was three years old, a story: "Two giants once ate up a river, so each river said: 'Get bigger so that the giants won't be able to eat you up.' "—"A big river," the analyst adds, "equals a big penis 'which holds lots of water.' "

If this example is read with the findings presented in the preceding section in mind (to which the exclamation points that are mine are meant to refer), it describes, again: shame, a primitive form of social fear and the phobic attitude toward the urethral-erotic discharge of cannibalistic libido. In addition, however, it illustrates the infantile theory of erection. The elevator phobia finally may illustrate the "presaging" mentioned above; for the elevator moving upward against gravity inside the "house," symbolizes erection belonging to a genital organization.

B. THE FANTASY OF CLITORIS URINATION

This fantasy is extremely frequent, perhaps ubiquitous, in the phallic organization. If the clitoris is the substratum of the phallus, it must do as the phallus does and yield urethral-erotic discharge. Its proximity to the urethra in a covert region obviously facilitates the illusion. A surprising characteristic of the fantasy is its long persistence. Adolescent girls, or girls of college age or above, will eventually inspect themselves while urinating in order "to find out where the urine really comes from"; but on occasion the analyst observes a much older female in whom the fantasy has been retained.

A sexually experienced woman of middle age, who alternated between intercourse and clitoris masturbation, reports waking up from a dream with a strong urinary urge. "When I went to the bathroom," she continues, "I noticed suddenly (after sitting on the toilet for several moments) that no urine or very little of it was coming out. I looked at the clitoris to see what had happened." She told this naively, without any critique, and as though it had been the most natural thing to do.

The persistence of the fantasy of clitoris urination becomes understandable when one considers its background: the fantastic equation, intrinsic to an "infantile genital organization," of continence with a phallic and of incontinence with a castrated make-up. The phallus is to the owner of this organization what the bung is to the barrel, and anatomy permits this particular one of its functions to be perpetuated in fantasies even if others had to be given up.[8]

Cf. Anny Katan (94): "In all cases of enuresis we find the fantasy that the genitals are damaged and, like a broken water-tap, cannot retain urine."

C. THE FANTASY OF AN "UNCASTRATED" CONSTITUTION

The antithesis phallic-castrated, characterizing as it does the phallic phase, is not inclusive because it disregards the frequent fantasy of an "uncastrated," i.e., neither phallic nor castrated, constitution. The common occurrence of this fantasy is documented by the fact that it dictated in antiquity (and often even today) the treatment of the female genital by the sculptor. Here the male genital is reproduced realistically, and in all detail, while the female genital is—omitted. The abdominal wall is continued solidly to the insertion of the thighs, and there is nothing to intimate the existence of any genital whatsoever.[9] It

[8] I have the feeling that the words spoken by "Dora's" father (34) in her first dream: "I do not wish that I and my two children burn up because of your jewelry case" allow (since "the dreamer dreams in the last analysis of himself") for a narcissistic overdetermination. The dream speech would then contain the female dreamer's idea, expressed symbolically, that enuretic incontinence is the result of the loss of the male organ which one incurs when one is built like the mother. (The patient's first spontaneous association, that the brother must be given a chance to use the bathroom at night, sounds like a confirmation.)

[9] Cf., e.g., the Aphrodite of Kyrene in Rome, the marble torso of Aphrodite in Algiers, the Aphrodite girding herself with the sword of Mars in Florence, or

is this "nothing" that appears so frequently in the associations of patients where it often refers to the "uncastrated" appearance.[10] The latter is obtained by a withdrawal from the "reality" of the female genital area, and its fantastic replacement. "Nothing" may thus represent the denial of the female genital: the vulva is, as it were, first interpreted as castrated, then negated and eventually replaced. The replacement, however, representative of the denial, is total: the castrated organ is not equipped with a phallus but supplanted by skin.

The ontogenesis postulated here admits of illustration through material from a single analytic hour.

The patient was suffering from the impact of memories in which his mother, a woman of a psychotic make-up, had presented him with the fact of "castration" by exhibiting with spread legs at close range. He begins the hour by perceiving a nonextant smell of food in the analyst's office and an urge to perform fellatio on the object of his transference. Then he reports on a dream: He is lying in bed and on top of a certain psychotic man, the lower part of whose body is detached from the upper part and moves independently, while his genital region is like that of a store dummy without clothes. "You know, where there is just nothing." (Spontaneously, these are his words.) The man moves his lower region in such a fashion that the dreamer is able to perform rectal intercourse ending in an ejaculation. Upon waking up the patient suspects himself, erroneously as it turned out, of having had a nocturnal emission.

The associations to the dream, concerning the denial of castration through the choice of a phallic object and through rectal intercourse as instinctual aim, shall be omitted as impertinent to the present subject. The others were in the sequence in which they occurred:

---

the statue of Omphale at the side of Heracles in Paris. These are not examples of great art, they are chosen merely for ready reference to their photographs in the *Encyclopaedia Britannica* (under the general subject of "Sculpture"). I remember, however, the superb statue of an Egyptian Princess, whose tinted plaster cast adorned my office once, and also many sculptures of the female body by Maillol, some owned by friends, others in museums, without there being any difference in the point under discussion.

[10] Not simply to "the female genital," as Bertram D. Lewin has contended (Psa. Q., XVII, 1948).

(1) Subsequent to the dream, he had felt, for the first time, an arousement upon seeing an advertisement showing a girl with a girdle. He had never been able before to experience what his friends told him they did: a sexual reaction to such ads, and to girls in bathing suits which they found more exciting than nudes.

(2) He remembers, again, how he and a girl cousin showed each other their genitals at the age of seven; but again, he cannot recall what he saw except as a "blank."

(3) For the first time he remembers looking at his mother who sat on the bed while she dressed. He was two and a half years of age and his head came just on a level with her genitals. She got up, put her bloomers on and, for a moment, before she had pulled them up, "there is nothing but the hair." This astonished the child who had expected to see a penis on which he thought the mother had been sitting while she was on the bed.

If these associations are perused in reverse, i.e., in their historical sequence, they indicate that the mother is thought of as phallic before her castration is perceived. In latency this castration, which in the meantime must have become traumatic, can no longer be either acknowledged or denied by equipping the girl with a penis. The perceptive withdrawal from the castrated genital of the girl leaves a blank, which the dream replaces by the "uncastrated" complexion of a man, i.e., of an object which should have a penis but which has "nothing" instead. To "affirm" the penis incorporatively (64) causes subsequently, in the waking state and the transference situation, the wish for fellatio.

The material for the fantasy of the "uncastrated complexion" can be found in at least two places in Freud's work.

(a) The "Wolf Man" (55D), who minimizes his shock upon seeing the little girl by calling her genital the "anterior behind" (der vordere Popo), ruminates later over Christ's behind and its functions. However, upon Nanja's information that Christ as a man had and did everything the others have and do he consoles himself, with the idea that the "behind was, after all, only the continuation of the legs." Thereby he abolishes the anal area in the manner of the fantasy under consideration.

(b) Another example, more direct because it lacks the displacement from front to back, is the fetish described by Freud (67) as a girdle which can also be worn as bathing trunks—"a piece of clothing which altogether covers the genitals. . . ." Supplementing Freud's analysis of this garment, one is led to assume the existence of both a regressive object relation to, and an identification with, the "uncastrated" female.

A contemporary materialization of the fantasy is the present-day female underdrawer, the "step-in," which, uncleft in the crotch and clinging to the lower part of the body, lends the same "uncastrated" complexion to its wearer. There are, of course, others of similar shape, real girdles with closed crotch, "briefs" with close-fitting elastic about the thighs, and fantastic ones, e.g., "iron pants," which a woman patient of my observation had imagined herself as wearing.

One patient, reported elsewhere (19), "after the partial abolishment of her illusory penis had enabled her to become conscious of her homosexuality, produced a fantasy in which a female partner, having waited impatiently for her to come home from work, was eager to perform cunnilingus. In this performance she fantasied herself as clad only in a dressing gown, noticing with astonishment that the act of disrobing had not, however, included the taking off of her underdrawers. Both dressing gown and cunnilingus furnish a phallic assurance against castration; the former in its symbolic role as a 'mantle,' the latter because the clitoris is erected and shown. It is the act of shedding the garment described above that is equivalent to castration and therefore, although implied, is not actually performed. First wearing and then not wearing the step-in, she has at no time removed it; and, by virtue of this omission, has exchanged directly a 'phallic' for an 'uncastrated' constitution."

In re: "nothing," one will recall the dialogue between Hamlet and Ophelia before and after the dumb-show.

Before the show:

    ¶ HAM. Ladie, shall I lye in your lap?
    ¶ OPHE. No my Lord.

¶ HAM. I meane, my Head upon your Lap?

¶ OPHE. I my Lord.

¶ HAM. Do you thinke I meant Country matters?

¶ OPHE. I thinke nothing, my Lord.

¶ HAM. That's a faire thought to ly between Maid's legs.

¶ OPHE. What is my Lord?

¶ HAM. *Nothing.*

After the show:

¶ OPHE. Will they tell us what this shew meant?

¶ HAM. I, or any shew that you'l shew him. Bee not you ashame'd to shew, hee'l not shame to tell you what it meanes.

¶ OPHE. You are *naught,* you are *naught* [120C].

"Naught" is a variation of "nothing" and at the same time, in Shakespeare's time, "naughty" (cf. Webster).

All illustrations presented here—from the sculpture of antiquity to the Elizabethan dialogue—demonstrate one determinant for the deletion of the female genital in the fantasy of the uncastrated complexion: a scoptophilic defense. There is nothing to show or to see. To appreciate this one must remember how often the phallus is displaced upon almost any part of the anatomy, subject to the (conscious or unconscious) wish to show or see. By deleting the genital the fantasy abolishes, as it were, the impulse and in so doing the problem of castration.

A patient experienced the most painful struggle in reporting that she had inspected her genital area the night before. She could not stop berating herself and expatiating on how only a thoroughly depraved individual could do such an utterly horrible thing. It was obvious, although not interpreted to her, that she had performed a displacement. Not the action but its result originally evoked the horror; not the seeing but what was seen: her castration. Soon afterwards she found herself strongly tempted to bring me a photograph of herself which she called "in the nude," but described as showing her in a clinging veil, i.e., with an "uncastrated" complexion.

However, there are other determinants. The "iron pants," owned fantastically by a celibate and extremely narcissistic female, were certainly a defense against masturbation. Tactile as well as visual cognizance of the castrated organ is, in this fashion, evaded.

Yet the most fundamental determinant becomes discernible only if one remembers the unconscious equation of incontinence with castration. (Cf. p. 171.) The abolishment of the female genital includes the abolishment of the urethra; where there was aperture there is integument, owing to the fantastic replacement of the genital area by skin. Thus the fantasy of an "uncastrated complexion" is that of continence not dependent upon the ownership of a phallus; being uncastrated, one is, so to speak, continent *a priori*.

> The patient with the "iron pants" fantasy exhibited not only the "symptom of the crossed legs" but at the same time the use of the phallic pleasure-organ described in the previous section (cf. pp. 144 ff.) overtly and in abundance. Her frequent crying, of the type described in the same section (cf. pp. 149 f.), was at one point spontaneously recognized by her as a "sort of orgasm," followed by calm and comfort. However, when the abstinence rule was eventually enforced she developed simultaneously two new transference symptoms: the need to eat, and to urinate before the hour. No longer "uncastrated," she felt threatened with getting hungry and having to urinate during the session, and protected herself through an admittedly prophylactic gratification of either impulse.
>
> Years ago when entering the Louvre from, as I recall, a side entrance, one met with, head on, a solitary painting: Ingre's *La Source,* the nude figure of a pretty girl, life-size, undeniably exhibiting the "uncastrated" appearance, while carrying on her left shoulder a vessel from which water poured forth in an enormous stream!

D. THE FANTASY OF THE PHALLUS EQUIPPED WITH A MOUTH

In the two myths, compared by Freud in his study *On the Acquisition of Power over Fire* (72) (cf. p. 154), two symbols are of particular interest because both represent *a primal fantasy* in which *the phallus appears as provided with a mouth*. They are the vulture and the snake. Yet so do many other symbolizations of the phallus; such as birds in general, flying insects, and all manner of creeping animals, children (the "little one") and the human figure. The frequent employment of these symbols testifies to the same primal fantasy which, *corrigeant la nature,* abolishes the discrepancy between erogeneity and libido, described above (cf. p. 152), and transfers the mouth upon the (urethral) orifice of the phallus.

I believe that this fantasy contains the explanation of two puzzling clinical observations made by Freud. (1) Why, one asks oneself, does the son who assumes the passive sexual role toward the father become castrated *in the act?* And (2), why is the phallic mother always the bad, the *destroying* mother? The answer: *because the phallic discharge is, in either case, that of oral-sadistic libido;* or, in terms of the fantasy, because the *phallus devours.*[11]

This is exemplifiable by two famous studies, one that Freud wrote, and a second in which he at least had a hand.

1. *The Devouring Paternal Phallus*

The first study, illustrative of the devouring phallus, owned by the *father,* is that of the "Wolf Man" and his nightmare (55E). Of the two wishes motivating the dream, Freud found one superficial and transient. This one adhered to day residues (the expectation of Christmas and of gifts), and was precipitated by impatience. The other wish, deeper and permanent during the phallic phase, was that for sexual gratification by the father. This second wish is, as Freud has expressed it, replaced in the dream by the wish to observe the primal scene, once so fasci-

11 The question as to whether or not a "wee-wee maker bites" is first raised, though not answered, in a conversation between the father and "Little Hans" after his tonsillectomy (!). Freud points here (38) merely to a somatic contribution to the passive version of the fantasy of being castrated through being bitten, by mentioning that pruritus of the glans penis is described as: "It bites me."

nating, again. The replacement is possible, one may add, because the passive dreamer had identified with the mother, the
passive partner in the primal scene, so that in observing it he
is emphatically gratified by the father.

However, one can arrive at Freud's interpretation of the second, the infantile dream wish, merely through the interpretation of symbols; and it is in so doing that one provides an example of the fantasy of the phallus having a mouth. I assume that
the reader is thoroughly familiar with Freud's study and quote
the dream text here only for the sake of convenience:

> "I dreamt that it was night and that I was lying in my bed.
> (My bed stood with its foot towards the window; in front of the
> window there was a row of old walnut trees. I know it was win-
> ter when I had the dream, and night-time.) Suddenly the win-
> dow opened of its own accord, and I was terrified to see that
> some white wolves were sitting on the big walnut tree in front
> of the window. There were six or seven of them. The wolves
> were quite white, and looked more like foxes or sheep-dogs, for
> they had big tails like foxes and they had their ears pricked [up]
> like dogs when they are attending to something. In great terror,
> evidently of being eaten up by the wolves, I screamed and woke
> up" (55F).

The tree, rooted in the earth (= the mother) is the paternal
phallus.[12] It is qualified as tall, as a nut tree, and as one of many,
all old; in other words, it is big and of age, it bears fruit, and
connotes "many times." This connotation, representing frequency through multiplicity, alludes, in the otherwise almost
static picture, to motion;[13] i.e., to the repeated occurrence of the
insertion (frictional movements). *The window* symbolizes the
"infantile genital" aperture of the "female" dreamer, whose bed
is in a position permitting no other interpretation.[14] The win-

12 Cf. Freud: *Gedankenassociation eines vierjährigen Kindes* ("Thought Associations of a Four-Year-Old Child") (57).

13 Cf. Freud: "The *temporal repetition* of an act is regularly shown in dreams
by the *numerical multiplicity* of an object" (31D).

14 Cf. Freud: *The Occurrence of Dreams of Material from Fairy Tales* (44).
Freud juxtaposes here the (likewise oedipal) dream of a young woman to that

dow opens—the only actual motion in the dream and directly expressive of the wish to be penetrated by the father—with the result of a further qualification of the paternal phallus: the tree representing it now becomes equipped with the wolves settled like birds, in its branches, in other words, *with the erective intent to devour*. It is to this qualification of the father's phallus as cannibalistic, that the dreamer reacts with a flurry of new ones: symbolic, pictorial, allusive, and indicative of intense dream work under the exigencies of extreme condensation. The antitheses prevalent in these representations are phallic-castrated (six or seven, etc.), devouring, and being devoured (foxes, and white *sheep*-dogs), biting, and not biting (dogs immobile, and dogs alert to the game). Yet the wolves remain wolves on the tree, which remains in front of the open window. Thus the censor has failed in enforcing either successful distortion of ideation or inhibition of affect; the unconscious infantile dream wish has proven stronger than both censor and the wish to sleep. Where the liberation of sexual affect, and the corresponding hallucination of action become unavoidable the former is, therefore, transformed into the anxiety affect, and the latter avoided through arousal. The phallic child has a nightmare because *the*

---

of the four-year-old "Wolf Man." Compare the beginnings of both, and note Freud's interpretation of the first.

(1) *Woman patient:* "She is in a wholly brown room."
(2) *Wolf Man:* "I dreamt that it is night and I lie in my bed."

Ad (1): (a) *Historic interpretation:* "The woodbrown room" is in the first place the bed, and through its relation to the dining room (reference to the patient's associations) "a marital bed."

(b) *Symbolic interpretation* ("deeper and a purely sexual content"): "the room is now the vagina. (The room is in her, the reverse in the dream.) The little (old) man . . . is the (father's) penis; the narrow door and the steep stairs confirm the conception of the situation as a representation of intercourse."

Ad (2): (a) *Historic interpretation:* consists here merely in a reference—to the dreamer's situation in observing the primal scene—because the representation is not, as in (1), indirect but a direct one. One could practically say that the Wolf Man begins his dream with Freud's interpretation of the woman patient's.

(b) *Symbolic interpretation:* the room is, again, in him—the reverse of the dream where he is in the room. Since the window is plain (lacking draperies, curtains, etc., representing so frequently the labia of the adult) and no vagina is symbolized (staircase), it is interpretable as the "mother's belly" (*Mutterleib*) in accordance with the conception of the phallic child.

father's phallus is about to castrate him through a cannibalistic invasion.[15]

2. *The Devouring Maternal Phallus*

The second study, illustrative of the devouring phallic organ, owned by the *mother,* is Abraham's *The Spider as a Dream Symbol* (5). It consists in a short article, and a postscript. In the former, the analyses of four dreams, three from one male patient, one from another, are utilized for a progressively over-determinative interpretation of the symbol with the result that "the spider represents in the first place the wicked mother who is formed like a man, and in the second place *the male genital attributed to her.*[16] In the latter, two remarks are quoted: one made by Nunberg, the other by Freud. "Nunberg laid stress on the fact that the spider kills its victim by sucking its blood, and *that this sucking served as a castration symbol* in the case observed [my italics], *i.e.,* it gave expression to the typical phantasy of losing the penis during the sexual act." The phallus, in other words, castrates again *by using its mouth.* Freud, as reported by Abraham, finally put the finishing touch to the picture: the female spider is actually far superior in size and power to the male, and it kills and *devours* the latter frequently during copulation.

Furnished with this knowledge it is not uninstructive to return from the postscript to the clinical data contained in the

[15] The reader will recall other corroborative material from Freud's study. The boy's previous identification with the *active* father in the primal scene (before the sister's seduction had made him passive) precipitated a *urethral-erotic* instinctual discharge at the sight of Grusha—an "edible" object (*Grusha*-pear). A "particularly good tasting" kind of pear enabled the child to transfer this object, or its pertinent parts, subsequently, upon a butterfly, because both pear and butterfly bore yellow stripes = *a pictorial allusion to urine.* Finally: the phobic attack around the time of the dream occurred at the moment when the yellow-striped swallowtail lighted on a flower (*beginning to use its mouth*); and the affect, common to both the "superficial" and the "deeper" wish motivating the dream, is in the last analysis recognizable as *cannibalistic impatience.*

[16] Italics this writer's. The author continues: "In this the spider's web represents the pubic hair and the single thread the male genital"—an interpretation of which I doubt that it has the general validity requisite to that of a symbol.

article proper. In both of the two dreams the spider is crushed: once by the woman's phallus (the maid's broom), and the other time (if we discount the censorial doubt) by the aperture of the *Mutterleib* of the dreamer.[17] Crushing, however, one is taught by analytic experience, is often dreamt or fantasied as an attenuation of biting (cf. p. 109); and Abraham identifies "the fantasies of crushing the penis" with those of "neurotic women with a marked *castration* complex"—women in whom the wish, not only to bite off the penis but to incorporate it as well, is demonstrable beyond doubt. Of the dream of the second patient, a dream of the mother's belly according to Abraham, it shall only be mentioned that it contained—reminiscent of the "Wolf Man's" story—a nondescript *butterfly* in which Abraham recognizes the "hidden female penis"; and of the third dream of the first patient, that the spider—as though to complete the analogy to the "Wolf Man"—had a "tuft of *yellow* hair on the upper part of each thigh." (Italics mine.)

This material, while merely alluding to the urethral-erotic discharge of cannibalistic libido, points unmistakably to the fact that the devouring organ is not the vagina dentata, which belongs to the "genital" phase, but the phallus of the "phallic" mother.[18]

17 Cf. footnote 10, above. The dreamer is an adult, not a child. The symbol is complicated through the allusive symbolization of vagina and rectum (the two rooms with a common wall).

18 The meritorious study by Sylvan Keiser on *Orality Displaced to the Urethra* (95) came to my attention only after the above subsection had been written. This author states—and he is the first to my knowledge to do so—that "It is remarkable that the penis fantasied in the vagina has been accepted as having an orally incorporating capacity and this same quality is attributed to the male penis, but without considering the urethra as a potential mouth.

"Though analytic authors describe the body as phallus . . . and the mouth as having the potential for unconscious representation of the functions of a urethra, the reversal of these roles is not discussed. That is, the penis as a body with the urethra symbolically assuming the ingestive functions of the mouth. In a general way, orally incorporating needs have been assigned to the penis, but a direct transition to the urethra has not been given due consideration. . . . The oral nature of the penis is consistent with Jones's idea that the penis penetrates to get at the things it wants to eat."

IV. A TRANSFERENCE DELUSION CONCERNING THE CASTRATION COMPLEX: THE "DÉJÀ RACONTÉ"[19]

A

One might not expect to find remarks on the *déjà raconté* in this place. My justification lies in my thesis. It appears, from what I can observe, that the phenomenon always concerns the castration complex: the memory, either recent or distant, that the patient is certain to have told before although he has not, alludes to castration. A few examples:

1. A male patient mentions that he "had told" me "before" how his *mother* had been in the habit of saying to him as a boy: "X. [name], take your *hand* out of your pocket." Shortly thereafter his associations concerning occasional masturbation during puberty with sand under the prepuce, bloodying the penis. His reaction to being informed of his self-deception was one of considerable dismay.

2. In the analysis of a female patient, the ordeals suffered before and after an emergency operation that had saved her life during the latency period, were repetitively and with strong affect recalled. It had been at night, and the euphoric child, "feeling fine," was rushed to the hospital "just for X-rays," as the mother explained, promising that they would shortly be back. Once in the hospital she was abandoned to the surgeons. As she was being prepared, wheeled into the operating room and anesthetized, she became frightened in the extreme, pleading with everyone to let her be with her mother until she became eventually unconscious. The periods in which this memory was emotionally relived until it was gradually, belatedly and incompletely transferred, were reminiscent of a cathartic rather than of a psychoanalytic treatment. On one such occasion the patient added a new detail in the form of a *déjà raconté*: passing a door

---

[19] The following section appeared under the title: "The *Déjà Raconté*: A Transference-Delusion Concerning the Castration Complex" in *The Psychoanalytic Quarterly*, Vol. XXV, pp. 215-227, 1956, and is reprinted here with the kind permission of the Editor.

while on the hospital stretcher she became terrified at seeing a white-clad doctor come out of it with blood *dripping* from his rubber-gloved *hands*. My remark that I had not heard this before did not shake her conviction that she had told it, and disappointed her deeply.

3. A female, who sees her physical self as unpresentable and inferior, finds hands a distinguishing feature in people and compliments herself on her own. They are her father's hands, good and strong, and the only part of her body with which she remained satisfied even after the outbreak of her neurosis. While musing about this, she thinks to herself: "Funny, I have never done anything [damaging] to them. . . ." A week later she refers back to the report of these thoughts and to the fact, which she is positive of having told at the time, that only one or two days afterwards, in the morning she had *spilled* hot coffee over one *hand* and burned it. This was actually an addition to the report; her reaction to being told so was one of anger and contemptuous disbelief. I must omit the material in which this *déjà raconté* was embedded; it dealt exclusively with the antithesis phallic-castrated, applied to the patient herself as well as to incest objects. In the interest of comparing examples further below, I shall merely mention that it contained a detachable rubber penis and a man's urination into a *jar*.

4. The near-rape episode recorded on p. 93 was also told as an attenuated *déjà raconté*. ("I *believe* I told you this before.") The patient could not, however, react to her error because, for technical reasons, it had not been brought to her attention. The analysis of this incident, and of others, left no doubt that rape— and sexual intercourse was always rape to this patient—represented a castrative mayhem. The prelude to the report had been a memory in which the three- or four-year-old child has asked her father: "What have you got in your pants?" and was twice cruelly cuffed in the face; the first time for asking the question and the second for crying over the slap.

5.[20] A woman begins her analytic hour with the report of a dream: she was sitting on a step wearing blue jeans and

20 This observation is not my own. I am indebted for it to a colleague whom, in the interest of the anonymity of this patient, I cannot thank by name.

spreading her legs apart. There is a girl sitting next to her who either has no hair on her head or else is holding a big glass *bottle* in her *hands*. The patient has a pleasant feeling of anticipation as she turns to the girl and begins to *rub* her head on the *bottle*. As she rubs, hair begins to grow on one side of the head or bottle. She has the feeling of failure about not being able to produce hair on the other side, but after rubbing again, hair grows on that side.

Thinking about the dream, she goes on to say that she had felt that it was related to losing a penis as a punishment for masturbation. When her son told her recently that a girl playmate of his had a sore on her body, the patient had thought that this meant that the little girl had no penis. The lad had also talked to her about having a child of their own—a girl child, "because he wanted to see how she grew"; which she had considered as expressive of the boy's wish "to see how a girl has no penis."

At this point the analyst asked his patient, who had persisted in being reluctant to talk about her sexuality, "What about your own masturbation?" She has told all about it, was the answer. She has stopped being masturbated by her husband after telling him several months ago that she did not want it any more. This was a *déjà raconté*: she had told no such thing but insisted, as my colleague writes, "with finality and absolute certainty," that she had. After a brief discussion of her sexual responses she furnishes, upon request, associations to the first part of the dream. I select from them the comfort she used to feel wearing blue jeans, which allowed her to spread her legs, and how much she liked being in them. This was followed by the memory of playing with the boys in the street wearing a catcher's glove, and becoming as proficient in throwing and catching as the boys with a "thrill of satisfaction."

It need hardly be pointed out that the castration appears here in two different forms: one more typical for the boy (although extant, as my experience had taught me, in practically every female), and the other specific for the girl. The first is that one has owned a penis and lost it through masturbation. (In the dream, which is a wish fulfillment, instead of losing it one obtains it through masturbation.) In later times the illusory penis is erected over the loss and we find the girl wearing pants, doing athletics and being "one of the boys." The second is "penis envy," acknowledgment of the inferiority of the clitoris and, because of it, the relinquishment of masturbation. In the present example it was the second form that became subject to a *déjà raconté*.

6. I append the nuclear portion of the classic example with which Freud originally illustrated his discovery of the *déjà raconté* (46): "A patient said to me in the course of his associations: 'When I was in the garden with a knife (that was when I was five years old) and cut through my little finger—oh, I only *thought* it was cut through—but I've told you about that already.'

"I assured him that I had no recollection of anything of the kind. He insisted with increasing conviction that it was impossible he could be mistaken. I finally . . . asked him in any case to repeat the story . . . .

" 'When I was five years old, I was playing in the garden near my nurse, and was carving with my pocket-knife in the bark of one of the walnut trees that also come into my dream.[1] Suddenly, to my unspeakable terror, I noticed that I had cut through the little finger of my (right or left?) hand, so that it was only hanging on by its skin. I felt no pain, but great fear. I did not venture to say anything to my nurse, who was only a few paces distant, but I sank down on the nearest seat and sat there incapable of casting another glance at my finger. At last I grew calm, took a look at the finger, and saw that it was entirely uninjured' " (46A).

7. It appears almost as though Freud himself had unconsciously been impressed with the fact that the *déjà raconté* concerns the castration complex, because he adds a second example, paralleling the content of the first without being a *déjà raconté*. The subject is, in fact, not even a patient but a male

[1] Cf. "The Occurrence in Dreams of Material from Fairy Tales" [44]. In telling the story again on a later occasion he made the following correction: "I don't believe I was cutting the tree. That was a confusion with another recollection, which must also have been hallucinatorily falsified, of having made a cut upon a tree with my knife and of *blood* having come out of the tree." [Freud's footnote.]

correspondent who reports two memories from his childhood (46). In one he inspects the genital of a little girl, and "notices very clearly" that she has "a penis like his own." In order to maintain this observation against others, e.g., of female statues, that would not bear it out, he has his own penis disappear between his thighs which he presses together—an "experiment," as he calls it, that explains why no penis need be visible in the girl. The second memory had, in contrast to the first, never been repressed and appeared always to him as of the greatest importance since it was one of the three recollections of his mother who died when he was very young. It may again be quoted verbatim: "My mother is standing in front of the wash-hand-stand and cleaning the glasses and washing-basin, while I am playing in the same room and committing some misdemeanour. As a punishment my hand is soundly slapped. Then to my very great horror I see that my little finger is falling off; and in fact it falls into the pail. Knowing that my mother is angry, I do not venture to say anything; but my terror grows still more intense when I see the pail carried off soon afterwards by the servant-maid. For a long time I was convinced that I had lost a finger—up to the time, I believe, at which I learnt to count' " (46B).

B

Freud's description of the *déjà raconté* requires a brief discussion and, in one point at least, an addendum. He calls the phenomenon not infrequent; in my experience it is rare. This need mean nothing; the explanation for it may be the much smaller number of patients that one analyzes today when analyses have become so much longer, or it may be due to his greater technical skill. His report on the apparent *déjà raconté,* in consequence of the analyst's paramnesia to be removed by self-analysis, requires that anyone like myself, who combines a good analytic memory with a general memory nowhere nearly comparable to Freud's, add instances where he answers his patient: "I do not remember having heard this; but it is possible that you mentioned it sometime, perhaps in the beginning, when it had not as yet any meaning for me and that I may have forgotten." Correspondingly there are instances where the patient will answer:

"I thought I had told it but if you say so maybe I haven't." This is important by contrast for it allows one to formulate: any instance in which either the analyst or the patient is ready to make a concession is not a *déjà raconté*.[21]

Freud's description, finally, of the patient's reaction to being informed of a *déjà raconté* is accurate but incomplete. I shall introduce the addendum to it by speculating about a fictitious event: if I were to advise my Irish maid, a respectable housewife and mother who thinks well of me, that I do not believe in the god she worships, that there is no historical proof of his having lived among men, and that the Renaissance pictures on my walls which she dusts so faithfully are there not because of what they depict but of how they depict it, I would provoke a two-fold reaction: I would, negatively, not shake her conviction, and, positively, disappoint her severely in me. It is incontestable to her that the Gospel tells us the truth; she simply knows it is so; and if I doubt it, I destroy common ground between us, leaving a chasm with me on the other side, and am no longer the good man she had thought me to be. To the first of these reactions, the patient upon being informed of a *déjà raconté* adds, *en miniature,* the second. He is not under the influence of a paramnesia but of a delusion, he simply knows he has told; and the confrontation with the reality, which is that he has not told, breaks, or at least infracts, his positive transference, leaving one with the feeling that one has abrogated a common bond. It depends on the character of the patient how explicitly he expresses this reaction; but, listening with free-floating attention, I have never missed it. The patient makes, subsequently, a "social recovery" *en miniature;* the incident loses its impact, and the positive transference is restored. Still later the content of the *déjà raconté* becomes analyzable but I, personally, have never found myself prompted by the material to remind the patient of his transient delusion and to attempt analyzing the *déjà raconté* itself.

[21] The logical reader may wish to dismiss Example 4 on the strength of this formulation.

C

I cannot furnish a theory of the *déjà raconté* and shall therefore confine myself to assembling some material for one. Before doing so I must gather and review critically Freud's own theoretical contributions because they are scattered in his work, and contain, I believe, one error. For convenience I shall distinguish between his remarks on the form, the experience of the phenomenon, and those on its content. The review of the former shall precede the review of the latter.

In his paper on the subject (46) Freud terms the *déjà raconté* a paramnesia and gives the superficial explanation that the patient had originally intended to tell and mistakes subsequently the intent for its execution. At the same time he groups this particular kind of *fausse reconnaissance* together with others, classified as different forms of the *déjà vu,* and refers to his previous treatment of this subject (33A). There he calls the *déjà vu* "a peculiar sensation or feeling [*eine eigentümliche Empfindung*]" but adds immediately that in terming it so he knows he is merely adopting a loose usage of language and that "it is probably [rather] a judgment, more specifically judgment of cognition [*Erkennungsurteil*]." Yet, he adds further "these cases have nevertheless a character quite peculiar to themselves [*einen ganz eigentümlichen Charakter*] and one must not disregard the fact that one never remembers what one is seeking, namely when and where one has seen the particular set-up before." Three and a half decades later (74) he calls both *déjà raconté* and *déjà vu* "deceptions" while comparing them to the states of alienation (*Entfremdungen*) of which he states that they are commonly described as "sensations" but are (actually) "apparently complicated processes, tied to certain contents and connected with decisions about these contents." Finally, "alienations, *déjà vu* and *déjà raconté* occur in the normal [as well as in the morbid individual] . . . yet they are of an abnormal structure as are the dreams. . . ."

I find much of this confusing and inconsistent; because it fails to avail itself of the distinguishing clinical characteristic described above. States of alienation—depersonalization and derealization (and apparently also the *déjà vu,* with which I have personally no experience)—are feelings that never influence the judgment of cognition: the individual *feels* that he is *not* himself but he *knows* all the time that he is; the environment *appears* to him as unreal but he doubts its reality *at no time.* This is incomparable with the *déjà raconté,* where the patient does not *"feel as though"* he had told his castrative experience before but where he *"knows"* that he has. To repeat: the alienations are sensations or feelings which do not impair cognitive judgment; the *déjà raconté* is a conviction that does—in other words, a delusion.[22]

My objection to Freud's treatment of the *experience* of the *déjà raconté* does not hold for his interpretations of its *content.* Here it is justifiable, and indeed profitable, to compare the *déjà raconté* with the *déjà vu,* and to oppose it to the alienations. Both *déjà vu* and *déjà raconté* are, as Freud expressed it, symptomatic of the *"reanimation of an unconscious impression,"* a *"fantasy that had been repressed"* onto a locale. "This would again be an occasion," Freud formulates the unconscious motivation "for awakening that (unconscious and unknown) fantasy[23] which at such and such time had formed itself in me in order to *improve the situation."*[24] When the *déjà vu* appears in a dream it represents, Freud has found, *the genital of the mother.* ("There is no other [locale] of which one can state with such certainty that one 'has been there before.'") In comparing, finally, *fausse reconnaissance,* i.e., *déjà vu* and *déjà raconté* with

---

[22] Freud has observed the *déjà vu* in dreams. I have, in some of these instances, almost been tempted to speak of a *déjà rêvé.* It is obvious that the distinction made above is naturally deleted here; for the dream is filled with delusions at all times, and the fact that a *déjà vu* is believed by the dreamer is a matter of course.

[23] Ferenczi's observation that this fantasy may also have been elaborated upon in a dream is not, even if it should prove to be true, an addition; for any fantasy can be dream material (33).

[24] These and subsequent italics in this section are mine.

"states of alienation," i.e., derealization and depersonalization,[25] Freud calls the latter the positive counterpart of the former. *Déjà vu* and *déjà raconté* are "illusions [*Täuschungen;* literally: deceptions] in which we want *to suppose something as belonging to our ego*, just as in the derealizations[26] we endeavor to exclude something from us."

This and what has been said before make it evident that the evaluation of the *déjà raconté* has developed in the four decades that the phenomenon has been known. It can no longer be looked upon as a parapraxia but is a delusion, for which Freud has left us but fragments of a general theory; and it is in a certain respect comparable to alienation, of which Freud (74) stated as late as 1936 that it is "still obscure and scientifically so little conquered." Some of his very first, and some of his last words about *déjà vu* and about alienation sound prophetic if applied to the *déjà raconté*, which is indeed "a judgment, more specifically a judgment of cognition" and a complicated process and "tied to certain contents and connected with decisions about these contents" (33). The contents, as was stated and illustrated above, concern the castration complex.

D

The establishment of a theory of the *déjà raconté* is, as the foregoing shows, quite a formidable task. In gathering material for it one finds oneself in a situation comparable—if it be permitted to liken small to great—to that of Freud when he wrestled with the theory of anxiety: one explores different approaches and finds that none leads far enough to reach the conclusion. I shall therefore merely enumerate them; and since Freud's example is so much more instructive than any of mine let it play the lead and my own the supporting role.

[25] I am changing Freud's terminology without changing his meaning. It is more convenient to use the one term "alienation" (*Entfremdung*) as comprehensive and inclusive of "derealization" and "depersonalization."

[26] This formula is improvable by the adoption of the terminology suggested in the previous footnote; because it holds true for depersonalization as well.

1. Freud has called the castration complex the "bedrock" of all psychological stratification. "This," he remarks (76): "is probably as it ought to be because for psychology biology plays really the role of the underlying bedrock." The fantasy of castration, in other words, is not only a primal fantasy and as such in part phylogenetic but particularly regressive. Its emergence from repression is therefore apt to induce a particularly strong ego regression in the patient.

It is thus that the *déjà raconté* occupies the singular position of a *typical transference delusion in the nonpsychotic*. Freud's patient testifies to the regression by preceding the delusion with a parapraxia that makes him talk for a brief moment like a psychotic. Here he is with both hands completely intact and says: "When I was playing at the age of five, in the garden, with a knife and cut through my little finger . . ." Yet he emerges immediately and becomes aware of his parapraxia: "—Oh, I only thought it was cut through—." However, this state is as brief as the previous one; and is followed with a renewed and deeper regression, in which the parapraxia becomes exchanged for the delusion of the *déjà raconté*: "But I have told you that already." The minute investigation of his behavior cannot be concluded in English; it requires the original wording in German: ". . . *aber das habe ich Ihnen* JA *schon erzählt.*" It is the here untranslatable *"ja,"* an expression of "affirmation" that, if one applies to it the first of Freud's fundamental findings on this subject (64) since the model for affirmation is incorporation, confirms at once that the *déjà raconté* is indeed a deception "in which we want to suppose something as belonging to our ego."

The question arises: what is this something? *I believe that it is, in the last analysis, the maternal breast, to the fantasy of whose incorporation the shock of castration has caused the patient to regress.*

Three arguments speak in favor of this hypothesis. In the first place both of Freud's examples, 6 and 7, suggest, and none of mine contradict, that it is as though the patient were saying: I am now transferring upon you someone to whom I have not told it before either. In his first example it is the nurse, *a mother substitute;* in the second it is the *mother.* In my own examples it is in 1, where the *mother* was obviously not told; in 2, the *mother* could not be told; 3, 4, and 5 cannot in this respect be discussed because the *déjà raconté* concerns the recent past and the childhood experience, repeated there, is not known. It may merely be noted that in 5, the not telling about masturbation is directly re-enacted in the transference. I must therefore confine myself to pointing out how remarkable the not telling in Freud's examples appears. A terrified child will ordinarily cry out and come running to the nurse who is "only a few paces away," or the mother who is "in the same room." Yet neither child did so, and they are both satisfied with a glib rationalization; one that he just "did not dare," the other that he "did not dare because he knew that the mother was angry." The reader is naturally aware of the explanation: the "playing with the knife" and the "committing of some misdemeanour" cover masturbation, which had caused the "little finger" to be lost and which cannot be confessed. In the second place, if Freud's opinion that the *déjà raconté* has a kinship to the *déjà vu* is correct and if the latter represents the genital of the mother, the former should represent her *breast; because having told concerns obviously the mouth.* In the third place, if it is a re-enactment in the transference, it may well concern *a fantasied union of mouths* such as one observes in instances other than that of the *déjà raconté,* between the patient's regressively infantile "oral" mouth and the analyst's mouth upon which the breast was transferred.

One will now understand why the patient is so deeply disappointed when he is told that he has not told, and why the analyst is abruptly made a stranger.

2. Analytic material is often resemblant to polyphony, and analytic interpretation to that of a score. Both analyst and conductor or player must evaluate the significance, in a given phrase, bar, or beat, of the representative of a part and afford it what he feels is its proper position. There is in Freud's and in

some of the other examples, the element "hand" and the element "liquid," of which I feel that their inconspicuousness is deceptive and conceals their significant nature. They should, I believe, be given prominence. In 6, the hand is evident and the liquid merely implied, inasmuch as a finger hanging on by its skin would bleed profusely; but later the tree bleeds instead. In 7, the hand is punished and the finger falls into a pail of water (*Wasserkübel*), which the maid shortly afterwards carried out. Example 1 is about hand and penis, but the penis bleeds. In 2, the hands are dripping blood. Example 3 tells about hot coffee poured over the hand, a detachable penis and urination into a jar. In 4, one may infer that the child would like to touch the father's penis before she is able to stop the flow of her tears. In 5, finally, at least the dream preceding the *déjà raconté* is one of rubbing, obviously with the hand or hands, and alludes to liquid through allusion to a bottle.

This is not incidental. It alludes to the fantastic equation (cf. p. 171) of continence with a phallic, and of incontinence with a castrated constitution in the mentality of the phallic child; and the equation explains, in its turn, the danger to his ego organization in consequence of the fear of castration, against which he is forced to protect himself through regression. It is as though he were obsessed with the thought: *I am in danger of re-experiencing castration in consequence of my infantile masturbation and of being destroyed by becoming incontinent through the loss of the phallus. To protect myself I have regressed to an early stage where owning the breast is what matters* (cf. pp. 73 ff.), *and having transferred upon you the early mother, have incorporated yours. To maintain myself at the same time ecologically* (cf. p. 159) *you must now let yourself become the victim of a* folie à deux *and join me in my delusion.*

It would appear that this imaginary transcription of the patient's unconscious thought explains much detail of the clinical picture of the *déjà raconté*.

3. One may nevertheless go on, asking oneself afresh: why is it so important to the patient to tell his castrative experience

for the second time "first"? What compels him not to know that he is telling it for the first time? Why must there be no first time that he tells it? I believe that the theory, discussed on the occasion of the reduplicate bisyllabic speech of the child (cf. pp. 104-107) and applied later to the rhetorical reduplication of Shylock's forensic speech (cf. p. 164) contains the answer. Clinical observation of repressed traumatic experience show one ever so often that the repressed is not merely, as Freud has shown us, excluded from the adult ego organization. *The repressed has often surrounded itself, as it were, with a fragment of infantile ego which, although it had been recognizable all the time characterologically and in symptoms, seizes suddenly, concomitant to the emergence of the repressed, the whole patient.* The shock of castration, to be relived in consequence of the "buoyancy of the repressed" and the removal of counter-cathexis through the analytic work, could not therefore be borne the first time. It is a *passive* experience and annihilative of the infantile ego. Its re-enactment the second time is an *active* one and is formative, not destructive, of ego. It is thus, I believe, that the patient can only indulge in it the second time "first."

4. If the *déjà raconté* is a delusion, a final approach to it should be that of a general theory of delusion. There are, however, only fragments of such a theory in existence, and the present context does not allow for their exposition.

V. CONCLUSION

It may surprise the reader to find the present chapter terminated—perhaps somewhat abruptly—at this point. But I have no more to say on the subject of the phallic phase.

It is, of course, tempting to consider a monographic treatment of the *castration complex*. One could show that the man's fear of castration is, paradoxically, often the stronger the more completely he has identified himself with the "castrated" woman; and that the woman's feeling of inferiority is frequently the more pronounced the more she has deluded herself about owning a phallus. One could demonstrate many of the countless displacements of the phallic and the castrated genital and of the innumerable manifestations of the phallic and of the castrated state. One could illustrate the precariousness of the phallus, whose existence is, in most instances, simultaneously affirmed and denied.

One might, furthermore, elaborate upon the *perversions* and exemplify in detail how *all* of them insure *both* sexes against the fear of castration. But in so doing I would not be able to say anything that has not been said, either explicitly or implicitly, by Freud. And the present volume is not intended to be didactic.

A word, finally, on the absence in the present volume of any observations concerning the *latency period*. They are lacking because I have made none; and the reason for that is method. The psychoanalysis of neurotics, and, occasionally of psychotics, reveals a disturbed latency, which in itself is equivalent to its absence. The appropriate method for investigating this period in the psychosexual development is the direct observation of normal, or near-normal, children.[27]

[27] I have found only one article in psychoanalytic literature whose author employs this method: Berta Bornstein: *On Latency* (10).

6

THE GENITAL PHASE

I. THE PERSISTENCE OF EARLIER PHASES IN THE GENITAL PHASE

The persistence of characteristics of earlier phases in the genital phase has been dealt with by Freud and Abraham so exhaustively that there is little for me to say. Freud, in his last summing up of the matter (77C) has described this phase as a "condition in which (1) *quite a few [manche] earlier libidinal cathexes have been preserved* [Italics mine], (2) others are included in the sexual functions as preparatory, auxiliary acts, whose gratification yields the so-called forepleasure, (3) [still] other strivings [*Strebungen*] are excluded from the organization, either altogether suppressed (repressed) or subjected to a different employment in the ego, forming character traits [or] undergoing [a variety of] sublimation[s] with a displacement of their aims."

In view of Freud's and Abraham's work, (2) and (3) do not call for exemplification; (1), however, requires brief comment and some illustration.

The preservation of orality in the genital phase, in the sense which Freud had in mind, is observable in the pleasure of eating, drinking and smoking, and in the practice of fellatio and cunnilingus. It is difficult to delimit the former from "sublimation with aim displacement," and the latter from the perversions. Yet beside the sublimated pleasure of the gourmet, there is the unsublimated pleasure of the gourmand who may, nevertheless, own a genital organization; and the performance, upon occasion, of cunnilingus is certainly not, that of fellatio probably not, necessarily morbid although "end pleasure" not merely "forepleasure" is obtained.

The preservation of *anality* has moved Freud to a little-known comment, which, besides concerning this particular subject, tells one in general what he had in mind. A letter to Dr. Friedrich S. Krauss (41) on the latter's sexological collection *Anthropophyteia* contains the following passage:

"Psychoanalysis has prompted us to contend that the anal region—normally and also in nonperverted individuals—is the seat of an erogenic sensibility and acts in certain respects completely like a genital. . . . The *Anthropophyteia* here assists psychoanalysis inasmuch as it shows how people dwell quite generally with pleasurable emphasis [*Lustbetonung*] upon this bodily region, its functions [*Verrichtungen*] and even the products of the latter. Were it different, all these stories would have to evoke revulsion in those who listen to them, or the whole mass of the people would have to be 'perverse' in the sense of a moralizing *psychopathia sexualis*."

One must naturally remember that the attitudes described here change according to time and environment. If a lady receives an enema while standing in audience before the King of France, this is not, two hundred years later, in harmony with our idea of propriety; and we have little taste for Sainte Beuve's report of a practical joke among courtiers involving laxation. On the other hand, we find Freud's description quite adequate if we apply it, e.g., even today, to a period of enforced celibacy in the life of a fighting army. Yet if the rectum is made "to act . . . completely like a genital" between sexual partners, at least more frequently than upon rare occasions, one has good reason to wonder whether such is compatible with mental health. I doubt that it is, when the act concerns man and woman; in the case of males I lack the broad clinical experience requisite to a judgment.

For the persistence of *phallicity* in the genital phase of the male I must draw attention to a phenomenon which, although known to everyone, has escaped analytic attention. It is the urinary erection after sleep. Under the influence of an unconscious infantile wish in a dream remembered or unremembered, the normal male, while asleep, can regress to an infantile sexual organization. The fact that neither erection nor urination yields pleasure should not prevent one from acknowledging that under the conditions mentioned above a temporarily phallic make-up is compatible with a genital constitution.[1]

It would appear that arousal dreams, followed not only by a urinary urge but by a urinary erection, are particularly apt to be forgotten; I, at least, have no illustrative material. I can, therefore, only refer to the "Dream of Count Thun" (31E) where the end of each of its three parts, and more emphatically and directly that of the third, suggests that the dreamer awoke not only, as he reports, with a urinary urge, but in the condition described above.

The existence of a urinary erection of the clitoris without sexual feeling, has, at least by one of my patients, been ascertained. I cannot, however, be sure of its compatibility with a genital organization. The persistence, generally, of sexual ex-

---

[1] Cf. Hamlet, at the time of his first monologue, is absorbed in oedipal fantasies of the primal scene—daydreams mobilized by the preceding scene of the play. He makes much of the mother's tears, her appetite, and her impatience: it is a predominantly oral-sadistic conception of the primal scene. Correspondingly, he describes himself as phallic; and complains of his urinary erection as he complains subsequently of the mother's misdeed. The compatibility of this temporarily phallic make-up with a genital organization is intimated by the idea of his ridding himself of the erection through masturbation:

¶HAM. Oh that this too too solid Flesh would melt,
    Thaw, and resolve it selfe into a Dew:
    Or that the Everlasting had not fixt
    His Cannon 'gainst Selfe—slaughter . . . [120D].

The Folio's "solid" denotes the hardness of the erection; the Quartos' "sallied": a rushing or bursting forth; and "selfe-slaughter," suicide, stands, as Freud (69) has discovered and Cohn (14) has elaborated upon, for masturbation.

The interpretation, obvious as it is, gains further support when one compares the passage with its abortive earliest two-line version in the first Quarto,

¶HAM. O that this too much griev'd and sallied flesh
    Would melt to nothing . . .

and in so doing, becomes aware that the later addition originated in a separate creative act of the poet.

citability of the clitoris and of its faculty, latent or manifest, of yielding end pleasure is, of course, a sign of the survival of a phallic characteristic in the genital phase.

One could, furthermore, say that the little girl's wish for a penis is gratified in the normal adult woman by her femininity; or, if one does not care whether or not one sounds somewhat absurd, that femininity is the equivalent, in the genital phase of the female, of the phallus.

> I remember a famous actress, who in the thirties embodied the ideal of female sexuality for the nation, expressing this in her own way: when the name of a well-known strip-tease beauty came up in an interview she said, contemptuously, that if one had "it" one did not have to strip. This "it" is evidently what made her what she was, and it is heir to the phallus.

On the other hand, it is evident that the transformation is *hardly ever completely successful;* for ever-changing feminine fashion—from the corset and the *cul de Paris* of the nineties to the sweater and girdle of today—reminds the woman that something, somewhere, *is not quite as it ought to be and needs something done to it:* colored, enlarged, exposed, or concealed, etc. Hair, cheeks, eyes, mouth, bosom, legs, heels, etc., have throughout feminine history been treated as though they were the castrated genital in displacement and therefore required restitution.

In justifying the brevity of the foregoing comments, I repeat that they concern only one single line of Freud's last remark on the subject—a remark virtually without precedent in his work. I have consequently dispensed with any comments upon the morbid persistence, as well as with most pregenital use of the genital, because both are regressive and, in general, not compatible with a full genital sexual organization.

II. A NEW EROGENIC ZONE, DISCHARGING AN OLD PARTIAL LIBIDO

Freud has characterized the genital phase essentially through the primacy of the fully developed genital zones and of their functions, as well as by the subordination of the latter to pro-creation. From the standpoint of a history of the psychosexual development of the human, this characterization appears incom-plete and in need of certain addenda based on a number of clin-ical observations.

One can say, to begin with, that the genital phase is distin-guished through *the acquisition of a new erogenic zone, oper-ated with an old partial libido*. This simple statement demands an elaborate elucidation. In entering upon it, one will find it natural to draw mainly upon the sexual life of the female be-cause her anatomy and physiology are so much more extensive than they are in the male. Yet the explanation will be circuitous, not merely long; and it may even be unsatisfactory, for I have found it nowhere as difficult as in this instance to cover the simultaneity of conditions through a sequence of their enu-meration.

The new zone should be characterized anatomically, pleasure-physiologically, and psychologically; and the last is equivalent to a description of the vicissitudes of preoedipal sexuality, i.e., the continuing of its functioning in a normal genital organiza-tion. The old partial libido should be shown to be newly em-ployed, and the attempt should be made to delimit this normal employment against a morbid, regressive one which interferes with, instead of sustaining, genital function. All of this should at the same time be fitted into the framework of Freud's theory of instinctual discharge, i.e., the theory of a psychosomatic oc-currence, effecting ejaculation and sexual affect (*Sexualaffekt*) in both partners.

I must, in view of the magnitude of this task, allow myself to use inhomogeneous sources, to present impressions where I lack proof, and to hope for a lenient reader. My results will be fragmentary at that.

Anatomically, the new erogenic zone acquired by the pubes-cent girl, consists of the *proximal two thirds of the vagina and the womb*.

It will be remembered, by contrast, that the distal third of the vagina is anatomically vestibular and pleasure-physiologically phallic. (Cf. p. 145.) This is why, for instance, certain women call their intercourse normal when closer investigation reveals that they respond to the man's frictions merely with the vestibular phallic pleasure organ, and with an orgasm that is, qualitatively, clitoridian. It is the participation in this response of the distal third of the vagina, besides the introitus, that supports their self-deception and allows them to remain unaware of the anesthesia of the two proximal thirds.

The old libido, engendered and discharged in this new erogenic zone, is *oral*. Freud has all but said so himself. "It is not without good reason," he wrote in one place (36B), "that the child sucking at his mother's breast has become the model for every love relation. The finding of an object is really a re-finding of it." And "it is at the height of the lover's paroxysm," he wrote elsewhere (55), "('I could devour you from love') . . . that the erotic aim of the oral organization re-appears."

III. A PRIMITIVE EROGENIC MODEL

Having lifted these remarks out of their context, one may attempt to replace them in that of a theory of instinctual discharge. Instinct is a psychosomatic concept; instinctual discharge must therefore be thought of as a psychosomatic occurrence. On the somatic side Freud has assumed—and we can certainly do no better—that sexual substances (*Sexualstoffe*), i.e., hormonal-metabolic products, accumulate in the zone, charge it, and produce psychological sexual stimulation. He found it somewhat strange (*einigermassen befremdend*) "that this one stimulus appears to demand abolishment by a second, applied to the same place" (36C).

I find it strange that Freud found it so, since it was he who established, as has been mentioned above, the nursling as the model. In describing the infant's sensual sucking (*Wonnesaugen*) which separates for the first time the oral-libidinal gratification from the intake of food, he calls the second "quasi-erogenic" zone which is sucked (such as, e.g., the thumb) "inferior," and a mere substitute for the lips themselves. His analysis of the matter culminates in the ingenious verbalization expressing the nursling's disappointment over this inferiority: "What a pity, that I cannot kiss myself" (36), i.e., profit from the employment of a full-fledged and dominant erogenic zone. If this formula is as profound as I believe it to be, it implies a continuous process: the lips are charged with sexual substances and the charge provokes vascular dilation, such as their turgor in the aroused mature woman allows one easily to observe. When the charge reaches a certain threshold a muscular reflex is set into motion which, in the case of the infant's imaginary kissing himself, would initiate discharge. The muscular action is of a spastic nature and the discharge of the sexual substance is one into the blood stream, accompanied by an unknown metabolic process and terminating in a gradual flowing back of the blood, ending the hyperemia. Sexual tension, climactic pleasure, and gratification are the psychological phases concomitant to this physiological sequence. *Here then is the most primitive hypothetical model for the instinctual discharge of an erogenic zone.*

A female patient, who had always been able to perform orgastically in intercourse, experienced, nevertheless not infrequently, nocturnal orgasms and maintained for a long time that she did not need partners. "I can do it all myself." Her complete enjoyment of intercourse was at first puzzling; for the neurotic is usually observed to be sexually deficient. During a long analysis it became clear that the better part of her sexuality had remained preoedipal—men were no more than nurses; while the fixation upon a mother devoid of all human feeling had forced the attractive girl, while desiring marriage and children, to stay single; and to transfer the early mouth upon the vagina.

It is this last fact that renders it possible to use one of her self-observations as an illustration for some of the points made above. She reports waking up on the verge of an orgasm from a dream in which she sees a certain man representing the transference object sitting down and writing love poetry to her. The excitement becomes strongest when she suddenly sees a page of handwriting of his such as she is accustomed to see upon entering the office. (It may be added that in life, mental stimulation by a man is of extreme importance to her; it is another form of being nursed which she both craves and fears. The fear is that of not being able to hold her own in the conversation; it is but another instance of her inability to give, by which her life is dominated: she receives.) Upon arousal, she engages in a combination of pressure and pulling up of the buttocks, extending toward the front until "something inside comes together" which leads to an orgasm, "high up inside." Careful questioning sustained the impression that what came together could only have been the vaginal walls,[2] so that, allowing for the displacement, one could borrow Freud's words, and say that this patient is literally able to "kiss herself."[3]

IV. ELABORATION UPON THE MODEL

When genitality is attained, and the discharge is brought about by sexual intercourse, a number of complications require elaboration upon the model. In the first place, the libido involved and commonly called "genital," is, as Freud has taught us, a composite. Forepleasure and auxiliary pleasure ("by-play," cf. p. 196) testify to contributions from *several* erogenic zones; there are, e.g., anal components in the olfactory, and anal and phallic ones in the scoptophilic enjoyment, as well as in the tactile excitation, active and passive, of the sexual partners' skin; the "kindling function" (Freud) of the clitoris is, of course, phallic. Nevertheless, the indispensability of the kiss, the particular excitability of the breast, the olfactory "intake," and, if the "unit of mouth and eye" (cf. pp. 55-60) be recalled, the better part of all scoptophilic contributions—all

---

[2] Apparently the most proximal portions, forming the fornices; whether or not a contraction of the uterus was involved could not be ascertained. But it is probable because in other instances the performance was assisted by manual pressure on the abdomen at about the place where the uterus ought to be.

[3] This is thrown into still more relief when one compares the oral-erotic performance described here, with the phallic one, also issuing from the buttocks, described on p. 146. I have omitted the analysis of the anal-erotic admixture of both character and masturbation as impertinent to the present illustration.

show the oral partial libido prevailing over all others in initiating and sustaining the act. The seizing upon each other by the partners is, finally, likewise an introjective gesture, and one that recalls the auxiliary role of the hand. (Cf. p. 60.)[4] In the second place, one must assume a libido regression during intercourse, and remember Freud's finding that a regression of the libido has to be thought of as accompanied by a defusion of instincts. (The far-reaching consequences of this assumption will be stated further below.) In the third place, one is compelled to suppose that the act is accompanied by a regression of ego, the description of which will be attempted hereinafter; the material for it can be found in a little-known place of Freud's work (51).

A. THE CONCEPT OF PARTIAL SUBJECT AND PARTIAL OBJECT

The ego of both the sexual subject and object regresses to what I suggest calling a "partial subject" and "partial object." *Subject* and *object* in these terms mean what they always mean: each partner is to his own self the subject, to the other an object. *Partial* denotes a reduction of ego, occurring gradually, and ending in a condition in which the ego, topographically, is but an appendage[5] of the genital zone, and, dynamically, the executive of its erogenic function.

Freud (51) has virtually described partial subject and partial object without naming them so; he speaks of "representations that derogatorily replace a whole person by one of their organs, e.g., the genitals," of "unconscious phantasies leading to the identification of the genitals with the whole person," and finally of "jocular idioms such as 'I am all ears.'" In doing so he implies that the ego can be found reduced to the partial subject, or partial object, of any erogenic zone but that the genital zone is preferred.

---

[4] The orality is apparently felt so strongly by the sensitive French, that *baiser* (= to kiss) has become slang for "having sexual intercourse" while *embrasser* (= to embrace) has come to mean kissing.

[5] For the term "partial object" in the sense of this definition, cf. p. 21, where Bismarck's dream and Leonardo's drawing represent "the mother, reduced to her sexual parts."

Both these facts are true, but since only the second is pertinent to the present topic, I shall quote and analyze only the second of his illustrations. It is a myth and its sculptural representation.

THE DRAWING OF BAUBO

From Freud: *A Mythological Parallel to a Visual Obsession.* Col. P., Vol. IV

The Legend: "According to Greek legend Demeter came to Eleusis in search of her daughter who had been abducted, and was taken in and housed by Dysaules and his wife Baubo; but in her great sorrow she refused to touch food or drink. By suddenly lifting up her clothes and exposing her body, however, the hostess Baubo made her laugh. A discussion of this anecdote, which is probably to be explained as a no longer intelligible magic ceremonial, is to be found in the fourth volume of Salomon Reinach's work, *Cultes, Mythes, et Religions,* 1912. In the same passage mention is also made of terracottas found in excavations at Priene in Asia Minor, which represent Baubo. They show the body of a woman without head or bosom, and with a face drawn on the abdomen: the lifted clothing frames this face like a crown of hair" (51A).

The Analysis of the Legend: The "magic ceremonial," contained in the legend, becomes intelligible again when one avails oneself of the assistance of the sculpture and of the clinical observation reported on p. 202. The Goddess of fertility, mourning the loss of her child and refusing to eat and drink, plays obviously the role of a daughter in the house of Dysaules and Baubo. What the mother shows her, is herself, reduced to a procreative partial subject. In so doing she consoles her by gesture: we mothers can have (other) children; no need to grieve (over this one). In attempting to explain why she is so successful that the aggrieved child turns to laughter, one cannot avoid separat-

ing actually inseparable phases of a process. For one thing, the
procreative partial subject, as the terracotta depicts it, dispenses
—as does all antique sculpture (cf. pp. 171 f.)—with the external
female genital; but so does my patient: both pelvic action and
manual pressure are exerted directly and selectively upon the
fornices and the womb. For another, the word "suddenly" appears in both legend and dream report: Demeter is taken by
surprise and so is my patient, who produces a "threshold symbolism" in her dream. Questioned about the "suddenly," she
explained that the page of handwriting appeared not in con-
tinuity with what she had been seeing but abruptly, and big,
"like a close-up" in front of her face. It may well have represented the breast; because in one of the subsequent hours she
"remembers" for the first time the nursing breast of the mother
with the milk overflowing on it. (The mother's lactation had
actually been excessive.) Both my dreamer and Demeter introjected the mother through the eye, the earliest auxiliary to the
mouth: my patient probably the "mamma," Demeter the procreative maternal partial subject. The effect was in both a
sudden cathectic displacement, releasing (counter-) cathectic
energy which became discharged orgastically in the case of the
patient, and through laughter in the case of Demeter.

The introjection was, of course, only a re-introjection; but it
was instrumental in an acute re-identification with the maternal
partial object, such as is requisite (see below) to the female
genital function. This bit of theory remains, however, incomplete if one fails to recognize that the maternal partial object is
preoedipal—it is, in Demeter's case, the mother reduced to the
(mother's) belly on legs—and to remember (cf. p. 76) that all
preoedipal sexuality consummates an identification.

¶   ¶   ¶

In order to complement the necessarily crude analytic discussion with the most subtle rendering of those experiences that
this discussion attempts to order, I would like to refer the reader
to the *Annunciation to Mary* by Rilke (112), whose art in saying the unsayable remains for our time unparalleled. Note: the
suddenness, and the ocularly procreative introjection; the clash-

ing of eyes between angel and virgin; the union seeing and what is seen; and, finally, the discharge: the singing.

MARIÄ VERKÜNDIGUNG	ANNUNCIATION TO MARY
Nicht dass ein Engel eintrat (das erkenn),	Not that an angel entered (mark that)
erschrechte sie. So wenig andre, wenn	was she frightened. No more that others when
ein Sonnenstrahl oder der Mond bei Nacht	a sunbeam or the moon at night
in ihrem Zimmer sich zu schaffen macht,	busies itself in the room,
auffahren—, pflegte sie an der Gestalt,	do startle—, would she, accustomed to the shape
in der ein Engel ging, sich zu entrüsten;	in which an angel goes, be indignant;
sie ahnte kaum dass dieser Aufenthalt	hardly aware (even) that this
mühsam für Engel ist. (O wenn wir wüssten,	is burdensome for angels. (O if we [but] knew
wie rein sie war. Hat eine Hirschkuh nicht,	how pure she was. Did not a hind
die, liegend, einmal sie im Wald eräugte,	that, reclining once espied her in the wood,
sich so in sie versehn, dass sich in ihr,	so lose itself in looking into her, that in her
ganz ohne Paarigen, das Einhorn zeugte,	quite without siring, was begot the unicorn,
das Tier aus Licht, das reine Tier—.)	beast of light, pure-beast—.)
Nicht, dass er eintrat, aber dass er dicht,	Not that he entered, but that he
der Engel, eines Jünglings Angesicht	the angel closely, so inclined the face of youth
so zu ihr neigte, dass sein Blick und der	about her that his glance and that
mit dem sie aufsah, so zusammenschlugen,	with which she looked upward, so clashed together,

als wäre draussen plötzlich alles leer	as though all outside suddenly were empty
und, was Millionen schauten, trieben, trugen,	and what millions see, do, bear,
hineingedrängt in sie: nur sie und er;	were crowded into them: only she and he;
Schaun und Geschautes, Aug und Augenweide	seeing and what is seen, eye and eye's delight
sonst nirgends als an dieser Stelle —: sieh,	nowhere else but at this point—: look,
dieses erschreckt. Und sie erschraken beide.	this does terrify. And terrified they were.
Dann sang der Engel seine Melodie.	Then the angel sang his melody.
	(Translation: E. and R. F.)

B.   THE FEMALE GENITAL PARTIAL SUBJECT: PART I

The partial subject discussed above is *pregenital;* it centers around the *Mutterleib* of the "uncastrated" mother, and exploits the child's ignorance of the vagina. The *genital* partial subject centers around the proximal portion of the vagina and the womb, and extends to the skeletal parts of the body requisite to performing the sexual act. One may compare it, after a fashion, to the "parturitive organ" (*Gebärorgan*), a term coined by the gynecologist Sellheim, who embodied under it all of the well-known anatomical changes of the genital tract during pregnancy, if one remembers that in the present instance the changes occur during intercourse, and are, with regard to the body, physiologic; with regard to the body-ego, cathectic.

If it is true that the ego, in general, as Freud has expressed it, "is in the first place [*vor allem*] a body ego," this is still more so in the ego when reduced to its genital parts and functions. Thus an investigation of the genital partial subject is essentially that of a regressive condition of the body-ego. If one appreciates that the regression occurs in the course of function, one is apt to recall Freud's late remark (73A) that it is possible that the "topographical differentiations [of the ego] . . . become altered and undergo a temporary involution during a function," and that "this seems to be true in particular with regard to the phylogenetically last and most tenuous one, the differentiation between ego and superego." The earliest parent is, as Freud has taught us, at the time of the dissolution of the oedipus complex, introjected and deposited in the superego. In the case of the girl, where the dissolution coincides with the entry into the genital phase, the earliest mother is, I have observed, simultaneously introjected and deposited in the body-ego. The seat of this deposition is the womb.

This is epitomized in the German word for the organ: *Gebärmutter* (parturitive mother; French: *matrice*). It is unfortunate that I must support this contention by various observations without the benefit of having dealt systematically with the body-ego, and with the symbol as representative of the elements of the body-ego. Yet the present volume is not devoted to these subjects; I shall therefore restrict myself to a brief remark about the relation between body and body-ego.

The body-ego, an essentially preconscious psychic formation, reflects the body through illusions about it; and its elements are representative not of organs indicable by a medical term but of functional—in the present case, pleasure-physiological—combinations of organs. It is in this sense that the statement: the womb is the seat of the earliest mother introjected into the body-ego, is to be understood. The reflection of the *Gebärmutter* in the body-ego differs from the uterus much in size and indefinably in shape; and in addition, it includes a proximal portion of, if not in some instances perhaps all, of the vagina. It appears to entertain, furthermore, certain relations that I have not too well understood, with the breast.

In order to illustrate this relation I shall again, as I did when quoting Freud with the Demeter example, oppose a legend to a clinical illustration.

The Legend: The Kojiki, or Record of Ancient Matters (712 A.D.), the oldest recorded history of Japan, describes how the

Sun-Goddess, Amaterasu O-mikami, ". . . had been offended by
the playfulness of her brother, and . . . in a fit of sulking had
hidden herself in a cave and had sealed the opening with a great
rock. Since the world was in darkness as a result of her concealment, the other gods assembled to persuade her to show her
face again. One of the assembly, Amano-Uzume-no-Mikoto
(translated by: 'Her Augustness Heavenly-Alarming-Female'),
elaborately clad, placed a sounding-board outside the cave and
stomped until it resounded, 'and doing as if possessed by a deity,
and pulling out the nipples of her breasts, pushed down the
skirt-string *usque ad privatas partes*.'

"This spectacle caused the gods (eight myriad of them) to
laugh until the Sun-Goddess, piqued by curiosity, looked to see
for herself what had caused the uproar. Once she had pushed
back the rock from the cave, she became interested. After she
had watched the performance for some time, she felt appeased,
and returned to her place in the heavens" (11).

A Clinical Observation: I was acquainted only recently with
this legend but felt gratified to be able to parallel it with a
clinical observation, recorded long ago. To draw the parallel to
its full length I must expand briefly upon the occurrence reported on p. 151. It will be immediately evident that here
again, the gods' discharge in laughter is, in the case of the
patient, orgastic. But there are a few other data that correspond.
The patient, much worried about the inferiority of her nipples,
had lived with a mother with small breasts and huge nipples,
which chronically protruded and fascinated the daughter. During her analysis she had lengthy and conflictuous dealings with
a mother figure who, on one occasion, absent-mindedly briefly
performed the exact exhibition of Amono-Uzume-no-Mikoto for
the benefit of the patient. There is, finally, an obvious contradiction in the legend: if "the world was in darkness as a result of
[the sun-goddess'] concealment," how could Uzume's act have
been seen? My patient's parents slept next to her until puberty,
but she maintained for years that she saw nothing, and could
not have, "since it had been too dark." In the beginning of her
analysis, the patient felt certain that she had never seen a man's
penis; when it later appeared that she was having intercourse

only in the dark, and she was asked about it, she was absolutely aghast at the outrageous implication of this question. Once in particular, when the lover wanted to bare her breasts, a violent tussle ensued and she held tightly onto her brassiere.

Analytic comment: I am aware that, in opposing the case to the legend, I am not making much of a point. I intended merely to illustrate the relation, of which I said that I did not sufficiently understand it,[6] of the genital partial subject to the breast. When one compares the Japanese to the Greek legend it appears that, in both, mourning is terminated through laughter in consequence of the ocular incorporation of a procreative partial subject. (The very contradiction to darkness lends emphasis to this scoptophilic introjection; how it is to be reconciled to the theory of mourning—and, if there were one, to that of laughter—can not here be discussed.) Yet while the older myth features the belly, the younger one features the breast in the partial object; not, however, without representing—compensatorily, as it were—birth in the subject by means of a partial-subjective symbolization through the cave from which the "child" gradually emerges.

In handing on this material to future workers one can hardly refrain from referring to the "rock" (cf. p. 210) with which the sun-goddess sealed her cave, and to the breast (cf. p. 24) with which Leonardo equipped so illogically the median section of the maternal partial object. Nor can one leave it unmentioned that the patient, adduced on pp. 202 and 206, stated several times that "there is a connection" between the breast and the upper portion of the vagina which she felt when she was excited;[7] and that Leonardo drew this connection in the shape of a duct (cf. p. 23), linking mammilla, mamma, and womb.

[6] Breast feeding is known to evoke occasional sexual feelings. Their analytic investigation, the knowledge of the conditions under which they arise, and, in particular, that of their seat should elucidate this relation.

[7] It is bewildering, but it must nevertheless be recorded, that this "connection" had an infantile model. The patient reported close to the beginning of her analysis how at the age of nine her mother saw her playing with her nipple and exclaimed: "Don't do that. You'll get sick from it!" It was only much later that she remembered obtaining vestibular sexual sensations from this play and said: "That was what frightened me and made me mind her."

C. REPRESENTATIONS OF THE PARTIAL SUBJECT

The representation of the female genital partial subject in the body-ego is, as is all representation, either direct or indirect; in the latter instance it is most often symbolic. I shall adduce hereinafter one clinical observation illustrative of the former, and several of the latter (numbering those to be discussed later under another heading).

1. A Direct Representation: "The Spot"

Example 1: I have once recorded (17), although without then understanding it, the role played by a certain part of her anatomy which she called "the spot," in the love life of a homosexual patient. This sexually excitable spot was "a circumscribed area . . . located in the middle of the abdomen about halfway between the upper edge of the pubis and the navel." It is only now that I know that the "spot" did not belong to the integument but was internal, and that I can identify it as representative of the combination of womb and fornices mentioned on p. 208. The patient who had a passive woman friend was accustomed first to sucking the latter's breast, then to lying on her, kissing her, tongue in mouth, finally straddling the thighs, while rubbing her genitals on them and touching the partner's. This performance precipitated an orgasm; but it did so only under one mandatory condition: the "spot" had to be borne upon manually or by the abdomen of the partner. "Hitting" this spot, while pressing her naked stomach on the woman's, was "what mattered" in the relation; and gave her the feeling that "nothing would touch or hurt you again if this spot was touched in this way."

All additional information about the spot, contained in the record, either supplies or reiterates properties of the procreative genital female partial subject. Having the spot touched reminded the patient of the "grumbling" in her mother's belly which, as a child, made her anxious lest a new sibling might be born; and the spot entertained a direct connection to both her own mouth and the sucking of the friend's breast. "Hitting the spot" was linked to kissing the friend by putting the tongue

> into her mouth "as far as you can go"; and the sucking of her breast to lying on her "nice, big, soft stomach." "But," she added, "there is something about being buried about this." Asked to explain, she translated her symbolic utterance: "I mean having her arms and legs around me . . . getting inside of her . . . wanting to be enveloped by her" which is "like being swallowed by her."

Need I comment again on the oral libido involved, the pre-oedipal aim, or the incorporation consummated in the performance? I think not. I should merely remark that the picture is not as complete as it would be if I could draw it from observation today. The role of the rest of the vagina, exclusive of the fornices, is, for instance, not clear; nor is the patient's breast even mentioned. One may infer that the vagina here plays a subordinate role; and find the partner's breast taking the place, as it were, of the patient's. ("What a pity that I cannot kiss myself . . .") One may note the accord of the survival of preoedipal sexuality in an adult with an erogenic combination consisting essentially of mouth, *Gebärmutter,* clitoris and "mother's belly." One may, finally, be aware how these parts seek the corresponding ones of the partner, so that the act leads eventually to an identification of partial subject and partial object.

¶ ¶ ¶

Here again the clinician's description may be complemented by the poet's, and an unsublimated by a sublimated performance. In Rilke's *Life of the Virgin Mary* (112) his *Visitation* follows the *Annunciation* (quoted above).

MARIÄ HEIMSUCHUNG	VISITATION OF MARY
Noch erging sie's leicht im An- beginne,	Still she walked it smoothly in the beginning,
doch im Steigen manchmal ward sie schon	Yet in climbing sometimes she was already
ihres wunderbaren Leibes inne,—	aware of her wondrous belly,—
und dann stand sie, atmend, auf den hohn	and then she stood, breathing, on the high

Judenbergen. Aber nicht das Land,	Hebrew mountains. Yet not the land,
ihre Fülle war um sie gebreitet	but her fullness was spread about her;
gehend fühlte sie: man über-schreitet	walking she felt: one never transcends
Nie die Grösse, die sie jetzt emp-fand.	the greatness that she now felt.
Und es drängte sie, die Hand zu legen	And she craved, to lay her hand
auf den andern Leib, der weiter war.	on the other belly, that was fur-ther [wider].
Und de Frauen schwankten sich entgegen	And the women swayed (the) one to the other
und berührten sich Gewand und Haar.	And touched each other garment and hair.
Jede, voll von ihrem Heiligtume,	Each, full of her heavenly load
schützte sich mit der Gevatterin.	Shielded self with kinswoman,
Ach der Heiland in ihr war noch Blume,	Ah the Savior in her still was bud,
doch den Täufer in dem Schoos der Muhme	But the Baptist in the cousin's womb
riss die Freude schon zum Hüpf-en hin.	already, joy-impelled, was leap-ing.

(Translation: E. and R. F.)

¶ ¶ ¶

The very same "spot" came dramatically into being in the re-analysis of a patient.

> In her first analysis she lay most frequently on her left side, often with her legs somewhat drawn up. I had allowed this because I thought that its various meanings in the transfer-ence—contact with me, sitting on my lap, being dropped from it at the end of the hour, etc.—had become evident and had been reduced to childhood patterns. In the beginning of her

second analysis I was able to recognize my permissiveness as a severe technical mistake. What I had overlooked was that the patient had exploited this position for an unnoticeable and unconscious masturbatory gratification of small quantities of sexual excitation which kept her sexuality in the transference suppressed. I explained this, termed it explicitly a mistake and invoked the abstinence rule against it. At first her reaction to having to lie on her back was that she felt numb from the waist down and felt as though she had no legs at all.

Soon, however, in the course of an hour whose content I fail to remember, she was seized with an extremely strong sexual urge of the kind of her nocturnal ones (cf. pp. 202 f.) and of which she was convinced that it would have become orgastic had she assisted it with a squeezing of thighs and a manual pressure on the "spot."

In order to recognize that it was again the introjection of the mother that mobilized the *Gebärmutter* I must give the following data: my office is fairly roomy, sunny, and "warm"; it has curtains, pictures, and always flowers or greens; it is the opposite of what is called "functional" in the modern architect's parlance. The patient, however, had insisted throughout her first analysis that it was nothing but "four walls," while occasionally explaining that it represented my wife to her, whom she had, on one or two occasions, seen in the apartment house hall, and whose appearance she had liked. When, in the second analysis, "the transference," as Freud expresses it, started to "furnish the energy quanta for the continuation of the treatment," she soon changed her mind, and began to enjoy the warmth, the aesthetic qualities, and what she called the *Gemüt* of the room. It was this replacement of a cold, unloving mother by a warm and loving one that made it possible to introject her into the womb in the transference situation. (For the mother's being "around" the individual instead of "in" her, see Freud's remark about it quoted on p. 179, fn., b.)

2. *Indirect Representations*

a. "Mother Comes In"

If, in the body-ego, the "womb" is the seat of the early mother who became located there by introjection, it is expectable that, under certain conditions, the mother will appear in projection as a symbolic representation of the "womb." This is indeed so: for instance, in menstrual dreams.

At the onset or at the cessation of a menstrual period the womb enters, relatively speaking, into or disappears from the body-ego in consequence of its relative prominence in the body as a result of the glandular cycle. In dreams symbolizing this entry the mother enters the room. (One can, of course, say to this, and to all other representations described in the section, that they reflect the partial *object* rather than the partial *subject;* but it is meaningless to say so, because the latter is established through introjection of the former with the result that they have eventually become the same.) I have hardly ever heard that such a dream occurred near the middle of the menses; it is almost always dreamt at the beginning or at the end. Why the recess of the womb in the body-ego should also be symbolized by the mother's entry, is not clear.

I shall present three examples. All of them, as well as the ones further appended, are taken from different patients.

Example 2: The first dream was probably dreamt immediately before, possibly immediately after, the onset of menstruation:

"I was in something like a resort hotel or apartment house where there were a lot of rooms, halls and people. I was with this man *Hugh* that I knew many years ago. I wanted more than anything to have intercourse with him and we were looking for a place where we could be alone. We went into his apartment and went to bed together. He kissed me, touched my genitals but that wasn't what I wanted. I wanted him inside of me and almost at once he put his penis in me. He touched *way up in-*

side of me and I had this tremendous sensation of *ecstasy* so overwhelming that I *cried out*. I've never known a feeling like that. It took all of me. Right afterward I suddenly wondered if I'd remembered to use a pessary and then decided that I didn't care anyway. I wanted him too much to stop. And then *his mother came into the apartment* at that moment and *we had to stop*. She didn't seem to realize what we were doing although she must have seen us. I was disappointed and worried because I thought now Hugh will not want to go on. He won't want me any more. I was really surprised to find he did want to go on and with me wanted to find a place where we could be alone. We went to my room but I shared it with two other people and one of them was there asleep. We put up a screen but this was no good and the dream just petered out. Somewhere before we went to bed in my room I did find out that I was wearing a diaphragm. When I woke, I knew the man in the dream was not this Hugh I had known."

The dream appears as one of "getting well," a *Genesungs-traum;* but it was actually one of those of which Freud has warned against thus interpreting them because they foreshadow nothing and are merely wish fulfillments. In her waking life the patient had only clitoris orgasms; vaginal stirrings turned into vaginal pain or concomitant rectal sensations. In the dream, under the menstrual impact, she fulfills the wish for a procreative orgastic gratification from the transference object (Hugh = you). The seat of the gratification is "the spot," located "way up inside" and in the middle of her orgastic experience (his) *"mother .comes in"* (to the apartment). In the latter part of the dream the mother is symbolized by the familiar "two (other) people" (cf. p. 18); although it is here not the mother who enters the room but the dreamer. (For further comment on this part, cf. p. 244, Ex. 2.)

Example 3: The second dream was dreamt on the last day of her menstruation by the mistress of a patient afflicted with ejaculatio praecox. She had told it to him, he wrote it down for me in a foreign language, and I have translated it word for word:

> "X dreamt that we lay together completely undressed, and that I, while amusing myself with her, had an ejaculation all over the rug. She was neither angry nor annoyed. But I put my head in rage on the pillow. She asked me why I was angry, and I said because I didn't want to come as yet; I wanted to hold off in order for it to last a little longer.
>
> "At that moment *her mother arrived*. She was in her nightgown, looked very well and smiled.
>
> "In the situation in which we found ourselves we did not know where to hide. But nothing happened."

Here the cessation of menstruation enabled the dreamer, of whom I know that she wanted to marry my patient and have a child by him, to a symbolic gratification of the same nature as that obtained in the first dream. To recognize this, one must possess oneself of three different data. (1) The equivalent of the word "arrive" occurs three times in the original dream report: "to come" is "arrive at enjoying," the mother "arrived," and "nothing happened" is "nothing has arrived." (2) The rug in a room, if it is a symbol at all, symbolizes, in my experience, the womb. (3) The dreamer herself was subject to a deep-seated disturbance, aggravated by the damming-up of much resentment justified by the shabby character of my patient. This and the fact that the report is a second-hand one may explain the paucity of affective experience in the first part of the dream.

Thus, when the lover "arrives," ejaculating into the "womb," the "mother arrives" and approves. The negation, where "nothing has arrived," is analogous to that in the preceding dream and will be commented upon in the same place. (Cf. p. 244.)

Example 4: The third dream is premenstrual. It is atypical because it attempts to elaborate upon a traumatic experience, but it displays, nevertheless, enough typical traits. The patient had had an upsetting experience with a mother figure, went eventually to sleep but was awakened by the "yipping of a dog and the squeaking of a car's brakes or tires." This led to a possibly hypnopompic experience. "The sound," she describes, "made me feel as though someone had grabbed the upper part of my womb and twisted it so that the neck cramped." Finally she falls asleep again and immediately afterwards has a long dream, which begins:

> "I was partly sleeping, and partly waking on a small bed in the same room with my mother. I wanted to go to sleep but was afraid to for fear that she would do something to me. She kept getting in and out of bed and pacing back and forth, *in and out of the room . . .*"

In addition, I append two experiences, in which the relation between menstruation and mother coming in has undergone variations.

Example 5: In the first one it is reversed. Certain unusual circumstances made it advisable to have the patient's mother come in for a consultation, to which the patient reacted with a dream (the details of which are inessential) of menstruation that occurred nowhere near her menstrual period.

Example 6: The second is the report on an analytic hour, containing much food for thought.

The patient's legs hurt again; the intensity and the seat of the pain varies, it may go down all the way to the instep and all the way up the thigh.

> Yesterday morning a *dream:* Company, all male, is gathered in her room; father among them. She is clad only in pajamas and begins to menstruate, blood is running down her leg and foot. She asks her father to reach into a cupboard behind her and to hand her her bathrobe, which he does.

Waking up, she finds that her menstruation has actually begun, staining pajamas and bedsheets. While she goes to the bathroom her mother comes into the room, to whom she tells what has happened and with whom she investigates whether the couch cover is also stained, which it wasn't.

The associations to the dream concern two day residues and a memory from adolescence that had never been repressed. Last night the father drove mother and daughter to visit friends and had one of his states of agitation. He complained first about snow which neither daughter nor mother could see, then about icy roads while there was only ice at the edges. His wife's suggestion to return home was answered with: "Oh, we're practically there," while they had done only ten minutes of an hour's ride. With the friends the father was perfectly "calm and nice," and driving back he had no complaints whatsoever. During the argument my patient was peculiarly passive, just watching the parents fight. Later on the father passed her in the hall, with the fly of his pajamas unbuttoned. She looked, would have liked to "see something," but it was too dark; all she saw was "a black triangle." In adolescence she suffered from the severest menstrual cramps, sat on the toilet in the bathroom separating her bedroom from the parents', and pressed her stomach moaning aloud in the hope that "mother would come in" and press the " 'spot' with her cool soft hands."

The analysis of the dream must begin with the acknowledgment that it is a "Dream of Nudity"; it contains the indispensable elements: the partial undress and the disinterested onlookers. At first sight it seems to contradict Freud's remark (31C): "I know of no example where the actual onlookers to those infantile exhibitions reappear in the dream," because the father is there. Second thought has, however, convinced me that the dream is no exception because the "black triangle" belongs actually to the mother who is the real object of the exhibition. This is borne out by the patient's behavior upon arousal as well as by her associations, even if one did not know that she is still fascinated by the mother's *regio pubis* when this lady, who dispenses with underdrawers, sheds her open girdle at night. With this in mind one becomes aware that the blood in the dream takes the path of the pain in the leg and that the ride screens the memory of the primal scene in which the patient looks on and identifies with the mother.

I have long and unsuccessfully wondered what "snow" stands for but when it was suggested[8] that it represents blood, I have more than once had the occasion to confirm this interpretation. Thus the father finds the "road," on which he "drives" to the "visit" and has practically "arrived," covered with blood. (Having visitors, *Besuch haben*, is a German colloquialism for having the menses.) The patient's last association is, in the context of this section, self-explanatory; except for the fact that when asked to localize the cramps, which she had wished her mother to soothe, she indicated exactly "the spot."

To sum up a rather complicated state of affairs: here is a menstrual dream in which the mother fails to come in because it is a "Dream of Nudity" where, for reasons unknown, the object of the exhibition is not allowed to appear. But she enters actually upon arousal and is made subject to an exhibition; to make up, as it were, for her exclusion from the dream.

b. The "Wave Dream"

Example 7: There is another typical indirect representation of the preoedipal partial subject; not, however, in terms of the womb but of the *Mutterleib,* the "mother's belly." It is the "Dream of the Waves," whose manifest contents permits so little variation that I present only one example; when one has heard one or two, one has practically heard them all:

> "I'm standing on a cliff—in one I was living with some people in a house on top of a cliff. The sea is at the foot of the cliff. The waves are very high and keep getting higher. I stand and watch them until they are splashing. Then I see an enormous wall of water approaching. It towers way over me and I'm panic-stricken. I try to run away then as it roars down on me, but I can't make it. The dream always breaks off there with the water right over me but never engulfing me. In the last dream, a few months ago, I was standing on a pebbly shore of a lake—like

8 Personal communication: Dr. Franz Cohn.

Lake Ontario—and I think the bluff was behind me, as it is on Lake Ontario. I watched the waves a long time not believing, I guess, they would reach me and yet I was frightened of them. And again a wall of water roars toward me all of a sudden and I try frantically to climb up the cliff knowing really I can't make it. Again the dream stops there."

The dream always stops there. It is, in all instances known to me, a repetitive dream and a nightmare; and the only variation consists in the occasional lack of the house with several persons in it. What my records fail to answer, because I did not know that I should question the dreamer, is whether the dream coincides typically with the period; the two quoted above were reported, but not necessarily dreamt, on the third day of menstruation.

The dreamer stands on a cliff—an association to the above-mentioned dream was her impulse last Sunday on a walk to throw herself into the Hudson River, which she interpreted spontaneously as the wish for a union with the mother—or she is in a house with someone in it, sometimes no one but herself. This is interpretable as a projection after the fashion set by Freud (cf. footnote 14, pp. 178 f.) and followed in the symbolic interpretation of the "Wolf Man's" nightmare (cf. p. 178): the mother (and the child or children) in the dreamer are around her in the dream. She is gradually being engulfed (cf. p. 213) by the waves, the *Mutterleib* of the mother, the sea. Why the dream is always a nightmare is not clear. I would hazard that it reproduces an early traumatic situation in which the mother's belly is filled with urine (cf. p. 169) and where there is no "womb," i.e., no place to deposit the mother (cf. p. 209) in the body-ego of the child. If this explains why the incorporative intent is traumatic, it does not explain its premature precipitation.

In the particular case of the patient, two of whose wave dreams are quoted above, I have material which may explain the precipitation. Her analysis had rather drastic results in certain areas of her life, and none in others. This was due to the persistent projection upon me of a vicious, perverse mother and a series of later phallic substitutes for her—a projection which she employed for abundant hypnotic evasions. I have elsewhere (20) reported upon her and on the fact that I did not recognize the evasion.

Re-analysis led to the origin of the hypnosis after it had abolished the evasion. At the ages of three and four to perhaps five, i.e., after the mother had given birth to the younger sibling and became pregnant with the youngest, a nocturnal ritual was established. The child used to wake up, call for the mother and they met at the bathroom. Both took their places: the child, wanting to urinate, on the toilet; the mother next to her on the edge of the bathtub. (The patient is sure of the ages, because she remembers how at first her legs stuck out straight and later were let down toward the floor.) The child is unable to urinate and the mother talks softly to her: "Just relax, darling, it will be all right," etc., while stroking her legs, sliding over her genitals, and her back down to the buttocks. It was semi-dark, only the hall light, covered with a towel, shone dimly. Under the influence of the voice and these "passes," which the child enjoyed, she slid gradually into a condition that the patient now spontaneously calls "hypnotic." The ritual ends with a urinary release, and subsequent to it, urination by the mother. The memory of it developed gradually and became eventually clear beyond doubt; it contained only one error: the relative location of toilet and bathtub were exchanged obviously in consequence of an "anal reversal" where right is substituted for left. (Cf. pp. 125 ff.)

The patient's masturbation remained infantile until she was twenty-one; clitoris stimulation yielded pleasure but no climax and was invariably followed by urination. After her first intercourse, during which she was anesthetic, she asked the partner to masturbate her; he refused, telling her she could do that herself. It was this episode that initiated orgastic "puberty masturbation." As for the mother, she kept the habit throughout adolescence and even adulthood, of sliding her hand affectionately way up on the inside of the daughter's leg; and when the patient later visited with the mother she had repeated a puzzling experience. They slept in separate bedrooms; but after the daughter had arisen at night and used the toilet in the common bathroom for urination, she heard the door of the mother's bedroom almost stealthily open and the mother go to the toilet herself.

I have appended these data from later times only to show the survival of what had begun with the ritual; it is the ritual that explains in this patient the premature mobilization of the incorporative intent. She was actually hypnotized by the mother in the phallic period; and of the hypnotist Freud has taught us that he induces the subject to introject him. Thus the child was compelled by the mother to introject her at a time when her body-ego had only a "mother's belly," no "womb." It would befit my hypothesis about the "wave dream" that this patient suffered from dreaming them throughout life.

Needless to add that the traumatic premature mobilization of the incorporative intent must, in other instances, have been brought about on occasions and by means different from the ones reported above; for the wave dream is not infrequent.

Several months after I had written the preceding section I heard for the first time in my experience a patient report two atypical wave dreams. The first of them was dreamt about two or three days before the onset, the second in the night after the cessation, of menstruation.

Dream 1: "I was sitting with X, my mother, Y, and several other unknown people. The face of Y was vague but he had white hair (which he actually has, I met him once fleetingly a few years ago). The boat was jogging along lightly and I was chatting very gaily with X. My mother was sitting quietly on the other side of the boat and talking to some of the unknown people. I was in quite a gay, chatty mood when suddenly I looked up and saw a gigantic black wave of ocean heading directly toward me. It was a mountainous wave—and I thought quickly—I'll hold my breath until it passes over me and I will be alright . . . I thought fleetingly of the others in the boat—but there wasn't time to do anything but start holding my breath—I was also hardly concerned with the others—I was intrigued with the idea that I would be able to save myself with this quick thinking. There was also a sort of feeling of thrill in the fact that I was going to conquer this hazard. With this, a slight fear—but it was challenging. Then the wave hit me, I held my breath, and this mountain was tremendous—much greater than I had anticipated . . . it didn't seem to pass over me—it stayed—My breath was running out . . . I was feeling desperate—the feeling of I couldn't hold it any longer—I must get air—and then I couldn't stand it any longer and I gasped. I felt as if my lungs were about to split and be filled with water. And then I awoke with my head under the blanket, actually gasping for air. I was exhausted and completely breathless."

I was unable to obtain associations except to one element: *the black wave*. To the patient this represents her "mother's vagina coming toward and engulfing" her. However, I think that memories which had emerged lately were elaborated upon in the dream. They concerned bizarre exhibitions of the psychotic mother for the benefit of the phallic child. In one of them the mother sits on the toilet with excessively spread legs, leans back, and urinates in such a fashion that most of it goes on the bathroom floor. The patient believes she saw a large clitoris from which the stream issued. In another memory that had, to the great astonishment of the patient, been recalled with complete clarity in the hour directly preceding the dream, the mother lies, in the nude, on a couch on a summer day with her legs drawn up and plays with herself while telephoning, "probably with a woman," for the benefit of the six-year-old child who looks on. Her facial expression, the fact that she reached no orgasm, and the patient's wish to touch the mother's genital are definitely remembered. The telephone, or telephoning, when a symbol, always represents masturbation.

It was the telephoning that made me suspect (correctly) that the memory screened another one of a similar but orgastic exhibition where the mother breathed heavily, which was elaborated upon in the dreamer's breathing difficulties at the end of the dream. Much of the child's reaction to this second exhibition—unmasterable excitement and extreme frustration—stemmed from a previous primal-scene observation that had permitted the seeing of an unusual amount of detail.

It is at this point that the material agrees well with the general theory of the preoedipal phase as discussed by Ruth Mack Brunswick in her paper (12) written in collaboration with Freud. In studying the child's interpretation of the primal scene one must bear in mind, as the author has expressed it, "the child's capacity for projecting its own desires upon others . . . the counterpart of the passive fantasy of being suckled is [therefore] the active oral fantasy of suckling . . . By the time," she adds, "[that] the active wish to touch the mother's genital is formed, inhibiting influences and prohibitions have usually become sufficiently strong to limit the child in fact though not in fantasy, and not even always in fact to a wish to *see* the mother's genital . . ." (12A). What the author omits is what I have tried to demonstrate in many places in the present monograph: the oral wishes toward the preoedipal mother object, regardless as to whether they concern the mouth itself or its auxiliary, the eye, are intended to consummate an identification. The material following this premenstrual wave dream concerned, therefore, almost exclusively the beginning of puberty and many different ways of having become the mother.[9]

If cannibalistic incorporation, as Freud has found, is the

---

[9] Two illustrations, one where *touching* and one where *seeing* dominates the picture:

(1) On the day when these lines were written a man patient began his hour by reporting that he had been greatly astonished when he saw his latest photograph because he looked so effeminate, which reminded him of a previous occasion on which he heard his voice on a record and found it feminine, high, and whining. He then referred to the end of the last hour before the week end, but could not remember its content. It had concerned a "suspicion," spontaneously verbalized by the patient, that the mother, who definitely had a psychotic make-up and had engaged in many unusual intimacies with him as child and young adolescent, might have allowed him to touch her genitals in the phallic phase.

(2) A woman patient at age ten met the girl who soon became her best friend, and they decided, as youngsters will, to mingle their blood in token of their friendship. Walking through the woods with a pin to be employed for the purpose, they came to feel that this was what everyone did, that they would be different; so they buried the pin in the ground and urinated on it in turn while the other excitedly looked on. It was the mixing of urine on the same spot on the ground that had consciously been substituted for the mixing of blood; the scoptophilic consummation of the intended identification had remained unconscious.

model for identification and if it is also true, as I have observed and attempted to show (cf. pp. 152 ff.), that cannibalistic libido can find a urethral-erotic discharge, some of the associations to the dream in the text (the mother's "phallic" urination) as well as the friendship ritual described in the footnote acquires additional meaning.

> *Dream 2:* "I was jogging through a body of water in a small outboard motorboat with an oldish man who had very kind warm eyes and a comfortable face. I felt very protected by him —He was wearing a slicker and a rain hat and he gave me a feeling of complete capability . . . (suddenly reminds me of a day I went rowing with Z about —— years ago, just the two of us—I had the same feeling—I was discussing Z; on Monday night before this dream). The sea began to get rougher and the water began to splash over the sides of the boat—this man told me not to worry and if a wave came near me to hold my breath until it passed over—and all was well. I had a feeling of great confidence in this man—and as if he had saved me . . . When I awoke (right after this) the man was you and I was thinking of Monday's hour—my great feelings of devastation, but your very warm comfort."

I am not free to report all the associations but must select from them:

To "the man": The analyst who will help her through upheavals. (The "very warm comfort" had followed an hour of character analysis that had upset the patient greatly because she believed character to be unchangeable and inborn. The comfort consisted in nothing but the information that this is not so and that morbid character traits can and must be analyzed just as anything else.) Then a father figure and a certain memory of him which is reproduced in the dream.

To *"the large wave":* The mother's vulva again; but, more prominently, the mother's *derrière*. I interpret that, in view of this last association and of some other material that had lately begun to come up, the repeated emphasis in both dreams on the dreamer's holding her breath must contain the denial of an olfactory gratification. This evokes a hitherto repressed memory in which the child is allowed to come into the mother's bed and to bury her nose in between the mother's buttocks, although with a sheet between them. The olfactory gratification is recalled in detail, followed by the spontaneous question whether or not the child touched the maternal genital at some of those occasions. Knowing the mother's complete inability to gratify the child orally as an infant (she remarks spontaneously in this hour that the mother's breasts were forbidding, said "no," and that she hated the nipples), it is very convincing that the breasts had subsequently to be transferred onto the buttocks, which the patient characterizes as "the only cuddley place" on the mother's body. It is obvious that here the incorporation is not consummated either through mouth proper or eye but is nevertheless accomplished through an appendage of the oral-erotic zone. At the same time passively incorporative anal-erotic experiences and the gratification obtained from them were remembered: the insertion of enema nozzle, suppositories and thermometer by the mother, who on those occasions, in contrast to others, was skillful and gentle, and evoked a "pleasant" feeling "like wanting to go to sleep" in the child.

Here I raised the question: was this hypnotic? The patient's answer remains inconclusive. But I have indirect evidence that it was. Her treatment is a reanalysis; her first analysis had had only limited results because of a passivity that I could not conquer. This had been due to two technical mistakes on my part: one was that I had, as mentioned earlier, allowed the patient to lie on the couch in precisely the position that she now describes as the mother's, and did not recognize this as an acting out. The other was that I had not recognized her abundant "hypnotic evasions" (cf. p. 287, footnote) because I did not know then enough about this particular form of resistance.

To "vulva": Several associations, from which I choose a sudden "feeling" that the mother is squatting over the patient, vulva impending over her face, is coming down on her, and finally encloses her.

I think that the reader studying the preceding material will find that the theory of the typical wave dream that I have tried to establish (cf. pp. 222 f.) explains these atypical wave dreams as well. Among the factors that make them atypical—i.e., different from the typical ones, recorded first—I would suspect the radical difference in the erogeneity of both patients which goes back to the first five years of life.

In the first patient the erogeneity was the usual one, at least inasmuch as the clitoris, the child's "executive" organ furnished sexual stimulation, which was discharged in subsequent urination (cf. pp. 223 f.)—a regime that, although belatedly, was exchanged for orgastic clitoris masturbation. Vaginally this patient was frigid; sexual intercourse induced at first no feeling, later merely vaginal or rectal pain. She showed, in fact, a strange, although not infrequently observed, disinterest in the vagina. In the second patient the state of affairs was reversed. Her vagina became sexually mobilized—it is not exactly known how or when—somewhere during the first five years of life. A colleague, with whom I once discussed this aspect of the case, told me that she had seen such a vaginal mobilization in girls who had undergone tonsillectomy at an early age.[10] My patient underwent this operation at thirteen months, and came to be able to recall how she consoled herself in the hospital with clitoris masturbation. She felt from then on that "there was something wrong with her mouth" and her mother subsequently never failed to assure her that her mouth was ugly. With the onset of latency she abandoned the clitoris so completely that its sensitivity was restored only after years of analysis.

I have elsewhere (18) described that her mouth became transferred onto the vagina; but I did not know then that the transfer, at least partially, had been effected that early. It is imaginable that in consequence of it this child was in some measure better equipped, then are children with the ordinary infantile sexual constitution, to deposit the mother in her body-

10 Personal communication: Dr. Phyllis Greenacre.

ego; and that this might account for the atypicality of her wave dreams, the second of which is not even a nightmare.

D. THE ORALITY OF THE LIBIDO EMPLOYED

1. *Menstrual Dreams*

That it is the preoedipal mother, who in the process of the formation of the female genital partial subject, becomes introjected with the result of an identification, is in good accord with the assumption that the partial subject is charged with, and discharges, oral libido. Evidence for this assumption was presented on p. 204; further evidence abounds in the analytic material about the "spot," the direct representation of the *Gebärmutter* recorded on pp. 212 ff. In the case of indirect representation, however, through "mother's entry," and the "wave," such evidence is either lacking or so circumstantial that it can hardly be made convincing. One has to turn to other menstrual dreams in order to find the orality undisguised.

Three Examples from Three Different Patients

Example 8 (Patient A): "I dreamed we were having a steak dinner at the Cooke's home. I started to compliment Mrs. Cooke but I started my sentence by saying, 'Mrs. Steak . . .' To get myself out of the embarrassment (mistake) I turned to Mr. Cooke and told how Henry the Eighth had been so impressed with the first steak that he had had the cut knighted—and made it Sir Loin.

"We also seemed to be playing a game like chess using little fleshy fingers bent at right angles for chessmen.

"When I woke up I found myself menstruating."

One need hardly mention that steak, often enjoyed almost raw, is a particularly "cannibalistic" food; and that the introjection of the mother, besides being alluded to through her name as such, is alluded to once more in the dream report through "mistake" (= me steak = my steak) even if the dreamer had not spent her childhood, as she did, among Irish people.

Example 9 (Patient B): The second example concerns the report on a day residue and two menstrual dreams contained in my files. The first of them was apparently dreamt before the beginning of menstruation, the second on the first, the second or possibly even the third day.

"Bought some cold sliced roast beef for dinner on March 4th . . . looked at it when I unwrapped it and it repelled me—was too rare and looked bloody—thought no more about it but I didn't eat it. March 5. Woke up that morning about 9 and felt as though I had started to menstruate. I was afraid that some blood had gotten on my pajamas—looked at them and found no stains. Put a tampax in me and went back to sleep—had the following dream:

"X [girl friend] and I were standing in the street [city street] slicing meat off the side of a dead horse. I was carefully examining the pieces of meat when I suddenly had the feeling I was doing something wrong. Turning from the horse, I walked up the street to see if anyone were watching—my eye rested at a parked car in which my father and mother were sitting—they didn't see me—relieved, I walked back to where the horse had been lying. X had disappeared and someone was dragging the animal along by a rope which was tied around its neck. This was the first time I had a full view of the dead horse. It was disgusting . . . I almost felt nauseous. Woke up."

Dream of March 7 or 8: "I was lying on a couch in my dentist's office . . . I was there to have a tooth extracted. The doctor and the nurse were standing over me telling me that this was a new kind of anesthetic . . . I was merely to relax and shortly I would fall asleep—but nothing happened. I felt completely relaxed but sleep wouldn't come. The dentist said he couldn't understand it and that if this didn't work, he'd have to give me Novocain . . . I could see lots of blood, pieces of loose gum falling out with hunks of tooth . . . a very gory mess. I was also worried because this new type of anesthesia hadn't worked on me . . . it worked on everyone else. Why was I different?

"Think I woke up."

The abundant orality need not be pointed out. Yet a few remarks on the dreams and the dreamer appear of interest. Neither dream was analyzable because the dreamer could not, at that time, perform free association. She could only discuss problems, report dreams, incidents, feelings or produce oral-erotic silence. (Cf. pp. 293 ff.) Nevertheless, if the first dream is compared to the preceding one in Example 8, dreamt by another patient, it becomes evident that the mother, to be incorporated through eating and represented through allusion and picturization by "Mrs. Steak" is in the other represented symbolically by the horse. (Cf. pp. 16 and 247.) The day residue, elaborated upon in this symbolization, is sliced roast beef for dinner; and the disgust and the nausea in the dream are reaction formations against the cannibalistic intent.

The second dream is dominated by the fear of castration; but the castration is oral. It is really a dream of analysis—the patient had, a month ago, dreamt "I was in your office but it wasn't your real analytic room" . . . instead a dentist's office—and the day residue is the "unfinished thought": why can I not associate if everyone else can? But she cannot; because the analyst wants to extract associations from her mouth, mutilating her like the dentist, and prove her mother right, who used to show the child menstrual clotting and explain it as pieces of ovary that had been torn away. Her silences, incorporative of the analyst (cf. p. 72) who represented the breast, and defensive against mutilation (cf. pp. 74 f.) prevailed at all times; but it took the menstrual period to bring the cannibalism, active and passive respectively, into a dream.

Example 10 (Patient C): The third example stems from a very resistive patient whose morbidly punitive superego denied her a positive transference when awake, and, as censor, compelled her to excessive secondary elaboration when asleep. I shall therefore, in order to simplify matters merely quote from the dream; and, in order to be convincing, put it into the context of the hour in which it was reported.

On the eve of the hour she had noticed the beginning of her period and, without sexual excitation, had suddenly "felt that she should masturbate." She did so, ending up in the vaginal use of a toothbrush container, and a locally restricted climax. During all of it she felt anger, and after it the urge to hurl the container away. If the toothbrush is one allusion to the orality of the libido, the absence, for the first time, of a respiratory symptom during this hour is another. In addition, the patient had recently had excessive urges to eat. (In a more detailed description of the symptomatology and its analysis I could show the reintrojection of the mother.) Subsequently a dream, the locale of which was a church:

"It seemed as though I were small but I do not know whether I was a child or just little in size. I was clambering high up on a very large, arched, stained glass window which was much larger than I. The bottom of the window was far below my feet and its top was high above my head. My body against the glass took up a comparatively small space on the window . . ."

There follow two primal scene representations, both in their oral-erotic conception: in the first a couple, "at a huge organ," sang together and "the blending of the male and female voices was very beautiful"; in the second the minister walks down the aisle of the church with the open Bible in his hands, i.e., about to read.

The dream continues: ". . . I was left dangling at the window, far above the floor of the church, clutching the moulding that separated the panes of glass. I flattened myself against the window to make myself as inconspicuous as possible. I dared not move for if I did I might attract the minister's attention, but I was also scared *not* to move, being afraid I couldn't hang on much longer and that I would fall the long distance to the floor. Then when I looked down I saw that almost directly below me there was a large rectangular table around which a number of men and women were seated. A bald-headed man was passing a large white bowl of mashed potatoes to another person. Then I was afraid that if I fell, I might fall on the table.

"Then I woke up."

This menstrual dream is dominated by the representation of birth. The dreamer, instead of getting the mother into her, is therefore in the mother, dangling at the church's "large [!], arched, stained [!] glass [!] window" and about to "fall down" (!). Yet the fall will be one onto a table (!), and into a meal. The group at the table is merely seated, but the analyst, alluded to through his baldness, is passing the potatoes; and if she falls she would obviously supply what is missing: the meat course. She evades into arousal. Her very next dream has the analyst instead of the minister reading from a book, explaining the word "cod-piece" and the dreamer taking a small bite from his shoulder.

It would appear that these three dreams, representative as they are, give further incontrovertible evidence of the cannibalistic libido elaborated upon by the *Gebärmutter,* acquired in puberty as a new erogenic zone.

I append the report of a father on his almost twelve-year-old daughter who at the time had not yet shown any physical signs of the puberty she was about to enter. The family had a table conversation about "civilization"—a topic that the son (a younger child) had brought home from school. In the course of it the girl asks suddenly: *"Daddy, is civilization why parents do not eat their children?"* Subsequent to this the top of a *medicine bottle* is lost and the father helps the child look for it under the bed, where it is found. However, the girl asks him whether God had helped them find it; and the father guesses—and is confirmed by the daughter—that she had been praying to God for the recovery of the bottle top. He explains that they found it because they searched, not because of her prayer, and God's assistance.

There is, obviously, an oral-sadistic as well as an oral-erotic fantasy preparatory to the emergence of the new erogenic zone. The former fantasy is explicit; the latter is only alluded to by the medicine bottle and the prayer, of which I have for long entertained the notion that its instinctual nature is oral-erotic.

About six weeks after the little episode recorded above the girl began to develop breasts.

2. *A Typical Complaint Concerning the First Menstruation*

Freud has found a ubiquitous accusation against the mother: she had not supplied enough milk, has not nursed the child long enough. I have observed a complaint that, if perhaps not ubiquitous, is nevertheless rarely missing: it concerns the role of the mother at the patient's first menstruation. The wording varies: the mother has not enlightened the patient, or she has not told early enough, or she has told but the daughter has treated the enlightenment as *non arrivé;* in one particular instance she must have told, yet what she said is completely forgotten. The variations, as can be seen, are extreme; in the last two cases denial and amnesia take the place of the complaint. Nevertheless, there is almost invariably something wrong with the mother's telling the child about her first menstruation.

> *Example 11:* Paradigmatic material, selected from two sequent analytic hours, shall precede the analysis of the complaint.
>
> *First hour:* The patient had awakened at 4:30 A.M. noticing the onset of her period and experiencing a feeling "as though she had inhaled and could not now exhale but had to hold her breath in her pelvis." She was compelled to get up to go to the toilet several times with loose movements and urination. The symptoms vanished while she had her breakfast coffee and read the paper. All of this is reported in an extremely forced type of speech; each word is separated from the next and literally squeezed out. She is evidently still "holding her breath" and, as far as the pelvis is concerned, imitating a scanty menstrual flow. (Upon questioning she confirms the fact that the flow is actually of this kind.)
>
> Asked to associate to her symptoms, she remembers how at the time of her first menstruation at thirteen she had a backache, lay on the couch with her mother sitting next to her, sewing on a machine and telling her about the menses, which the backache had led her to expect to begin, and "announcing

that from now on there would be a sick time every month."
(They actually started a few months later.) While this went on,
the patient read a paper and pretended not to pay any attention because she resented the mother's not having told her this
earlier. Not that she had not known it; on the contrary: she
had been showered with sexual information by her schoolmates
and had seen many times a manufacturer's pamphlet advertised
with the title: *What to Tell Your Daughter When She Is
Twelve.* This led her to expect that on her twelfth birthday,
the "mother would come in" with the story. (Cf. pp. 216-221.)

The omitted material concerned a conflict about giving birth
that found symptomatic expression in the bowel movements
and one about returning to the womb.

Second hour: I shall confine my report mainly to the inception of this session. She had yesterday completely forgotten to
tell me her "most important" association to the menstrual symptoms. The "holding her breath in the pelvis" is the holding of
her breath when, at ten, she once awoke and noticed that the
(psychotic) mother, with whom she slept, had introduced a
finger into the girl's genital. This incident, in which the daughter "played possum" and pretended to be still asleep, had always been remembered; it was told in the very beginning of
the analysis. But it is only now that an essential addition to it
is recalled: the mother had not, as the original version alleged,
inserted only a finger tip into the vestibular region, but had slid
her whole finger into the length of the vagina.

When it was pointed out to her that the remaining repression concerned two points: the termination of the performance (which is typical for memories of this kind) and her
participation in it, the patient associated a previously reported
dream, which elaborates on the childhood experience in terms
of the transference. (I am remiss in not having noted its relation to the menstrual period.) "I was lying in bed and you were
and were not beside me . . . I kept talking and talking interminably and all the while I talked you were rubbing my
genitals with your finger . . . I felt much physical excitement
and pleasure from your stimulation . . . but the pleasure became
so intense that I did not think I could bear it for another
second and I wanted you to stop rubbing your finger over the

clitoris and labia and insert it into the vagina. For the purpose of directing your finger into the vagina, I guess, I gave a great lurch, but instead, I lurched myself into being awake. I think that I actually did lurch in my sleep."

Analytic Comment: The orality in this material abounds. The mother, who in the patient's childhood had entered the upper part of the vagina, touching "the spot," is at the onset of menstruation reintrojected: she is, fantastically, inhaled and retained in the pelvic region. (I remember another patient who, when she first menstruated, was loath to be in the same room with her mother and held her breath because she "could not tolerate breathing the air with that woman"—a complaint which, at the time when I heard it, I did not understand.) The oral-sadistic libido, collateral to the oral-erotic one is altogether discharged through urination (cf. pp. 152 ff.); having breakfast replaces the intake through breathing and abolishes the complaint. The simultaneous reading of the paper—both in the scene at thirteen and on the morning before the session—is, of course, an ocular introjection of the symbolically represented mother ("paper": Freud). In the dream, finally, "talking and talking interminably"—although this time on the part of the dreamer with the mother object merely agreeing[11]—accompanies the increasing desire for vaginal introjection. It is in this material that the memory of the complaint is encased.

The analysis of the complaint is, as the clinical record shows, simple. Telling the child is to be understood as an oral activity and vehicular to the mother's introjection into the *Gebärmutter,* which makes its appearance in the body-ego on the occasion of the first menstruation. In the neurotic woman this introjection has failed or has subsequently been canceled out, which is why the proximal vaginal portion is anesthetic, hypoesthetic and/or its procreative function denied, abridged, or misplaced.[12] It is not without justification if the patient accuses a mother, lacking in love, for failing to lend herself to this form of identification, requisite to a genital organization. It is merely

[11] Told in the omitted part of the report on the dream.
[12] I am alluding here to the sterile woman, the girl who cannot marry, the frigid, and the unmarried mother.

deceptive that this accusation takes the innocent form of the complaint.

3. *Pregnancy and Giving Birth*

If the reader finds the following section on orality with regard to the procreative aspect of the genital partial subject unsatisfactory, it is because of the relative lack of clinical observation. I have never had the occasion to analyze a woman while she conceived, went through her pregnancy, and gave birth. I can therefore cite only shreds of evidence and must take them from where I have found them.

a. They are perhaps best introduced by a fragment of conversation between Timon and Apemantus.

¶ TIM. Wilt dine with me Apemantus?
¶ APE. No: I eat not Lords.
¶ TIM. And thou should'st, thoud'st anger Ladies.
¶ APE. O they eate Lords;
          So they come by great bellies.
¶ TIM. That's a lascivious apprehension [130].

"Lascivious" means that it concerns earthly, as distinct from heavenly love;[13] in other words, the genital, procreative partial subject alone, and the latter "eats" and in so doing, conceives.

b. Simmel (133) notes that "the vaginal anaesthesia of the frigid woman is a means of defense against the devouring tendency of the vagina, the demands of which unconsciously have been fused with the demands of the mouth." Clinical observation confirms that without leaving room for doubt; and there are reports where it seems that when analysis has undone the fusion, impregnation has occurred, and the two are legitimately considered cause and effect. In an indeterminate number of instances, however, physiology may divorce itself from psychology; hence the many vaginally frigid women who are able to conceive.

13 Webster's moralizing explanation that lust derives from L. *lascivus* = wanton, contains the same distinction. "Lust" denotes bodily appetite; "specifically, and most commonly, sexual desire as violent or degrading passion."

c. Freud's double interpretation of the phobic expectation of "Little Hans" implies an interpretative cross-reference that makes the latent orality in the process of giving birth manifest. In his summing up of the case, Freud determines that of the two fears—"the horse will bite" and "the horse will fall down" —the latter is the deeper one; both, however, the biting and the falling horse are the father who punishes Hans for his bad desires. Yet the "falling horse was . . . not only the dying father but also the mother in the act of giving birth." Freud calls this interpretation "the perhaps . . . most unassailable part [of the analysis]" (38). But, one may add, in the interpretation of the deeper "falling down" (*niederkommen*) = giving birth, the biting is disregarded by Freud; yet it should not be, because it supplies the orality to the parturition.

d. Under the datelines of April 14 and 15, Little Hans tells his father a "phantasy in which he persisted with much obstinacy and which he embellished with much detail" about his little sister Hanna's traveling with the family in a box the summer *before* her birth. Freud remarks: "The effrontery with which Hans related this phantasy and the countless extravagant lies with which he interwove it were anything but meaningless. All of this was intended as a revenge upon his father, against whom he harboured a grudge for having misled him with the stork fable. It was just as though he had meant to say: 'If you really thought I was as stupid as all that, and expected me to believe that the stork brought Hanna, then in return I expect *you* to accept *my* inventions as the truth'" (38C).

This is undoubtedly true. But there are elements in the fantasy that have additional meaning. I shall quote them and ask the reader to supply the context by studying the rest of the conversation.

" '*I:* "What did Hanna eat inside the box?"

" '*Hans:* "They put in bread-and-butter for her, and herring, and radishes" [a Gmunden supper], "and as Hanna rode along she buttered her bread-and-butter and ate fifty times."

" '*I:* "Didn't Hanna scream?"

" '*Hans:* "Sat quite still inside."

" '*I:* "Didn't she push about?"

" '*Hans:* "No, she kept on eating all the time and didn't štir once. Two big mugs of coffee she drank up—until by morning it was all gone, and she left the dung behind in the box, the leaves of the two radishes and the knife for cutting the radishes. She gobbled everything up like a hare: one minute and it was all finished. It *was* a funny scramble. I and Hanna even rode along in the box; I slept the whole night in the box." (We did in fact, two years ago, go to Gmunden by night.) "And Mummy rode in the railway carriage. All the time we ate also in the carriage, too; it *was* fun . . . Hey, what I'm telling you isn't true."

" '*I:* "What isn't true?"

" '*Hans:* "None of it is. Say, let's put Hanna and me in the box[1] and I'll wee-wee into the box. I'll just wee-wee into my pants; I don't care a bit; it isn't shameful at all. You know, that isn't a joke; but it's great fun, though' " (38D).

If Hans, as Freud discovered, had noticed his mother's enlarged abdomen and knew about pregnancy, in other words, about Hanna's having been with them "in the box" on the summer vacation, he had also—as the above fragment shows—observed the pregnant mother's increase of appetite and her craving for spicy food, the bulemia, and *picae gravidarum*. The mother eats more, since she eats for herself and the child;[14] and stimulation and alteration of appetite by the pregnant womb is another bit of evidence for the orality involved in the procreative function. The reader of the preceding chapters will not be surprised to find that the fantasy of the phallic boy supplies the breasts ("two big mugs of coffee") the cannibalistic impatience ("She gobbled everything up like a hare: one minute and it was all finished") and, in the end, the pleasurable urethral-erotic discharge.

     e. In conclusion a direct clinical observation: it is the report of a patient on her experiences, one particular day, between

[1] 'The box standing in the front hall which we had taken to Gmunden as luggage.' [Freud's footnote.]

[14] Cf. Lisbeth about Bärbelchen who got herself pregnant in *Faust I*:
. . . *Es stinkt*
Sie füttert zwei wenn sie nur isst und trinkt.
(It stinks [cf. Hanna's "dung"!] She's feeding
two now when she eats and drinks.)

after luncheon and after dinner. She came home from her
analytic hour, an hour in which she had again been confronted
with her difficulty in communicating with the analyst, ate
lunch and lay down on her couch. She slept for two hours and
was subsequently for about thirty minutes half awake, thinking
how she had been unable to tell her lover that she knew he did
not really want to see her any more. "I felt very discouraged"
her report continues, "I had a strong feeling of how much I
wanted to tell you everything. It seemed to me that I'd been
wanting to tell everything for a very long time. I began to cry.
Opposing that desire came a quick feeling that I shouldn't do
that—it was humiliating, dangerous, somehow shocking, I
guess. I'm not sure just what goes into that feeling . . . I became
very restless. I wanted something to relieve that feeling, but I
didn't know what. Nothing answered it. Shortly after this I
became aware of this strong urge in my mouth and throat. I
don't know how to describe it except it *felt like a sexual urge
only it concerned my mouth and throat*. It was for a few moments a very strong feeling. I had a definite feeling of relief
for a short time after that. Then the restlessness returned worse
than ever. I got up and discovered that I *had started to menstruate*. That startled me at first because I hadn't expected it
and had had no warning cramps. When I figured out the dates,
I realized that it was probably only a few days early, which is
usual.

"I couldn't keep my mind on anything, had no energy and
yet I couldn't relax. I was in the predicament of being unable
to do nothing and yet there seemed to be nothing I could do.
A sad state to be in, don't you think? Then *my throat began
to get sore on the left side*. The soreness continued all evening.
After a while X [roommate] came home. I still felt a little depressed although I felt better when I had someone to talk to.
I hadn't thought I wanted anyone around. We had *dinner*
and abruptly afterward X *told me she was pregnant* and had
to do something about it. *Immediately my restlessness and un-
happiness vanished*. I was cheerful, able to concentrate on her
problem and what we could do. I was pleased about it—not, I
think, because I wanted her to be in a jam but *for some special
personal reason of my own . . .*"

The orality in this material need hardly be pointed out; nor does the rest of the material require comment—were it not for the fact that it recapitulates almost everything that has been said in the preceding pages. It is again the onset of menstruation that stimulates oral desire. The latter takes first the conflictuous form of telling or not telling everything to the analyst, at that time the mother in the transference (cf. pp. 235 f., and the dream on p. 236); and changes subsequently to a strong sexual urge in mouth and throat of an otherwise indefinable nature. It is this urge that gives way to restlessness and the awareness that the period had begun. The patient, asked to write her experience down, interpolates into the description of her condition, which bears resemblance to that of an agitated depression, the gratuitous question, "Don't you think?" followed immediately by reporting the sore throat. (I have observed in analysis that such questions are expressive of oral cravings: the answer should be put into the mouth. (See the discussion of this subject on pp. 92-96.) Then the "mother comes in"—it is the name of the roommate that identifies her as the oral mother—and the patient feels better because she has someone to talk to and to eat with, besides experiencing what could be called a symbolic alleviation. Immediately after the common, i.e., the mutual, meal (cf. p. 124) X reveals herself actually as a mother, and with a "belly that was further" (cf. p. 214) than the patient's. Talk and meal acquire at once the significance of her introjection; and abruptly the patient's condition is cured.

E. THE FEMALE GENITAL PROCREATIVE PARTIAL SUBJECT: PART II

To complete the description of the female genital partial subject, it is necessary to give a long introduction in order to make a small point. It also requires a patient reader who is willing to go, once more, over ten of the examples contained in this chapter and to re-examine them with regard to their affect. It will then become apparent that they show the discharge of aggression, partly oral-sadistic and partly defused. In the case of most of them the material presented is sufficient: only two of them, Examples 1 and 5, demand brief addenda.

1. *A Review of the Preceding Examples in Regard to the Discharge of Affect*

I need hardly dwell on the necessity of introducing and illustrating a point concerning normality, with pathology. It is our method: Freud has shown that in most instances only its morbid distortions allow insight into the structure of a normal condition.

Example 1 (pp. 212 f.): One will remember: "There is something about being buried" in the union of mouth and stomachs, and "it is . . . like being swallowed" by the partner. However, more information can, by way of addenda about the "being swallowed," be drawn from the record (17). The friend "is a lady . . . if there ever was one—a real aristocrat. But you should see her gobbling the food at my house; you should see the greed with which she smokes cigarettes, or eats candy, and it is always my food, my candy . . ." The patient is compelled to call the woman every night, and recognizes this behavior as compulsive. She has to do this because—and here she is groping —there is a certain feeling connected with it, a feeling that "something would happen" if she did not. The woman friend would "explode," would "get me by the throat," would "swallow me." "Yes, a big animal swallowing a little animal, that's what it is. She would eat me, and would explode into little pieces."

It is easy to see in this instance that part of the record quoted here complements the one quoted previously by adding the oral-sadistic instinct component to the oral-erotic one. One must assume that their separate verbalization is expressive of their unreconciled coexistence which is the consequence of a regressive defusion of instincts.

Example 2 (pp. 216 f.): Here the aggression, set free as a result of defusion, has a very different effect: it causes doubt, inhibition and procrastination. This combination is symptomatic of a libido regression to the anal-sadistic stage, which indeed dominated the patient. I have transcribed her dream report in two paragraphs in order to throw the coexistence of libido and aggression into relief. In the first paragraph all is libido; the second is filled with aggression which, instead of being discharged, is turned back onto the self: the originally unambiguous procreative intent becomes ambiguous by "doubting" (wonders about the pessary) inhibited (had to stop), and negated ("H. won't want to go on, won't want me any more"). When the libido makes another attempt at prevailing it is stifled by the aggression with the result that the dream ends as a typical variant of the "dream of inhibition" (*Hemmungstraum*) described by Freud (31F).[15]

Example 3 (pp. 217 f.): Here the defused aggression intruded directly as rage. At first the libido has again full sway: the rug, "all over" which the partner ejaculates, symbolizes the womb; and the dream thus fulfills the wish for impregnation. (That the rage is the partner's who resents his being premature is another wish fulfillment; the dreamer wishes the passive and selfish lover to be interested in her gratification.) The mother's arrival is, again, followed by a negation, resembling the inhibition in the preceding example ("nothing happened").

Example 4 (pp. 218 f.): Here the defusion allows all free aggression to be directed toward the womb for the production of a painful conversion symptom in a state that is probably hypnopompic but at any rate not the state of sleep. In the dream the aggression is fused with libido: the wish for the mother, the womb, and the fear of them are in balance; which is probably why the mother not only does "come in" but alternates between coming in and going out.

Defused and fused aggression are, in other words, separated by prevailing in two different states; and by concerning one time the womb and the other its symbolization.

Example 5 (p. 219): The brief extract must be enlarged by the practically full text of the dream: My mother and I were sitting next to each other in a double bed, taking dictation from a Miss Boucher. She was standing in the far corner of my parents' bedroom—my mother and I were cozy and warm in the

---

[15] I have observed this variant often, although I have never described it: the inhibition, instead of being owned by the dreamer, is projected upon the environment where circumstances foil his intent.

bed as we wrote in our notebooks—we finished writing—Miss Boucher disappeared, the lights went out. A short time later I felt wet—turned on the light and found the sheets soaked with my menstrual blood. My mother looked at them with a revolted expression and said 'Get out of this bed!' I felt terribly ashamed and started to get out."

In the beginning the libido has full sway: the dreamer enjoys a peaceful union with the mother, promoted by a mother figure whose name is not only French but directly representative of the mouth (*bouche* = mouth). In the end the aggression takes over: the dreamer is scolded by the mother who cancels the union, ejecting her as it were, and she experiences a strong feeling of shame.

Example 6 (pp. 219 ff.): This dream is devoid of all affect. The latter appears only in the associations; particularly in the memory from adolescence: the aggression in the extremely painful conversion symptom and the libido in the preoedipal wish to be touched, remedially, by the mother.

Example 8 (p. 230): The aggression appears in the cannibalistic intent; the libido is merely implied in the employment of humor and in the mitigation to a game. With regard to affect the last two examples are instructive. For one thing the suppression of affect is in both dreams rather successful; for another they are arousal dreams, avoiding a possibly imminent liberation of affect through waking up; and, finally, neither was analyzed so that no associations could render the affect manifest that was suppressed in the dream.

Example 9 (p. 231): In the prelude to the dream libido and aggression are obviously defused. While the former is mobilized, masturbatorily, to the point of a climax, the latter precipitates anger and finds a motor outlet in the hurling of the container. In the dream the libido creates beauty; the aggression, passive cannibalistic desire.

Example 10 (p. 232): The "Analytic Comment" (cf. p. 234) implies the defusion in the oral-libidinal discharge through inhaling and the oral-aggressive discharge through urination.

2. *A Second Review of the Same Examples with Regard to the Subject or Object Respectively of the Oral-Sadistic or Defused Aggression*

May I try the reader's patience still further? I would ask him to review the ten examples a second time in order to see that the *genital procreative partial subject is the subject or object, respectively, of the oral-sadistic defused aggression*. I have previously (p. 86) stated the impression that the death instinct is not only original with but intrinsic to the second oral stage. I went on to say that "the mouth of this stage is transferable onto all subsequently dominant erogenic zones, and that it is the degree to which it persists or is revived regressively that determines the manifestations of the instinct." (The urethral-erotic discharge of cannibalistic aggression was the one notable exception.) The pathological instances, used for study preliminary to that of the normal function, are instances of this kind. Oral-sadistic and defused aggression is demonstrably discharged by the genital partial subject which, although it is not the mouth, is nevertheless centered around the erogenic zone, acquired in puberty, that elaborates upon oral libido.

In the first example the sexual woman partner "gobbles" the woman patient's food greedily, and is a big animal swallowing a little animal, eating the patient and exploding into little pieces. In the second example, while the dreamer wanted the partner ardently, his mother came in *at that moment* and they had to stop, in other words, the countercathectic inhibitory aggression is inseparable from the emergence of the partial subject. In the third example rage is mobilized and *at that moment* the mother arrives. (Both women spontaneously used these same words.) And, again, upon the mother's arriving nothing "arrived," i.e., simultaneity of partial subject and countercathectic inhibition. In the fourth example it is the womb itself which, while being felt, is twisted into a cramp. In the fifth example it is the mother, with whom the dreamer is warm and cozy in bed, who punishes her for having the menses and, revolted, orders her out of bed. In the sixth example the womb is the

seat of severe menstrual cramps and the mother never responds
to the call for the desired remedial introjection. In the seventh
example it is the *Mutterleib* of the mother, the waves, that roar
toward the dreamer, terrify her and threaten her with engulf-
ment. In the eighth example the mother, as "Mrs. Steak," is
the object of the cannibalistic desire. In the ninth example the
object of the active desire is the symbolized mother, the horse;
and of the passive, the patient. In the tenth the vaginal climax
in the "spot" precipitates violent anger; and the dreamer, subsequently, is threatened with being borne into a passively cannibalistic fate. In the eleventh, the oral-erotic inhaling and holding
of the breath in the pelvis is accompanied by frequent urination
discharging the oral aggression, and in the scene from the thir-
teenth year, the girl menstruates while having a backache.

3. *Regressive Anal-Sadistic Interference with Menstruation*

We are now almost prepared to equip the female genital
partial subject, anatomically, for the discharge of defused aggression. Almost—but not quite: for there are data derived
from everyday observation which must first be disposed of. The
interference with the menstrual function is, obviously, often
an anal one: the intestinal tract is regressively fantasied as procreative (cf. the *Lumpf,* the fecal child of "Little Hans"); and
the periodic mobilization of the womb is accompanied by intestinal cramps, irregularities of elimination, and headaches.

I shall exemplify by comparing excerpts from fantasies and
from dreams of three different patients:

Patient A reports: "For several nights I entertained myself
before going to sleep with a fantasy, the central theme of which
was food. I had escaped with my husband—a very vague figure
—to a log cabin in an extremely isolated and inaccessible region
of the Rockies. It could be reached only on horseback, and since
the time was winter, it is actually cut off from contact with the
outside world. The fantasy presupposed some acute danger
such as revolution in the outside world to account for the necessity of escape. The time is quite specific. It is always dinner time

or early evening. There is a violent blizzard outside which enhances the warmth and comfort and security inside. The cabin is attractive and modern and does not entail much in the way of pioneer hardships. However, the chief support for the feeling of security is the fact that we have enough food stored away for an indefinite length of time. There is a large amount and a pretty wide variety of food. I am not interested in specific meals but rather in the idea of food, in the amounts and kinds that we have. For example, in storerooms there are potatoes, carrots, onions, and all kinds of storable vegetables. More fragile foods are canned, and there are shelves lined with them. There are hams, bacon, and fresh, frozen meat. We have a cow so there is milk, cream, butter and cheese. We have chickens so there are fresh eggs.

"After this fantasy had recurred for two or three nights came the day when I had preliminary and premature menstrual cramps . . . That was on a Wednesday. Friday night I was in the midst of enjoying the fantasy when a fragment of a picture abruptly appeared, seemingly from out of nowhere. I slid in easily, and for a second I didn't really absorb what it was. When I did, I was startled and frightened. It was very clear, very specific and seemed more like a memory than a fantasy. It was simply a picture of a small section of a room. There was an old-fashioned heating stove, not very well cared for. There was a small area of floor and wall. The floor had wide, softwood planks as old houses do. The planks were rough, worn, and unpainted. My impression was that this might be a storeroom or some outbuilding of a farm not finished for living purposes. On the floor just a short distance from the stove were three large brown rats. At first they did not move, and I did not recognize them immediately. They seemed to be eating something. It was like looking down on cows grazing. Then the rats moved, and I recognized them. I was frightened, and my own idea was to escape. With that the picture vanished.

"The next day I had more cramps. Sunday morning I started to menstruate—four days early. I had slightly more severe cramps than usual. The menstrual flow started a little differently than usual, almost with spurts. Since I had the flu last summer, the menstrual flow had been very slight, much less than normal. This time, however, the flow was if anything more profuse than normal."

In the first paragraph she describes a menstrual fantasy of the "return to the womb." (The abundant orality need not be pointed out.) It is mobilized by the earliest, pre-premenstrual stages of the womb's entering the body-ego, for which the patient has normal tolerance; and it is therefore enjoyable, peaceful. All aggression is fused: "it is always dinner time," oral-erotic and oral-sadistic libido are offered their normal potential discharge in the "idea of food," while the blizzard outside (= the menstrual flow—cf. p. 221) but "enhances the warmth and comfort" of the expanded womb.

In the second paragraph she reports menstrual cramps; and with them an abrupt and frightening intrusion, the equivalent of a threshold symbolism in a dream. The intrusion was hypnagogic: the environment suddenly narrowed down to a small section of a room; floor and wall, old-fashioned, not very well cared for, the planks rough, worn and unpainted and not finished for living. This, even without the rats, is immediately recognizable, as the rectum. The tolerance of the patient's body-ego for the appearance in it of the womb is exceeded and a cathectic displacement upon the rectum is enforced; with the result that this erogenic organ arrogates the place in the body-ego, previously occupied by the womb. The replacement reflects itself once more in the momentary appearance of the frightening rats as peacefully grazing cows.[16] Rectal contractions and the irrational wish to escape from some unnamed enclosure were frequent with this patient, even when fully awake.

The third paragraph supplies the complementary information of increased menstrual cramps and of the precipitation of it all by a relatively expansive period.

Patient B reports two dreams from two successive nights, after the last of which her menstrual period came to an end. Her dysmenorrhea had improved but had in part been re-

---

16 The rats are "brown" (picturization) and "three" (symbolization). For the compatibility of a phallic organization with a libido regression to the anal-sadistic stage, cf. Freud's *"A Child is Being Beaten"* (56); for the rat symbolism his *Notes upon a Case of Obsessional Neurosis* (39), especially Chapter G; and for the persistence of orality in anal erogeneity, pp. 111 ff. of the present volume.

placed by oligomenorrhea, which the thirty-five-year-old woman takes for the beginning of the menopause. She is afflicted with a fistula recti. (Cf. pp. 112 ff.)

In the first dream a male acquaintance gave her a bouquet of tea roses.

". . . I took them from him but seemed to be entirely indifferent about the gift and the giver. Later he gave me another bouquet. This one was made up of vegetables—beets, carrots, peas, all packed together in decorative fashion, the way they sometimes appear in the windows of Longchamps. (Tomatoes were in the bouquet—that was the vegetable I couldn't remember when I reported the dream.) I was equally indifferent in receiving this bouquet."

In the second dream an expensive woman dressmaker offers her a dress, which she is too poor to buy.

". . . But I noticed a lace blouse which I thought I could afford. It was made of fine lace, quite transparent. I looked at it and planned to make some nice-looking under-blouse to wear beneath it—something colored. The blouse was white. Then I heard a noise. It proved to be a rat running around in a saucepan full of boiled potatoes in my kitchen. I seized the rat around the neck and choked it. While doing so, it occurred to me that I ought to put it in a glass of water and drown it. I did this and while I held it in the water, it seemed to me more of a mouse than a rat. X [her husband] then seemed to go over to the saucepan full of potatoes as though he were going to eat them. At one and the same time I seemed to think I must warn him that a rat had been running around in the potatoes and they must be thrown away, and, what an awful thing it was that the potatoes must be wasted . . ."

The dream ends with a reference to the mother's catching her (at some forbidden sexual activity) by unexpectedly "coming into the house."

It does not seem that these dreams, when compared to the fantasy, need much comment. In the first, again the abundance of food; as a representation of the breast the, at first forgotten, tomato (*pomo d'oro*). In the second, at the point where the underwear is to be colored, again the rat and the choking, analogous to the narrowing of the room in the preceding example. In conclusion, the drownings, the eating and the "waste."

Patient C tells the dream of a house: "It is well-built, sturdy, and nicely kept. The doors and the windows are closed but there are friendly people inside. It seems to be my home. It sits on a point of land and is surrounded by the sea on two sides. High tide rises to its front steps, but the waves do not wash it away. There are four large lighted lamps at the four corners of the roof, and these seem decorative and friendly, although a little odd. They emphasize the friendliness and healthiness of the atmosphere. The house says: 'Come on in here.' "

Asked to associate to the dream, she recalls the fantasy, recurrent over many years, of another house, which she describes, while comparing "dream house" and "fantasy house" to each other.

"The Fantasy House is vacant and looks in bad repair. It is dark grey and weather-beaten, and has overrun vines and weeds growing around the porch. Several of the front steps are broken, and the shutters are falling off. It used to be occupied, but it is now vacant and probably haunted. Cobwebs grow everywhere. This house frightens me and I look fearfully at it. I listen for sounds inside and there are none and the silence is ominous.

"The Fantasy House is dead, cold and frightening by comparison with the Dream House which is alive, warm and friendly. Both are square with porches running all around. Both are dark grey, but the Fantasy House is the grey of neglect, dust and death while the Dream House is a shiny enamel grey, recently painted and in good condition. The Fantasy House is overgrown with shrubbery. The Dream House is at the edge of the sea with coarse sea grass all around but no trees or flowers. I feel drawn to both of these houses and curious about them. The Fantasy House makes me feel worried and anxious. The Dream House does not. The Dream House is not healthy, it had been inhabited once; it is now filled only with cobwebs and ghosts. But there is that damn thing in the cellar: it has the shape of a serpent; is it a dragon? A demon?"

The "Dream House" represents the *Mutterleib*: it is a home and it has friendly people inside (cf. p. 221); even the waves, rising to it (cf. p. 221) cause no anxiety whatsoever, and the house asks for someone to "come in." One could call the dream of this house the affective opposite of the "wave dream" and suspect that the absence of trees and flowers and the presence only of sea grass, mentioned so explicitly by the dreamer, alludes to the very earliest growth of pubic hair. (I neglected to ask whether the fantasy might have begun with pubescence.)

What is the Fantasy House? Certainly not, except for the cellar, the rectum. One ought to call it, I think, the *Mutterleib* in a regressively anal-sadistic conception.[17] It is shabby and in disorder, cold, frightening, full of dust and death and in its cellar there is a snake;[18] while the Dream House is warm and alive.

The "Fantasy House" is of long standing. So are the menstrual prodromata of the patient which never fail her although she enjoys otherwise unusually good health. They last for three days and consist in being fatigued, having what she calls "that unique feeling" and a "being pulled down," which she describes upon being questioned as a feeling of weight in the upper part of the vagina, the "spot." On the night, however, of the morning when she reported the "dream house" (dreamt, I do not know why, nine days previously) she experienced a surprise: she began to menstruate for the first time in her life without warning. While the period started exactly on time, all prodromata had been absent.

It had, again, been anal-sadistic libido that has sustained the (mild) dysmenorrhea; better still: aggression, defused in consequence of the regression of the libido.

4. *Oral-Sadistic Interference with Menstruation: The "Kreuz"*

Having acknowledged anal-sadistic interference with menstruation one cannot but expect that there is oral-sadistic inter-

[17] Analogous to, e.g., the anal-sadistic conception of the primal scene.

[18] The snake is what might be called a tripartite symbol: it is phallic (Freud), anal (Simmel, F. Cohn, personal communications); and oral (my own observation: the bite).

ference as well, the result of a further regression, accompanied by a higher degree of defusion. If the system for the discharge of aggression is the musculature (Freud), one recognizes that uterus, vagina and tubes are hollow muscular organs. Tubes and uterus in particular seem to be capable of producing spastic reactions, perceivable as well-localized hypogastric pains. However, there is the hardly ever absent complaint of a backache the seat of which must be added to the "pleasure anatomy" of the female genital partial subject. The ache is located in the sacral region, the small of the back; the muscles whose spasm is requisite to it are those of the *os sacrum,* a bone which the anatomists qualify by an adjective with the double meaning of "sacred" as well as "cursed." (See, e.g., the widespread American idiom for menstruation, the "curse.") The German name for the bone is *Kreuzbein* (cross-bone) and the name for the sacral region is *Kreuz* (cross). The almost ubiquitous symptom is the more in need of an explanation since its seat is not that of any sexual organ but a purely muscular area: I suggest that this area be considered a part of the genital partial subject, to which— as its participation is dysmenorrhea shows—it evidently belongs, and with which it seems to share the capacity for discharging defused aggression.

To demonstrate this with the use of analytic material alone is difficult because the *Kreuz* is rarely either directly, or indirectly, represented.

a. I might adduce the experience of a patient, who in the middle of an analytic hour exclaims: "Now I know why I have to lie on my back when I masturbate . . ." Asked for an explanation, she describes the ability to produce an orgasm "way up inside" through purely vestibular manipulation without participation of the rest of the vagina. What had suddenly struck her was a mandatory condition, of which she had previously remained unaware: she makes the sacral and the abdominal muscles move toward each other in order to exert pressure upon the "spot." This is, however the only time in my observation that the participation of the *Kreuz* in a sexual performance has become conscious.

b. The patient with the "premenstrual" backache at thirteen (cf. p. 235), who was completely ignorant of my ideas about the *Kreuz*, wondered spontaneously if perhaps it had not been "the intention of my body to menstruate then but that in my resentment I held back." (Cf. p. 263.)

c. The representation of the *Kreuz* in a dream is, likewise, so rare that I have only one example:

"I dreamed that a large fat woman had accidentally shot her husband. She was distressed about it. A bloody *cross* in a circle drawn on the wall seemed to show where he had been killed. I was lying in bed and the lady moved across my body. I had a strong sexual feeling as though ready to give in to the temptation of having a sexual experience with her on top of me. Then I woke up."

The dreamer is another one who as a child had been seduced by a psychotic mother. She had lately remembered that the activities were confined to the times around the mother's menstrual period. The two premenstrual dreams—the one quoted above, preceding the onset by a day, and another to be quoted below, preceding it by a few hours—reproduce, when combined, the experience: the mother had the daughter at the time of latency suck her breast forcefully, with an orgastic effect. Bizarre exhibitions, concerning breast and "cloaca," which fascinated the child, took the place of a "foreplay." In associating to the dream new details of the performance are remembered; among them the mother's copious urination after the act and the fact that it all began after the father, an alcoholic in his terminal phase, had eliminated himself from the home. Yet the dream had left the patient with a "blinding" headache and a pain in the neck, which could, as previous experience had taught her, be abolished through masturbation with fantasies, elaborating upon the traumatic experience. However, she had decided to refrain and to analyze instead. The assocation, after which the pain ceased, concerned manifestly the recent past: her solitary enjoyment of several cups of coffee and of the landscape, coastline and sea, spread out before her, in the early morning. Following this, she insists that her urine has the odor of coffee and remembers how pleasant the coffee smelled when on Sunday mornings the mother, getting up ahead of the child, had prepared it. There were no associations to the cross proper.

The second dream: "I dreamed I was sucking my own left nipple. I had a strong sexual feeling throughout the clitoris and labia by pressing my thighs together. This excitement woke me up.

"A few hours later I started to menstruate."

Analytic comment: One could say that in the first dream the mother, after the father is killed, initiates sexually an incorporation (see the similar case discussed on p. 212) which appears in the second dream as an identification. But in order to understand why the pain vanished when it did, one must possess oneself of two observations; the first, a bit of common knowledge by now, and the second, told me by a colleague[19] but subsequently confirmed on occasion. "Head and neck" can be a displacement symbol for the phallus (or in the "body-as-phallus" for the glans). This, of course, neither invalidates their historical meaning which belongs in the present case to details of the breast-sucking activities, not reported above, or the punitive determinant of so many conversion symptoms. The accompanying impairment of vision denies the incorporation in terms of the eye, the associate of the mouth. The "dream of the beautiful landscape," my informant has taught me, is a dream of reconciliation with the female genital, which had once been considered as castrated and ugly. I found this to be true, although not confined to the dream. In the present instance the maternal partial subject, symbolized by a seascape, is remedially introjected through the eye while the coffee supplies the mouth with the "milk" that the breast would not yield again, as it had done in the earliest, happiest times. The fantasy of urinating the coffee implies a fantasy of the *Mutterleib,* from which issues what had been drunk; and the cessation of the conversion symptom is due to a normal if transient "identification with the castrated mother" (17).

I am to blame for not having asked the dreamer to associate to the cross. But I am almost certain what the association would

19 Personal communication by Ruth Mack Brunswick.

have been,[20] because it dotted the analysis for many years and only the hour, reported above, brought its elucidation. The girl had, in puberty, found among the mother's belongings, and appropriated, a crucifix with a glass peephole in the middle, through which one could see Virgin and Child. Once while looking through it she had experienced the fright of her life: an agonal feeling, difficult to describe, of an imminent, almost mortal, danger of loosing a part of herself, which she would be unable to retrieve. I cannot, in the context of this volume, give the theory for this phenomenon, which belongs to the states of alienation (*Entfremdungen*). However, it appears evident that the image of the phallic child, looking or reaching for the breast of the mother, precipitated, in the course of mobilizing the repressed memory of the traumatic experiences, an acute fright of castration. Yet this happened on the occasion of an incorporative employment of the "cross."

As a collateral to the first dream, it may be instructive to enumerate the prodromata of this patient. They were, in the sequence in which she reported them upon being asked:

1. A slight swelling of the breasts and a somewhat increased sensitivity of the nipples.

2. Backache. (*Q*. In the small of the back? *A*. Yes.)

3. Cramps. (*Q*. Where? *A*. In the uterus.)

4. Violent headaches, often causing nausea. (*Q*. Head and neck? *A*. Yes.)

5. Clotting. (Not, of course, a prodroma.) It will be noted that she juxtaposes spontaneously, the ache in the sacral region and the cramps in that of the womb. The analysis has subsequently abolished all of it except the first.

d. I append here a dream from fiction which may serve as another illustration. I must, however, precede it with excerpts from the story itself in order to furnish the background requisite for its interpretation.

---

[20] This guess was later proven correct. A supplementary analysis of the patient afforded me at a certain point the opportunity to remind her of the dream, which she remembered and of the lack of associations to the cross. She associated immediately the episode reported in the text, furnishing the addendum that, when one looked from the other side through the peephole, one saw Christ on the cross.

Olenka, the heroine of Tchekov's near-masterpiece, *The Darling* (140), identifies with whomever she marries or consorts with. However, Olenka is childless; in the end she adopts, although not legally, the son of her former lover by his wife, and identifies now with him, as she had with his father.

The description of her second marriage is perfect; I quote from it the background material for the dream:

"Pustovalov and Olenka got on very well together when they were married.

"Usually he sat in the office till dinner-time, then he went out on business, while Olenka took his place, and sat in the office till evening, making up accounts and booking orders.

" 'Timber gets dearer every year; the price rises twenty per cent,' she would say to her customers and friends. 'Only fancy, we used to sell local timber, and so Vassitchka always has to go for wood to the Mogilev district. And the freight!' she would add, covering her cheeks with her hands in horror. 'The freight!'

"It seemed to her that she had been in the timber trade for ages and ages, and that the most important and necessary thing in life was timber; and there was something intimate and touching to her in the very sound of words such as 'baulk,' 'post,' 'beam,' 'pole,' 'scantling,' 'batten,' 'lath,' 'plank,' etc. . . . Her husband's ideas were hers . . .

"On Saturdays Pustovalov and she used to go to the evening service; on holidays to early mass, and they walked side by side with softened faces as they came home from church. There was a pleasant fragrance about them both, and her silk dress rustled agreeably. At home they drank tea, with fancy bread and jams of various kinds, and afterwards they ate pie. Every day at twelve o'clock there was a savoury smell of beet-root soup and of mutton or duck in their yard, and on fast-days of fish, and no one could pass the gate without feeling hungry. In the office the samovar was always boiling, and customers were regaled with tea and crackers. Once a week the couple went to the baths and returned side by side, both red in the face.

" 'Yes, we have nothing to complain of, thank God,' Olenka used to say to her acquaintances. 'I wish everyone were as well off as Vassitchka and I.' "

It is easy to see that, although she is the husband's mother, he is, at the same time, hers. ". . . *we* used to sell local timber . . ." refers obviously to a time before she had even known him, and the gesture of horror is easily that of woman being imitated by her child. The "intimate and touching" sounds are a child's, to whom the mother taught words to which it has not become quite accustomed and which are perhaps just a little too big for it. There is, further the holiday idyll, the childlike enjoyment of special foods and the common bath. However, Olenka has an evidently recurring nightmare: "At night when she was asleep she dreamed of perfect mountains of planks and boards, and long strings of wagons, carting timber somewhere far away. She dreamed that a whole regiment of twelve-arshine, five-vershok[21] beams, standing on end, was marching upon the timber-yard; that long beams and boards knocked together with the resounding crash of dry wood, kept falling and getting up again, piling themselves on each other. Olenka cried out in her sleep, and Pustovalov said to her tenderly: 'Olenka, what's the matter, darling, *cross* yourself!' "

This is a dream that permits a virtually complete interpretation without the dreamer's associations, because the dream work employs practically nothing but symbolizations. It is, as the first sentence shows, a dream of *Verkehr* (cf. p. 17) with the mother. Transportation stands, as does traffic, for intercourse (Freud); and wood for the mother. At this point it appears worth while to trace the wording of Freud's interpretation of this symbol: ". . . boards," he writes, "are also women, probably because of the antithesis, which cancels the curves of their bodies. Wood, anyway, seems from its linguistic connections to be a representative of the female substance (matter). [". . . *ein Vertreter des weiblichen Stoffes (Materie)* . . ."]. The name of the island of 'Madeira' means 'wood' in Portuguese" (31G). In another place (32) he speaks of "symbols," such as "wood for the woman's body (*Frauenleib*)." I must, to prepare for my comment upon these interpretations, interpolate here a remark on Freud's style. Everyone recognizes his accuracy, but there are important places in his work where he is vague. I am con-

[21] Russian measurements.

vinced that this vagueness is deliberate; for, when clinical observation has taught me something apparently new, I have often found it prepared for, if not implied, in the very ambiguities of certain of Freud's formulations. The one quoted above is an instance of this kind. As far as the boards in the dream are "boards," they are women; and considering the representation of frequency through multiplicity as well as the representation through opposites, mentioned by Freud in the case of the board, they are one woman, possessed by feminine bulges with whom Olenka has often had traffic. (Breasts and belly are, after all, prime targets for the child's interest in her mother.) As far as the boards are "wood" they are "feminine substance (matter)"; and *Frauenleib* which, although its main meaning is "woman's body," carries the overdeterminant "woman's belly."[22] Can this, if you combine the three interpretations mean anything but the maternal partial object?

Having exhausted the first sentence of the report of the dream, the second is easy to understand. It describes the attempt of introjection, interfered with by defused aggression. Thus, instead of introjecting the partial object, the partial subject is invaded by it; wood crushes on wood, and instead of joining, piles up. The attempt by the childless dreamer herself to fulfill the evidently forbidden wish to transform the partial object into the partial subject through introjecting it—in other words, to identify with the mother in order to be one—ends in failure; and anxiety takes the place of gratification. Is it surprising that a writer capable of inventing so perfect a dream does not fail at the point where the tortured dreamer cries out, to produce the "cross"?

e. Both the fictitious husband's reaction to his wife's fictitious nightmare, and my patient's associations to her dream contain a reference to the crucifix, the "cross" of the Christian religion. Georg Groddeck, a Protestant, of whom I know because he told me so, that he was anxious not to be thought of as antireligious, first expressed the opinion that the crucifix symbolizes the mother. This sounds reasonable (see above) since the cross is a wooden one, and has the shape of a human about to embrace;

22 *Leibschmerz* = e.g., "bellyache."

it implies, however, that it is a mother who kills her son. Those unwilling to consider such implications because dogma has erased every trace of it, need merely study Freud's review of Sartiaux (43) and the article "Artemis" in the *Encyclopaedia Britannica:* Mary's ancestors are an Asiatic mother-goddess and the Greek Artemis, fused together to the Ephesian Diana, "a female with many breasts, the symbol of productivity" or indicating "the all-nourishing mother." From the waist to her feet, however, "her image resembles a pillar, narrowing downwards and sculptured all round with rows of animals (lions, rams and bulls)." Artemis' development up to the time (8th century B.C.?) of her identification with the Asiatic deity is itself a long story, ranging from the huntress, demanding human sacrifice to the goddess of childbirth protecting mother and child. Her association with Hekate, goddess of night, and of the underworld—the abode of the dead—is an early one; her virginity is a late addition. With regard to the other ancestor, Freud remarks elsewhere (45) that all the "great mother-goddesses of the Oriental people seem to have been procreatresses as well as (female) annihilators, goddesses of life and of fertilization as well as of death." The phallic image of the Ephesian Artemis with her breasts to be sucked on the upper half of her body and the animals, eating and to be eaten, on the lower appears a sculptural condensation of a development in whose subsequent course, from Diana to Mary, only the oral-erotic qualities of the deity were preserved while the oral-sadistic ones were repressed. Following Freud in his eventual application of the concept of repression to collective thought, the cross and its legend would represent a "return of the repressed," such as we encounter it in the analysis of the individual, i.e., an unconscious thought amenable to interpretation. It is the context of the present chapter that suggests—even if it does no more than suggest—that the interpretation of the cross be the sacral "organ," equipped for the discharge of oral-sadistic aggression, the *Kreuz.*

It is one thing to gain impressions and another thing to convey them. The above material is scanty; some readers may even feel that it is relatively inconclusive. It is for this reason that I have persuaded myself to add two more clinical observations, pointing to the connection between *Kreuz* and both *Gebär-mutter* and *Mutterleib,* in spite of the fact that the method with which they were made is not analytic, and to conclude the section with a few observations on the Nurse in *Romeo and Juliet.*

f. A well-informed and intuitive social worker who had under her care a child of eleven or twelve whom we shall call Joan, felt that the girl was ready to menstruate but could not because of the mother's distinct preference for the nine-year-old brother whom we shall call Jonathan because their actual names resembled each other in the same fashion. Since the mother was chronically sick, the children needed foster care and the worker eventually found separate foster homes for them from which they could visit each other. Joan was placed in the home of a happily married couple with several small children, and her foster mother loved her for the attractive girl that she was. But there were still the visits to the mother, who on her sick bed behaved no differently than she always had: she drew Jonathan to her and left Joan standing alone.

"It was on the way home," the report reads, "from one of these visits to the hospital that Joan and I had our little talk. We had left Jonathan in his foster home in a different town and I was taking Joan back to her home. I think it must have been winter time, because in the late afternoon or early evening it was already dark or almost dark in the car. What with needing to pay some attention to driving, and with the darkness, I had little idea of Joan's facial expression, but I know she made little verbal response. I did not expect her to be able to . . . I told her that the foster mother had told me about her aches (or whatever it was) and that she thought that maybe this meant that Joan would soon begin to menstruate. This meant she was growing up and becoming a woman, and that every month she would have a menstrual period. (The foster mother had explained physical aspects of menstruation to the girl.) I tried to express *for* Joan that it was tough having a little brother who seemed to get a lot of attention because he was little and more of a baby than she was, and that sometimes it must seem as though there wasn't much advantage in growing up into a woman. But she could do some things he couldn't because she was bigger and older and a girl. The foster mother liked her a lot, wanted her to grow up, and hoped that some day Joan would want to be married and have babies of her own, just as the foster mother did. (I knew that Joan liked the foster parents' young child, or children, whichever it was) . . ." Soon afterward Joan had her first menstruation.[23]

It is hardly necessary to translate this report into psycho-analytic parlance and to say that Joan could not become a young woman because she could not identify with a mother who only loved a child with a penis. I find it particularly intuitive of the worker that she chose a situation, resembling the analytic one, inasmuch as its medium was the spoken word; while in addition, employing the symbolism of riding together. The reason why I am quoting the little story is that the only complaint of the child, who for psychological reasons had to curb her physiological maturation to the extent of denying her womb, were *backaches*.

g. As a medical man in the 1920's I shared with other German physicians an interest in physiotherapy and the pathology of the muscles. I learned from several institutions methods of "medical reflex massage"—differentiated therapeutic procedures not to be confused with the "Swedish" stroking and kneading of the *masseuse*. At the same time pathologists, both in America and abroad, demonstrated histologically, the "rheumatic" lesion to which the muscle reacts functionally with a spastic response called *Hartspann*.[24] These were, briefly, the sources from which I developed for my professional use a technique of reflex massage, which made it possible to ferret out hidden muscular spasms, to remove them selectively, and so to exercise secondarily a therapeutic influence on the lesions. It turned out that many internal conditions caused pathology of the integument, that the two maintained each other, and that spasms in distant locations

[23] I am indebted for this report to Professor Elizabeth Meyer of the New York School for Social Work.

[24] Untranslatable. It denotes muscular tautness with the resultant of the muscle having become hard, although not necessarily painful.

were related in such a fashion that it was impossible to remove one before having removed the other.

The relation of sacral and abdominal musculature is a case of this kind. Some abdominal cramps can be abolished by working on the insertions of the musculature of the belly (costal arch, pubic bone, sometimes extending into the rib cage and the musculature of the axilla), and on the *Hartspann* in the umbilical area. But there are others where one obtains no result until one has first removed the often hidden and painless, but nevertheless *severe spasms of the musculature of the sacral region*. Here the inhibiting influence of the *Kreuz* on the *Mutterleib* seems to become palpable, and it is as though one felt it directly under one's hands.

It has again been the morbid rather than the normal function that brought the *Kreuz* to attention. In the presence of pain one may assume that aggression is discharged in it; but its more frequent and certainly more important morbid function is that of binding aggression and, by virtue of its connection with the abdominal portion of the genital partial subject, inhibiting—countercathectically, as it were—the libidinal discharge or even the charge with libido. In the case of sexual functioning this is hardly demonstrable; but in instances of prodromal backache and initial oligomenorrhea, with or without a delay, one hears on occasion that the eventually normal flow and cessation of all backache is accompanied by a marked increase in well-being as compared, not to a premenstrual time, but to the rest of the month. The woman describes herself as less inhibited and more outgoing, less neutral and more feminine, in other words, as a more libidinal person.

h. Juliet's nurse, a youthful but abstinent widow, is to me one of the most convincing human beings in fiction. Stage tradition has falsified her completely by casting her as an old woman. If one computes her age relative to Juliet's, one finds her anywhere between twenty-eight and thirty-three or thirty-five—in the midst of the menarche.

To the young men who tease her (see below) she appears "old"; but would they tease her as they do were she so? I can-

not present her analysis here, except for the remark that she is
to Juliet—at times and *mutatis mutandis*—what Mozart's Papageno is to Tamino. (Cf. pp. 277 f.) There are, however, two
sequent scenes in the first of which, sent by Juliet to get a
message, she meets with Romeo and his friends, while in the
second she is to deliver the message to Juliet. The young gentle-
men give her a rough time, taking her for a "bawd" and assault-
ing her with their libidinous banter. She tries very hard to
remain a lady until they leave; but, left alone with Romeo and
her servant-chaperone Peter, she can no longer contain herself
so sexually stirred up is she. She breaks out against Mercutio
who has been teasing her the worst.

> ¶ NUR. And a speake anything against me, Ile take him
> downe, & a were lustier than he is, and twentie such Jacks: and
> if I cannot, Ile fine those that shall: scurvie knave, I am none
> of his flurt-gils, I am none of his skaines mates, and thou must
> stand by too and suffer every knave to use me at his pleasure.
> ¶ PET. I saw no man use you at his pleasure: if I had, my
> weapon should quickly been out . . . [128A].

In the subsequent scene, to which for the present purpose
the foregoing one is only the prelude, Juliet most anxiously
awaits the return of her messenger; and when he finally arrives,
craves the message from Romeo about their impending marriage. But the Nurse leaves her on tenterhooks, teases and
tortures her, partly from envy and partly because she has to
curb her own mobilized sexuality, which has been further increased upon talking to Romeo, in identification with Juliet:

> ¶ NUR. I am a weary, give me leave a while,
> Fie how my bones ake, what a jaunt have I had?
> ¶ JUL. I would thou had'st my bones, and I thy newes:
> Nay come I pray thee speake, good good Nurse speake.
> ¶ NUR. Jesu what hast? can you not stay a while?
> Do you not see that I am out of breath.
> ¶ JUL. How art you out of breath, when thou has breath
> To say to me, that you art out of breath?
> The excuse that thou doest make in this delay,
> Is longer then the tale thou dost excuse.

Is thy newes good or bad? answere to that,
Say either, and Ile stay the circumstance:
Let me be satisfied, ist good or bad?
    ¶ NUR. Well, you have made a simple choice, you
know not how to chuse a man: *Romeo,* no not he though
his face be better then any mans, yet his legs
excels all mens, and for a hand, and a foote, and a body,
though they be not to be talkt on, yet they are past
compare: he is not the flower of curtesie, but Ile warrant
him as gentle as a Lambe: go thy waies wench, serve
God, What have you din'd at home?
    ¶ JUL. No no: but all this I did know before
What saies he of our marriage? what of that?
    ¶ NUR. Lord how my head ackes, what a head have I?
I beates as it would fall in twenty peeces.
My backe o th'other side: o my backe, my backe:
Beshrew your heart for sending me about
To catch my death with jaunting up and downe.
    ¶ JUL. Ifaith: I am sorrie that you art not well.
Sweet, sweet, sweet Nurse, tell me what saies my Love?
    ¶ NUR. Your Love saies like an honest Gentleman,
And a courteous, and a kind, and a handsome,
And I warrant a vertuous: where is your Mother?
    ¶ JUL. Where is my Mother?
Why she is within, where should she be?
How odly though repli'st:
Your Love saies like an honest Gentleman:
Where is your Mother? [128B].

Here it is all again—I do not know how much of it I must
point out once more to the reader of this volume: Juliet's
(cannibalistic) impatience (most outspoken in the monologue
preceding the scene, which I have not quoted); the Nurse's description of Romeo in terms of a sexual partial subject, terminated by the completely gratuitous mention of "dinner"; the
"backache" and what it curbs: the "mother," symbolizing the
"womb" in the girl who is becoming a woman, and in the
woman who identifies with the girl. (¶ NUR. Your Love saies . . .
. . . . Where is your Mother?/ ¶ JUL. Where is my Mother?/ Why

she is *within*, where should she be?/) In the present context, the citation of the *backache* is the reason I have quoted the dialogue. The scene containing it becomes, by the way, still more lively a document if one is aware of the *aktual*-neurotic foundation of most of the Nurse's conversions; in particular that originally described by Freud as "one upon the rheumatic muscles . . ." (30).

I hope that others will add new and perhaps more convincing observations. The ones presented above are all that I can advance at this point in an attempt at persuading the reader to consider the *Kreuz* as a part of the female genital partial subject.

F. ON THE MALE GENITAL PARTIAL SUBJECT

The elaborate sexual anatomy and physiology of the female stands in contrast to the simplicity of the male. He does not either menstruate or conceive, bear, deliver, or lactate; the anatomy and physiology of his sexual organs serve no other purpose than that of ejaculation. The only organ that represents itself as a genital in his body-ego is the penis; the testes belong physiologically to the anal zone.[25] In puberty he does not acquire a new erogenic zone but is affected by the alteration of an old one; after the testes have matured physiologically, the penis upon sexual stimulation erects fully, and the urethra ejects semen. I believe that this requires an identification with the father, analogous to that of the woman with the mother, but I am unable to trace it.

Clinically I have obtained but hints. I remember two men who only in the course of analysis became able to recognize that the (unerected) penis had the same size as the father's.

Another man voiced in the beginning of his analysis the complaint that his penis did not erect at an angle but came out straight, parallel, as it were, to the floor. This condition, which for years had him worried that he would fail with the woman,

---

25 I observed this independently long ago; and I was later told (personal communication: Ruth Mack Brunswick) that Freud held the same opinion. I am not certain that he has expressed it in print.

was exploited unconsciously for the reproduction of the incomplete erection, "elongation" as he called it, in response to a seduction during the phallic phase. However, the same man—he was married and had a little child—became intermittently seized by the thought: "I am a father? Why that is impossible, that cannot be: it's absurd . . ."

I believe also that the altered zone discharges oral libido, but again I have no conclusive observations.

A vulgar German idiom comes to mind, which expressed this directly. It has the young man, eager for the sexual act, exclaim: "****** [vulgarism for the female genital] on the table! ****** [vulgarism for the male genital] wants to breakfast!"

When the manuscript of this volume was practically on its way to the printer I happened to read a travel essay on Andalusia (98) in which it is told how a girl passes a group of Cordovan men. "All round the square," writes the sensitive author, "under the African palms, old men wearing black Cordobese hats, sat in stiff rows like figures at a judgment. Late in their life though it may have been, these ancients still had a sharp eye for a pretty woman. As Kati walked by, they looked at her hard from under their hats. '*Behold!*' said one, '*how like a ham she is.*' '*Oh, for a knife and fork!*' cried a second. 'Silence,' growled a third. 'Don't you see that she is a married woman?' 'Ah,' said the first with a sigh, '*but that she were a widow for only five hours.*'" (Italics mine.)

With regard to the discharge of aggression, the penis is not, as is the vagina, a muscle; only the seminal ducts and the urethra are muscularly equipped. Yet their reflex action is purely peristaltic and as such not quite comparable to that of vagina and womb. It is in good accord with this anatomical and physiological difference, as well as with the psychological one of greater native activity, that the general skeletal musculature of the male—in pursuit, embrace, and the performance of frictions—discharges more aggression than does that of the female.

Thus if I define the male genital partial subject, in analogy with the female (cf. p. 266), as centering around the penis and extending to the skeletal parts of the body, requisite to performing the sexual act, I have not said much although I think I have spoken the truth. In the interest of a subsequent contribution toward a theory of coition (cf. pp. 272 ff.) it is naturally essential to be aware of the psychological connotations of the term "penis" discovered by Freud. They are not exhausted in the unconscious equation "feces = money = gift = child = penis" because, to quote Freud's own words (73B), "the interest in this part of the body has . . . a perhaps still more powerful *oral* root, since after the discontinuation of nursing the penis inherits also from the nipple of the maternal organ." As for the *Kreuz,* I have observed its inhibiting influence upon the charge with libido of the genital of the male only once.

A patient, who transferred certain phases of his overt homosexual past very intensely, for a while had erections on his way to the analyst, which however vanished when he entered the door of the building. After an extended period of resistance (which impressed one—incongruously so, it seemed—as repression resistance rather than transference resistance) he began an hour by reporting "a new symptom": a spastic pain in the small of his back, centering around the spine and inducing some restriction of motility. The most comfortable position was lying flat on his back "just like here." In the first part of this hour a hitherto repressed memory, in which he lays hold of the erected penis of a certain adult who himself was lying on his back is recalled vividly and with a fair amount of detail. This precipitates twice in succession a brief erection. Subsequently the patient feels a desire for autofellatio, which was easily demonstrable as a sequel to the memory at age five or six: he had performed fellatio on the man. *At this point the backache is gone.*

In one of the subsequent hours, in which an earlier memory of a seduction prior to the experience mentioned above was being worked through, the patient who had come without any cramp felt it suddenly reappear in response to a fleeting erection. Toward the end of the hour he experienced what he called "a controversy going on" between the small of his back and his penis, in other words, between cramp in the *Kreuz* and libidinal charge of the membrum.

Plato's famous description (108) of the "appetites" of the "lawless wild-beast nature" that is "in all of us, even in good men" and "peers out in sleep" furnishes, I believe, a further elaboration: "I mean those which are awake when the reasoning and human and ruling power is asleep. Then the wild beast within us, gorged with meat or drink, starts up and having shaken off sleep, goes forth and satisfies his desires; and there is no conceivable folly or crime—*not excepting incest or any other unnatural union, or parricide, or the eating of forbidden food* [My italics]—which at such a time, when he has parted company with all shame and sense, a man may not be ready to commit."

In the first place the author speaks about man as distinct from woman, and in the second he describes the temporary involution of the superego. (Cf. p. 208.) In the parenthetic thought between the dashes, finally, he completes what I believe is the most astute description of the male genital partial subject. By putting the eating of forbidden food on a par with incest and parricide he records the orality of the libido; in mentioning parricide he alludes to the (subsequent) identification with the father; and in juxtaposing incest with parricide he epitomizes the oedipal nature of the genital partial subject in the male.

Clinically one is indeed impressed with the more oedipal make-up of man as compared to woman; although one cannot be certain how much of this difference is dependent upon time and place. Take the case of a neurotic fixation on the mother and its typical manifestations in the transference. The man is apt to establish immediately a father transference with all the consequences described so elaborately by Freud. It is only after much analysis that behind, and at times beside, the father, the patient transfers his preoedipal sexuality and his mother. The woman will, in most instances, transfer her mother at once upon the male analyst and equip him with her individual features. Her bondage to this mother, and now to the analyst to whom she must come, no matter how negative her transference be, is distinctly preoedipal; it is the small child's inability to exist alone, without mother. Here a good deal of analysis and of progress is needed before the father, and with him oedipal sexuality, can effectively be transferred. Not to be misunderstood, I must add that even if she also effects a transference of the father immediately, perhaps even vociferously, one gains the impression that this, compared to that of the mother, is relatively superficial.

I know the limited value of such generalizations, and I have seen exceptions to this one, but I still think the impression is not invalid.

I am of course fully aware of the far-reaching consequences of my interpretation of Plato's description, which implies a persistence of oedipal sexuality in the normal male. Yet Freud's tentative "destruction of the Oedipal strivings in the Id" (63) has always impressed me as a hypothesis made *ad hoc*. For one thing we know of no other instance where anything in the id is destroyed; and for another we have no reason to assume that incestuous dreams, often but little distorted, are pathognomonic for the neurosis.[26] Our normal "nocturnal psychosis" disregards, as does psychosis itself, the incest barrier, requisite as it is to civilization,[27] and reveals behind it the incestuous wish. However, if one is aware that the *object* of the *male* partial subject is the female genital partial *subject*—that the partial subject in either sex under the regressive conditions requisite to orgastic gratification, strives for the partial object—one will appreciate that, in the *folie-à-deux* here concerned, the incest barrier does not apply: the "mother, reduced to her sexual parts," is simply

[26] Cf. Freud's classic formulation of the subject at the end of his "Introductory Lecture" XXI (52).

[27] Plato's context is sociological. One will remember that the description quoted above is a deliberate psychological divagation. He indulges in it because he feels that without it his sociological inquiry "will always be confused" (*loc. cit.*).

a female, and the superego, in consequence of its "involution in the course of the function" (Freud), lends its energy to the procreative intent.

This intent is ascribed, as it were, to a late Greek mythical figure which must be looked upon, I believe, as a *direct* representation of the male partial subject. Rose (113) describes Priapus as "an obscene little deity, a daimon of fertility, . . . a more or less *grotesquely misshapen man,* with a *huge* and *erect* phallus." Here it is as though the erection had practically absorbed the man, or the man were but an appendage of the erection.

With regard to *indirect* representations, it would appear that certain symbolizations of the penis, such as, e.g., the bird, might better be looked upon as symbols of the male genital partial subject; which is why, e.g., Zeus, stripped as it were of his regalia, visits Leda in the shape of a swan. One particular representation of the male partial subject, the horse-half of the "centaur," has aroused my curiosity to the point of making inquiries relative to it. Yet I could not obtain any answers. I am therefore dependent upon merely saying what I think.

Of these mythical creatures Webster states that they are thought of as "wild and coarse," and that their "animal nature" is "shown by their bodies, being half man and half horse." Since the horse is a symbol for the incest object (cf. p. 16), a man who is sexually horse is incestuous, in the sense explained above. (The battles of the Centaurs were primarily battles for the possession of a King's bride.) Mammals are incestuous; in the case of the horse, as in that of other domesticated animals, man has learned to employ incest for breeding, giving it sanction as it were. Satyrs, half-man, half-goat, are, of course, a case similar to that of the centaur.

Sin, in the last analysis, is oedipal sin; stating it so is, of course, but a way of paraphrasing Freud's discovery that the feeling of guilt has its deepest root in the oedipus complex. Thus the Devil, the impersonation of sin, is still satyr inasmuch as his left (*sic!*) foot is cloven;[28] and Mephistopheles, Goethe's famous devil, is by the same token still centaur for he has the foot of a horse. The irrational disinclination of the Western, the Christian, world to eat horsemeat, finally is, in the light of Plato's triad, "incest, parricide, and the eating of forbidden food" not altogether surprising.[29]

The relative paucity of data on the male genital partial subject, as compared to the female, needs no apology; it is explainable and has been explained above, by the relative lack of occasion for clinical observation.

All in all: should the reader feel that positing a partial subject is actually taking a metapsychological (topographical) step in disguise and that there must be conditions whose study permits one an accounting for and a naming of the rest of the ego (in the narrow sense of the term), I agree. Chapter II of the second volume will be devoted to this matter.

V. TOWARD A THEORY OF COITION

The difficulty in sketching a theory of coition—the prime sexual function of the genital phase—lies in the number and in the disparity of the clinical data, elaborated upon through hypothesis, that require coordination. Most of these have been either quoted, extended or presented afresh in the preceding pages; and much of the present short section may therefore read like a repetition.

For a starting point one must go back to the "Primitive

28 This does not contradict that he stems from Hephaistos, nor that the limping has the meaning of castration.

29 Since the Negro is another symbolization of the incest object, it is quite logical that Iago, rousing Desdemona's father in order to tell him that his daughter has eloped with the Moor, speaks of devil and horse and threatens him with equine descendants (119).

¶ IA. Sir: you are one of those that will not serve God, if the devill bid you. Because we come to do you service, and you thinke we are Ruffians, you'le have your daughter cover'd with a Barbary horse, you'le have your Nephewes neigh to you, you'le have Coursers for Cozens: and Gennets for Germaines.

Erogenic Model," constructed from Freud's descriptions, and remember the "inferiority" of the second, quasi-erogenic zone that the nursling who "cannot kiss himself" substitutes for his lips. "The inferiority of this second site," Freud explains (36D), "will later be one of the motives for seeking the homologous parts, the lips, of another person." This second site is, of course, a substitute for the mother's breast and its establishment signifies that the orality, sucking and incorporation, is about to become gradually independent of the function of feeding. It is thus really "not without good reason," as Freud explains (cf. p. 201), "that the child's sucking of the mother's breast has become the model for every love relation" and that "the finding of an object is actually a re-finding of it."

This would imply that what is *refound in the genital sexual union, is the breast.* (The frequent mobilization of hunger through sexual intercourse is common knowledge.) With regard to the instinctual aim, Freud has been quoted (cf. p. 201) as stating that "at the height of the lover's paroxysm . . . the erotic aim of the oral organization reappears," and as adducing the idiom "I could devour you from love" as an illustration. It is here that his observation has been extended. The newly-acquired erogenic zone, characterizing the genital phase, was shown to discharge oral libido in others of its functions (menstruation, pregnancy, giving birth) with the result that the orgastic reappearance of the oral instinctual aim becomes part of a context. Yet this context remains incomplete if it does not include the regression of ego to partial subject and partial object (cf. pp. 204, 208 ff.) and the defusion of instincts, accompanying the regression and necessitating the discharge of aggression as well as libido in the sexual act.[30]

30 The latter was, of course, known to Freud. As early as 1909 he introduces ambivalence, while commenting on the coexistence in Little Hans of fervent love for and death wishes against his father, and states that *"these antithetic feelings usually become conscious in the adult only at the height of erotic passion"* (Italics mine) (38E). Taking advantage of his later enlargement and refinement of theory, one substitutes "aggression" for "death wishes"; and in so doing justifies the word "conscious," which would otherwise apply only to the exceptional case of the lust-murderer, who is evidently psychotic.

The theory of this act is the theory of a normal function.[31] The fact that the function is in certain respects a regressive one does not make it any less normal than, e.g., the much more regressive function of sleep, with which in so many languages it is metaphorically equated. The normality of the performance depends upon the sexual constitution of the partners, not their relation. The latter may be purely carnal or one of love; their association, in either instance, begins with a state of "infatuation," of which Freud has observed that it causes the person to divest himself of narcissistic libido and to transfer it onto the object. In the course of the sexual act this libido is retrieved. But it is retrieved *by an ego that in the course of regression* (cf. p. 204) *has become partial subject, capable of incorporating the partial object.*[32] Economically this amounts to the tremendous concentration of libido, requisite to its discharge. Since the genital is, in the main, instrumental in discharging the libido, the concentration employs naturally cathectic quantities invested previously in the body and consequently the body-ego. The "fleeting but unmistakable loss of consciousness which can be felt at the climax of any intense sexual gratification" (37a) is an economic result of this libido displacement. Topographically one must further assume that the *genitals of partial subject and partial object fuse and orgastically equate themselves*

31 I have therefore omitted reference to all literature dealing with its disturbances as well as my own observations of the latter.

32 This explains an otherwise whimsical penstroke in the portrait of Rosaline, Romeo's hopeless love. The young man has indeed relinquished almost all of his narcissism to this girl, who became thereby—*a priori*—the most beautiful in Verona. To his friend, Romeo without narcissism is dead and must be conjured back to life with the image of the beloved:

¶ MER. I conjure thee by Rosaline's bright eyes,
    By her High forehead, and her Scarlet lip . . .

It is here that the pen reverses itself as though the draftsman, at the thought of the lips, had suddenly been seized with the notion that it is not the social but the intimate Rosaline—not the *object* but the *partial object*—that holds promise of restoring his friend. Thus Mercutio finishes his portrait:

    By her fine foote, straight leg, and Quivering thigh,
    And the demeanes, that there adjacent lie,
    That in thy likeness though appeare to us [128C].

in the body-ego. I suggest the term "zone equation" for this occurrence.

Thus, if the nursling originally wanted to kiss himself, man or woman make the other's genital eventually their own; and if the nipple is at first but the mouth in the state of gratification (cf. p. 56), the partner's genital is, at last, but one's own in the same condition. Yet the discharge of regressively oral libido in the end entails discharge of defused aggression. In the case of the woman, whose sexual organ is a muscle, it is as though the vagina becomes gradually aware of what Freud has called "the more powerful oral root" of its "interest" in the penis, which has "inherited from the nipple," and discharges oral-sadistic aggression as well as oral-erotic libido in the contraction of its proximal portion. Pelvic and skeletal musculature, of course, lend forceful assistance in the discharge of aggression; and in so doing may pave the way for the spreading of the orgastic sensation throughout the body. In the man the general muscular discharge of aggression dominates the sexual picture. Since this organ is not a muscle he cannot "suck" or "bite" with it; his mode of oral-erotic stimulation, the frictions, are rather derivative of the nursling's rhythmical "pulling" of areas of skin, which Freud has recognized as a substitute for, and an extension of, sucking (36E).

A patient once produced a repressed primal-scene memory that contained the empathic discharge of oral-sadistic libido on the part of the observing child.

The little girl between the age of two and three lay on her side in her crib, close to the parental bed, and got a distinct view of the father's erection in profile while he descended on the mother. She remembers wanting to call out to the mother, warning her of the danger. While she sees, as she puts it, the father "crashing down" on the mother her thumb goes into her mouth and is *at first sucked and then bitten* so as to "steel herself" against the experience. Once the father is on the mother, the latter is no longer seen, her body being totally obscured by him who "covers the whole bed." There is no memory of any frictions; and, when the parents eventually relax, the girl *urinates,* thumb still in her mouth, but the *thumb is now again sucked.* After that she gives it up to hold off the wet pajamas with both hands.

It is hardly necessary to point out to the reader of the present volume that the mother becomes invisible because she is swallowed by the father; and that the thumb is sucked in the end because the biting impulse is now discharged through urination.

In the very end, however, *the anatomical and physiological difference is canceled out psychologically through the "equation"* described (just before the clinical insert) *of the genital-erogenic zones.*[33]

The foregoing sketch has been limited to the sexual act in the narrowest sense of the word. It has dispensed, lest it be too repetitious, with foreplay and by-play (cf. p. 203) and the physiology of instinctual discharge (cf. p. 201), of which no more is known in the case of the genital than in that of any other erogenic zone. It is possible that the intent maintaining, if not initiating, the act is always, unconsciously at least, procreative. With regard to the zone equation, one may finally assume that the libido in the course of regression becomes eventually preoedipal and regard the equation, in the last analysis, as but another instance of the preoedipal consummation of an identification.

VI. POSTSCRIPTUM: NOTES ON AN ARIA AND DIALOGUE FROM "THE MAGIC FLUTE"

A grandiose artistic representation of the zone equation is, I believe, the duet between Papageno and Papagena in Mozart's

---

[33] If the reader studies this beautiful passage from *Measure for Measure,* he will find the description pervaded by the idea of zone equation:

¶LUC. . . . Your brother, and his lover have embrac'd;
As those that feed, grow full: as blossoming Time
That from the seedness, the bare fallow brings
To teeming foyson: even so her plenteous wombe
Expresseth his full Tilth, and husbandry [124B].

Magic Flute, portions of the score of which are appended and commented upon as a "coda" to this chapter.

To make it understandable one must recall who Papageno is. He comes from Fairyland: a birdcatcher who is a sort of human bird himself (cf. p. 271) covered with feathers; a preromantic Germanic Caliban, if you will, yet without guile or evil. He makes his entrance with an aria depicting love as preoedipal love:

> Wenn alle Mädchen wären mein,
> So tauschte ich brav Zucker ein,
> Die, welche mir am liebsten wär',
> Der gäb' ich gleich den Zucker her.
> Und küsste sie mich zärtlich dann,
> Wär' sie mein Weib und ich ihr Mann.
> Sie schlief an meiner Seite ein,
> Ich wiegte wie ein Kind sie ein [105A].
> (He would like to catch all the girls, keep the one he loves best, give her sugar and kiss her; they would be man and wife, she would nestle beside him, and he would rock her to sleep like a child.)

Upon meeting Tamino, the fairy prince, who eventually gains Tamina, the fairy princess, Papageno plays throughout the opera the part of Tamino's partial subject. When he tells Tamina that Tamino has fallen in love with her portrait and is hurriedly on his way to find her he says, instead of the expected "I," "we":

> . . . This great love for you has been the crack of the whip that hastened *our* footsteps along the road. Now *we* are here, to tell you lots of nice, pleasant things, take you in *our* arms and bear you to your mother's palace, if possible as quickly as *we* came, or even more quickly [Italics mine] [105B].

The famous love duet at the end of this dialogue (in which the reader will not have missed either the "mother" or the cannibalistic impatience) is sung by him and Tamina; and when later asked whether he too longs, as does Tamino, for wisdom he answers: no "I am a sort of nature-man, satisfied if I can eat, drink and sleep—and of course, if I could some day put my hand on a pretty little sweetheart—." In the trials that the two must undergo, to be initiated and win their women, Papageno fails all, because he is incontinent orally where oral continence is demanded: they must not eat, drink or speak, nor even see their beloved. He is eventually forgiven and, after Tamino is united with Tamina, finds his mate: Papagena. She appears at first as an old woman, dancing, leaning on a stick; she gives him to drink and coerces him into marriage with her. Whereupon she changes into a young fairy girl, feathered like himself, and promptly disappears. Papageno is desolate and about to commit suicide (masturbation) since he cannot get any girl, when suddenly three cupids produce Papagena, who at last is now his.

After the briefest of ritornellos the duet, symbolizing their union: it begins with the first syllable of their names, which is identical and with it in hastening alternation the partners "palpate" each other; it becomes interwoven between them because baritone and soprano alternate instead of singing together. The tempo increases with an ingenious exploitation of the beat and the gradual transformation of quarter notes into eighths; the phrases are imitative and they overlap for the first time by half a bar only when the syllable actually precedes the name, each partner singing the other's.

EXAMPLE 1

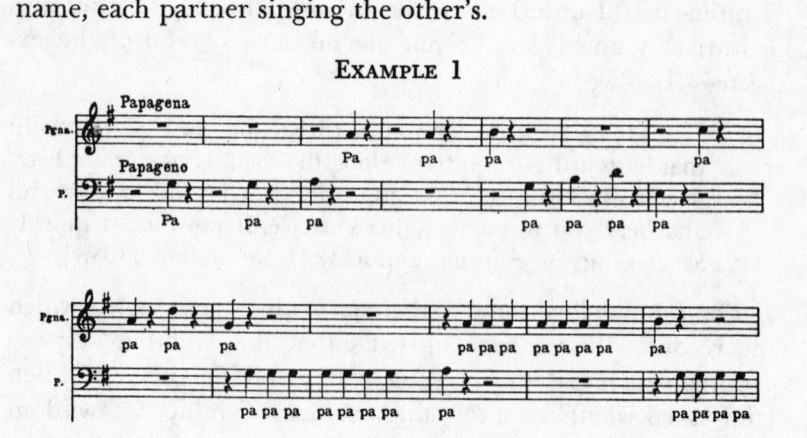

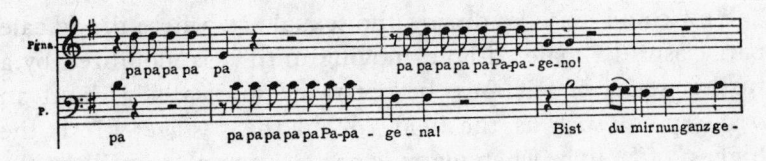

There is naturally no proof in such matters; but the more I have studied the ineffably beautiful yet musically rather simple aria, which expresses the love for each other, praises "the highest of feelings," and abandons itself to the ecstatic contemplation of having an abundance of children, the more have I become convinced that the experience of the zone equation in the act has made its imprint upon text and music. (They are both Mozart's, as is documented by a note from Schikaneder to him.) The beginning, quoted above, where the "Pa-Pa," etc., of one voice slides in between that of the other, until they gradually overlap and become simultaneous, sets the pattern and leads to passages such as this one, devoted to the anticipation of progeny. "First a little Papageno, then a little Papagena, then again a Papageno, then again a Papagena, Papageno, Papagena, etc.":

EXAMPLE 2

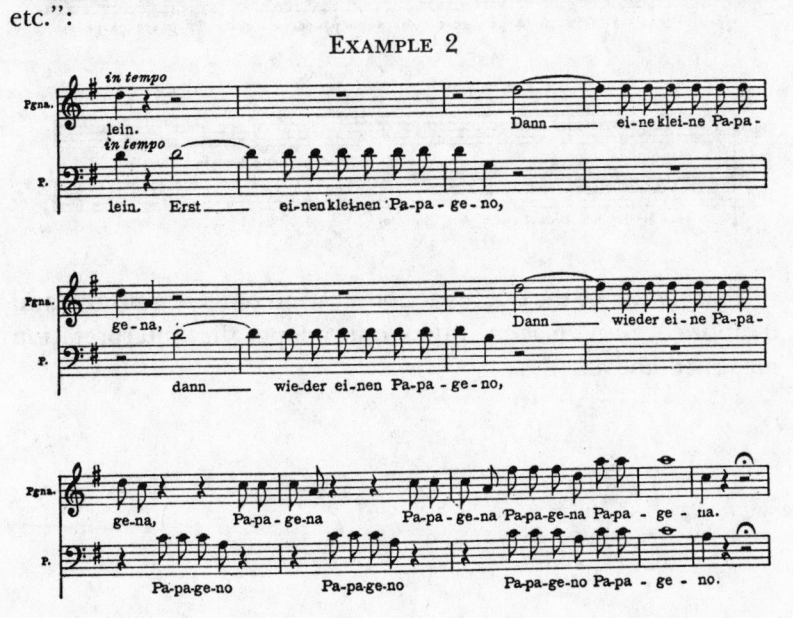

How could episodes during the sexual act, where the female part clasps the male without moving until it is mobilized by a further series of frictions, be portrayed musically without an organ point such as the held "d" in the passage: "It is the highest of feelings when many Papa . . . geno(a) . . . will be the parents' blessing"? And how could the male imitate this (in the tenor) so meaningfully unless it were representative of the zone equation? (The repetition is not given in the example.)

EXAMPLE 3

etc., Continuing:

The ending of the duet is a modification of its beginning; and it appears anticlimactic unless one adopts the interpretation suggested above:

EXAMPLE 4

PART THREE

PART THREE

7

ON EROGENIC
(REGRESSIVELY PARTIAL-EROTIC) LANGUAGE

> *But what else is language & utterance, and discourse &*
> *persuasion, and argument in man, then the vertues of a*
> *well constituted body and minde, little lesse naturall then*
> *his very sensual actions?*
>
> —GEORGE PUTTENHAM (1589)

The following brief chapter takes the place of an appendix.
It has been added for two reasons. In the first place it describes
functional characteristics of certain erogenic zones that have become directly observable in consequence of their displacement
upon the speech apparatus, where they modify verbalization.
In the second place, any observation concerning verbalization
should be of interest to the analyst whom his patient furnishes
"analytic material" almost exclusively by means of verbalization.

Erogenic language could, of course, have been described on
the occasion of the different phases of psychosexual development, characterized by the dominance of those erogenic zones
that are later capable of producing such language. Regressively
partial-erotic language is, after all, but another symptom of regression. I have, nevertheless, preferred to treat the subject
en bloc because it requires a separate introduction and because
I wished to facilitate a comparison of the different language
types with each other, as an assistance to their description.

285

I. INTRODUCTION

In introducing the subject it is convenient to distinguish between language and speech. This distinction is neither subtle nor theoretical; it is approximate only, and it is practical: language is that part of verbalization that reaches the ear, speech that part that carries the thought.

The notation of language if fragmentary; that of speech is complete. And the notation of language, incomplete as it is, is effected chiefly through punctuation.

Question mark and exclamation mark, e.g., influence both volume and inflection; colon, semicolon and period introduce certain pauses bearing qualities of finality in varying degree. Dashes and parentheses transcribe a different kind of pause, where, with a holding of breath, as it were, the meaning too is held over. In conclusion: speech essentially conveys ideation and language, affect.

Freud (50) has found that "affects and feelings correspond to processes of discharge, whose ultimate expressions are perceived as sensations." In so doing he has connected erogeneity with verbalization, inasmuch as affect—and that includes affect that has found verbal or vocal expression—is reducible theoretically to instinctual discharge. Theoretically it should therefore be possible to correlate affect with "affectivity" (Freud); practically, however, it has, in most instances, remained impossible to do so: there are but a few erogenic or quasi-erogenic combinations (such as, e.g., those producing the sexual affect) whose functioning can be named as responsible for the precipitation of a particular affect.

The foregoing concerns normal language; and it has mainly been stated in order to delimit morbid partial-erotic language —the subject of the present chapter—from normal language and to sketch the background for describing the former.

Partial-erotic language is regressive: it does not express affect, but is symptomatic of the intrusion into language of an erogenic process displaced upon the speech apparatus and forcing the latter to emulate a particular erogenic zone.[1]

There are different types of regressive partial-erotic language. They are exhibited only by individuals in whom certain partial-erotic excretory activities have retained or regained—either permanently or temporarily—their original sexual function. These individuals present the corresponding neurotic symptoms or perversions (pollakisuria, anuria, diarrhea, constipation, urinary games, the masturbatory employment of enemas, etc.), and their speech apparatus appears as conditioned, in its performance, by the functional characteristics of the particular excretory activity whose erogenic role it is forced to play. An alteration in their erogenic regime does not fail to reflect itself in a corresponding change in their language; and if and when analysis causes them to relinquish this "partial-erotic" disturbance or abuse, their speech becomes normal.

The general premise for the observation of specific types of erogenic language was first formulated by Ella Freeman Sharpe who wrote (132): "When the ego stabilizes . . . [the] achievement of body control and it becomes automatic, the emotions of anger and pleasure, which heretofore accompanied bodily discharges, must be dealt with in other ways. At the same time as sphincter control over anus and urethra is being established, the child is acquiring the power of speech and so an avenue of 'outerance' present from birth becomes of immense importance. First of all the discharge of feeling tension, when this is no longer relieved by physical discharge, can take place through speech. The activity of speaking is substituted for the physical activity, now restricted at other openings of the body, while words themselves become the very substitutes for the bodily substances . . ."

---

[1] I have dealt with this subject, at least in part, seven years ago in an article (18) from which I shall borrow some formulations. My paper contains, however, one error. Wherever the clinical picture of partial-erotic language shows traits in the patient's behavior that I compared to the effects of sedation or mild hypnosis, these are not characteristics of such language, but symptomatic of "a hypnotic evasion," dealt with in a later paper (20).

It is evident that if speaking is to be looked upon as a substitute for sphincter action, silence must be considered as the equivalent of sphincter closure. Temporary cessation of speech must, consequently, under certain conditions cause the retention of words as the substitute for an excretory product; and it must be possible to identify a particular form of silence as the equivalent of the closure of a particular sphincter. In other words: as there are different forms of regressive erogenic language, there are different forms of regressive erogenic silence; and the latter are coordinate to the former.

It can be said of all erogenic language that it interferes with the normal give and take of a conversation. In describing and illustrating briefly the main types of partial-erotic language that I have observed I must report that some language types are more distinctly observable than are others; and that mixed types are generally more frequent than pure ones and apt to confuse the clinical picture. Within the framework of the present volume it should, finally, hardly be necessary to repeat that these types of regressive language are not partial-*libidinal* but partial-*erotic*. It is not the partial libido discharged, but the particular erogenic zone discharging it whose functional characteristics the speech apparatus is forced to copy. And it is the copying by the speech apparatus of different erogenic zones that distinguishes one type of regressive language from another.

II. URETHRAL-EROTIC LANGUAGE

A. INCONTINENCE TYPE

It is characterized by an incessant flow of words, extreme dilution of analytic material, ineffectual punctuation, and lack of silence.

A female patient, paradigmatic for this type of language, had reacted to the inception of her treatment with an attack of urinary incontinence during coition. She used to "swim" into the anteroom, began talking as soon as she entered the office, and insisted upon closing the door herself, sometimes in such a fashion as to suggest the click of the lock on the door of a bath-room. The tempo of speaking was excessively rapid, the speed uniform and the flight of ideas extreme. At the end of the session she persisted in talking while getting up from the couch, left the door of the anteroom open, put on hat and coat conspicuously and resumed continence, as it were, only with the closing of the outer door.

B. PHALLIC TYPE

This type is almost impossible to describe because of its close resemblance to normal language. One can say only that there is a marked insistence upon speaking rather than listening, that the language is oratorical, and that speaking is noticeably enjoyed. It is forcefully articulated and there can be no objection to calling this language exhibitionistic.

The language of the female patient with the fantasy of clitoris urination (cf. pp. 170 f.) was representative of this type. She had pollakisuria, considered using the bathroom sixteen times daily as normal, and offered in one of the first analytic hours to show the analyst her left breast. She spoke *at* one, rather than *to* one, in perfect phrases with clauses and subclauses but in a strident voice, frequently smacking her lips at the end. Questions like "What do you think of that?" were constant attempts to obtain voyeuristic approval; and the telling of many anecdotes gave her the chance to exhibit her imitations.

Silences in phallic urethral-erotic language resemble those that the public speaker interpolates for effect; and with regard to punctuation one might point both to the dominance of the exclamation mark and to a certain prominence of the question mark in the verbalization. I admit that, as far as the language proper is concerned, this is not much of a description; but, as I said above, this language type does not lend itself very well to being described.

C. MIXED TYPE

The description of a mixture of the incontinence type and the phallic type of urethral-erotic regressive language has been given in another place. (Cf. pp. 153 f.) The "obstinate urge to talk, connected in most cases with a feeling of overflowing" described by Abraham (6) in individuals presenting "frequently . . . a neurotically exaggerated urge to urinate" belongs to the same mixed language type; and the reader of the present volume, familiar with the urethral-erotic discharge of cannibalistic libido, will not be surprised to find Abraham calling his observation that of an oral trait.[2]

III. ANAL-EROTIC LANGUAGE

This is the most distinctly observable type of regressive partial-erotic language. It is the language collateral to compulsive speech, although this relation is not reversable: I have never heard anal-erotic language without compulsive speech, but I have heard compulsive speech without anal-erotic language. While pitch and tone color vary in different individuals the language shows always a peculiar monotony, and is extremely halting. In order to characterize it more accurately than by merely calling it "verbal constipation," one may state that the small vertical punctuation marks—comma, semicolon, colon and period—have, in this language, become "malignant." They not only pervade it excessively, but they have left their normal positions—framing clauses, ending a part of the whole of a sentence, introducing specification of content, etc.—and now separate any word or series of words from the next; they are sometimes found even inside the single word. At the same time the punctuation has grown, as it were, to the extent of effecting pauses much longer than it would ordinarily, and of frequently terminating a mutilated series of words which it deprives of the chance of ever becoming a sentence.

In transcribing anal-erotic regressive language for the sake of illustration one cannot use much punctuation; for while one could notate their displacement one cannot notate their growth.

[2] I know, of course, that he calls it oral-*erotic* but I must disagree with him; he was, after all, not aware of the urethral-erotic discharge of oral *libido*.

I shall therefore simply use horizontal lines for the indication of the seat and the approximate length of the pauses.

Here is the beginning of an analytic hour of a male patient:

> "... The.
> .... I want to describe something ....
> as it is. .... And then talking makes it not so. ....
> ...."

A further characteristic, rarely missing in regressive anal-erotic language, is the frequent interpolation of a quasi interjection, transcribable as "er," "uh" or "ah," and imitative, so it appears, of flatus. A more or less explosive "but," followed by a long pause, is also not infrequent.

> Here is a sentence of the female whose pleasure physiology was described on p. 146 after she had become able, in a measure, to take to sexual relations:
>
> "..........................
> And then......ah........ah we kissed........ah, ah........
> the idea of this man's body near me....................play-
> ing with me.........................was nice........."

There is finally, on occasion, an abundance of participles in this type of regressive language as though the patient had to separate strivings from their subject. Instead of saying, for instance, "I felt warm," she—I have not noticed this in men—will say, "There is this feeling of being warm."

> Here is a transcript, in which another patient describes her feelings after the previous analytic hour:
>
> "Why, I don't know....
> yesterday when I came home..............first there was this
> feeling of excitement, then........of this wanting to........
> uh......I don't know..........throughout my whole insides
> ....of being very much alive..................
> this wanting to be with somebody........."

The error to be avoided in listening to this type of language is to mistake the halting verbalization as expressive of groping for words. It has nothing to do with that; the scheme is simply that somebody wants to say "Yesterday when I had my piano lesson" because this is the thought definitely on his mind, but instead he will say: "Ah..........yesterday when.......... ah..........I had..........my..........piano lesson." He will do so because his language has to emulate the peristaltic characteristics of a regressively sexualized anal-erotic zone. The pauses thus obtained are of course manifestations of anal-erotic silence, imitating a closure of the powerful sphincter ani. They are, therefore, unbreakable and their duration varies extremely; the patient engaged in such silence is tense, either rigid and motionless, or moving in what appears as distress. He is absorbed in a struggle either for or against verbalization; and in extreme instances speech interrupts silence rather than silence speech.

In the case of one patient, who presented upon occasion intestinal rumbling, it became possible, once or twice, to coordinate her regressive language with the peristaltic motions which she felt.

Once, when her language had again been excessively analerotic throughout several hours, producing not only long pauses between sentences but also a radical breaking up of every sentence itself, she reported upon her failure with many people to obtain from them a certain favor. She had noticed two symptoms in the course of her efforts: several intermittent stools before asking someone, and the inability to stretch out or continue the conversation after she had delivered herself of her request. I explained in nontechnical terms how erogeneity had here become behavior: the anus closes tightly after each short stool and so does the conversation; and I commented, again without being technical, on her narcissistic regression: she has no contact, cannot ingratiate herself and asks her question "by rote."

While discussing this and listening to further associations I suddenly notice that her language is now rather fluid. I call it to her attention.

She: But there are still pauses between the sentences.
I: But none inside.

It is obvious what had happened: the interpretation of the influence of the patient's regressive erogeneity upon her speech had, for the time being, canceled the better part of that upon her language.

No other type of regressively partial-erotic language demonstrates as convincingly as do anal-erotic language and silence that the resistance to free associations is in certain patients *overdetermined by a fear of incontinence in displacement.* How to deal with this fear depends entirely on the nature of the case. In the male patient, for instance, from whom the first sample was taken (cf. p. 291), I left the language alone until toward the end of his analysis, when it was easy to show it to him as just another of his intestinal symptoms and to explain its nature. His speech immediately became fluid. In the female patient presented above the interference of anal-erotic silence with verbalization was so excessive that it had to be dealt with much earlier: the pauses, when added up, took up a substantial part of the fifty minutes reserved for her analytic hour.

IV. ORAL-EROTIC SILENCE

There is no oral-erotic language, there is only an oral-erotic silence. The erogenic zone emulated by the speech apparatus is here the "earliest mouth"; and the patient engaged in this type of silence, has temporarily reverted to being an "infant," whose very name, as is commonly known, derives from the fact that he cannot speak. Regressive oral-erotic silence is not therefore either an interruption or a disruption of speech but rather a temporary replacement of verbalization by silence. It occurs without recognizable motivation, and conveys to the listener the impression that the patient had suddenly physically "absented" himself. The analysand exhibits no signs of struggle or conflict whatsoever, lies either perfectly still or is quietly engaged in some form of pantomime, informing either directly or indirectly (e.g., symbolically) of an erogenic occurrence. The silence appears "interminable," and can indeed rarely be terminated through admonition; its eventual termination is essentially a spontaneous one. The patient may inform one afterwards, credibly, of genuine and truly inconquerable inability to speak. If the speech apparatus is to be thought of as emulating the once dominant oral-erotic zone, one must assume that the passive ingestive function of this zone ("sucking") excludes the excretory performance of speaking, and that the collateral active and aggressive instinct component (biting) manifests itself in the abrupt severance of the subject from the object of what might be called a "primal" form of transference, in which the analyst plays the role of the breast. The speech apparatus does not, in other words, in this instance emulate sphincter action, but the mouth reverts instead to its previous existence in an early infantile ego.

> The theory of oral-erotic silence—the cannibalistic reincorporation of the breast in consequence of a regression to the second oral phase—has been given on pp. 72 f.; and the transference difficulties of the paradigmatic patient have been described on pp. 73 ff. It may be of interest to record further that in her case the abstinence rule had to be applied to seeing (visiting) her mother. For the "seeing" here was really seeing; and the eye became to such a degree the auxiliary to the mouth (cf. pp. 55 ff.) that the patient could gradually experience a visual "fascination" (her word) with the mother, and learn how this gratification was obtained at the expense of a workable transference.

The description of erogenic language will—as does all analytic description—become meaningful only to the analyst who is able to verify its existence in patients of his own. In order to do so, he would have to sharpen a natively good ear and revive in himself some of that interest in the spoken word that captivated the Elizabethans. "As your single words may be many waies transfigured," writes one of them (109), "to make the meetre or verse more tuneable and melodius, so also may your whole and entire clauses be in such sort contrived by the order of their construction as the eare may receive a certaine recreation, although the mind for any noveltie of sense be little or nothing affected. And therefore all your figures of grammaticall construction, I accompt them but merely auricular in that they reach no furder than the eare." Regressively partial-erotic language, a morbid formation, is not of course either "tunable" or "melodious"; but the ear, capable of perceiving it and of distinguishing between the different types, is the same that is able to derive "recreation" from artful speech, such as for instance from the infinite subtleties of the Shakespearean line.

BIBLIOGRAPHY

Key to Abbreviations

Col. P. Collected Papers, by Sigmund Freud. London: Hogarth Press. Vols. I and II, 1924; Vols. III and IV, 1925; Vol. V, 1950.

Int. J. Psa. International Journal of Psycho-Analysis

Int. Z. Psa. Internationale Zeitschrift für Psychoanalyse

J. Am. Psa. Journal of the American Psychoanalytic Association

Psa. Q. The Psychoanalytic Quarterly

Psa. St. Ch. The Psychoanalytic Study of the Child. Edited by Ruth S. Eissler, Anna Freud, Heinz Hartmann, Ernst Kris. New York: International Universities Press. Vols. I-X, 1945-1955.

Sel. P. Selected Papers on Psycho-Analysis, by Karl Abraham. London: Hogarth Press, 1927.

Stand. Ed. The Standard Edition of the Complete Psychological Works of Sigmund Freud. London: Hogarth Press. Vols. IV, V and VII, 1953; Vols. II, X and XVII, 1955.

1. ABRAHAM, K.: *Restrictions and Transformations of Scoptophilia in Psycho-neurotics; with Remarks on Analogous Phenomena in Folk-Psychology* (1913). Sel. P., pp. 169-234.
2. ———— *Ejaculatio Praecox* (1917). Sel. P., pp. 280-298.
3. ———— *The Narcissistic Evaluation of Excretory Processes in Dreams and Neurosis* (1920). Sel. P., pp. 318-322.
4. ———— *Contributions to the Theory of the Anal Character* (1921). Sel. P., pp. 370-392.
5. ———— *The Spider as a Dream Symbol* (1922). Sel. P., pp. 326-332.
6. ———— *The Influence of Oral Erotism on Character-Formation* (1924). Sel. P., pp. 393-406.
7. ————*A Short Study of the Development of the Libido, viewed in the Light of Mental Disorders* (1924). Sel. P., pp. 418-501.
8. BACH, J. S.: *Mass in B Minor.* New York: Schirmer. Vocal Score #18, Aria: p. 135.
9. BORNSTEIN, B.: *The Analysis of a Phobic Child: Some Problems of Theory and Technique in Child Analysis.* Psa. St. Ch., III/IV, 1949.
10. ———— *On Latency.* Psa. St. Ch., VI, 1951.
11. BOWERS, F.: *Japanese Theatre.* New York: Hermitage House, 1952, p. 3.

12. BRUNSWICK, R. M.: *The Preoedipal Phase of the Libido Development* (1940). In: *The Psychoanalytic Reader,* ed. R. Fliess. New York: International Universities Press, 1948.
    A: pp. 273-274.
13. CASTIGLIONI, A.: *A History of Medicine.* New York: Knopf, 1941.
14. COHN, F.: *Practical Approach to the Problem of the Narcissistic Neuroses.* Psa. Q., IX, 1940.
15. COUPERIN, F.: *Soeur Monique.* Pieces de Clavecin.
16. *Encyclopaedia Britannica,* 14th edition.
17. FLIESS, R.: *Knocking on Wood: A Note on the Preoedipal Nature of the Magic Effect.* Psa. Q., XIII, 1944.
18. ———— *Silence and Verbalization: A Supplement to the "Analytic Rule."* Int. J. Psa., XXX, 1949.
19. ———— *Countertransference and Counteridentification.* J. Am. Psa., I, 1953.
20. ———— *The Hypnotic Evasion: A Clinical Observation.* Psa. Q., XXII, 1953.
21. ———— *On the "Spoken Word" in the Dream.* Chapter V in: *The Revival of Interest in the Dream.* New York: International Universities Press, 1953.
    A: pp. 147ff.
22. FRAZER, J.: *The Golden Bough,* I. New York: Macmillan, 1922. Cf. Index: "Stones."
23. FREUD, ANNA: *Indications for Child Analysis.* Psa. St. Ch., I, 1945.
24. ———— *The Psychoanalytic Study of Infantile Feeding Disturbances.* Psa. St. Ch., II, 1946.
25. ———— *Observations on Child Development.* Psa. St. Ch., VI, 1951.
26. ———— *The Mutual Influences in the Development of Ego and Id: Introduction to the Discussion.* Psa. St. Ch., VII, 1952.
27. ———— *The Role of Bodily Illness in the Mental Life of Children.* Psa. St. Ch., VII, 1952.
28. ———— *Problems of Infantile Neurosis: A Discussion.* Psa. St. Ch., IX, 1954.
29. FREUD, SIGMUND: *On Aphasia* (1891). New York: International Universities Press, 1953.
30. ———— *The Justification for Detaching from Neurasthenia a Particular Syndrome: The Anxiety-Neurosis* (1894). Col. P., I, pp. 76-106.
31. ———— *The Interpretation of Dreams* (1900). Stand. Ed., IV, V.
    A: "A Dream of Bismarck's [1900]." Vol. V, Ch. VI, E, xi.
    B: Vol. V, Ch. VI, G, vii.
    C: Vol. IV, Ch. V, D.
    D: Vol. V, p. 373.
    E: Vol. IV, Ch. V, B, ii.
    F: Vol. IV, Ch. V, D; Ch. VI, C.
    G: Vol. V, p. 355.

32. FREUD: *On Dreams* (1901). Stand. Ed., V.
33. ———— *The Psychopathology of Everyday Life* (1901). In: *The Basic Writings of Sigmund Freud.* New York: Random House, 1938.
    A: Sec. xii.
34. ———— *Fragment of an Analysis of a Case of Hysteria* (1905 [1901]). Stand. Ed., VII.
35. ———— *Wit and Its Relation to the Unconscious* (1905). In: *The Basic Writings of Sigmund Freud.* New York: Random House, 1938.
36. ———— *Three Essays on the Theory of Sexuality* (1905). Stand. Ed., VII.
    A: p. 217.
    B: "The Transformation of Puberty," Ch. III.
    C: "Infantile Sexuality," Ch. II, 4.
    D: p. 183.
    E: "Infantile Sexuality," Ch. II.
37. ———— *Character and Anal Erotism* (1908). Col. P., II, pp. 45-50.
37a. ———— *General Remarks on Hysterical Attacks* (1909). Col. P., II, p. 103.
38. ———— *Analysis of a Phobia in a Five-Year-Old Boy* (1909). Stand. Ed., X.
    A: pp. 82-83.
    B: p. 37.
    C: p. 129.
    D: p. 77.
    E. p. 113.
39. ———— *Notes upon a Case of Obsessional Neurosis* (1909). Stand. Ed., X.
    A: p. 326.
40. ———— *Leonardo da Vinci: A Psychosexual Study of an Infantile Reminiscence* (1910). New York: Moffat, Yard, 1916.
41. ———— *Brief an Dr. Friedrich S. Krauss über die Anthropophyteia* (1910). Gesammelte Werke, VIII. London: Imago Publishing Co., 1943, pp. 224-225.
42. ———— *Formulations Regarding the Two Principles in Mental Functioning* (1911). Col. P., IV, pp. 13-21.
43. ———— *Gross ist die Diana der Epheser* (1912). Gesammelte Werke, VIII. London: Imago Publishing Co., 1943, pp. 360-361.
44. ———— *The Occurrence in Dreams of Material from Fairy-Tales* (1913). Col. P., IV, pp. 236-243.
45. ———— *The Theme of the Three Caskets* (1913). Col. P., IV, pp. 244-256.
46. ———— *Fausse Reconnaissance ('Déjà Raconté') in Psycho-Analytic Treatment* (1913). Col. P., II, pp. 334-341.
    A: pp. 337-338.
    B: p. 340.

47. FREUD: *On Narcissism: An Introduction* (1914). Col. P., IV, pp. 30-59.

48. ———— *Instincts and Their Vicissitudes* (1915). Col. P., IV, pp. 60-83.

49. ———— *Repression* (1915). Col. P., IV, pp. 84-97.

50. ———— *The Unconscious* (1915). Col. P., IV, pp. 98-136.

51. ———— *A Mythological Parallel to a Visual Obsession* (1916). Col. P., IV, pp. 345-346.
    A: p. 346.

52. ———— *A General Introduction to Psychoanalysis* (1916/17). New York: Liveright, 1935.

53. ———— *Mourning and Melancholia* (1917). Col. P., IV, pp. 152-170.

54. ———— *Contributions to the Psychology of Love. The Taboo of Virginity* (1918). Col. P., IV, pp. 217-235.

55. ———— *From the History of an Infantile Neurosis* (1918 [1914]). Stand. Ed., XVII.
    A: Sec. viii.
    B: Sec. ix.
    C: p. 572.
    D: Sec. vi.
    E: Sec. iv, fn.
    F: p. 498.

56. ———— *'A Child Is Being Beaten'* (1919). Col. P., II, pp. 172-201.
    A: p. 201.
    B: p. 184.

57. ———— *Associations of a Four-Year-Old Child* (1920). Stand. Ed., XVIII, p. 266.

58. ———— *Dreams and Telepathy* (1922). Col. P., IV, p. 428.

59. ———— *Medusa's Head* (1922). Col. P., V, pp. 105-106.

60. ———— *Two Encyclopaedia Articles: (A) Psycho-Analysis; (B) The Libido Theory* (1922). Col. P., V, pp. 107-135.

61. ———— *The Ego and the Id* (1923). London: Hogarth Press, 1927.
    A: Ch. IV.
    B: Ch. V.
    C: pp. 61-63.

62. ———— *The Infantile Genital Organization of the Libido* (1923). Col. P.: II, pp. 244-249.

63. ———— *The Passing of the Oedipus-Complex* (1924), Col. P., II, pp. 269-276.

64. ———— *Negation* (1925). Col. P., V, pp. 181-185.

65. ———— *Some Psychological Consequences of the Anatomical Distinction between the Sexes* (1925). Col. P., V, p. 193.

66. ———— *Inhibition, Symptom and Anxiety* (1926). London: Hogarth Press, 1936.

67. ———— *Fetishism* (1927). Col. P., V, pp. 198-204.

68. ———— *Humour* (1928). Col. P., V, pp. 215-221.

69. ———— *Dostoevsky and Parricide* (1928). Col. P., V, pp. 222-242.

70. FREUD: *Civilisation and Its Discontents* (1930). London: Hogarth Press, 1930.
    A: Ch. VI.
    B: Ch. VIII.
    C: Ch. VII.
    D: Ch. IV.

71. ———— *Female Sexuality* (1931). Col. P., V, pp. 252-272.
    A: pp. 254-255.

72. ———— *The Acquisition of Power over Fire* (1932). Col. P., V, pp. 288-294.

73. ———— *New Introductory Lectures on Psychoanalysis* (1932). New York: Norton, 1933.
    A: "Anatomy of the Psychic Personality," Ch. III (xxxi).
    B: "Anxiety and the Instinctual Life," Ch. IV (xxxii).
    C: "Revision of the Theory of Dreams," Ch. I (xxix).

74. ———— *A Disturbance of Memory on the Acropolis* (1936). Col. P., V, pp. 302-312.

75. ———— *Entwurf zu einem Brief an Thomas Mann* (Draft of a Letter to Thomas Mann) (1936). Int. Z. Psa., XXVI, 1941, p. 218. (Trans. this writer.)

76. ———— *Analysis Terminable and Interminable* (1937). Col. P., V, pp. 316-357.

77. ———— *An Outline of Psychoanalysis* (1938). New York: Norton, 1949.
    A: Ch. I.
    B: Ch. II.
    C: Ch. III.
    D: p. 84 (partly retransl.).

78. ———— *Moses and Monotheism* (1939). New York: Knopf, 1939.
    A: pp. 156 ff.
    B: p. 138.

79. ———— *Schriften aus dem Nachlass* (1941). Gesammelte Werke, XVII. London: Imago Publishing Co., 1941, p. 151.

80. GADDIANO, A.: *Life of Leonardo*. Quoted in "Leonardo da Vinci." London: Paidon Press, 1943.

81. Genesis, XXII:i-iii.

82. GLOVER, E.: *The Concept of Dissociation*. Int. J. Psa., XXIV, 1943.

83. GOETHE: *Faust,* Part I.

84. HARTMANN, H.: *Comments on the Psychoanalytic Theory of the Ego.* Psa. St. Ch., V, 1950.

85. HENDRICK, I.: *Contributions of Psychoanalysis to the Study of Psychosis.* J.A.M.A., CXIII, 1939.

86. HOFFER, W.: *Mouth, Hand, and Ego-Integration.* Psa. St. Ch., III/IV, 1949.

87. ———— *Oral Aggressiveness and Ego Development.* Int. J. Psa., XXXI, 1950.
    A: p. 158.

88. HOFFER, W.: *Psychoanalysis. Practical and Research Aspects.* Baltimore: Williams & Wilkins, 1955, p. 24.

89. ISAIAH, A. B. and SHARFMAN, B.: *The Pentateuch of Rashi's Commentary.* Brooklyn, N. Y.: S. S. and R. Publishing Co., 1949.
    A: p. 204.

90. ISAKOWER, O.: *On the Pathopsychology of Falling Asleep.* Int. J. Psa., XIX, 1938.

91. ———— *On the Exceptional Position of the Auditory Sphere.* Int. J. Psa., XX, 1939.

92. JONES, E.: Quoted by Abraham (4).

93. JOSEPH, Sister Miriam: *Shakespeare's Use of the Arts of Language.* New York: Columbia University Press, 1947.

94. KATAN, A.: *Experience with Enuretics.* Psa. St. Ch., II, 1946.

95. KEISER, S.: *Orality Displaced to the Urethra.* J. Am. Psa., II, 1954.

96. KRIS, E.: *Some Comments and Observations on Early Autoerotic Activity.* Psa. St. Ch., VI, 1951.

97. LANDOWSKA, W.: "Masterpieces for Harpsicord." *A Treasury of Harpsichord Music.* Victor Album, M/DM #1181.

98. LEE, L.: *A Rose for Winter: Travels in Andalusia.* New York: Morrow, n.d. (1956?).

99. LEONARDO DA VINCI: Windsor Mss. (R. 1358). In: *The Mind of Leonardo da Vinci,* by E. McCurdy. New York: Dodd, Mead, 1939, Ch. III.

100. ———— Arundel Mss. (Folio 156V). In: *The Notebooks of Leonardo da Vinci,* ed. and tr. E. McCurdy. New York: Reynal & Hitchcock, 1939, Ch. I.

102. MAHLER, M. S. and GOSLINER, B. J.: *On Symbiotic Child Psychosis: Genetic, Dynamic and Restitutive Aspects.* Psa. St. Ch., X, 1955.

103. MONTAIGNE, M.: "Of Cannibals." *Essays.* London, Oxford, 1927.

104. MOZART: *Sonata in C Major.* Koechel 545. New York: Kalmus.

105. ———— *The Magic Flute.*
    A: II, #21.
    B: I, Dialogue.

106. NUNBERG, H.: *Allgemeine Neurosenlehre auf psychoanalytischer Grundlage.* Bern-Berlin: Hans Huber, 1932.
    A. English edition: *Principles of Psychoanalysis: Their Application to the Neuroses.* New York: International Universities Press, 1955.

107. PASCAL, B.: *Lettres Provinciales.*

108. PLATO: *The Republic,* IX.

109. PUTTENHAM, G.: *Arte of English Poesie.* London, 1589.

110. REICH, A.: *The Discussion of 1912 on Masturbation and Our Present-day Views.* Psa. St. Ch., VI, 1951.

111. RIBBLE, M.: *Disorganizing Factors in Infant Personality.* Am. J. Psychiat., XCVIII, 1941.

112. RILKE, R. M.: *Das Marien-Leben.* Leipzig: Insel Verlag, 1912.

113. ROSE, H. J.: *Handbook of Greek Mythology*. New York: Dutton, 1929.

114. SCHILDER, P.: *Medizinische Psychologie*. Berlin: Springer, 1924. (English: *Medical Psychology*, tr. D. Rapaport. New York: International Universities Press, 1953.)

115. SCHLICK, M.: "Naturphilosophie." *Lehrbuch der Philosophie*. Berlin: Ullstein, 1925.

116. SHAKESPEARE, W.: *A Winter's Tale*, V:i.

117. ———— *Coriolanus*.
> A: IV:v.
> B: IV:iii.

118. ———— *Cymbeline*, V:iv.

119. ———— *Othello*, I:i.

120. ———— *Hamlet*.
> A: IV:iv.
> B: I:iv.
> C: III:ii.
> D: I:ii.

121. ———— *Henry V*, I:i.

122. ———— *Julius Caesar*, I:ii.

123. ———— *Macbeth*.
> A: V:i.
> B: I:ii.

124. ———— *Measure for Measure*.
> A: II:ii.
> B: I:i.

125. ———— *Merchant of Venice*.
> A: IV:i.
> B: I:iii.
> C: IV:i.

126. ———— *Midsummer Night's Dream*.
> A: I:i.

127. ———— *Othello*.

128. ———— *Romeo and Juliet*.
> A: II:iv.
> B: II:v.
> C: II:ii.

129. ———— *The Tempest*, I:ii.

130. ———— *Timon of Athens*, I:ii.

131. ———— *Twelfth Night*, III:i.

132. SHARPE, E. F.: *Psycho-physical Problems Revealed in Language: An Examination of Metaphor*. Int. J. Psa., XXI, 1940.

133. SIMMEL, E.: *Self-Preservation and the Death Instinct*. Psa. Q., XIII, 1944.

134. SPERBER, H.: *Über den Einfluss sexueller Momente auf Entstehung und Entwicklung der Sprache* (On the Influence of Sexual Factors on the Origin and Development of Language). Imago, I, 1912.

135. SPITZ, R. A.: *Anaclitic Depression*. Psa. St. Ch., II, 1946.

136. ———— *Anxiety in Infancy: A Study of Its Manifestations in the First Year of Life*. Int. J. Psa., XXXI, 1950.

137. ———— *The Primal Cavity: A Contribution to the Genesis of Perception and Its Role for Psychoanalytic Theory*. Psa. St. Ch., X, 1955.

138. STERBA, E.: *Analysis of Psychogenic Constipation in a Two-Year-Old*. Psa. St. Ch., III/IV, 1949.

139. TAUSK, V.: *On the Origin of the "Influencing Machine" in Schizophrenia* (1919). In: *The Psychoanalytic Reader*, ed. R. Fliess. New York: International Universities Press, 1948.

140. TCHEKOV, A.: *The Darling, and Other Stories*, tr. C. Garnett. London: Chatto & Windus, 1921.

141. WANGH, M.: *Othello: The Tragedy of Iago*. Psa. Q., XIX, 1950.

INDEX

Case material and illustrations to the various (partial-libidinal) phases are listed after each phase or phase group, in the order in which they occur.

Abraham, K., 4, 49, 53-54, 111, 115, 117, 137, 150, 196, 290, 297, 302
  on affect and defecation, 123
  on ambition, 152
  on anal-sadistic manifestations, 120, 124-125, 162
  on cathectic displacement, 25-26
  on ejaculatio praecox, 161
  on fantasies of crushing penis, 181
  on incest prohibition, 21
  on passive sexual aim, 63
  on phallic "partial love," etc., 73
  on spider as dream symbol, 180-181
  on urge to talk, 153, 290
Accident proneness, 115, 117
Acting out, 92, 108, 228
Activity
  in first oral phase, 60-65
  transformation of passive experience into, 107, 194
Addict, 70
Aesthetic pleasure (sublimated), 103
Affect
  "archaic," and sphincter control, 121-124
  becoming conscious, 127
  cannibalistic, *see* Impatience
  and defecation, 123
  discharge of, 243-245, 286-287
  and erogenous zone, 143, 286
  inhibition of, 43-44, 179
  and instinctive idea, 107-108
  and language, 286-287
  and masturbation, 146
  and musical thought, 139
  quantum, 43, 107, 143
  sexual, 200, 286
  "signal-" (rage), 123
"Affectivity" (Freud) and language, 286
Affirmation, 57, 173, 191
Aggression
  aims of, 49

  and superego formation, 34-35, 38-40
  assumption of primary, 3-8
  defused, 243-247, 252-253, 259, 275
  discharge of, 72, 101, 242-245, 253, 260, 262, 267, 275
  in melancholia, 4-5
  "neutralized," 42, 64
  oral-sadistic, 242-247, 260, 275
  turned upon the self, 244
  see also Cannibalistic libido, Death instinct, Destructive instinct, Hostility, Rage
Aim inhibition (cannibalistic), 88
Aktual-neurotic, 149, 266
Alienation, states of, 188-190, 256
Amaterasu-O-mikame, 210
Ambition, 152-153
Ambivalence, and oral-sadistic libido, 273
"Anaclitic" depression, 72 f.
Anal-sadistic phase (s)
  affect (archaic), control of, 121-128
  anal-erotic elaboration upon cannibalistic and oral-erotic libido (Freud, Abraham), 111-144
  anal-erotic elaboration upon instinctual strivings, 124
  anal-erotic object, 116-121
  anal-erotic zone, 124, 132, 143
  anal-erotic zone, cathectic displacement to, 25-26
  anal reversal, 125-128
  anal-sadistic development and the ear, 131-137
  constipation, delusion about, 116
  distinction between first and second, 111, 115, 124
  ear, controlling speech, posture, etc., 137-139
  ego nuclei and, 70, 123-124
  ego, preservation of, and anal sphincter, 124

Anal-sadistic phase (s) *(con't)*
persistence of, in later phases, *see below*
persistence of orality in, 111-121, 124
persistence of orality in language in, 132-137
Portia's second injunction, 125
regression to, 47-49, 92, 138, 243, 249 fn.
rectal procreation, fantasy of, 120
sphincter "morality," *see* Affect *above*
"spoken" word, fear of, 134-137
thought, motor characteristics of, 128-131
thought and musical thought, 138-144
see also Cannibalism, Phallic phase, Genital phase
Anal-sadistic phases: Clinical and Illustrative Material
fistula recti, 112-114
excessive enemas, 114 f.
child afraid of toilet, 116
cannibalistic impatience, 117
feces, animation of, 117 fn.
man in the dark, 118
refusal to defecate, 118
constipation a "pilot" symptom, 119
Viola, coin and Clown, 120 f.
Shylock and Laban's sheep, 121
Abraham's little Hungarian boy, 123
melancholic carrying thousands in currency, 124
brothers eating with letter scale (Abraham), 125
Portia's second injunction against Shylock, 125
anal reversal and name, 126 f.
Rat Man, 127
Hamlet and the Captain, 128 f.
Cassius swimming with Caesar, 129 fn.
Macbeth against Norway, 129 fn.
Rodin's "Thinker," 130
"the ayre a chartered Libertine," 133 fn.
Mephistopheles and the Freshman, 133
a modern myth of the analyst, 134 f.
spoken word, fear of, 135 f.
Hamlet's soliloquy, 136 f.

Viola and the Clown, 137
"Anthropophyteia," 197
Anxiety, 107, 123, 160, 179, 190
first appearance of, in oral-sadistic phase, 79-80
Aphasia, 105 fn.
Appetites (Plato), 269
"Archaic experience" (Little Hans), 12-40
Art, 65, 102, 171-172
Atavist, *see* Cannibalism, Shylock's
Auditory sphere, 36-37, 131-143; *see also* Ear, Hearing
Autoerotism, 53, 61, 69-70; *see also* Masturbation
Autohypnosis (and "voice of super-ego"), 38
Autopsic encumbrance, xix
Auxiliary acts, *see* By-play

Bach, J. S., 139-141, 297
Backache
and menstruation, 235, 247
and *Kreuz*, 262-263
and Juliet's Nurse, 265
in male, 268-269
Baubo (and Dysaules), 205
Beating fantasies, 47, 62, 150
Bible, 20-21, 31, 98-101, 121
Bibring, E., 64
Birth
anal concept of, 15, 117, 120-121, 236, 247
oral concept of, 120, 238-239, 273
phallic concept of, 22
representation of, 211, 234
trauma of, 79
urethral-erotic concept of, 22, 28
see also Child, Fantasies
Bismarck, 19-21, 26, 27, 204
Bisyllabic reduplication, 104-107, 164, 168, 194
Biting, 91, 104, 108, 153, 275
and cannibalistic intent toward nipple, 112-114
and child in anaclitic depression, 72 f.
and death instinct, 86 f.
and (jaw) activity (Hoffer), 72 fn.
see also Anal-sadistic phases, Cannibalism, Castration, Oral phase (second)

Bladder, 25-26
  loss of control of, 132, 158-159; *see also* Incontinence
  stone, 28-30
  see also Urethral erotism, Urination
Bleeding, limitation of, 30-31; *see also* Castration, Symbolism
Body
  and body-ego, 209
  identification with organs, 147-148
  as phallus, 16, 18-19, 102, 181, 255
  see also Mother
Body-ego, 44, 48, 128, 131, 208-209
  introjection of mother into, 209, 212, 215-216, 224, 229-230, 237, 249
  and libido, xviii, 274-275
  regressive conditions of, 208-209
  and womb, 249
Bornstein, B., 170, 195, 297
Bowers, F., 210, 297
Breast, 206
  analyst becomes, 96
  and cannibalistic strivings in child, 161
  and *déjà raconté*, 191-193
  feeding, sexually stimulating, 211
  and first oral phase, 56, 60, 62-64, 69-70
  and *Gebärmutter*, 209-213
  "having and being," 71, 73-76, 193
  Mephistopheles and the Freshman, 133
  and oedipus complex, 65
  refound, in genital sexual union, 273
  and second oral phase, 71-77, 78, 80, 86, 101 fn.
  sucking of, 254-255
  see also Mouth, Nipple, Oral phases, Portia's Injunctions, Transference
Breath, holding of, 227-228, 235-237, 247
Brody, M., 100-101
Brown, I., xv
Brunswick, R. M., xviii, 114, 226, 255, 266, 298
By-play, 196, 203, 276

Cannibalism, Cannibalistic desire, Cannibalistic
  absence (relative) of—manifestations in child, 78 f.

affect of (impatience), 88, 107-110, 117, 164-168, 170
aggression, urethral-erotic discharge of, 245-246
aim inhibition (and aim displacement), 78, 88-89
castration and, 180, 232
and communion, 98-101, 127
and delusion of indigestion, 163
ejaculatio praecox and discharge of —libido, 161
enuresis and ontogenesis of, 161
and execution, 97-98
and forms of violence, *see* Aim inhibition *above*
impatience, *see* Affect *above*
incontinence and, 164-168; *see also* Incontinence
Leonardo's exhortation against, 99 fn.
libido, anal-erotic elaboration upon, 111-116, 125, 165-166
libido, urethral-erotic, elaboration upon, 88, 152-168, 226, 237, 240, 290
Montaigne on, 98 fn.
ontogenesis of, and enuresis, 161
persistence (collective) of—desire, 97-101
persistence (in individuals) of—desire, 97-101
Portia's injunctions against, 80-86, 125
prohibition against speaking, and, 99
Rashi's Commentary, 100 fn., 101 fn.
Sacrifice of Abraham, 98-99
Shylock's, 80-86, 125, 164
transsubstantiation and, 100-101
urethral incontinence and, *see* Libido, Shylock *above*
see also Biting, Devouring, Eating, Ejaculatio praecox, Fear, Oral *and* Phallic phases
Castiglioni, A., 28-29, 298
Castrated-phallic, 144-145, 165, 171-176, 179, 183
Castration, Castration complex
  becomes murder, 31
  and biting, 96, 177, 181
  through cannibalistic invasion, 177-181, 232

Castration, Castration complex (con't)
a (castrative) "dream of analysis," 232
=death, 159
denial of, 166, 172-175
and déjà raconté, 182-194
fright (shock of), 166-167, 191-194, 256
and (infantile) masturbation, 191-194
and masturbation, 184-185
and phallic organization, 95-96, 144-145
primal fantasy of, 30, 191
and sound, 167
—wish of "Little Hans," 13
Cause-effect, reveral of, 127-128
Centaurs, 271-272
Character
analysis, 94, 227
defect, 70
Character traits, 196
anal, 88, 125
and cannibalistic libido, 88-89, 152-153
and deafness, 138
urethral-erotic, 152-153
Child
and anxiety (beginning of), 79
and lack of cannibalistic manifestations in, 78-80
=clitoris, 150
coitus play of, 10
direct observation of, xvi, 117, 132, 195
dream of, 178-180
fantasies about pregnancy and childbirth, 15-18, 22, 28, 117, 120-121, 169-170; see also Birth, Pregnancy
fear of animals in, 118; see also Little Hans, Phobia
fear of defecating, in, 116, 119
institutionalized, xvi, 72
invasions (cannibalistic) of, by parent, 88, 89
loss of newly acquired functions in, 132
reared without parents, 10-11
regression in, 132
speech of, 138
see also Infant, Seduction, Trauma
Chronology of development, xvi

Clitoris
clitoridian orgasm, 201
element in (pleasure-physiological) copy of rectum, 145-147
and feelings of inferiority, 147-150
urinary erection of, 198
urination, fantasy of, 170-171, 289
Cloaca
fantasy of, 161
regressive revival of, 146
Cohn, F., 137, 198, 221, 252, 298
Coition, theory of, 268, 272-281; see also Genital phase
Communion, 98-101, 127
Compulsion neurosis, 124
Compulsions, 76-77, 90, 112, 162, 243
Condensation, xviii-xix, 17, 123, 164, 179
Constipation, 115-116, 119, 287
"verbal," 290
Constitution
sexual, 146-147, 274; see also Fantasy "uncastrated," 175
Continence, 25-26, 41, 44, 123, 145-146, 148, 170, 193, 278
=phallic makeup, 148, 170, 193; see also Cannibalism
Conversion symptoms, 61, 113-114, 162, 244-245, 255, 266
Cooking, invention of, 155
Council of Trent, 98, 100-101
Countercathexis
and neutralized aggression, 42
and repression, 42, 194
Counteridentification, 33-35, 38
Counterpoint, 129
Couperin, F., 141, 298
Crucifix, as symbol of mother, 259-260
Crying, 149-150, 176
Cunnilingus, 196-197
Curiosity (scientific), 130

Daydreams, of a compulsive patient, 36
Death
fear of, 6
wishes, 15, 38, 273
see also Castration
Death instinct, 4, 6, 8, 45-46, 64-65
original in second oral phase, 71, 86, 246
and regressive revival of oral-sadistic mouth, 86-88

Death instinct (con't)
  see also Aggression, Destructive instinct, Instincts, Leonardo da Vinci
Defecation, 78, 106, 146
  fear of, 116-117, 119
  toilet-training, 122-123
Defense, scoptophilic, 175
Déjà raconté, 182-194
Déjà rêvé, 189
Déjà vu, 188, 192
Delusions
  about analyst, 39
  analysis of, 58
  and constipation, 116
  concerning the castration complex (déjà raconté) 168, 182-194; see also Transference
  genesis of, 69
  of inferiority, 147
  shared by father and son (Little Hans), 35
Demeter, 205-206, 209
Depersonalization, 189-190
Depression, 48, 149, 242
  anaclitic, 72-73
  in infancy, 5-6, 72-73, 117
  see also Melancholia
Derealization, 189-190
Desexualization, 46, 57, 65; see also Sublimation
Destructive instinct, 45-46; see also Aggression, Death instinct, Thanatos, Instinct
Development, deviation in chronology, xvi
Devil, the, 271 f.
Devouring, 78-79, 86-87, 99, 107, 153, 177-181, 273
Diana, 260
Displacement
  of biting impulse, 153
  of cannibalistic aim, 78, 88-89, 126, 153-154
  cathectic, 85, 125-128, 206, 249, 274
  of fear of incontinence upon language, 293
  from front to back, 173-174; see also Anal-sadistic phase (anal reversal)
  from genital to anal, 25-26, 125
  and identification, 147
  of phallic and castrated genital, 195, 199

in phobia, 33
of visual upon acoustic, 59
of visual upon tactile, 77
Doctor, passive devotion to, 89
Dora, xv, 171
Dream (s)
  affect in, 245
  alteration of symbols in, 167
  arousal, 81, 198, 245
  of "the beautiful landscape," 255
  of Bismarck, 19-21, 26, 27, 204
  of bridges, 148
  déjà vu in, 189
  of Dora, 171
  of enuretic child, 158
  fantasy material in, 189
  Freud's, see Freud (dreams of)
  fulfilling bodily need, 70
  of "getting well," 217
  incestuous, 270
  of inhibition, 244
  interpretation, 178-180
  menstrual, 91, 216-234, 245-247, 249-259
  of nudity, 220-221
  orgastic, 73-75, 91
  of primal scene, 118-119
  punishment in, 5
  representation of Kreuz in, 254-256
  spider as symbol in, 180-181
  spoken word in, 136, 171
  traumatic, 105, 168, 218-219, 222
  of waves, 221-230, 247, 252
  and wish, 16, 30, 217, 244
  of Wolf Man, 178-180
  see also Child, Symbolism
Dysmenorrhea, 249, 252-253

Ear, 96, 104-106, 167, 286
  and anal-sadistic development, 131-143
  survival of mouth in, 133
  see also Auditory sphere, Hearing
Eating, 78-80, 86, 95, 100-101, 124-125, 212-213, 243, 246, 251
  and being eaten, 78-79, 95, 114, 161
  disturbances, 78, 80, 115, 138, 155-158
  of forbidden food, 269, 272
  of God, 100-101
  and killing, 86, 166
  prohibitions against, 78, 80

Eating (con't)
together, 94-96, 124-125, 242; see also Communion
Ecology, phallic, 160, 166, 167, 193
Ego
and castration threat, 191, 193-194
delimitation from object, 71-75, 79
dissolution of, 124, 159-160
and double environment, 128, 131
formation, and affect control, 43-44, 122-123, 287
formation, and speech inception, 104-107
inception of, 57, 69-70, 123
and incorporation, 90
and introjection of father, 17
in melancholia, 4-5, 82, 85
narcissistic cathexis of, 73, 75
nascent (and object), 71-74
nuclei, 69-70, 123
and object, 71, 101
and partial object and subject, 204, 273-274
in phallic phase, 144, 158-160
reduction of, 204, 208
and reflex arc, 122
and repression, 194
in second oral phase, 71-75
and speech inception, 104-107, 132, 294
and superego, 34, 36-38, 48, 85
see also Regression, Body-ego
Ejaculation, 151, 172, 200, 266
and urethral-erotic discharge, 144
without mechanical stimulation, 76-77
Ejaculatio praecox, 61-64, 76-77, 161-163, 217, 244
Elizabethans, xv, 106-107, 295; see also Shakespeare
Emotions, see Affect
"Empathy," 101-104
End pleasure, 197, 199
Enlightenment, sexual, 235-236
Enuresis, 158, 161, 164, 171
Equilibrium, 138
Erection (urinary), 198
Erogeneity
of anal zone, 143
elaboration upon model of, 201-203, 273
and language, 283-291

and libido, xviii, 54, 161, 165, 177
and libido, distinction between, 48-49, 151-152
of phallus, 163
primitive model of, 201-203, 273
see also Erogenic zones, Mouth, and all phases
Erogenic zones, 45, 48-49, 111, 151-152, 266
and partial libido, 54, 199-202, 234-235, 246, 273
(quasi-) inferiority of second, 201-202, 273
see also Genital phase, Zone equation
Eros, 6, 45, 57
and activity, 65
Erythrophobia, 160
Eucharist, Holy Sacrament of, 100
Execution (queries on philosophy of), 97-98, 109
Exhibitionism, 91, 103, 113, 172-173, 205-206, 210-211, 220-221, 225, 254, 289
Eye, 55-60, 77, 90, 91, 119-120
—mouth unit, 101-104
substitution of ear for, 132-133
see also Mouth, Vision

Facial expression, 128-129
Fantasy
active and passive, in preoedipal phase, 226
of anal intercourse, 121
of clitoris urination, 170-171, 289
of cloaca, 146, 148, 161
and déjà vu, 189
of erection through filling penis with urine, 169-170
of incorporating the breast, 191
and masturbation, 27, 47-48, 61, 64, 91
vs. memory, xvii-xviii
menstrual, 247-249
oral, and emergence of new erogenic zone, 234-235
passive cannibalistic, 127
of phallus equipped with mouth, 176-181
of pregnancy, through filling "mother's belly" with urine, 169, 222
of return to womb, 160, 249

Fantasy *(con't)*
   of "uncastrated" constitution, 171-176
   see also Birth, Child, Primal fantasies
Fargeon, H., xv
Father
   "archaic" (Freud), 34
   "assistive," 17
   death wishes against, 15, 38, 273
   oedipal identification of child with, 17, 34-35, 37-40
   passive role to, 177-180
   religion, 99-101
   and superego, 34-35, 37-40, 82
   voice of, 37, 136-137
   see also Hamlet's Soliloquy, Superego
Fausse reconnaissance, 188-189
Faust, 133, 240, 272
Fear
   of associating freely, 161
   of being eaten, 78-79, 95, 114
   of exhibiting oneself, 148-149
   of loss of love, 122
   of poisoning, 116
   social, 160-161, 170
   of spoken word, 134-137
   see also Anxiety, Phobia
Feces
   and accident proneness, 117
   animate nature of, 116-118, 120, 134, 268
   and bisyllabic reduplication, 106
   and rectal procreation, fantasy of, 120-121, 247 ff.
Feeding, without love, 61-62, 74; *see also* Breast, Eating
Female, *see* Partial object *and* subject, Sexuality
Femininity, 199
   increase of, 263
Ferenczi, S., 39, 44, 189
Fertility rites, 28
Fetish (ism), 66, 118, 167, 174
Fire, 154-155, 165, 167, 176
Fistula recti, 112-114
Fixation
   in melancholia, 4
   on mother, 269
   and regression, 65, 124
Fliess, R., 298

Folie à deux, 35, 193, 270
Folklore, 159, 167
Fondling (and rocking), 60-62
Food
   denial of breast as, 78
   patient=food, 95
   as poison, 116
Foreplay (forepleasure) 112-114, 196-197, 203, 276
Forgetting, 235-236
   of names of persons, 137
   see also Déjà raconté
Franklin, B., xix
Frazer, J., 28, 298
Free association, 114, 148, 154, 161; *see also* Fear, Silence
Freud, Anna, xvi, xvii, 10-11, 53, 55-56, 70, 72, 78, 80, 89, 117, 132, 296
Freud, Sigmund
   on affect, 143, 146, 286
   on affirmation, 191
   on ambition, 152
   on amnesia removal, xiii
   on ambivalence, 38, 112, 273
   on anality, 197
   on anal-sadistic mentality etc., 112
   on "Anthropophyteia," 19
   on aphasia, 105
   on "archaic" father, 34
   on beating fantasies, 47, 150
   bibliographical references to, xiii, xvi, xvii, 298-301
   on body-ego, 44, 128, 148, 208
   case histories of, *see* Little Hans, Wolf Man, Rat Man, Dora
   on castration complex, 191
   on childhood, xvi, 41, 122
   on child's fear of animals, 118
   on child's fear of being eaten, 78-79
   on clitoris, 148
   on conversion (upon rheumatic muscles), 66
   on constancy principle, 5
   on death instinct, 4
   on definition of psychoanalysis, xiii
   on *déjà raconté*, 185-191
   on *déjà vu*, 188-189, 192
   on delay of instinctual gratification, 123
   on destruction of oedipal strivings in the id, 270

Freud, Sigmund (con't)
  on dream, 19-21, 148, 177-179, 188-189, 217, 220, 222, 244, 258, 270
  dreams of, 26-27, 30, 150, 198
  on dualistic theory of instincts, 3, 45-46, 49, 64-65
  on ego, 104, 159, 196, 208-209
  on fausse reconnaissance, 188-189
  on fear of poisoning, 116
  on fetish ("Glanz"), 118
  on fetish "girdle," 174
  on fire, 154, 165, 176
  on frequency represented through multiplicity, 59, 77, 178, 259
  on genital phase, 196, 199
  on "Having and Being in the child," 71
  on humor, 39, 85
  on hypnosis, 224
  on identification, 42, 226-227
  on infant's sucking, 201-202, 273
  on infatuation, 274
  on influence of civilization, 122, 159
  on instinctual discharge, 201
  on joke, 133
  on Leonardo da Vinci, 22-24
  on libido, 47, 196
  on Little Hans, see same
  on mastering the outside world, 107, 169
  on Medusa's head, 166
  on melancholia, 4
  on model of love relations, 201, 273
  on money, 268
  on mother-goddess, 260
  on negation, 61 fn.
  on neurosis, 270
  on neurotic, 40
  on object relation and identification, 71, 75, 76, 85
  on "organ representations," 29, 128, 131, 204
  on orgasm, 201, 273-374
  on origin of guilt, 38, 271
  on paranoia in female, 111-112
  on phallic sexuality (and mankind's prehistory), 29 fn.
  on phylogenetic inheritance, 9-11, 40-41, 43
  on prehistory of mankind, 29, 38, 40, 98-99
  on "preservation of fire," 154

  on projection, 79, 222
  on psychic energy, 45, 64-65
  on psychic organization, 122-123
  on psychological connotations of penis, 268
  on Rat Man, 127, 165
  on reappearance of orality in orgasm, 273
  on regression, 204
  on relation of biology to psychology, 191
  on representation of female genitalia, 22, 148
  on representation of mother, 179, 215
  on representation of whole person, 204
  on repression, 11, 41-44, 122, 194, 196, 260
  on reversal, 125-126
  on schizophrenic speech, 143
  on scoptophilia, 103
  on sexual instinct, 201
  on shame, 29 fn., 159, 167
  on sibling rivalry, 8
  on substitution of ear for eye, 133
  on suicide, 198 fn.
  on superego, 34-37, 39, 85, 122, 209, 271
  on symbolism of wood, 258-259
  on symbolization, 18, 178-179
  on system Pcpt-Cs, 122
  on thought processes, 123, 128, 130-131
  on totem feast, 101
  on transference, 74, 215
  on typical accusation against mother, 235
  on unconscious, 41
  on urethral eroticism, 29, 159, 169
  on Wolf Man, see same
  on women, 148
Frigidity, 156, 229, 237-238

Gaddiano, A., 301
Gastrointestinal symptoms, 162-163
Gebärmutter, defined, 208-209; see also Womb
Genesis, 98-101
Genital, Genital phase
  addenda to characterization of, 200 ff.
  affect (in examples of female partial subject), 243 ff.

Genital, Genital phase (con't)
aggression (in the same), 246 ff.
the breast refound, 273
cathexes (libidinal) preserved in, 196-199
ego regression (in coition), 273 ff.
erogenic zone (new) and an old partial libido, 200 ff.
female genital, omission of in sculpture, 171-172, 206
female genital, devaluation of, 58, 175
female genital (procreative) partial subject, 208-242
female genital (procreative) partial subject, 242-266
and folie à deux, 270
Gebärmutter (element in body-ego) defined, 208-209
Gebärmutter (represented by the "spot"), 212-216
Hartspann, defined, 262
the Kreuz, 252 ff.
the Kreuz in the male, 268-269
libido,— (components of, etc.), 203 204
Magic Flute Aria (and zone equation), 276 ff.
male genital partial subject, 266-272
menstruation and oral-sadistic interference with, 252 ff.
menstruation (regressive) anal-sadistic interference with, 247 f.
"mother comes in," 216-221
Mutterleib, 261-263; see also Mother
orality of libido (employed in female genital partial subject), 230-242
oral libido, elaboration upon (Plato), 269
partial subject (and object) defined, 204
partial subject and partial object (in coition), 274 ff.
preoedipal sexuality (survival of), 213
persistence of earlier phases in, 196-199, 203, 230-242, 242-247 ff., 266, 273
primitive model for discharge of erogenic zone, 202 ff.
the "spot," see Gebärmutter above
the wave dream, 221-232

zone, discharging partial libido, 199-201, 267
zone equation, 274-275; musical representation of, 276 ff.
Genital Phase, Clinical and Illustrative Material
"Oh that this too too solid Flesh would melt," 198 fn.
"I can do it all myself," 202
Baubo, 205-206
Rilke's "Annunciation," 207
a Japanese legend, 210
connection between nipple and clitoris, 211 fn.
the "spot" (example 1), 212
Rilke's "Visitation of Mary," 213
the "spot" in transference, 215
dream of "mother comes in," 216-217
dream of the mistress of a patient, 218
a premenstrual dream of "mother comes in," 219
a patient's mother "comes in" for consultation, 219
a "Dream of Nudity" (menstrual), 219
"dream of the waves," 221-222
two atypical "wave dreams," 224, 225
touching and seeing, 226 fn.
"Mrs. Steak," 230
the dead horse, 231
tooth extraction and fear of castration, 231
the patient dangling at church window, 233
"holding breath in pelvis," 235
(psychotic) mother touching the "spot," 236
Timon and Apemantus, 238
Little Hans and Hanna, 239
oral symptoms and a pregnancy, 241-242
the patient afraid of being eaten, 243
libido canceled by aggression, 244-245
fantasy of mountain house, 247
interference (via "rats") with menstruation, 248
dream of the vegetable bouquet, 250
dream of choking the rat, 250
"dream house" and the "fantasy house," 251

Genital Phase, Clinical (con't)
  the Kreuz and a sexual performance, 253
  dream of the bloody cross, 254
  "Olenka's dream," 257-258
  Mary, Artemis, and Hekate, 259-260
  a delayed first menstruation, 161
  a cramp in the sacral region, 262
  Juliet and the Nurse, 264-265
  three men's complaints, 266
  the Cordobese men, 267
  male with Kreuz symptom, 268
  Iago's threat, 272 fn.
  Romeo and Rosaline, 274 fn.
  a primal scene memory, 275
  a passage from Measure for Measure, 276 fn.
  zone equation and The Magic Flute, 277 ff.
Gesture, 128-129, 153
Gitelson, M., xx
Glover, E., 69, 301
God
  eating of, 100-101
  injunction against speaking name of, 99
  prohibition of making image of, 99
  prosthetic, 131
Goddess, of fertility, 205; see also Mother
Goethe, J. W., 133
Golden Calf, 100
Greenacre, P., 229
Groddeck, G., 259
Guilt
  and cannibalistic desires, 80
  and "masked masturbation," 146
  and oedipus complex, 271
  and social fear, 122

Hallucination, 179
Hamlet's Soliloquy, 136 f.
Hand
  and déjà raconté, 182-186, 193
  and mouth, 60, 103, 132, 153, 204
Harrison, G. B., xv
Hartmann, H., 42, 301
Hartspann (a muscular tautness), 262-263
Hatred, as original tie between humans, 101

Hearing, cessation of, during psychoanalysis, 92-96, 133; see also Deafness, Ear
Hendrick, I., 104-106, 301
Hippocratic oath, 16, 28-29
Hoffer, W., 11, 53, 55-57, 60, 70, 72, 101 fn., 167, 301-302
Homosexuality, 58, 151, 212, 268
Horse, see Little Hans, Symbolism
Hostility
  to competitor, 7
  to older brother, 8
Humor, 39-40, 165, 245
  lack of, 39, 82
  Shylock's, 85-86
Hunger, 61 fn.
Hyperemia, 202
Hypnagogic phenomena, 35-36, 66-67, 249
Hypnopompic phenomena, 35-36, 67, 219, 244
Hypnosis, 224
  mother- (Ferenczi), 39
"Hypnotic evasion," 135, 223, 228, 287

Id
  and destruction of oedipal strivings in, 270
  inherited traces of, 41, 43
  and instincts, 45-46
  and superego, 37-38
Identification
  and accident proneness, 115, 117
  with aggressor, 89
  of analyst with patient's ego, see Counteridentification
  and cannibalistic re-incorporation, 90-92
  with castrated mother, 255
  consummation of, 76-78, 206, 226, 276
  with father, 266, 269
  with feces, 117, 119
  of genital with whole person, 204
  of genital (male) with breast, 77
  and incorporation, 118, 226-227, 255
  with maternal partial object, 206, 215, 230
  with mother object, 22, 259, 262
  via mouth, 96-97
  of name with its owner, 137
  and narcissistic identity, 75-78
  and object relation, 71, 75-78, 85

Identification (con't)
of oedipal child, 17, 42
of partial subject and partial object, 213
of person with clitoris, 147-148
with preoedipal mother, 63, 76, 114
primary, 42-44, 75, 79, 101-105, 122-123
regressive, 75-78
secondary, 42-44
and superego formation, 34-35, 37-38, 85
see also Incorporation, Introjection
Illusion, 85, 163
Imitation, 57, 102-103
Impatience, cannibalistic, 88, 107-111, 115, 152, 154, 180 fn., 240, 265, 277; see also Cannibalism
Incest barrier breakdown, xvi
Incest object, 16, 21
Incest prohibition, 35, 269-270, 272
Incontinence, 77, 160, 164-168, 171, 193, 278, 288-290
=castration, 171
=castration=death, 159-160, 166, 176, 193
displacement upon anal sphincter, 124
ecology, 159
and feelings of inferiority, 150
insurance against, 170
urethral, 29, 132, 154, 159-159
see also Bladder, Cannibalism, Continence, Ejaculatio praecox, Language, Oral phase (second), Phallic phase
Incorporation
consummation of, 213, 228
and elimination, 111
model for affirmation, 191
ocular, 103-104, 211, 255
olfactory, 167, 203
oral, 57, 72, 80, 90-92, 99, 101, 226-227, 294
and projection, 118
see also Identification, Introjection
Infancy, 55-58
anxiety in, 79
deprivations in, 60-61
Infants, direct observation of, 55-58, 60-61, 72, 101, 167

Inferiority, typical ideas of, 144, 147-150, 194-195
Ingres' "La Source," 176
Inhalation, discharging oral libido, 245
Inhibition, 243-244
of cannibalistic aim, 78, 88-89, 162
countercathectic, 246, 263
see also Affect
"Innate attitudes," 10
Instincts, and theory of
and affect, 107-108, 123
aim of, 76, 122, 165
of animals, 10
cathexis, 43
components of, 86-87, 107
defusion of, 4-5, 204, 242-245, 273
delay of gratification of, 123
derivatives, 48-49
discharge of, 200-202, 276
dualistic hypothesis of, 3-8, 49
energy of, 45-47
fusion of, 4, 46, 49, 101
"neutralization" of, xx, 42
oral-sadistic and oral-erotic, 243
origin of, 45, 46, 49
regression in melancholia, 4-5
sexual, 45-47
see also Aggression, Death instinct, Libido, Psychic energy
Intercourse, 203-204, 210, 273, 280; see also Coition
Interest, psychology of, 120-121
Interpretation, 192
Introitus, 145, 201
Introjection, 4, 90, 99, 209, 242, 247
and hypnosis, 224
and identification, 17, 259
of mother into Gebärmutter, 208-209; see also Womb
ocular, 206, 211, 237, 255
re-, 206
see also Incorporation, Identification, Womb
Isaiah, A. B. (and B. Sharfman), 31, 100, 302
Isakower, O., 35-36, 66, 302

Jealousy
oedipal, 11, 15
oral, 66
Jones, E., xviii, 25, 125, 181, 302
Joseph, Sister M., 302

Judgment of cognition, 188-190
Jung, C. G., 9

Katan, A., 158, 171, 302
Keiser, S., 181, 302
Kinesthesia, 120, 131
Kissing
  and biting, 91, 104, 153
  "oneself," 202-203, 212-213, 273, 275
Kittredge, G. L., xv
Kojiki, 209
Krauss, F. S., 197
Kreuz, 252-266, 268-269; *see also* Partial subject
Kris, E., xvii, 55, 61-62, 302
Kulka, E., 126

Labyrinth (perceptions), 60-61, 138
Landowska, W., 139-140, 300
Language
  acquisition of, 41-42, 44, 104-107, 122, 132
  erogenic (anal-erotic types), 290-293
  erogenic, types of (Sharpe), 287
  erogenic (urethral-erotic), 288-290
  and music, 139-143
  persistence of orality in, 132-134
  see also Anal-sadistic phases, Bisyllabic reduplication, Silence, Speech
Latency, disturbed, 195
Laughter, terminating mourning, 205-206, 210-211
Lee, L., 267, 302
Legends, *see* Myth
Leonardo da Vinci, 7-9, 99, 302
  and "death instinct," 8 fn.
  drawing of, 22-27, 204, 211
Libidinal phases
  overlapping of, 53
  persistence of earlier in later, 53-54
  see also all phases, Erogenic zones
Libido
  erogeneity and, distinction between, 49-49, 151-152
  Freud's three definitions, 44-49
  in melancholia, 4-5
  see also all phases, Instincts, Regression, Sexuality
Listen, inability to, 134
Lithotomy (and Hippocratic oath), 28-29

Little Hans, 11-19, 30-35, 38-40, 67, 117, 120, 164, 177, 239-240, 247, 273
Locomotion (R. Spitz and A. Freud), 72 fn.
Lumpf (fecal child—Little Hans), 16, 247

Mahler, M. S., 55, 61, 70, 72, 302
Maillol, A., 172
Male
  (hypothetical) identification with father, 266
  identification with female, 144, 150, 194
  see also Sexuality
"Man in the dark," 118-119
Mary, ancestors of, 260
Masturbation, 151, 155, 215, 245, 253-254
  Bismarck's dream, 19 ff.
  and *déjà raconté*, 183
  and discharge in urination, 76-77, 223, 229
  and (early mobilization) of vagina, 229
  and exchange of, for sexual intercourse, 17-18
  exhibitionistic nature of fantasies of, 61-62
  and fear of castration, 184-185, 192-194
  "hypnotic"—(by mother), 223
  and incorporation, 91
  of infant, 76
  and Leonardo's drawing, 24
  and persistence of second anal phase in phallic, 145
  orality of libido in, 233
  phallic (and partial object), 19-28
  in phallic phase, 78, 229
  by (psychotic) mother, 76
  and second beating fantasy (Freud), 47
  telephoning symbol for, 225
  and tonsillectomy, 229
  urination and, 27
  vaginal, 149
  in women, 145-147, 149, 229
  see also Castration, Fantasies
Mathematics, 130
McCurdy, E., 302
  (*see* Leonardo)

Mephistopheles, 133
Melancholia, 4-6, 124; *see also* Depression
  Antonio's, 81-83, 85
Memory (traces), 128, 155-158; *see also Déjà raconté*
Mendacity, 39, 82, 84
Menstruation, 245-247
  dreams related to, 216-238
  and oral desire, 241-242
  oral-sadistic interference with, 252-266
  regressive anal-sadistic interference with, 247-252
  typical complaint concerning first, 235-238
  see also Dreams
Meyer, E., 262
Michelangelo, 7
Modulation, symbolic, 31-32
Money, 120-121, 165; *see also* Interest
Monotheism, 101
Montaigne, M., 98, 302
"Morality" (first, and housekeeping brothers), 125
Moses, 20-21
Mother
  Baubo (maternal partial object), 205
  belly of (*Mutterleib*), 179, 204-206, 208; (defined), 213, 221, 224-230
  breath held against, 237
  and cannibalistic aim-displacement, 88
  complaint (typical) against, 235
  failure to introject, 221-222, 237
  fear of being eaten by, 78-79, 158
  fear of being engulfed by (Wave dreams), 221-229
  feeding on daughters (Freud), 93
  Gebärmutter, 208-209; *see also* Womb
  goddess, 65, 260
  "hypnotizing," 39, 223, 224
  introjection of preoedipal, 206, 209, 212, 215-216, 224, 229-230
  loss of, 79, 104-106
  oedipal vs. preoedipal, 144, 226
  phallic, 173, 177, 181
  preoedipal dependence upon, 111, 114, 160, 269-270
  reduction to sexual parts, 21, 24, 204, 270
  representation by stone, 19-30

  separation from, 72-73, 104-105, 117
  symbiotic relation with child, 70
  touching maternal genital, 225-226, 228
  union with, 244
  violent impulses toward, 88, 115
  see also Breast, Parents, Partial subject *and* object, Representations, Seduction, "Spot," Symbolism, Wave dream, Womb
Motility, 120
  and "anaclitic depression," 72 fns.
  and ego, 121-123
  restriction of, in anal-sadistic phase, 160 ff.
  in second oral phase, 101-103
Motor activity, and archaic affect, 44, 123, 160; *see also* Thought
Mouth, 167, 287-295
  and death instinct, 86-88
  and *déjà raconté*, 192-193
  -eye unit, 55-60, 77, 91, 101-104, 119-120, 132, 203, 294
  as vehicle of identification, 90-91
  incorporative employment of (for subsequent speech), 72, 104-107
  and nipple, 56, 275
  phallus equipped with, 176-181
  oral-sadistic (regressive revival of), 86-88
  sucking (intrauterine, Hoffer), 56
  transfer of— (of second oral phase), 246-247
  transfer of "maternal organ" upon analyst's, 96
  transfer upon vagina, 229-230
  see also Eye, Nipple, Oral phases
Mozart, W. A., 139-140, 142, 264, 276-281, 300
Musculature, 45, 64, 122-123, 160, 202, 253, 267, 275
  and oral-sadistic libido, 72, 101-102
  pathology of, 262
Music, 129, 139-143, 276-281
Mutterleib, see Mother, belly of
Myth (ology), 154, 159, 167, 176, 205-206, 209-211
  of analyst, 134

Name, forgetting of, 137
Napoleon, 8
Narcissism, and autoerotism, 69-70

Nausea, 95-96, 163, 232, 256

Negation, 61, 218, 244

Negro ("man in the dark"), 118-119

Neurosis
  fixation in narcissistic, 124
  and incestuous dreams, 270
  infantile, 47, 54
  onset of, 54
  and phylogenesis, 9, 11, 40

Nietzsche, F., 97

Nightmare, 177-180, 222, 258-259

Nipple, 66, 96, 116, 133, 210
  and cannibalistic drive toward, 86, 108, 111-114
  and ego formation, 69-70
  and mouth, 56, 275
  see also Breast, Cannibalism, Mouth, Oral phases

Nunberg, H., 117-118, 180, 302

Object
  activity and passivity toward, in oral phase, 61
  body as, 61-63
  destroying vs. sparing of, 150
  and feces, 106, 111-119, 123, 162, 165
  incipient, 57
  killing fathers, 136-137
  loss of, 4, 71, 104-105, 116-119
  and nascent ego, 71-75, 104-107
  need-satisfying, 56, 70
  oedipal, 77
  oral qualities of anal-erotic, 116-121
  preoedipal, 63-64, 70, 76-78, 106
  representations, 128, 131
  see also Identification, Partial object, Partial subject

Object relation
  lack of, 70
  oral model of, 201, 273

Obsessional neurosis, 127; see also Compulsion, Compulsive neurosis

Oedipus complex, 76, 209, 271
  deeper layers of, 65-69

Ontogenesis, 11, 15-16; see also Phylogenesis

Oral phases
  actings out and, 92
  activity, 60-65, 72 fn.
  affect-quantum, 107
  "anaclitic depression" (Spitz), 72-73
  anxiety, inception of, 79

  and art, "empathic" consummation of, 103
  bisyllabic reduplication, see Speech below
  breast, "Having and Being" (Freud, posthumous), 71, 73-76, 193
  cannibalistic desire, 78-101
  cathexes (early), and needs, 56, 70
  and death instinct, 86 ff.
  distinction between first and second, 78
  ego (nascent), and object, 71-75
  eye-mouth unit, 101-104
  first, 55-70
  identity (narcissistic), 75-78
  impatience, 88, 102-111, 115
  melancholia (and first—), 4-6
  mother object, 106-107
  mouth-eye unit, 55-60
  oral sadism (archaic) impact of, 166
  persistence of, in later phases, 53, 82, 104, 111-121, 124, 132-134, 138, 145-151, 151-168, 196-201, 230-242, 267, 269, 273
  preoedipal strivings, aim of, 75-77
  regression (to first), 60-64, 65-69, 73, 77, 82, 104, 138
  regression (to second), 82, 132, 167-168, 294
  rocking (and fondling), 61
  second, 71-111
  second, distinguished from all other phases, 78
  and speech, beginning of, 104-107
  superego (morbid), nucleus of, 90
  "weaning trauma," 92-97
  see also Biting, Breast, Cannibalism, Mother, Mouth, other phases

Oral Phase (first): Clinical and Illustrative Material
  mouth and eye, perceptory unit (Spitz), 56
  infant's domination by need (A. Freud), 56 fn.
  incipient ego reaction to incipient object, 57
  wish for the use of the mouth, 58-60
  early deprivation and a passive man, 61-62
  ejaculatio praecox, 63-64
  Desdemona's handkerchief, 66-69

Oral phase (Second): Clinical and Illustrative Material
  jaw activity (Hoffer), 72 fn.
  general activity in (Spitz, A. Freud), 72
  the "anaclitic depression" (Spitz), 72-73
  a patient "starves" the analyst, 73-75
  a male represented by women, 75-76
  preoedipal strivings and identification, 76-77
  Portia's first injunction against Shylock, 80-82, 86
  Antonio submits to Shylock, 82-86
  Aufidius' fight (with Coriolanus), 86
  the impulse to bite and the impulse to devour, 87-88
  the pinching mother, 88
  hate and strong identification, 89
  cannibalistic re-incorporation, 90-92
  the "weaning trauma" in the transference, 93-95
  an example from *Midsummer Night's Dream*, 96 fn.
  Posthumous and his jailer, 98
  Montaigne on cannibalism, 98 fn.
  Abraham's sacrifice, 98-99
  Leonardo's exhortation against cannibalism, 99 fn.
  Rashi's Commentary on passage from Genesis, 100 fn.
  oral-sadistic instinctual discharge in babies (Hoffer), 101 fn.
  the mouth-eye unit, 102
  "Ma-ma, go-go do-do" (Hendrick), 104
  the Elizabethan stage, 106 fn.
  patients with "cannibalistic impatience," 108-110
  Isabella's plea for delay, 109 fn.
Organ representations, 29, 128, 131
Orgasm, 150-151, 201-203, 212-217, 253, 270
  and distal third of vagina, 200-201
  and incest, 270
  and (incontinent) first anal phase, 150-151
  and theory of coition, 273-274
  as "withdrawal symptom," 74
Orphic rites, 29
Os Sacrum (Kreuz), 253

Pain, psychological meaning of, 89
Paramnesia, 186-188
Paranoia, in female, 111-112
Paranoid reactions, 112, 114, 138, 162
Parapraxia, 30-31, 112, 126-127, 183, 190-191
Parent (s)
  archaic, and superego, 34-39, 85
  as invaders, 91-92
  libidinal and destructive, 85-86
  psychotic, xviii
Parricide, 34, 38, 136-137, 269, 272
Partial object, 211, 216, 270
  Baubo, 205
  concept of, 204-208
  defined, 21
  Leonardo's drawing and, 24, 211
  maternal, 21, 24-25, 205, 211, 216, 259
  regression to, 211, 273-274
Partial subject
  aggression, discharge of, and 246-247
  affect, discharge of, and, 243-246
  concept of, 204-208
  ego regression to, 273-274
  female genital (procreative, *Gebärmutter*), 208-266
  female pregenital (*Mutterleib*), 205-208, 221 ff.
  identification with partial object, 213
  and the *Kreuz*, 252-266
  male, 266-272
  in regressive conditions, 270-271
  representation (direct) of female (the "spot"), 212-215, 230
  representation (indirect) of female, 212, 216-230
  see also Genital phase, Mother, Symbolism, Wave dreams, Womb
Parturition, orality of, 238-242
Parturitive organ (*Gebärmutter*), 208
Pascal, B., xix, 142, 302
Passivity
  in first oral phase, 60-65, 76
  in men, 61-64, 76, 161
Penis
  anatomical substratum for phallus, 144
  and breast, 77
  envy, xvi, 185
  =feces=money=gift=child, 268
  loss of, through masturbation, 184-185, 193

Penis (con't)
and nipple, 96, 102, 268
oral root of interest in, 181, 268-269
phallic and genital —, distinction between, 144
psychological connotations of, 268
represented in body-ego, 266
symbolizations of, 271-272
vagina compared to, 267, 275
see also Phallic phase, Phallus

Perception, 132
in infancy, 56-60, 102
internal vs. external, 128, 131
"modality of primal" (Spitz), 60

Perversion
in psychotic parent, xvii
and the addict, 70

Phallic, Phallic phase
and ambition, 152-153
and cannibalistic libido (urethral-erotic discharge of), 151-168
clitoris urination, fantasy of, 170-171
déjà raconté (transference delusion), 182-184
ego organization ("infantile"), dissolution of, 159
and ejaculatio praecox, 161-163
erection, infantile theory of, 170
and ideas of inferiority, 147-150
("infantile") ego organization in, 158-163
—masturbation, confession of, 150
—masturbation (and partial object), 19-28
persistence of second anal-sadistic phase in, 144-150
persistence of second oral phase in, 151-168
phallus equipped with a mouth, 176-182
and "Preservation of Fire" (Freud), 154-155
rectum, a — (pleasure-physiological) copy of, 145-147
Shylock's speech, analysis of, 163-168
stone, interpretation of, 19-30
"uncastrated" constitution, fantasy of, 171-176
urge to talk, 153-154
see also Cannibalism, Fantasies, Phallus, Penis

Phallic phase: Clinical and Illustrative Material
"masturbatory" exercise of pleasure-physiological "organ," 146
identification of person with this "organ," 149-150
biting, urination and ambition, 152-153
excessive talking, 153
primal scene material, 155, 156
frequent urination and lasting inhibition of eating meat, 155-157
infantile enuresis, 158
fear of urination and free association, 161
a passive male, 162-163
Shylock's speech, 165
child afraid of sea-bathing, 169
4½-year-old boy's retention, 170
clitoris urination, 170
the "uncastrated" constitution, 172-175
Ophelia and Hamlet, 174, 175
continence and the "uncastrated" constitution, 176
the Wolf Man's nightmare, 178
woman patient's dream (Freud), 179 fn.
the Wolf Man and Grusha (=pear), 180 fn.
the devouring maternal phallus, 180, 181 fn.
examples of déjà raconté, 182, 186

Phallus
and cannibalistic act, 80
clitoris as substratum of, 144, 170
erogeneity of (and ejaculatio praecox), 163
and feelings of guilt, 86
and femininity (in female genital phase), 199
imaginary, 144, 173 ff., 194 f.
maternal devouring, 180 f.
paternal devouring, 177 ff.
and Priapus, 271
symbolizations of, 16, 19, 154, 177
"wee-wee maker" biting, 177 fn.
see also Cannibalism, Ejaculatio praecox, Fantasy, Penis, Phallic phase, Urination

Philosophy of execution, 97

Phobia, 160-161
   in child, 169-170; *see also* Little Hans
   Shylock's comparison of phobic, 164, 166
   see also Erythrophobia
Phylogenesis, and ontogenesis, 16, 44, 86
Phylogenetic inheritance
   Abraham and the Angel, 31
   and "assistive" father, 17
   and Hippocratic oath, 28-29; *also footnotes*
   hypothesis of, 8-44
   Lady Macbeth's hallucinatory "dialogue," 31
   Little Han's dialogue, 13-14
   the "stone" (Frazer's *Golden Bough*), 29 fn.
   toe-stubbing, parapraxia of, 30-31
Physics, 130
Physiology, 144-145, 147, 200-201, 238, 266-267, 276; *see also* Pleasure
Picturization, 18, 232, 249
"Pilot" symptom, 119
Plato, 269-270, 302
Pleasure
   -anatomy, 253
   auxiliary, *see* By-play
   -physiology, 29, 145-149, 165, 167, 176, 200-202, 209, 291
Polytheism, 101
Portia's injunctions, 80-86, 125
Posture, 62, 74, 101-102, 129-130, 214-215, 228
   control of, by ear, 137-138
Preconscious, and repression, 42, 44
Pregenitality, reversion to, 47
Pregnancy, 15-18, 22, 169, 238-242, 273
Prehistory
   of individual, 9, 159
   of mankind, 29, 38, 40, 98-99
   see also Phylogenetic inheritance, Freud
Priapus, 271-272
Primal fantasies, 9, 30, 191
   concerning phallic phase, 144, 168-181
Procreation, 271, 276
Projection, 244
   and identification, 75, 118, 226
   and impatience, 110

"material," 118
of mother as "womb," 216
and recognition, 148-149
and superego, 34-35, 39-40, 82, 85, 135-136
and transference, 87, 135, 222-223
Prometheus, 154
Psychic energy, 45-47, 143
   displaceable and neutral, 64-65
   neutralization of, xx
Psychoanalysis
   clinical method and research, xx
   method of research in, xiii-xiv
   remarks on technique of, 92-95, 149
Psychosexual development
   chronology of, xvi-xvii
   see also Sexuality *and* Libidinal phases
Psychosis, xvii-xviii
   "nocturnal" (and incest barrier), 270
   see also Parents
Purging, 16
   of the Jews, 121 fn.
Puttenham, G., 285, 295, 302
Pythagorean rites, 29

Quantum, *see* Affect
Question (-answer game), 94-95, 114-115, 165, 242

Rashi, 31, 100
Rat Man, 127, 165
Reaction formation (Freud), 124, 232
Reality testing, 130-131
Rectum, 120, 151, 165, 203-204, 249, 252
   and phallic pleasure-physiological copy of, 145-147
   replacing womb, 249
Reduplication, rhetorical, 168, 194; *see also* Bisyllabic reduplication
Reflex arc, 122
Reflex massage, 262-263
Regression
   and defusion of instincts, 204, 242-243, 273
   of ego, 63, 85, 191, 204, 208 ff., 273-274
   and fantasy of castration, 191, 193
   from identification to incorporation, 101

Regression (con't)
    of libido, 4-5, 47-49, 62-64, 92, 96,
        132, 204, 243, 249, 252, 276
    narcissistic, 292
    partial, 123
    and partial-erotic language, 285
    see also Body-ego, Child, Fixation,
        Phylogenetic inheritance, and all
        phases
Reich, A., 146, 302
Reitler, R., 22-25
Repetition
    compulsion, 12, 92, 96
    restitution through, 168
Repression
    and archaic inheritance, 41
    "buoyancy of repressed," 194
    following into, 41
    of idea vs. affect, 108
    organic (Freud), 41-42
    "primal," 41-44, 122-123
    and shock of castration, 191, 194
Resistance
    to free association, 161, 293
    the "hypnotic evasion," 228, 287 fn.
    not hearing as, 92-97, 133
    transference — vs. repression —, 87
    see also Transference
Reversal, 125-126; see also Anal-sadis-
    tic phases (anal reversal), Right
    and left, Time
Rheumatic muscles, see Reflex mas-
    sage
Ribble, M., 60, 303
Right and left, reversal of, 125-126, 223
Rilke, R. M., 206-208, 213-214, 303
Rocking, see Fondling
Rodin, A., 130
Rose, H. J., 271, 303

Sachs, H., 19-21
Sacrifice, 31, 100, 154
Sadism, 49
Satyrs, 271
Schilder, P., 47, 303
Schizophrenia (and compulsion), 124
Schlick, M., 131, 303
Schnitzler, A., 160
Scoptophilia, 77, 101-104, 130, 203, 226
    fn.
Screen memory, 101, 225

Sculpture, 171-172, 205; see also Cas-
    tration
Secondary elaboration, 232
Seduction, of children, xvii-xviii, 59,
    76, 91, 112-113, 223, 225, 236, 254,
    267, 268
Seeing, 226, 294; see also Eye, Scopto-
    philia, Vision
Self-mutilation (through defecation)
    fear of, 116
Self-reproaches, in melancholia, 4-5
Sexuality
    female, 28, 144-149, 200, 202
    male, compared to female, 267, 275-
        276
    oedipal, 269-270
    preoedipal, 28, 200, 202, 206, 213,
        226, 269-270, 276, 277-278
Shakespeare, W., xv-xvi, xix, 66, 83,
    109, 128-129, 295, 303
    A Winter's Tale, 57, 303
    Coriolanus, 86-87, 303
    Cymbeline, 98, 303
    Hamlet, 128-129, 136-137, 174-175,
        198, 303
    Henry V, 133, 139, 303
    Julius Caesar, 129, 303
    Macbeth, 31, 129, 303
    Measure for Measure, 109, 276, 303
    Merchant of Venice, 80-86, 121, 125,
        159, 163-168, 194, 303; Portia's in-
        junction, 80-82, 86, 125; Shylock's
        speech, 163-168, 194
    Midsummer Night's Dream, 96-97,
        303
    Othello, 66-69, 272, 303
    Romeo and Juliet, 261, 263-266, 274,
        303; Juliet's nurse, 263-266
    Tempest, 107, 303
    Timon of Athens, 238, 303
    Twelfth Night, 120-121, 137, 303
Shame, 167, 170, 245
    ecology of, 159
Sharfman, B., 31, 100, 302
Sharpe, E. F., 287, 303
Sibling rivalry (Freud), 8
Silence (regressive)
    anal-erotic, 292-293
    oral-erotic (regressive), 293-295
    oral-erotic (theory of), 72-75, 91, 232
    types of, 288-289
    see also Hearing

Simmel, E., 238, 252, 303

Sleep, 104, 170, 269-270, 274; see also Hypnagogic and Hypnopompic phenomena

Smiling, in infancy, 57-58

Socrates ("Cratylus"), 126

Sounds, and castration, 167

Speech
  and anal-sadistic phase, 132-134
  apparatus, 285, 287, 293-294
  compulsive, 290
  control of, by ear, 137-138
  distinguished from language, 286
  distortion of analyst's, 92-96
  and hypnagogic phenomena, 35-36
  inaudible, 129
  inception of, 69, 72, 104-107, 132, 287
  inhibition of, 115
  loss of, in child (A. Freud), 132 fn.
  not hearing analyst's, 92-96
  received through mouth instead of ear, 92-96, 167
  and schizophrenia, 36, 105, 143
  Shylock's reduplicative, 164
  see also Bisyllabic reduplication, Language, Silence, Superego, Voice

Sperber, H., 148, 304

Sphincter
  anal, 111, 113-115, 123, 126-127, 160-161, 166, 287
  control, and language, 287-288, 290
  morality, 44, 121-125
  sucking function of, 115-116, 123

Spitz, R. A., 5, 55-58, 60-61, 72, 79, 304

"Spoken word," fear of, 134-137

"Spot," 212-215, 217, 220-221, 230, 237, 247, 252, 253; see also Partial Subject

Stone, enigma of, 19-30

Sterba, E., 119, 304

Sublimation, 103, 130, 213
  with aim displacement, 196-197

Submission, to archaic parent, 39, 85

Sucking, 60-61, 64-65, 78, 201, 212-213, 275
  as castration symbol (Nunberg), 180
  (child) sucking and love relation (Freud), 210, 273
  the eye and, 103-104
  of finger (Hoffer), 6
  intrauterine, 56

(sucking) mouth and the ear, 134, 134 fn.
  of thumb, 202, 275-276

Suicide of melancholic, 4-6, 81-82

Sun-goddess, 210

Superego
  and aphasic speech, 105
  archaic nucleus of, 39-40, 82, 85, 90, 135
  formation of, 34-39, 85, 122, 209
  and introjection of father, 17, 135-137
  in melancholia, 4-5, 82, 85
  precursors of, 122
  punitive, 232
  temporary involution of, 269, 271
  "voice of," 32, 35-40, 135-136
  see also Ego

Surgery, 182-183

Symbolism
  of bird, 271, 277
  of bladder stone, 28-29
  of breast (by food), 78 fn.
  of bridge (Freud), 26, 148
  of cat (Freud), 166
  of cave (Freud), 211
  of Centaur, 271
  of "falling," 15, 22, 117, 239
  of father's body, 32
  of flying insects, 177
  of hair (Freud), 166-167
  of head and neck, 255
  of horse, 13-18, 232, 239, 247, 271-272
  of house (Freud), 165, 170, 251-252
  of "knocking on wood," 19
  on mantle (Freud), 174
  of mother, 15-18, 21-22, 25-28, 212-229, 232, 237, 259, 265
  of "mother comes in," 216-221, 230, 236, 242, 244, 246
  of mouse (Freud), 166
  of Negro, 118-119, 272
  of paper (Freud), 237
  of rat (Freud), 165, 249
  of riding together (Freud), 262
  of room (Freud), 179, 181
  of rug, 218, 244
  of snake (Freud, Simmel, Cohn, R. F.), 177, 252
  of snow (Cohn), 221, 249
  of spider (Abraham), 180-181
  of staircase (Freud), 179
  of stone (rock), 13, 19-31, 211

Symbolism (*con't*)
of telephoning, 90-91, 225
of "three" (Freud), 249
of traffic (transportation, Freud), 17, 258-259
of tree, 178
of two people, 18, 217
of wood for mother (Freud), 12, 21, 258-259
of vulture (Freud), 177

Talking, excessive (urge to), 153-154, 157, 237, 288-290
Tausk, V., 167, 304
Tchekov, A., 257-258, 304
Teeth, 72, 80, 87, 108
Telephoning, *see* Symbolism
Thought (processes), 123
abstract, 130
delay through, 110
latent and manifest, 128-129
motor characteristics of, 128-131, 138
pathological, 143
and speech, 128, 138, 286
thought and musical —, 129, 139-143
as trial action, 128, 139
Threshold symbolism, 206, 249
Time
and space, 130-131
reversal in, 125-128
Toilet training, 132 fn.
and first "morality," 122
Tonsillectomy, 177, 229
Totem, 99
Touching, 102-103, 225-226, 228, 245
Transference, 172-173, 187, 214-215
of breast of mother, 192
and a delusion, 182-194
of male and female, 269-270
maternal breast in the, 91
—neurosis and regression, 124
positive, 187, 232
"primal" form of, 74-75, 294
repetition in, 55, 192
resistance, —, 87, 92-96, 268
and urinary urge, 145-146
"weaning trauma" re-enacted in, 88, 92-97, 108
Transsubstantiation, 100, 127
Trauma (traumatic experience)
in childhood, 9, 11, 117, 134, 194
elaboration in dream, 218-219, 222

elaboration in masturbatory fantasies, 254
see also Birth, Dream, Seduction, Weaning

Unconscious (Freud), 11, 41
Upright gait
acquisition of, 41, 44, 122
control of, by ear, 137-138
Urethral erotism, 22, 26, 29, 152, 154, 168, 229; *see also* Cannibalism, Masturbation, Phallic phase
Urination, 27-29, 102, 152, 226 fn., 227
clitoral, fantasy of, 170
and continence, 145, 176
with erection, 77
Mutterleib, fantasy of, and, 254-255
observation of, by child, 76, 169, 227, 254
and phallic urethral language, 289-290
and retention, 169-170
seduction of child while urinating, 223
and urinary discharge through tears, 149-150
see also Abraham, Cannibalism, Incontinence, Language, Speech, Urethral erotism
Uterus, 203 fn., 253, 256
seat of deposition of earliest mother, 209

Vagina, 145, 149, 200-201, 225, 252-253
anesthesia of (Simmel), 238
and breast, 209-211, 213
early mobilization of (and tonsillectomy), 229
engulfing mother's, 225
and mouth, 102, 229-230, 275
and new erogenic zone, 200
as part of (phallic) pleasure-physiological "organ," 145, 149, 201
Verbal ideas, and repression, 42
Verbalization, 123, 128, 136, 243, 285
replaced by (regressive) silence, 293-294
see also Language, Speech
Verbigeration, 105
Violence, forms of, and cannibalism, 88-89

Voice, dependence upon, 38-40; *see also* Speech, Superego
Voltaire, 55
Vulva, 22, 145-147, 172, 227-229

Wangh, M., 66, 304
War (and death instinct), 6-7
"Weaning trauma"
  and male passivity, 61
  typical re-enactment in transference, 92-97, 108
"Withdrawal" symptoms, 74, 92-96
Wolf Man, xv, 10, 76, 173-174, 177-181, 222
Womb, 160, 211-221, 224, 244, 249, 255, 265
  anal-sadistic conception of, 252
  and body-ego, 209, 216, 222, 237
  Gebärmutter, 208-209, 234; *see also* Partial subject (female), Partial object
  and new erogenic zone, 200, 234, 246
  as seat of introjected earliest mother, 209, 215-216, 230, 237
  see also Mother, Genital Phase, Partial subject *and* object, the "Spot"
Word
  images and ego, 104-107, 128, 132
  images and superego, 36-37
  as an object (name), 137
  as part of body, 134-137, 167
  remainders, 128
  into script, 136-137
  "spoken word," 134-137
Writing vs. fear of hearing, 134-135
Wulff, M., 66

Zeus, 271
Zone equation, 275-276, 276-281